Fly-Fishing
the South
Atlantic Coast

Fly-Fishing the South Atlantic Coast

Where to Find Game Fish from North Carolina's Outer Banks to the Florida Keys

Jimmy Jacobs

BACK COUNTRY

Backcountry Guides
Woodstock, Vermont

Library of Congress Cataloging-in-Publication Data
Jacobs, Jimmy.
Fly-fishing the South Atlantic coast : where to find game fish from
North Carolina's outer banks to the Florida Keys / Jimmy Jacobs.— 1st ed.
p. cm
ISBN 0-88150-433-5 (alk. paper)
1. Saltwater fly fishing—South Atlantic States—Guidebooks. 2. Marine
fishes—South Atlantic States. 3. South Atlantic States—Guidebooks. I. Title.
SH464.S64 J23 2000
799.1'66148—dc21   00-037908

Maps by Paul Woodward, © 2000 The Countryman Press
Book design by Faith Hague
Cover and title page photographs by Jimmy Jacobs
Interior photographs by Jimmy Jacobs, Tom Evans, Polly Dean, Paul Vanderford,
and Zane Jacobs
Illustrations by A. L. Ripley

Backcountry Guides is a division of The Countryman Press,
P.O. Box 748, Woodstock, Vermont 05091
Distributed by W. W. Norton & Company, Inc.,
500 Fifth Avenue, New York, NY 10110

Printed in the United States of America

10 9 8 7 6 5 4 3 2 1

Dedication

To Martha and R. L.,
who joined me in learning about saltwater fishing
on the Bulow Creek Bridge

and in memory of
Clyde "LeRoy" Powell
He was "bad to fish"

Special thanks to the folks who pointed the way or let me tag along
on angling adventures that contributed to this book, including:

Polly Dean
Jerry Gerardi
Brent Jacobs
Zane Jacobs
Mike Walsh
LeRoy Powell
Vernon Reynolds
Tom Twyford
Bill Vanderford
Robert Wiggers

Contents

*Small redfish, most often called "puppy drum" in the Carolinas,
are one of the most frequent catches for fly-rodders.*

PART I

Introduction

The allure of saltwater fishing is hard to explain. Why would any freshwater angler abandon the cozy confines of rivers and lakes to toss a fishing line into the sea? Freshwater haunts are finite enough that, over the years, you can get to know them in an intimate way, making fishing there a somewhat predictable effort. On the other hand, saltwater bays, sounds, and oceans are so large that you can never master all their angling mysteries.

Yet fishing in the brine casts its spell over practically any angler who happens to find him- or herself on the shores of salty waters. This appeal probably has its roots in the same desire that for centuries caused young boys to run away to the sea, chasing dreams of the sailing or pirate life. There is no denying that the romance of the sea finds its way into the blood of many angling sportsmen and -women.

Of course, romanticized and poetic yearnings aside, there are some valid reasons that anglers find themselves attracted to salt water. As a rule, the beaches, bays, and backwaters of our coastlines provide some of the most beautiful vistas in America. They are a joy to visit regardless of whether or not the fish are biting. The salt air and water also have such an invigorating effect that, again, you often hardly notice if the fishing action begins to lag.

Finally, there is that thrilling knowledge hiding on the edge of consciousness that in salt water you never know what may take your bait or lure next. Lore and literature are filled with our collective flights of fantasy on the subject, whether it is the tale of Hemingway's Santiago battling the great fish, Ahab in pursuit of Moby Dick, or Quint challenging Jaws. We know there are behemoths in salt water, and on the next cast one of them may take our bait! That knowledge lends an irresistible appeal to saltwater angling, and fly-casters are not immune to the siren call of the monsters of the deep. The possibility of battling truly large and strong fish is a large part of what draws fly-casters to the shore.

The history of saltwater fly-fishing is a surprisingly long one. There exist some mentions of saltwater fly-casting in Britain that date back to the start of the 19th century. In this country shad and striped bass were the targets of fly-casters in the Mid-Atlantic and New England areas as far back as the 1830s. Prior to the turn of the 20th century a host of early fly-fishing writers, among them Dr. James Henshall, Frank Forester, and Mary Orvis Marbury, were discussing the sport in relation to Florida and the Texas coast.

The first actual description of a fish taken from the brine on a fly concerns an 80-pound tarpon caught by an angler and writer named A. W. Dimock around the turn of the century at Homosassa on Florida's Gulf Coast. Still, for a long period after that event, saltwater fish were not considered normal targets for fly-casters.

That began to change during the 1930s, especially in the Florida Keys, when more anglers began seriously experimenting with the sport. During World War II, when many of the men working as guides in the Keys were away in military service, some women took over the reins of innovation in the sport. Sisters Beulah Cass, Frankie Albright, and "Bonefish" Bonnie Smith gained particular renown as fly-fishing guides during that time.

It was not until the end of World War II, however, that interest in tackling saltwater game fish with the long rod began to attract widespread interest. Much of the action in these early days was centered on the Florida Keys. The year-round good weather, shallow flats, crystal-clear water, and presence of big bonefish, tarpon, and snook near shore all combined to make South Florida the perfect cradle of modern saltwater fly-fishing.

One pioneer of the sport who was instrumental in introducing and popularizing the sport during the 1950s was legendary fly-caster and fishing writer Joe Brooks. He had already gained fame as a fly-fisherman before he began reporting the excitement of catching a variety of saltwater fish on fly-rods.

Close on Brooks's heels were other renowned anglers led by Frank Woolner, Lee Wulff, Stu Apte, and Lefty Kreh. Kreh, the longtime outdoor writer for Baltimore newspapers, has probably been the most widely known and influential saltwater fly-caster of the second half of the 20th century—and into the 21st. Not only has he pursued saltwater game fish with a fly-rod all over the globe, but he has been an innovator in the sport's techniques as well. The Lefty's Deceiver fly pattern that he created is one of the most versatile saltwater lures for fly-rodding ever designed. In fact, the fly's popularity is such that it was featured on a U.S. postage stamp back in 1991!

The enthusiasm these men generated for saltwater fly-casting has since infected a couple of ensuing generations of sportsmen, particularly along the South Atlantic Coast of the United States. South Florida may have been the cradle of the modern version of the sport, but it is now practiced all the way up to the Outer Banks of North Carolina and shows no signs of declining in popularity.

My own introduction to saltwater fly-fishing came as a result of stumbling into the Monroe County Library in Islamorada, Florida, on a rainy May afternoon about a decade ago. The day's fishing was a washout, so my interest in history drew me to that hall of books. In a dusty file cabinet I came across yellowing copies of magazine articles penned by Zane Grey in the second decade of the 20th century, detailing his pursuit of game fish in Florida's Middle Keys. Though his reputation was founded on writing enduring western novels, Grey was also a renowned big-game angler and co-founder of the International Game Fish Association. After reading of his pursuit of barracuda along Indian Key Fill and bonefish in the vicinity of today's Long Key State Recreation Area, I resolved to try to re-create his boatless fishing trips in modern-day versions.

It was almost a year before I was back in the area to pursue my quest. Just as Grey had done nearly 80 years earlier, I cast for barracuda from the shore of the Indian Key Fill just west of Islamorada, but with no luck. Later that same day I waded the shallow flats for bonefish off the Atlantic side of Long Key, near the site of the old Long Key Fishing Club where the novelist often visited. Though I spooked the only bonefish I encountered at this location, I did hook and land a couple of barracuda on flies. The adrenaline rush of fighting these toothy, aggressive fish, which turned aerial acrobats when hooked, was enough to set the hook of saltwater fly-fishing firmly into me as well.

Since that initial adventure I have fished for a wide variety of saltwater denizens with fly-casting gear along the Southeast Coast of the United States. From North Carolina's Outer Banks to the Florida Keys, I have pursued redfish, spotted seatrout, snook, tarpon, bluefish, bonefish, and permit with a fly-rod. Along the way, less glamorous blue runner, mangrove snapper, barracuda, needlefish, jack crevalle, Spanish mackerel, and ladyfish species have taken an interest in my flies. This variety of species is another factor in the sport's allure—not only do you never know what size the next catch may be, you can never be sure what species it will be, either.

Despite the many factors that make saltwater fly-fishing such an appealing proposition, the sport has its drawbacks. When you take up the sport, it is best to realize up front that you are putting yourself at a great disadvantage. If your goal is to catch as many of the biggest fish as is possible, then fly-fishing gear is not your best choice. The very limited casting range possible with a fly-rod is a distinct disadvantage. The amount of effort and energy needed for casting heavyweight rods and lines also requires you to have a pretty good idea where the fish actually are before beginning to cast. Blind-casting into the ocean can be a very tiring and frustrating endeavor!

There *are* some special situations in which fly-casting gear is the best suited for saltwater fishing—but these are the exceptions. In saltwater fly-fishing, the challenge of how the fish are caught is more important than how many or how big they are. If you recognize and accept this premise, fly-fishing in the brine can be a most rewarding hobby.

Once you are comfortable with the challenges that saltwater fly-casting presents, the next problems you will face are where to fish and for which species. Answering these two questions is the primary objective of this guidebook.

Surprisingly, the bulk of southern saltwater anglers need a bit of help with these questions. More than 77 percent of Georgia's saltwater anglers live over 100 miles from the nearest salt water! The figure is probably not much different in the Carolinas. Of course, any saltwater angler hailing from the landlocked southern states must of necessity travel to unfamiliar shores. Finally, in Florida the very length of the state's coastline makes gaining knowledge of all the prime fishing locations a daunting affair. An angler from Jacksonville visiting Miami may feel he has entered another world. Simply put, most anglers who fish in saltwater along the South Atlantic Coast have traveled from some distance and are not familiar with the area.

Added to this is the fact that successful saltwater fly-casting calls for some very specific conditions. At first glance you would expect finding saltwater fly-fishing destinations to be easy. After all, just look at how long the coastline is and how big our ocean, bays, inlets, rivers, and tidal creeks are—there seem to be endless tracts of water! The truth of the matter, however, is

ZANE JACOBS

There are many places on tidal rivers and streams where fly-casters can find targets for casting, even from the shore.

that a shorebound or wading fly-caster has only limited access to the South Atlantic shore. The three major limiting factors for shorebound fly-casters are marshes, mangroves, and private land. From North Florida up through Georgia and the Carolinas, a great deal of shoreline is made up of salt marshes. Usually these marshes border tidal creeks, rivers, or inlets and contain soft mud that makes walking in them all but impossible. They effectively create a barrier between the angler and the water. In Central to South Florida mangrove shorelines create very similar situations. And, of course, where the shore of a body of salt water is privately owned (except for ocean beaches up to the high-tide mark), you must have the permission of the landowner to cross any property or fish from shore.

In spite of these drawbacks, there are plenty of spots where a fly-fisherman can stand in one place and cast all day long. But to be successful, fly-casting must be a mobile pursuit. Covering as much fish-holding water as possible is the best way to improve your odds of catching a nomadic saltwater fish on a fly. For this reason, the destinations for shorebound fly-casters described in this book are all places where there is a large-enough expanse of water available to keep you busy for at least several hours of fishing.

Spotted seatrout are ubiquitous along the entire coast, from North Carolina to the upper Florida Keys.

The scope of this book, however, is not limited to directing shorebound anglers to good fly-fishing places. If you have a small boat at your disposal, your options for getting to the fish improve greatly. But given the thousands of miles of South Atlantic Coast, it would be impossible to note every bend in a tidal creek or bit of bayside shoreline that holds fish at some time of the year. In discussing the places for fly-casting from small boats, I have focused on destinations where visiting anglers are most likely to find themselves: major resort areas, cities, and parks. Naturally, if a particular stretch of coast is rather remote but offers truly outstanding saltwater fly-casting opportunities, it too is covered.

With regard to the species of fish discussed in later chapters, I cover those most often targeted and caught by fly-casters on inshore waters. Some that are susceptible to flies but not often pursued are also mentioned. Offshore ventures for big-game prey that require large, expensive boats and advanced levels of seamanship, however, fall outside the realm of this book, since that is a specialized subject.

The area covered in this book runs from the North Carolina–Virginia border south to Key West, Florida. In this region fly-fishing destinations on beaches, coastal rivers or creeks, ocean inlets, sounds, and tidal flats are described. Whether your next saltwater fly-fishing adventure takes you to the azure flats of the Florida Keys, the tidal marshes of Georgia's Golden Isles, or the sounds and beaches of the Carolina coast, you should find information in the following pages to make your trip and your fishing a bit easier and more successful.

Maps

Regardless of what type of fishing you choose to try, finding the best fishing locations and the access points to these waters are of prime importance to your success. Often the desired information can be obtained by contacting local tackle shops, talking to state fisheries personnel, or simply asking other anglers. Still, these methods can be rather hit or miss. After all, not every bait clerk, biologist, or fisherman is a master of creating verbal or illustrated maps.

Tackle stores can often provide maps to area hot spots along the shore, but these will ordinarily cover only a very limited piece of the coast—assuming that they are available at all.

On the other hand, it is possible to obtain maps and other information from the various states along the coast, which will make the problem of finding the best fishing much easier. First of all, the best maps available showing the roads and landmarks along the shore are the *Atlas & Gazetteers* produced by the DeLorme Mapping Company of Freeport, Maine. These very detailed map books are now available for Florida, Georgia, North Carolina, and South Carolina. They show major highways, secondary roads, and many dirt paths and trails to the water. Most boat landings and ramps are identified as well.

About the only weakness of the DeLorme maps with regard to coastal areas is that many tidal creeks, inlets, and bays are not named. Fortunately, the coastal charts produced by the National Oceanic and Atmospheric Administration (NOAA) of the U.S. government are also available to the public. These provide all the names of bodies of water that are missing from the DeLorme maps.

Finally, each of the four states covered in this book has a marine resources agency that provides lists of boat landings and ramps the state owns or maintains for public use. These are available either by mail or via the Internet.

The locator maps accompanying the individual chapters in the book show towns, major highways, and landmarks that, when used in conjunction with the material mentioned earlier, should make understanding the text and finding the fishing destinations more practical as well.

Map Sources

The maps listed below are available from public agencies or private companies for a fee. Contact the individual company or agency for details.

DeLorme Mapping Company
P.O. Box 298
Yarmouth, ME 04906
207-846-7000

DeLorme is a private company producing Atlas & Gazetteers *by state. These are the most comprehensive maps of land areas available from private sources. They show the names of major highways, secondary roads, and many landmarks along the shore.* Atlas & Gazetteers *are available for Florida, Georgia, North Carolina, and South Carolina.*

National Oceanic and Atmospheric Administration
Distribution Division (N/ACC3)
National Ocean Survey
6501 Lafayette Avenue
Riverdale, MD 20737-1199
1-800-638-8975 or 301-436-6990

This federal agency is charged with maintaining accurate navigational charts of coastal waters of the United States. These charts are the most detailed maps covering shoreline waters and are available for the coasts of Florida, Georgia, North Carolina, and South Carolina. They contain the names of bays, tidal creeks and rivers, passes, and sounds, as well as providing water depths. The charts, however, are rather expensive.

University of Georgia
Marine Extension Service
715 Bay Street
Brunswick, GA 31520
912-264-7268

This unit, a branch of the University of Georgia, produces a "Guide to Coastal Fishing in Georgia" map for each county on the coast of the state. These pinpoint areas that ordinarily hold game fish, identifying them by species. It covers tidal creeks and rivers, sounds and inlets, and near-shore waters. Some of these maps have recently been updated, but others are as much as 20 years old.

CHAPTER 1

Fishing Locations

In many ways fly-casting in salt water along the South Atlantic Coast has much in common with any other kind of fishing venture. At the heart of the matter lies the problem of finding the fish. Unless you are casting your fly to where the fish are, your chances of provoking a strike are small. Therefore, the first order of business is finding the species of fish you are trying to catch.

Having made that point, it is also worth noting that fishing in salt water in general, and fly-fishing in the brine in particular, presents some problems not faced when fishing in fresh water. Above all else, the fact that so many saltwater species are quite nomadic makes them different from their fresh-water cousins. These saltwater predators are not as likely to have a "home" as are freshwater species. A good feeding lie in a trout stream is quickly taken over by another fish if the original resident is caught. The same is true of a prime holding area for a largemouth bass under a boat dock or beside a sunken stump in a freshwater lake. A change of water level or severe swing in weather conditions may make these freshwater fish move, but when normal conditions return, the fish are prone to do so as well. Under usual cir-cumstances, these prime spots have fish in them.

The same cannot be said of saltwater fish, particularly with regard to the species targeted by fly-fishermen in shallow, inshore waters. These species favor certain feeding areas in which they forage, but not specific spots within that area. It is much more normal to find them roving through the area as singles or in schools. One exception to this rule can be found in the reef-

ZANE JACOBS

Wading into the surf from beaches or around inlets is an underutilized method of pursuing game fish along the southeast coast.

dwelling fish that congregate around rock or coral bottoms and around wrecked ships or other artificial reefs. These species, however, are ordinarily in deep water and make poor targets for fly-casting.

Adding to the difficulty of finding nomadic saltwater game fish is the influence exerted on them by the changing tides. Tidal marshes, flats, bays, and creeks are the nurseries of the sea. They are the spawning grounds where the food chain begins, which ultimately culminates with game fish we seek. As the tides sweep into these places, the deeper water allows safe access to large, hungry predators. Once the tide begins to fall, the game fish move back out of these areas, lurking in deeper water around the edges, waiting for the moving water to wash food species to them. Because of this cycle, many of the species we seek are in constant motion with the tides, as well as moving around seeking the most fertile feeding grounds.

Yet there are times when we pick the best tide phase, go to an area where fishing is often good, and still come back with an empty stringer because the roaming predators and bait fish were elsewhere. Such a situation is particularly difficult if you are not fly-casting from a boat, since moving to a new location to fish is not always easy or possible on foot. Needless to say, having access to a boat provides a lot more fly-fishing opportunities.

Due to the nomadic characteristics of the fish, saltwater anglers do not ordinarily prospect by blind-casting into open water. This is especially true of the fly-caster. Repeated casting with heavyweight fly gear can be frustrating—

and tiring—unless there is some reason to suspect there are hungry fish present. Since the fish roam so much, they could show up almost anywhere, and given the size of the Atlantic Ocean, our coastal sounds, and miles of tidal rivers and creeks, there is a great deal of water in which they can roam!

The answer to this riddle of where to fish can best be solved by angling in the spots that, under normal circumstances, hold bait fish and other sources of food. Certain bottom structures and types of underwater topography provide good feeding and hiding places for bait fish, or they offer fertile ground for other kinds of forage that attract game fish. Granted, even the presence of bait in these sites does not guarantee that the fish you want to catch are there as well, but the odds of finding the fish in them are much greater than in places less inviting to the predator and the prey.

Especially for fly-casters, who are limited in the amount of water they can cover due to the shorter casting range than is enjoyed by anglers using spinning lures or bait rigs, narrowing the search for fish to these prime areas is very important. When fishing a destination for the first time, try to find the sites most likely to hold fish, even if fish are not betraying their presence by rolling on the surface.

Be aware, however, that the following descriptions and tactics are all stated in generalized terms. Each fishing site has its specific challenges. Often several of the situations described are found in conjunction. For instance, stone riprap lining the shore of an ocean inlet usually holds bait fish and small crustaceans, which attract game fish. But if that same shore opens onto a tidal flat immediately inside the inlet, rising tides can draw the bait off the riprap to forage on the flat as it floods. When that happens, the predators follow the bait to the flat. Obviously, this alters the dynamics of the angling in this location, requiring flexibility in the approach you use. Still, the following information should be of use as you figure out where to begin your search for saltwater game fish on a fly-rod.

Piers, Docks, and Bridges

Some of the most obvious places to begin the search for hungry game fish are around the many man-made structures often found in the water. The pilings supporting bridges, fishing piers, and boat docks all serve as home or feeding grounds for a wide variety of marine life. The supporting posts of abandoned and collapsed structures serve the same purpose. Barnacles, plankton, and other residents of the lowest levels of the food chain abound around these wooden or concrete pillars. These creatures, in turn, attract larger crustaceans and small fish. Thus the climb up the rungs of the ladder of the food chain begins. Eventually the predatory game fish appear as well. These larger predators also use the structures in the water as cover for ambushing smaller unwary critters.

In virtually all cases these structures offer the best possibilities for successful fishing when the tides are moving the water. Ebb or flood tides when the water is standing still are ordinarily the least-productive fishing times. On the other hand, when the tide is either rising or falling, the pilings tend to attract fish. This is partially due to the fact that moving water dislodges small crabs, shrimp, and fish from hiding places on the structures, leaving them vulnerable.

As a general rule, casting to the downcurrent side of these obstructions is most effective. The eddies formed on this side of the pilings offer refuge from the current for bait fish, but also congregate them where the predators can find them. The game fish often get into the eddies as well; rather than wasting any energy fighting the moving water, they can wait to dart out and grab any food brought to them by the current.

The two best methods of fishing such a site are to bring the fly through the eddies, or to cast upcurrent of the pilings and run the fly down past where the game fish is (hopefully) hiding in the slack water.

There are a couple of drawbacks to fly-fishing around piers, docks and bridges. Ordinarily such structures are built in deep water. If you are shore-bound or wading, the pilings nearest shore are the only ones you can reach with a cast.

Since the structures are ordinarily built high above the water, they do not make practical platforms from which to fly-cast, either. Fly-casting is very much a sea-level endeavor. It is difficult to properly present a fly in a real-life manner when casting from a high perch.

Finally, piers, bridges, and docks are favorite spots for bait-fishermen. Their lines—draped from the structures into the water—often limit the space that you can target. Snagging one of those lines with your fly can cause either embarrassment or heated words with the owner of the line.

Tidal Creeks

The entire South Atlantic Coast region is crisscrossed by tidal creeks that meander through salt marshes. Sometimes these streams cut through higher ground, but even in these cases they ordinarily have a fringe of marsh grasses along the shore.

Especially important are the mouths of tidal creeks—where a main creek empties into a bay, sound, or river, or where smaller tributary creeks or ditches intersect a secondary creek. In other words, these can be the mouths of very big creeks or of very small ones. Either way, the conditions that attract fish are present.

Again, these areas depend on tidal flow to make them good spots to fish. When a flood tide is just beginning, game fish stack up at the entrance to these creeks, waiting for the water depth to rise to the point at which they feel secure in entering. Their purpose in running up the creek is to feed. Once the water rises, they can get back into the marsh grasses along the shore, where much of the rich marine life lives. As they wait for the rising tide, the fish are usually willing to get a jump on the feeding if something tempting is offered to them.

Once the tide has peaked and begins to fall, the fish will again congregate at the creek mouth. This time they are waiting for the water running out of the marshes to bring forage items to them—the saltwater game fish's idea of fast-food delivery. Small crabs, shrimp, and minnows swept out of the grasses by the falling tide are carried downstream. The reason the game fish pick the mouth of the creek to feed is that they can avoid being stranded back up in the creek by the falling tide.

The obvious way to fish these sites is to run a fly downstream, imitating the bait fish, shrimp, or crabs being pulled along with the current.

You will also tend to find game fish in deeper holes where there is a bend in the creek. This is especially common during colder winter weather, but also occurs during the heat of the day on bright summer afternoons.

These holes are created because currents encountering a change in course on the stream tend to gouge out either the shore, the bottom, or both. The added depth holds heat in the water during the winter, and allows less heat-producing light penetration in the hotter months. The more moderate temperature levels attract the fish to the holes. Naturally, any bait fish wandering into such a site that is occupied by a school of predators may end up regretting the move. It is just such a blunder that your fly should try to imitate when casting to these holes.

If you do not have a boat, reaching the mouths, bends, and holes on tidal creeks can be difficult. The bottoms of such streams are often composed of soft mud that makes wading difficult or impossible. Marshes limit shoreline access as well. But when you do find such sites that are accessible from shore, they can be consistent producers of fly-fishing action for you.

Shell Bars

Another important holding area for game fish is around submerged or exposed shell bars—mounds of oyster shells that may be either live or simply empty shells. Quite often these sites are a mixture of the two, with the shells of other species mixed in. In many cases you can find a bar at low tide, when some of the shells are above the water at low tide and the rest below the surface. In other cases the entire bar of shells is submerged during all water levels. Usually the shellfish making up these bars are eastern oysters, which are native to the entire coastline of the southeastern states.

As with virtually any hard surface in salt water, shell beds produce or attract many of the invertebrates that serve as food for larger marine creatures. Thus shrimp, crabs, and minnows gather around the shell bars to feed as well as to find shelter in the crevices created by the jumble of shells. As you would expect, when these bait species gather, they attract the predators.

Anytime there is current flowing over or by a shell bar there are likely to be game fish around, looking for an easy meal. If it is a bar that is partially or totally exposed during low water levels, try casting to it just after it becomes submerged on the rising tide. The fish move up on top of such bars looking for food when the water rises.

Tidal Flats

Some of the most productive fishing locations on the southeastern coast are tidal flats. These expanses of very shallow water—often only a foot or two deep—are generally at their best when the tide is high or at least rising. As a rule, all such flats shrink to only inches of water at ebb tide. Additionally, in many cases—especially in marsh or mud flats—they will be completely dry at low tide.

When there is water on the flats, the game fish move in to search for bait fish, shrimp, and other crustaceans. Very often the water is so shallow and clear that sight-casting to cruising or feeding fish is possible. Even on mud flats with discolored water, the lack of depth means that fish may give away their presence: Their tails break the surface as they feed on the bottom in a head-down position. Anglers refer to this phenomenon as tailing.

Tidal flats are most often associated with fishing in South Florida, specifically from Cape Canaveral down to the Florida Keys. The sand, grass, and marl shallows found there provide hundreds of square miles of fish-

A canoe can be very handy for reaching fish just offshore.

holding water. The very clear waters in this area make fly-casting to the various flats species a most practical fishing alternative.

Farther north, opportunities also exist for this type of fishing, though under slightly different circumstances. Here it is the mud flats found in association with marshes along the coast from North Carolina down to North Florida that are the scene of the action. In the backs of bays and especially at the heads of creeks, where the streams rise from the marsh, shallow flats are covered with only a foot or two of water at high tide. These shallows are scoured by game species when the water is high in their pursuit of food. The wakes created by cruising fish and the tails protruding from the surface are the signs to watch for in these places, since the generally poor water clarity offers little chance of actually seeing the fish in the water.

Whether in gin-clear or mud-stained waters, flats fishing is a sport that calls for sighting the quarry before casting. Anytime the water level is right on tidal flats, it is time to don polarized sunglasses (to cut through the surface glare) and begin looking for signs of game fish. Once you spot the fish, whether they are cruising or feeding, the trick is to figure out which way they are moving, then cast ahead of them. Use a fly that imitates the prey of the particular fish you are after and cast so that it comes close enough to be noticed, but not so close it will spook the fish. This type of fly-casting can be the most frustrating in the sport, but also the most exciting and rewarding.

Fishing on tidal flats, especially those covered with sea grasses, often calls for using topwater flies. Either a popping or skipping bug can provide some exciting action, particularly on days with low-light conditions, such as cloud

*Large skipping bugs are just one of the saltwater flies
that attract a variety of predators.*

cover. Since these flies float, there is less likelihood of them hanging up in the grasses. Also, since the water is so shallow, enticing the fish to come to the surface is not particularly hard—they are already practically there anyway!

The other practical option for fishing grass flats is to use a weedless fly. This is generally a streamer pattern with a short piece of heavy monofilament line or light wire arranged as a weed guard extending from the eye of the hook out to the point. This guard fends off the weeds, keeping them from getting hung on the hook's point.

Regardless of the exact composition of the flats, if they have a solid bottom for wading you can walk to good fly-casting spots that boating anglers cannot reach because of the shallow water. These flats have always been the domain of the wading angler.

Another reason wading can be advantageous is it allows you to keep a lower profile on the water than is possible in a boat. The movements of anglers in a boat are visible at long distances through the clear water of South Florida's flats. Wading means that less of you is above the surface—thus your movements are less visible to the fish. Most fish can see what is going on above the water, much the way you see movement in the water. Their field of vision is distorted by the surface, the same as yours. If you look straight down at water from a 90-degree angle, you can see into it better than if you look at the surface from a lesser angle. The smaller the angle in relation to the level plane of the surface, the less able you are to discern what is going on in the water. This holds true for fish looking from the other direction as well. The more you increase the angle by approaching them and exposing more of yourself above the water, the more likely they are to detect your movements.

Ocean Inlets

In most ways ocean inlets resemble the mouths of tidal creeks with regard to how and why they attract game fish. The difference is scale: The area covered as well as the force and volume of the water flow are greater. Basically, an ocean inlet (also sometimes referred to as a pass) is the gap between two barrier islands. This gap connects sounds or rivers on the inland side of the isles with the open ocean on their outer side.

Game fish visit these inlets in search of food on the same schedules they visit tidal creeks. During rising tides they enter from the ocean, moving inland with the advancing water. During falling tides the predators appear on the ocean side, where they await food being swept out to them. Of course, these are generalities that can be altered by the exact circumstances of the particular inlet. Quite often the inlets have been bridged, have piers or docks just inside their mouths, or even have tidal flats on the inland side. These combinations alter the exact dynamics of each inlet.

An additional factor that attracts game fish to inlets is the conflicting currents that clash there. Waters coming out of the sounds, rivers, or creeks meet the incoming tides, causing tidal or current rips in the water. As the waters meet from different directions, they often form areas of turbulent water with whitecapped surfaces, known as tidal rips. The water action also gouges out holes in the sand on the bottom. Such strong interaction also dislodges and leaves helpless smaller fish and crustaceans, making them easy prey for predatory fish.

Because of the direction of wind and wave action along the southeastern coast, tidal rips are most frequently found at the southern ends of barrier islands. They are closest to shore and most easily reached on incoming tides.

Another feature sometimes found at ocean inlets is riprap, a man-made structure composed of rocks piled along the shore to prevent bank erosion from the wave action of boat traffic passing through the inlet. Depending on the situation, these rocks can be anything from bowling-ball sized, to the size of a small automobile. Needless to say, the rocks—and the crevices within a wall of them—make great structures for producing and hiding bait species. Game fish generally are found cruising such shores in search of food during moving tides.

Jetties are other man-made structures often found around inlets. These long piles of rocks that stretch out into the open water prevent wave action from passing boats from eroding adjacent beaches. Some jetties are exposed above the waterline during all tidal levels, while others may be submerged during flood stages.

Jetties vary in length from just a few hundred yards to 3 miles. In most cases the abovewater portions are less than a mile long. Still, fishing from jetties offers the best opportunity for anglers without a boat to get out beyond the surf and toss flies at species ordinarily found in the open ocean, such as Spanish mackerel and bluefish.

Watch for schools of these game fish pushing bait to the surface during feeding frenzies. The fleeing bait fish and swirling water caused by the predators' attacks provide easy targets for placing your casts in the middle of the action. Another sign that gives away the location of such action is groups of gulls circling and diving to the surface to pick up stunned bait fish. At times this kind of feeding activity at the surface continues for more than an hour, allowing you to simply follow the fish as they move along the jetty.

In some cases the tops of jetties are paved, providing anglers great casting platforms from which to fish. Other jetties simply remain jumbles of various-sized rocks. Be careful, for these unpaved ones can be quite slippery and treacherous to navigate on foot.

Ocean passes require the same fly-casting techniques as do creek mouths. Casting streamers across the current during rising tides is a good option, while running a fly down the current during falling tides works better. Running the fly with the current, regardless of which way it is moving, is the best tactic when fishing along riprap.

Beach Tidal Pools and Washes

One of the most exasperating situations faced by saltwater anglers is trying to catch fish on the beach. Surf-casting can, under the right conditions, be exciting and productive. But you are challenging the Atlantic Ocean—which is a very big pond! Along its shore the beaches all look alike. There are simply miles of sand, with waves lapping on the sloping shore and virtually no structures to hold fish. Also, given the fact that the fish constantly move along this shore, if there is no obvious surface feeding going on, exactly where should you begin your search?

One tactic for finding fish consistently when surf casting is to locate tidal pools. These are areas where the wave action has gouged out low places along the beach that hold water even after the tide has receded. When the tide comes back in, it covers them to form deeper holes along the beach. The best time for fishing such spots is during incoming tides, when the rising water first covers the spit of sand that separates the pool from the surf. Predators move in at this time in search of prey species in the pool, and often continue to patrol these deeper areas as the tide continues to rise.

An additional advantage of these pools, from the point of view of the angler, is that they are usually quite close to shore, even at high tide. Often they are easily reached by fly-casters standing in only inches of water. On the other hand, these pools come and go with the shifting beach sands and water currents. As a result, today's good fishing spot may be tomorrow's flat beach.

Of course, not all tidal pools are created equal. The deeper ones offer the better fishing opportunities. Still, it goes without saying that if you see a pool with obvious signs of fish, such as pushed wakes or fish breaking the surface chasing minnows, cast there first.

Stripping minnow-imitating streamers through these pools is a good way to test them. Since such pools are generally not overly large or abundant, they can be quickly covered by a fly-caster. Even blind-casting in them is a practical strategy, if no fish are showing themselves, since they represent such limited target areas.

When the tide is receding, look for the washes where the water from the tidal pools is running back to the ocean. These small streams of water suck food items with them, and hungry game fish are likely to be found in the deeper water just offshore of them.

Stripping a fly across the current where it is first striking deeper water is a good approach to tidal washes. Still, because there are often crosscurrents and churning water in the surf, any angle or direction of retrieve may provoke a strike in these locations. It is always a good idea to work the site thoroughly with your casts before moving on.

Small jetties (also referred to as groins) are another feature sometimes found on beaches. Usually placed along the beach on barrier islands to hold eroding sand in place, they are particularly common toward the ends of islands near smaller inlets or creek mouths. They are very similar to the larger jetties at ocean inlets, but on a smaller scale. Since their rocky edges do not extend as far out into the water, the best time to fish along these groins tends to be during rising tides. Again, these may be composed of rocks that are paved on top, of unpaved rocks, or even of combinations of rock and timbers.

CHAPTER 2

The Fish

Over the past 40 years anglers have pretty much proven that virtually any saltwater fish can be taken on a fly-rod under certain conditions. From the regal billfish of the Gulf Stream to the lowly bottom feeders of the back bays, all species can, in the right situations, become vulnerable to a well-presented fly. Of course, the specific conditions vary from fish to fish, and some species are very rarely found in locations or situations where a fly-caster can successfully entice them.

On the other hand, six species of fish found in various areas along the South Atlantic Coast are susceptible to fly-fishing tactics, are commonly targeted by fly-fishers, and are frequently found in shallow, easily reached inshore waters. These are red drum, spotted seatrout, tarpon, snook, bonefish, and permit.

Another eight species are also found in the same areas and can be rather easily enticed to strike a fly, but are not often pursued by fly-fishermen. These are striped bass, bluefish, mangrove snapper, ladyfish, barracuda, jack crevalle, little tunny (false albacore), and Atlantic bonito.

Finally, another nine species can be taken on flies but are normally only hooked as incidental catches because they so infrequently show up in shallow water, are small in size, or have feeding habits that make them tough to target with flies. In spite of these drawbacks, black drum, cobia, flounder, pompano, sheepshead, Spanish mackerel, tripletail, weakfish, and whiting can be fly-rod targets at certain times.

All the world records mentioned below for these fish species are taken from the statistics of the International Game Fish Association (IGFA).

Red Drum *(Sciaenops ocellatus)*

If a poll were taken along the southern Atlantic seaboard, it would probably reveal that red drum are the second most popular saltwater fish pursued by anglers, finishing just behind the spotted seatrout. Among fly-casters, however, that ranking would probably be reversed. The favor with which fly-fishers look at the red drum is based on its ability to reach gargantuan sizes and the fact that the fish love to feed on shallow flats, making them very good targets for fly-casting. It does not hurt their rating that they also make delicious table fare.

Red drum are known by several other names in certain areas of their range, which stretches from the Virginia coast down to the Florida Keys and around the Gulf of Mexico to the Texas shore. In Florida and the Gulf states they are usually called redfish or simply reds. Other names in favor along the Atlantic Coast are channel bass and spottail bass. Especially along the coast of the Carolinas, smaller red drum are called puppy drum, while the larger members of the species are referred to as bull reds (even though these are usually females).

Ranging from copper to bronze colored, red drum always have a black spot at the base of their caudal fin, which accounts for the nickname spottail bass. Additionally, it is not uncommon for some fish to have several other black spots that are not uniform in size or shape spread along their sides.

For the most part, the red drum found along the South Atlantic Coast are not migratory. Instead, they tend to remain in tidal creeks or rivers for their first four years until they reach about 15 pounds. Then they begin to move to inshore ocean waters, forming schools that return to the sounds and bays to feed.

The exceptions to this rule can be found on the northern fringe of their range. While the smaller red drum there maintain their sedentary habits, in North Carolina there is a migration of bull reds along the beaches of the Outer Banks, moving south in the fall and back north in the spring.

Along beaches red drum are found around tidal rips where conflicting currents clash, or in the deeper washed-out holes at the outer edge of the surf. In bays, rivers, and creeks look for them around marsh grass at high tide and around any beds of live or dead oyster shells. The ideal shallow flat on which to locate red drum has marsh grass along one edge and deep water on the other.

Most of the fly-fishing opportunities for red drum occur when they are on shallow flats, where they feed on shrimp, crabs, and minnows. On flats that are covered with grass, the fish sometimes assume a head-down position in the vegetation while feeding, often leaving their tails sticking out of the water. This is known as tailing and is one way to locate feeding red drum. On mud flats these fish also give away their position by creating "muds" as they stir up the silt on the bottom in their quest for food. Finally, when a school of reds is cruising in the shallows, the fish create waves on the surface as their backs push the water before them. These waves are commonly referred to as humps or wakes, and the fish are said to be humping or waking.

Although red drum have the underslung jaw that is characteristic of bottom-feeding species, they take flies that are presented anywhere in the water column, from top to bottom. The most exciting way to catch them is on topwater popping bugs, but colorful Bendbacks, Clouser Minnows, Lefty's Deceivers, and other colorful streamer flies are more dependably successful. When sight-casting to tailing, humping, or mudding reds, it is necessary to cast the fly very close to the fish. Though red drum are quite wary in shallow water and are spooked by noise and shadows, they have poor eyesight. Thus the fly needs to be presented close to a fish, with a quick retrieve to attract the drum's attention.

The current all-tackle world record for red drum is held by Dave G. Deuel for a 94-pound, 2-ounce fish. It was caught in the surf on the Outer Banks at Avon, North Carolina, on November 7, 1984.

Spotted Seatrout *(Cynoscion nebulosus)*

As noted earlier, among all fishermen along the South Atlantic Coast spotted seatrout have been the number one target for years. Their popularity is founded on their abundance, wide range, and willingness to strike a variety of baits and lures, plus their fine taste (although they do not freeze well and should be eaten fresh). These fish are sometimes called speckled trout, specks, or simply trout by the anglers who target them. Larger specimens of this species are sometimes called yellowmouths because of the color around their mouths.

Spotted seatrout are found all along the southern Atlantic seaboard, from North Carolina's sounds south to the Florida Keys. Throughout this range they can be found along beaches, particularly in the fall and winter, but are much more abundant in tidal creeks, rivers, and bays. They are common on shallow sea-grass flats as well. With the exception of some migratory fish that

JIMMY JACOBS

Seatrout swim in the sounds of coastal North Carolina throughout the year.

move south from the Chesapeake Bay into the Carolinas in the winter, seatrout are relative homebodies. Research has found that they spend most of their lives within a mile or two of the estuary where they were spawned.

Though there are several related species that resemble this rather slender-framed member of the drum family, the seatrout's hallmark spots make it easily identifiable. These round black spots occur in random patterns along the back and sides of the fish, and are also found on the tail and dorsal fin. The very similar weakfish is also found along the South Atlantic Coast and is the fish most commonly confused with the seatrout. The weakfish, however, has only faint speckles on its sides and no spots at all on its tail or fins.

Throughout its range the spotted seatrout is abundant in sizes of up to 6 pounds. Any fish larger than this is considered a trophy catch and is often referred to as a "gator trout." In the southernmost portion of the waters inhabited by seatrout—and particularly in Florida's Indian River Lagoon in the vicinity of Cocoa, Melbourne, and Vero Beach—fish of more than 10 pounds are taken regularly. The all-tackle world record for this species is held by Craig F. Carson for a 17-pound, 7-ounce spotted seatrout caught at Fort Pierce, Florida, on May 11, 1995.

Speckled trout are excellent quarry to challenge with a fly-rod. They readily attack brightly colored streamers; many fly-casters favor red-and-yellow or red-and-white color combinations. But seatrout will strike any number of fly hues, particularly when they are actively feeding. These fish feed at varying depths, from the bottom to the surface, making it possible to attract them to topwater popping bugs in a variety of colors.

Seatrout do show a preference for a fly that is retrieved slowly, whether a streamer or a popping bug. When you spot a fish approaching your fly, however, you should speed up your retrieve to resemble a fleeing bait fish. Seatrout are noted for their proclivity for making quick dashes at a fly near the boat or shore, just as an angler is about to pick it up for a new cast.

In spite of their following among anglers, seatrout are not particularly impressive fighters once hooked. They are more prone to thrash on the surface than to make strong runs or leap from the water. They must be played with care as well, since their mouths are notoriously soft, making it easy for hooks to pull loose. The popularity of spotted seatrout is built on their abundance and edibility rather than their ferocious nature.

Tarpon *(Megalops atlanticus)*

It comes as a bit of a surprise to many anglers to discover that the tarpon is probably the third most popular target of fly-casters throughout the entire southern Atlantic seaboard. This is because these rugged fighters are more often thought of in association with the semitropical waters of South Florida. Yet during the summer months they can be found along the coast all the way up to North Carolina. As the popularity of saltwater fly-casting has spread, anglers have begun working on techniques for taking tarpon even in the murky waters in the more northerly portions of this range.

One obvious reason that tarpon attract a following wherever they are found is their size. Fish of more than 100 pounds are not at all uncommon throughout their range, with the world record for the species standing at 283 pounds, 4 ounces. That fish was taken by Yvon Victor Sebag on April 16, 1991, at Sherbro Island, Sierra Leone, on the African coast.

On the other hand, the tarpon's popularity is not at all based on edibility. Only a starving angler would try to stomach the flesh of these fish.

Although tarpon, which are also known as silver kings and poons, are most often found inshore in saltwater environs, the smaller ones in particular are at home in brackish water and not averse to venturing even into fresh water. The canal systems of South Florida are noted for holding smaller "baby" tarpon of up to 30 pounds year-round, while the older fish move offshore during cool weather and inshore when it is warm. From

North Florida to North Carolina, however, the larger fish are migratory. They move north along the coast as the water warms in the summer, returning to South Florida or the Caribbean in the winter. In a few instances tarpon have become year-round residents of the warm-water outflows of electric power plants along the southeastern coast.

Within salt water, tarpon can be found throughout the entire range of habitats. They frequent flats when feeding, patrol river or creek channels, swim in bays and inlets, and even run in pods along beaches. The young of the species are spawned offshore but move close to mangrove-lined shores of South Florida for their first six or seven years, until they reach about 4 feet long. They then join the adults in the annual migrations along the coast.

It is tough to mistake a tarpon for any other species. These sleek, silver fish are covered with large scales that look like an armor coating. The last spine in their dorsal fins is extended into a long filament-like appendage that flows behind the fin. The cavernous maw of the tarpon is also extremely tough, making setting a hook a difficult task once the fish strikes a lure.

The tarpon's physiology is rather primitive as well. They have an air bladder that lets them gulp air by rolling on the surface, supplementing the oxygen taken through their gills from the water. For this reason, these fish sometimes show up even in water that is stagnant and contains little oxygen. Surprisingly, although tarpon appear to be moving in a definitive direction when they roll, they most often settle back to the same spot after rolling. Thus surface rolling gives away their location to observant anglers. In fact, in the absence of this behavior, targeting tarpon with a fly-rod in the deeper, murkier waters along the Georgia and Carolina coasts would be a very difficult undertaking, since locating the fish can be daunting. In these areas most of the tarpon are found around ocean inlets or passes between barrier islands. On the other hand, in the shallows of South Florida flats or along beaches, sight-casting to visible fish in the clearer water becomes more practical. Tarpon make a particularly good quarry for fly-casters as well, because they are surface feeders. They do take cut baits from the bottom at times, but the majority of their feeding occurs near the top of the water column.

When you tackle tarpon on a fly-rod, your gear needs to be just as big and rugged as the fish are. Rods, reels, and lines in the 8- to 10-weight range are fine for fish of up to 30 or 40 pounds. Anything bigger needs a rig of 10- to 13-weight if you hope to land the fish in a reasonable length of time. Leaders also need to be stout and in the 30- to 50-pound-test range. These should have a foot-long, 80- to 100-pound-test shock tippet attached to the end. Tarpon have very rough, abrasive mouths that wear through lighter tippets during the extended battle they put up. With heavier terminal tackle, tarpon of more than 100 pounds can be taken.

When it comes to flies, larger-sized streamers are also necessary. Hooks in size 1/0 are needed for even the smallest tarpon, with 3/0 the standard size when fish of 15 to 40 pounds are encountered. For still-larger tarpon, most anglers opt for flies tied on huge 5/0 hooks. Although silver kings take flies in a veritable rainbow of color patterns, there are several that have consistently produced fish for a number of years. Red-and-yellow, red-and-white, and blue-and-white combinations are basic to your tarpon fly box.

These flies should be cast in front of the fish and retrieved in slow, 12-inch line strips. Tarpon like a slow-moving lure and often follow close behind it for a few moments before rushing in for the strike. Once a fish takes the fly, it is important to very quickly jerk your rod and line several times as hard as possible, which varies according to how stout your tackle is. This robust setting of the hook is necessary for two reasons. First, it keeps the fly from getting too deep into the tarpon's throat. If the hook lodges there, the fish's lips can reach far enough up the line to apply their abrasive power above the shock tippet, ensuring that you will lose the battle due to a broken line. Second, a tarpon's jaw is so tough that you need a lot of power to drive in the point of the hook.

The first thing a hooked tarpon tries to do is dislodge the fly by leaping into the air. There are often several of these jumps early in the battle and they can be spectacular—or frightening if the fish is big and near the boat when it becomes airborne. This is the part of the fight when most tarpon are lost, and it is often because the angler does not "bow" to the fish. When the tarpon leaves the water you must dip your rod tip toward the surface, which is most easily accomplished by performing a bowing motion. This provides enough slack line to accommodate the leap and lessens the pressure on the hook—while still maintaining enough pressure to keep it from coming free. Once the early jumps are completed, most tarpon will make long circling runs. With truly big fish, this portion of the battle can last up to an hour on even the heaviest tackle. Landing a tarpon of more than 100 pounds on a fly-rod is considered by many anglers to be inshore saltwater fly-casting's ultimate challenge.

Snook *(Centropomus undecimalis)*

The snook is highly prized and actively pursued by fly-casters throughout its range. It would rank much closer to the top of the list of Southeast Coast anglers' favorites if it were not for its rather limited habitat preference. Snook, which are sometimes referred to as rabalo or linesides, are tropical to semi-tropical creatures. Abundant throughout Central America and the lower Gulf of Mexico, they are rarely found north of the Georgia-Florida border along the eastern seaboard. The lack of favored habitat such as mangrove shores is one reason for their limited range, while their susceptibility to cold weather is another. During unseasonable cold snaps in North Florida, snook die-offs are not uncommon.

Snook have a slender frame that is ordinarily silver in color. A pronounced black line runs along the side of the fish from the back of the gill plate all the way to the tail. This feature accounts for the nickname linesides. Also of note are the very sharp edges found just inside the snook's gill plates. These often cut fishing lines when the fish thrash after being hooked. They can deliver nasty cuts to fingers as well if you try to hoist a snook by its gill plate.

As mentioned earlier, snook are most at home along mangrove-lined shores, but they are also found around submerged structures such as bridge, pier, and boat-dock pilings, or trees that have fallen in the water. Additionally, they can be found in sandy holes on grass flats or, at certain times of the year, cruising along beaches. They rarely venture out past the surf line in the ocean.

Fishing for snook is much like pursuing largemouth bass in fresh water. The tactics are very similar, and the habits of the snook closely resemble those of that very popular freshwater game fish. The differences are that snook get much bigger—and they fight like a largemouth bass on steroids!

Although most specimens are less than 10 pounds, snook weighing 20 to 30 pounds are commonly caught along the South Florida coast. The St. Lucie Inlet area accounts for some even bigger snook; fish of up to 40 pounds have been caught in those waters. Still, truly huge snook are most often taken along the coast of Central America. The IGFA record for snook stands at 53 pounds, 10 ounces. The fish was boated at Parismina Ranch, Costa Rica, by Gilbert Ponzi on October 18, 1978.

Since snook feed on a wide variety of fish, shrimp, and other crustaceans at all depths from the surface to the bottom, they offer a range of options for taking them on flies. Popping bugs worked on the surface draw explosive strikes from these game fish, but you must work the lure rather slowly. It should be cast, popped, then allowed to sit motionless for several seconds; then the pop-and-pause process is repeated. When you fish for snook with streamers, use hooks of sizes 1/0 to 3/0, with red-and-yellow, blue-and-white, and red-and-white being the most popular hues. Even larger crab-patterned flies will sometimes attract hungry snook.

Ordinarily the rods and reels used for snook fishing need be no heavier than 7- to 9-weight, unless you are targeting the largest specimens of the species. It is advisable, regardless of the size of the snook you expect to encounter, to use a shock tippet of 30-pound-test monofilament line at the end of your leader. This should keep a hooked snook from using its gill plates to slice the line during the battle.

Bonefish *(Albula vulpes)*

Bonefish have been highly valued as game fish (even though in this country they are considered too bony to be eaten) since early in the 20th century, when Zane Gray wrote of his pursuits of the "gray ghost of the flats" in the Florida Keys. This fish's long, line-sizzling runs of up to 200 yards when hooked are legendary among flats anglers. It is little wonder that the discovery that the bonefish will take a fly led to its position as one of the most popular species for targeting with a long rod. This ranking is even more impressive since this tropical species is limited in range to extreme southeastern Florida and the Keys in U.S. waters. Finding a bonefish north of Palm Beach on the east coast of the Sunshine State or in Florida Bay proper on the western side of the Keys is a rarity. Yet anglers flock to the Keys, the Caribbean islands, Central and South America, and some of the South Pacific isles where the fish are found, mainly because many saltwater fishermen count their fly-casting careers incomplete until they tangle with the legendary bonefish. For such a storied species, bonefish have surprisingly few colloquial nicknames. Ordinarily they are simply called bonefish or bones. These names, however, are quite accurate, because the fish have very primitive, bony bodies. Silvery in color, they have sloping foreheads and small downward-facing mouths designed for feeding on the bottom.

For such a popular fish, bones do not achieve the great sizes common to other saltwater game fish. On average these fish run in the 3- to 8-pound range. Usually they are found in pods or schools of similarly sized individuals, but the largest fish tend to travel solo or in pairs. The all-tackle world record for bonefish is held by D. Gama Higgs with a 19-pound bone caught off the coast of Zululand, South Africa, on July 8, 1953.

Though most common in the waters of the Caribbean islands and along the coast of Central America, on the western side of the Atlantic Ocean the largest bonefish are found along the South Florida shore and in the Keys.

Especially in Biscayne Bay near Miami, fish of more than 10 pounds show up regularly.

One reason for the bonefish's popularity is its habitat. These fish spend most of their feeding time in quite shallow water on tidal flats. They are often found cruising, tailing, or mudding while facing into rising tides. They will also feed into the wind if it is blowing hard enough to move the water during periods of slack tide. Even when tailing, bonefish are constantly on the move as they search their environment for small crabs, shrimp, or sea worms.

Fishing for bones is ordinarily a sight-casting endeavor. Casting to deeper channels along the edge of flats just prior to the beginning of a flood tide or during periods of cool weather can also be fruitful. Still, casting to visible fish in as little as 1 to 2 feet of water typically provides the challenge and thrill on which this species' reputation is built.

Many anglers who pursue bonefish go after them in vessels called flats boats. These craft were specifically designed for use in the extreme shallows where bonefish are common. The boats are wide, stable casting platforms that can run at high speed in open water, but they are also able to be poled over quite shallow flats. On the stern of the boat is a raised poling platform that sits above the outboard engine. This raised position provides for easier use of a 16- to 20-foot pole to propel the craft slowly and quietly on the flats. It also provides a better vantage point for searching for the fish in the surrounding shallow water.

On the other hand, many fly-casters opt for getting into the water and wading when chasing bonefish. Though this method cuts down on the amount of water that you can cover while looking for the fish, it does offer some advantages as well. Bonefish are noted for being quite wary and easily spooked in shallow water, and they are especially sensitive to noise. Even the sound created by a mild chop on the water splashing against the hull of the boat can send these fish scurrying to deep water. By wading carefully and silently along a flat, you can often get very close to pods of feeding bonefish.

Another reason wading can be advantageous is that a fly-caster can keep a lower profile on the water. The movements and shadows of boat anglers are visible at long distances through the clear water of South Florida's flats. Wading means that less of you is above the surface, so you are less visible to the fish.

As mentioned earlier, bonefish are bottom feeders, and quite effective ones. When downcurrent during a strong tidal flow, they have such an acute sense of smell that they can detect shrimp baits up to 100 feet away. On the other hand, they are not noted for having a great range of vision. For this reason, a fly must be cast close to a feeding fish, but it must land delicately enough to keep from creating a noise.

Once your fly is in the water, the best retrieve is to move it with slow, foot-long line strips. Sometimes bonefish will dart up to a fly moving in this manner, then slow down to follow it. If this happens, a quick, hard jerk on the line to make the fly look like it is trying to escape can provoke an attack from a hesitant fish.

The flies to use for bonefish are generally smaller than for other saltwater quarry. Hook sizes vary from 6 to 1/0, and the flies should be weighted to make them sink fast. Since bonefish feed on the bottom and it is necessary to get the fly close to them, it is also imperative that you get it down to the bottom quickly before the fish move away. Some fly patterns thus incorporate epoxy heads or lead eyes into their design for quick sinking.

Although crab patterns or weighted streamers like the Clouser Minnow can catch the attention of hungry bonefish, shrimp-patterned flies are the staple of this fishery. Patterns like the Crazy Charlie, Snapping Shrimp, and Bonefish Special imitate crustaceans and are designed for skipping right along the bottom. Most are tied so that the hook point faces up when retrieved, making them less likely to snag on the bottom.

Permit *(Trachinotus falcatus)*

The final major game fish targeted by fly-casters on the South Atlantic Coast is the permit. Many anglers using fly-fishing gear, also consider it the greatest challenge. Extremely wary when on shallow flats, permit can also be quite picky eaters. But once hooked, these members of the jack family put up a rugged fight. Though smaller permit of up to 10 to 12 pounds are purported to be quite delectable, larger fish are said to have rather coarse flesh. Still, most permit caught by anglers, especially on the flats, are released to fight again another day.

Like the bonefish, permit are tropical fish; only the most northerly portion of their regular habitat is found in U.S. waters. In fact, it is rare to find these fish north of Marco Island along the Gulf Coast of Florida, or north of Palm Beach on the Atlantic side of the peninsula. Farther south, permit occasionally appear in the Bahama Islands and are at times seen as far south as the Los Rocques Islands off the Venezuelan coast. More consistent populations of juvenile permit occur along the shores of the Yucatán Peninsula in Mexico. With regard to Florida's waters, the greatest concentrations of these fish are found in the Content Keys of Florida Bay, around Key West, and farther west in the remote Marquesas Keys.

Permit are routinely caught in sizes ranging from 5 pounds up to about 25 pounds, but can grow to more than twice that weight. The all-tackle standard for the species was set on June 30, 1997, when Thomas Sebestyen boated a 58-pound, 2-ounce specimen while fishing near Fort Lauderdale, Florida.

Although permit are known to school on nearshore reefs and shipwrecks, they do not represent viable targets for fly-casters in these locations. It is when they patrol the channel edges bordering flats or move up onto these flats to feed that permit begin to attract the attention of fly-fishermen. In these environs permit are ordinarily found singly or in small groups. When in groups, they are more vulnerable to anglers, since the fish are very competitive when feeding. These fish can be approached in a flats boat or by wading, using the same techniques described earlier for bonefishing. But, as also mentioned earlier, permit are much warier and more difficult to approach in shallow water.

Though usually found in the same waters as bonefish, permit are very easily distinguished from the bones. The permit has a much deeper-set, rounded body, as opposed to the sleek bullet shape of the bonefish. While both species can sometimes be found tailing in the same areas, the tail of a bonefish appears silver when above the surface of the water, while that of a permit looks black. Though most commonly permit have an overall silvery appearance, they can vary a great deal in hue, taking on a range of blue, green, or gold tints.

Ordinarily bottom feeders, permit are consistently attracted to a rather limited range of flies. At times they will strike a weighted streamer or take a shrimp pattern cast near them. By far the most popular and effective flies for permit are crab patterns, since these mimic the crustaceans that make up the bulk of this species' diet. Tied on hook sizes 8 to 1/0, patterns like the McCrab or Janssen's Floating Blue Crab can be quite effective.

Though permit are bottom feeders, often seen using their snouts to root along sand or marl flats in a nose-down, tailing position, the most effective presentation of crab flies does not take place on the seafloor. If the fish are cruising, drop your cast 10 to 15 feet ahead of them in the direction they are moving. If they are tailing, your cast needs to land closer, only about 5 feet from the targeted permit. Either way, the fly's entry into the water should produce a gentle splashing sound but not an explosive splat. Immediately give the fly a jerk with the rod, causing it to dart several inches just under the surface, then let it sink to the bottom. If the fish does not immediately rush the fly, give it another sharp jerk. Once a permit makes up its mind, it does not hesitate to grab a crab pattern—helping the fish make up its mind is the difficult part. If the permit follows the fly to the bottom, be prepared to set the hook as soon as you feel tension on the line. Permit are noted for quickly realizing their mistake in taking an inedible bundle of feathers and fur into their mouths. They can spit it back out just as fast as they inhaled it.

Ready Targets

Eight other fish that occur along the South Atlantic Coast are less frequently targeted by fly-casters but make rather easy marks for such fishing gear. As a result, they are ordinarily taken inadvertently. An angler who chooses to pursue them, however, can have great success.

The first two of these are **bluefish** *(Pomatomus saltatrix)* and **striped bass** *(Morone saxatilis)*. Though both are cool-water species that readily attack flies, their habits and ranges along the South Atlantic Coast make them unpredictable fish to catch on a fly-rod. Both are most available to anglers when the weather is at its worst along the North Carolina coast, where they are most prevalent.

Bluefish, also known as blues or Taylor blues (smaller fish along the North Carolina coast), are the more widespread of the two, occurring in fall and winter migratory schools from the Outer Banks of North Carolina south to the Miami–Fort Lauderdale area of Florida. Though often found in bays and inlets, it is only when they concentrate in feeding schools along beaches that it is practical to really target them. When such feeding occurs, fish breaking the surface, gulls circling and diving above the melee, and other fish frantically trying to flee the blues make spotting the schools easy.

Smaller bluefish are often called snappers, while fish of more than 10 pounds are called choppers. These nicknames stem from the wicked set of teeth bluefish possess. Be aware that these fish will bite you both in and out of the water if they get the chance. They will also strike any kind of streamer or topwater fly when they are feeding. You will need wire leaders to catch them, because of their teeth.

Bluefish are common throughout their range during cooler months in the 2- to 3-pound size class, with fish of double-digit weights far more common along the North Carolina coast. Any blue of more than 20 pounds

JIMMY JACOBS

*Striped bass are one of the main targets of fly-casters along the shores
of Bodie, Hatteras, and Ocracoke Islands.*

is a trophy. The world record for the species stands at 31 pounds, 12 ounces. That chopper was caught by James M. Hussey at Hatteras Inlet, North Carolina, on January 30, 1972.

Striped bass are sometimes referred to as stripers, linesides, or rockfish. Like bluefish, they are found in migratory schools in the fall along North

Carolina beaches. Circling seabirds and stripers breaking the surface are clues helping you locate their feeding frenzies. From South Carolina down to the St. Johns River in North Florida, smaller striped bass inhabit freshwater rivers and brackish estuaries but virtually never venture into bays or the open ocean.

Because they are rugged fighters that make runs of more than 100 yards when hooked, landing striped bass requires 10- to 13-weight fly-rods. The most productive flies for these fish are larger streamers, especially those that have a lot of white in the pattern.

Striped bass of 8 to 15 pounds are common throughout their range, with fish of up to 50 pounds taken regularly in North Carolina. The world record for this species was hooked on September 21, 1982, at Atlantic City, New Jersey, by Albert R. McReynolds. The fish weighed 78 pounds, 8 ounces.

Another fish that provides great fly-rod sport—but in a rather localized setting—is the **little tunny** *(Euthynnus alletteratus)*. This fish is more often called false albacore than any other name, but may also be referred to as an albie, a fat Albert, or a bloody mackerel. The species shows up along the North Carolina coast from April through December, with peak fishing taking place in the fall months. The fish are most often encountered just off inlets, with the area around Cape Lookout drawing the most fishing attention. Hooking such a fish is akin to tangling with a compact car on light tackle. Reels for this fishing should have at least 200 yards of backing, because these powerful fish are prone to make long runs. Since the fishing for fat Alberts takes place in open waters near inlets, it consists almost exclusively of fishing from boats.

Streamer flies 2 to 3 inches long that imitate silversides or glass minnows attract albies of up to 18 pounds in Carolina waters. The world record for little tunny is held by Jean Yves Chatard for a 35-pound, 2-ounce albie taken at Cape de Garde, Algeria, on December 14, 1988.

Closely related to the little tunny is the **Atlantic bonito** *(Sarda sarda)*. Bonito are smaller than false albacore but just as sporting on lighter fly tackle. They can be found 15 to 20 miles offshore all along the South Atlantic coast, but are most popular with fly-fishermen when they move in along the southeastern coast of North Carolina in March and April or in south Florida in May through September. Though they sometimes stray close to inlet jetties, they are most often caught slightly offshore from small boats, in many of the same areas where false albacore are found later in the year.

The bonito are sleek-bodied members of the mackerel family. They are steel blue to blue-green on their backs, silvery on the lower portion of their bodies, and have dark stripes running lengthwise at a slightly oblique angle along the top half of their sides. A large fish of this species would be about 36 inches long and weigh from 10 to 12 pounds.

Bonito display much of the same preference for fly patterns that is exhibited by little tunny and put up an equally rugged fight. The world record for Atlantic bonito is held by D. Gama Higgs for an 18-pound 4-ounce fish taken on July 8, 1953 off Faial Island in the Azore Islands.

During the summer months **jack crevalle** *(Caranx hippos)* and **ladyfish** *(Elops saurus)* are both found along the entire southeastern U.S. coast. They are likely to inhale virtually any fly that comes near them.

Jack crevalle are most often found along channel edges or on deeper flats. Although the world record for jack crevalle is 57 pounds, 14 ounces, taken by Leon D. Richard at Southwest Pass in Louisiana on August 15, 1997, most fish caught have run between 3 and 15 pounds. Still, they are strong fish that put up a tenacious, bulldog fight.

Ladyfish run even smaller, averaging only a pound or two each. The IGFA record is 6 pounds, with two anglers tied for that mark. Michael Baz caught the first from the Loxahatchee River in Jupiter, Florida, on December 20, 1997, while Ian Arthur de Sulocki matched that catch on January 24, 1999 while fishing in Sepetiba Bay, Brazil. These fish are ordinarily found in tidal creeks or inshore bays, rarely venturing onto flats. When hooked, ladyfish are spectacular leapers, often clearing the water several times during the struggle.

More localized in their range, **barracuda** *(Sphyraena barracuda)* and **mangrove snapper** *(Lutjanus griseus)* are common in South Florida in locations that often put them in the vicinity of fly-casters' offerings.

The barracuda is actually quite widespread along the Atlantic shore, but it is usually found offshore in deep water—except in the Miami and Florida Keys areas. There these toothy fish inhabit shallow flats and are the most dependable of all targets for anglers. Only an unseasonable winter cold snap will make them stop biting. They will hit any fly, including topwater versions. But the retrieve has to be fast to interest them, and wire leaders are sometimes needed to deal with their fearsome dentures. The record for barracuda is 85 pounds, taken at Christmas Island in the Republic of Kiribati, on April 11, 1992, by John W. Helfrich. On the flats, fish of up to 7 or 8 pounds are more often encountered. These smaller 'cuda make fast, erratic runs and readily take to the air when hooked in shallow water.

Mangrove snapper, also known as gray snapper, are found around offshore reefs, inshore bridge and pier pilings, in bays, and on flats. They are the most abundant fish of the snapper family found in U.S. waters and readily take streamers or smaller bonefish-style flies. Their range, however, is limited to Florida waters, and they are commonly caught by fly-casters only in their shallow-water haunts.

The mangrove snapper makes great table fare but rarely reaches larger sizes. Fish of 10 to 12 inches long are most common; they barely reach a pound in weight. The record for the species, however, is 17 pounds. It was taken by Steve Maddox on June 14, 1992, while fishing at Port Canaveral, Florida.

Gray snapper are easily identified once caught. When in an agitated state from their struggle to escape, a bold dark stripe appears from the tip of the nose, through the eye, and extending back to the gill plate.

Occasional Catches

Three fish that are found in open ocean waters but also sometimes encountered near the surface in bays and inlets are **cobia** *(Rachycentron canadum)*, **Spanish mackerel,** and **tripletail** *(Lobotes surinamensis)*. When found inshore, all can be taken on fly-rods.

The cobia, also known as ling, lemonfish, crabeater, cabio, black salmon, black kingfish, and sergeant fish, ranges from the Chesapeake Bay all along the Southeast and Gulf Coasts. Dark brown on their backs with a single black stripe down their sides, cobia look much like sharks in the water and are often mistaken for that species. Extremely migratory, they are fond of hanging around buoys and floating debris. In the spring they are most vulnerable to flies when you spot them following in the wake of rays on shallow flats. At times cobia will hit almost any fly, but long, stringy patterns resembling eels are most effective.

The world record for cobia is 135 pounds, 9 ounces. It was caught by Peter William Goulding on July 9, 1985, at Shark Bay, Western Australia.

Spanish mackerel *(Scomberomorus maculatus)* is one of the smaller members of the mackerel family. These sleek-bodied fish are found along the entire South Atlantic coast, usually in large schools of similarly sized individuals. They have a blue-green tinted back and silver sides covered with irregularly shaped, vivid gold spots. Although generally found several miles offshore, schools of the fish show up sporadically around inlets and jetties in the spring through fall.

The only time they are practical targets for fly-casting is when chasing schools of baitfish on the surface. In these situations a variety of streamer flies can attract vicious strikes from the Spanish mackerel. Their jaws are lined with a set of very sharp teeth, so care is needed when unhooking them.

The average Spanish mackerel weighs 2–4 pounds, but fish of more than 10 pounds can be caught. The world record Spanish tipped the scales at 13 pounds and was caught by Robert Cranton on November 4, 1987, at Ocracoke Inlet, North Carolina.

Tripletail are rather odd fish whose top and bottom rear fins extend far enough back to make them appear to have three tails. These surface feeders, also known as blackfish, are drab brown in color and are found in the Atlantic Ocean from North Carolina south to Argentina, as well as in the Gulf of Mexico. Usually found around floating weeds or other debris, they have the peculiar habit of floating on the surface on their sides, looking much like a big dead leaf. Sight-casting to such floaters with streamers or shrimp patterns is the only practical fly-fishing for tripletail.

The average tripletail weighs 2 to 5 pounds, but the IGFA standard is 42 pounds, 5 ounces for a fish taken off Zululand, South Africa, on June 7, 1989, by Steve Hand.

The **weakfish** *(Cynoscion regalis)* is quite similar to the spotted seatrout but, due to its habits, is not regularly available in places that fly-casters can reach. Weakfish have small speckles on their sides, as opposed to the seatrout's bold spots. Also, unlike the seatrout, weakfish never have any spots on their fins. In New England and Mid-Atlantic areas weakfish migrate to shallow inshore water and beaches in the spring and summer, spending the rest of the year in very deep water. This movement occurs along North Carolina's Outer Banks as well, making the fish vulnerable to inshore fly-casters.

Weakfish commonly weigh from 2 to 10 pounds, but the world-record mark stands at 19 pounds, 2 ounces for a fish landed by Dennis Roger Rooney on October 11, 1984, at Jones Beach Inlet on Long Island, New York. That mark, however, was tied by William E. Thomas while fishing in Delaware Bay, Delaware, on May 20, 1989.

From southern North Carolina down to South Florida weakfish continue to be present, but they are smaller and rarely frequent bay or estuaries. Though they will take the same flies that attract seatrout, weakfish simply do not offer fly-fishermen many opportunities to target them.

Southern flounder *(Paralichthys lethostigma)* and **black drum** *(Pogonias cromis)* are two species regularly encountered in tidal creeks and rivers, bays, and inlets along the southern coast, in most of the places that either red drum or spotted seatrout are found. For this reason, they are sometimes taken on flies intended for those game fish. Both of these are bottom feeders, however, so ordinarily it is a weighted streamer fished deep that will tempt them. It is quite rare for a fly-caster to purposefully target either species. In the case of flounder this is because the fly must be fished excruciatingly slowly along the bottom, which is not an exciting angling method. On the other hand, black drum do not readily take artificial baits except when actively feeding on shallow flats, where they are only infrequently found.

Flounder are easily recognized since they are flat fish that have both eyes on the same side of their head. They lay half-buried in the sand or mud on the bottom, eyes protruding from the sediment as they wait to ambush passing shrimp, minnows, or crabs. The world record for southern flounder is 20 pounds, 9 ounces, which was caught at Nassau Sound, Florida, on December 23, 1983. Larenza W. Mungin was the record-shattering angler.

Black drum are closely related to red drum and are often found in the same areas. They tend to be stockier fish and, when young, have five vertical black bars on their sides. These fade with age, leaving the fish a silver-gray color. Especially in Florida's Indian River and Mosquito Lagoon areas, schools of big black drum are known to cruise shallow flats, offering the best fly-fishing opportunities for this species.

Black drum average 5 to 50 pounds, with the world record for the species at 113 pounds, 1 ounce. Gerald M. Townsend hooked that fish on July 15, 1975, while fishing off Lewes, Delaware.

A couple of species often found on beaches or in bays along the Southeast Atlantic Coast are **Florida pompano** *(Trachinotus carolinus)* and **whiting** *(Menticirrhus americanus)*. Both are bottom feeders not easily taken on flies, but if you choose to target them, the feat is possible. Though both are relatively small, they are plentiful and also excellent table fare, making them worth the effort to catch.

The pompano is very similar to a young permit and ranges from North Carolina around Florida and into the Gulf of Mexico. Within this range, however, these roundish, gold- and silver-hued fish are relatively uncommon along the southern shore of South Carolina and the entire Georgia coast. This species likes rough bottoms along beaches composed of broken shells. Such bottom composition is rare on the shallow, gently sloping beaches of the barrier islands of these areas. On the other hand, summer migrations of pompano are common on the shores of North Carolina and Florida.

Pompano average only 1 to 2 pounds each, but the world record stands at

8 pounds, 1 ounce. That fish was caught on March 19, 1984, by Chester E. Dietrick while fishing at Flagler Beach, Florida.

Whiting, which are called sea mullet in North Carolina and occasionally referred to as southern kingfish, have rounded snouts, small downward-pointing mouths, and short barbels on their chins. Slender, silver-colored fish, whiting are found all along the South Atlantic Coast and in the Gulf of Mexico. Northern kingfish are occasionally found throughout this range as well; they can be differentiated by the seven or eight dark vertical bands across their sides. The first two of these bands form a V-shape just behind the fish's head.

Whiting of more than 1½ pounds are rare. The largest ever recorded on sport-fishing tackle was a 2-pound, 5-ounce whiting taken at Rodanthe, North Carolina, on July 29, 1999 by Michael Graham.

The trick for taking both pompano and whiting on a fly is finding the fish in tidal washouts near the beach, where it is easily possible to cast to them. Then a weighted imitation of a mole crab (also known as a sand flea) bounced along the bottom can provoke a strike from either species.

The final species of fish that merits mentioning in connection with South Atlantic Coast fly-fishing is the **sheepshead** *(Archosargus probato-cephalus)*. Bottom feeders that are rarely targeted by fly-casters, sheepshead are found around offshore reefs and wrecks, on grass flats, but especially around pilings and other hard, inshore structures.

Sheepshead have broad bodies with black and white vertical bars. They possess strong, flat, protruding teeth with which they grind up mollusks and crustaceans. Though they are very difficult to catch on flies, the feat is possible using crab patterns.

Sheepshead are ordinarily encountered in sizes ranging from 1 to 5 pounds. Wayne Desselle took the world record for the species while fishing at Bayou St. John near New Orleans, Louisiana, on April 16, 1982. His fish tipped the scales at 21 pounds, 4 ounces.

CHAPTER 3

Gear, Flies, and Safety

It will probably come as no surprise that fly-fishing in salt water calls for some specialized equipment. Although many fly-casters make their first tentative presentations in the brine using medium-weight freshwater fly-fishing rigs, they soon learn that the conditions on the coast require different gear if the fishing is to be efficient and enjoyable. As a general rule of thumb, saltwater fly-casting gear needs to be heavier and more rugged than its freshwater counterparts.

The four major factors from which these requirements stem are the corrosive nature of salt water, the almost constant winds blowing in coastal areas, the need to cast heavier flies for longer distances, and the fact that the fish are bigger and stronger in salt water. In virtually all situations you will encounter, several of these considerations will come into play. It's a good idea to start out with the right gear.

Rods

Choosing a saltwater fly-rod is one of your most important decisions in preparing to challenge fish in a coastal environment. Many tackle manufacturers now offer quality rods built specifically for use in salt water, most of which share several characteristics. The first of these has to do with the handle. The reel seat—that portion of the rod handle where the reel attaches—is often made of wood on better freshwater rods. A saltwater model demands something that stands up better to the brine. Light anodized aluminum is a popular choice. Besides the standard grip found on freshwater fly-rod handles, either a cork or rubber fighting butt is usually attached. A fighting butt is a protrusion from the end of the handle, extending out from the back of the reel seat. Since the possibility of hooking big fish is constant, so is the need to endure a long battle with such a fish. With a lighter freshwater rod, that fight would put a lot of pressure on your forearms. With a rod designed for salt water, however, you can brace the fighting butt against your stomach or abdomen to increase pressure on the fish and relax the strain on your arms. When your fly is firmly attached to a 40-pound redfish or even a 100-pound tarpon, the wisdom of having a fighting butt will become very apparent!

The length and weight of your chosen rod are also major considerations. These two factors are extremely important when it comes to casting into the wind or casting large flies for long distances. When you are fishing in salt water, a fly-rod 8 feet long is the bare minimum, and most experienced anglers will argue for at least a 9-foot rod. Particularly in the heavier-weight models, rods of 10 to 12 feet are also available—and in some cases necessary. The extra length provides more leverage for punching casts into or across the wind. And rest assured, it is a rare day when wind is not a factor in saltwater fly-fishing.

With regard to weight of the rod, 7-weight is about the lightest regularly manufactured for saltwater use. More common are 8- to 10-weights, with rods of up to 14-weight available. Anything over 10-weight, however, is probably overkill unless you are targeting 100-plus-pound tarpon or huge offshore species of fish.

For a general all-purpose rod that will meet the bulk of the saltwater challenges you will face, a 9-weight, 9-foot rod will suffice. It has enough length to provide casting leverage into the wind and is heavy enough to cast the larger 3- to 4-inch weighted flies that the fishing sometimes demands.

Fortunately, the development of rod materials has kept up with the demand for rugged equipment. The use of lightweight graphite composites in rods has allowed builders to incorporate the durability needed to fight big fish and harsh conditions, while keeping the rods light enough that they do not completely wear you out in a day of casting.

Also, the guides through which the line is threaded on saltwater rods are now made from a variety of very corrosion-resistant materials, ranging from aluminum oxide to chrome-plated stainless steel to titanium carbonitride. Regardless of their composition, the important thing is to make sure that on the rod you choose, the guides are made of a type of metal that will not easily rust.

One other consideration in choosing a rod is the number of sections into which it will break down. Most rods are two-piece models, which leaves you with transporting a rod case at least 4½ feet long. This can be a nuisance in cars and is definitely cumbersome on an airplane. For this reason, the slightly more expensive four-piece travel rods are more convenient and worth the extra money, particularly if you must travel any distance to get to your saltwater fishing destination.

Reels

The reels needed for saltwater fly-fishing share some of the traits that the sport demands of rods. A saltwater fly-reel must be made of materials that are resistant to rust and corrosion. It must also be larger and able to handle heavier lines than freshwater models. Finally, its drag system must be a good one.

A wide range of tackle manufacturers now offer reels specifically designed for salt water. These run the gamut from moderately priced to truly expensive. As with most things, you get what you pay for. The major concern is meeting the minimum standards for this type of fishing.

The first concern is the durability of the reel. Today most are made of anodized aluminum, a silicon-aluminum compound, or graphite. Some even have a polyurethane finish as well. These light compounds make it possible to produce large but lightweight reels that are very resistant to the corrosive effects of salt water and heavy use. Picking any reel that the tackle company describes as designed for salt water is a fairly safe bet these days, as long as its described capacities match the fish you plan to pursue. In other words, you can get into trouble if you chose the lightest, most inexpensive model in the sales lineup while targeting megasized tarpon that weigh in excess of 100 pounds. Match the reel to the fight you expect!

The second concern is the size of the reel. Saltwater fly-fishing demands larger reels than are necessary in fresh water. There are two reasons why bigger is better for this sport. First of all, since heavier-weight lines are needed for casting, these lines have larger diameters. Forty yards of 9-weight fly-line simply needs a bigger spool for storage than does the same length of 6-weight line.

Another important point with regard to the size of the reel is the need to have very long sections of backing for the fly-line. Backing is the nylon or braided fishing line attached to the fly-line at one end and to the spool of the reel at the other. It is much smaller in diameter than fly-line, thus more of it will fit on a reel spool. When you hook a big fish that makes a long run, backing gives you more line to use during the fight.

One of the more common comments from anglers who have just hooked their first big saltwater fish on a fly-rod is that they had never seen their backing before. Since it is covered by the fly-line on the reel, backing remains hidden unless a big fish takes a lot of line in a run. When you are battling freshwater fish, backing rarely comes into play. It is a different story, however, in the brine. Redfish, tarpon, and particularly bonefish are noted for taking off on 150- to 200-yard runs when hooked. To keep them from breaking off, having plenty of backing on a fly-reel is important. Your reel needs to be big enough to handle a heavyweight fly-line, and several hundred yards of backing.

The final consideration when picking a reel for saltwater fly-casting is its drag system. Simply put, a drag system is the mechanism built into the reel that puts pressure on the spool to slow line removal. Depending on the system you use, the drag applied to the line may or may not be mechanically adjustable.

One of the standard clichés about freshwater fly-reels is that they are simply something on which to store your line. Again, this stems from the fact that the waters are usually confined and the fish smaller. It is rare that a freshwater angler actually uses the reel and its drag system to fight a fish.

Salt water is a different story. It is not unusual to have fish begin stripping line from the reel while making several long runs. If your drag system is not up to this situation, it can literally burn out from the friction and even lock up, assuring the loss of the fish.

There are several basic types of drag systems employed in fly-reels. The first and simplest is an exposed outer rim on the line spool. This allows you to use your hand to put pressure on the edge of the revolving spool to slow its revolutions—an action usually referred to as palming. In many reels this exposed-rim feature is present even though the reel has a more sophisticated built-in drag system as well. This way you can put even more pressure on a fish during a run. Needless to say, when a truly big fish is hooked, an exposed-rim drag alone can be almost useless. Palming a reel under these conditions is a good way to either get friction burns on your hand or bust a knuckle on the spinning reel handle.

The second type of drag is composed of either a single- or a double-pawl mechanism within the reel. Obviously, a double-pawl setup is a bit more efficient, but it does add more parts and expense to the construction of the reel. In this type of reel the action of the pawl engaging a cogged wheel on the spool applies pressure to slow the removal of line. The amount of pressure the pawl puts on the wheel, and thus the spool, can usually be adjusted.

A more sophisticated type of drag is a disc setup. A disc drag applies pressure to the spool through contact between the spool's cogged wheel and the cogged edge of a metal disc. This tends to create a smoother and more efficient drag that can also be adjusted by tightening the tension on the disc.

Finally, some reels are coming on the market that employ a pawl-engaged clutch system. These reels have an adjustable cork-composite friction drag pad that applies the pressure to the spinning spool.

Regardless of which reel you choose, it should have a minimum of a pawl drag; a better choice is a disc system. All the drag components should also be made of rust-resistant materials—usually stainless steel, but such exotic materials as copper-beryllium compounds are also used.

Lines

There are several considerations to take into account when you pick a fly-line for use in salt water. Many companies now manufacture line designed to handle the rigors of the harsh saltwater environment and still deliver maximum performance with regard to durability and casting distance. The major point is to pick a fly-line designed for salt water.

The three basic types of fly-lines are level, double-tapered, and weight-forward. A level line is the same diameter from one end to the other. A double-tapered line is thickest in the middle, getting narrower in width toward either end. A weight-forward line is thinnest where it attaches to the backing, getting progressively thicker toward the end that attaches to the leader. In virtually all instances the weight-forward design is best for saltwater fly-casting. Having the heaviest portion of the line at the end makes casting heavy flies easier, plus it adds to your ability to push casts into the wind.

Lines also come in sinking, sink-tip, and floating varieties. Though there are some instances when a sinking line or sink-tip line (only the last 10 to 20 feet of an otherwise floating line is weighted) may be useful or necessary, a floating line is a good all-purpose choice since, as a rule, most saltwater fly-fishing is done in shallow water or near the surface in deeper areas.

Finally, the weight of the line must be matched to what your rod and reel are designed to handle. Of course, the weight of a fly-line—*9-weight,* for example—has nothing to do with break-point tensions, as is the case with monofilament fishing lines. The numbers designating weight are assigned from standards established by the American Fishing Tackle Manufacturers' Association back in 1960 and are based on the weight in grains of the first 30 feet of the fly line. These range from a 1-weight line weighing 60 grains up through a 14-weight that weighs 380 grains. All of which, from the average angler's standpoint, is a rather academic point.

What really counts in the real world of fly-casting is to make sure the weight number of the line matches that printed on your rod and reel.

Leaders

In essence, a leader is a piece of monofilament fishing line attached to the end of the fly-line. Since fly-line is so thick and heavy, it is not designed to have a fly directly attached to it; the leader thus provides a link to the fly. Since this leader is much less bulky than the fly line, it allows for a more delicate delivery of the fly to the water. When cast correctly, the leader should allow the fly to enter the water without creating enough commotion to spook nearby fish.

The length of leader material you use depends on the length of your rod, the type of fly you are using, and the conditions under which you are fishing. As a rule, the leader will be about as long as the rod, but heavier streamer flies may call for shorter lengths. Shorter leaders are also more practical when you are trying to cast a bulky fly under windy conditions.

Usually, leaders are tapered, with the butt section that attaches to the fly line being somewhat heavier than the tippet that ties to the fly. Such tapered leaders can be purchased from most fly-fishing shops, or you can make your own by connecting several sections of decreasingly heavy monofilament line. For standard saltwater use, the butt sections run anywhere from 30- to 40-pound test, decreasing to about 8- to 12-pound test at the tippet. Lighter tippets than these are rather impractical for salt water and are ordinarily used only by anglers in pursuit of line-class world records. It may be impressive to land a big saltwater fish on a 6-pound leader, but the odds are you will lose a large number of hooked fish in the process.

One exception to this tapered-leader rule is the use of a shock tippet on the end of the leader. In the case of battling fish that put up rugged fights and have wicked sets of teeth or sharp gill plates (either of which can cut through light line), a short piece of much-heavier monofilament can be attached at the terminal end of the leader. This combination allows for easier casting of the normal tapered leader, while providing a rugged tip that can stand up to the abuse and punishment of the fight.

Shock tippets may range from 30- to 40-pound test for big redfish or snook, up to 100-pound line for large tarpon. It is even possible to use a short wire leader on the end of the monofilament. This may be necessary in some situations for boating large barracuda or bluefish. Just be aware that using the wire usually cuts down on the number of strikes you get from most fish. The exception to this rule is found in tangling with very aggressive bluefish. In this case a shiny, silver-colored wire shock tippet may actually induce strikes.

Flies

Probably the most important consideration in fly-casting in salt water, other than picking a spot where fish are located, is the selection of the flies you use to attract the fish. Even if you have a totally mismatched rod, reel, line, and leader, if you still manage to put the right fly near a fish there is a good chance that it will bite. All of that other gear is designed to make getting the fly to the fish easier and more efficient, but the bottom line is still delivering the right fly to the hungry fish.

When casting into salt water, the object is to use flies that imitate the usual food sources of the fish being targeted. For inshore species, picking the proper flies is not an overly taxing or scientific endeavor. Several saltwater critters make up a large portion of the forage for game fish: smaller bait fish, crabs, and shrimp. Based on this, stocking your fly box with a small selection of imitations of these creatures can cover most of the situations you encounter.

Streamers—flies designed to imitate bait fish swimming through the water—come in a wide variety of patterns. These are ordinarily cast and retrieved with short strips of the line to create movement that looks like a swimming fish.

The color of feathers and other materials used in tying streamers can be matched to the hues of the natural bait fish to further enhance the appeal of these flies. On the other hand, sometimes the most garish of color combinations that look like nothing that lives in salt water are more effective. This is particularly true if you are casting around schooling bait fish. The whole purpose of schooling is to make it more difficult for a predator to pick out a single fish to attack. Obviously, a fish of the same size as the others, but oddly colored, is more easily seen and singled out by the game fish.

All of which points out that having a basic selection of three or four proven streamer patterns in a variety of sizes and colors is your best bet for stocking your fly box. It is not really necessary to turn your box into a veritable ark containing two of every fly ever created.

A good all-purpose selection of streamers for southern waters should include several Lefty's Deceivers in blue-and-white, red-and-white, and yellow-and-red. Also add to the box some Clouser Minnows in chartreuse-

JIMMY JACOBS

A variety of colorful streamers can attract the attention of predatory species all along the Southeast Coast.

and-white, olive-and-white, and red-and-white. Finally, carry a few Bend-Backs in yellow-and-white combinations. Try to include each of these in a couple of different hook sizes.

These streamers can attract the attention of seatrout, redfish, snook, tarpon, bluefish, jack, flounder, or virtually any other predatory fish that happens to be near when the fly hits the water.

Another group of flies that are quite versatile for fishing the South Atlantic Coast are shrimp patterns. Most of these originated for use on bonefish in South Florida, but they attract other species like seatrout, redfish, jack, mangrove snapper, and even pompano as well. Usually these flies are smaller than streamers. When you are sight-casting in shallow water, they can be tossed in front of feeding fish, allowed to sink, and then skipped across the bottom like a fleeing shrimp when the predators approach. In dingier water fishing them with short strips of the line—much as you would a streamer—can also be effective.

Crab flies, though they do not particularly resemble shrimp patterns, can be cast and retrieved in similar manners. As their name implies, these fur and feather creations are designed to look like small crabs. Species such as permit, redfish, and snook are often quite susceptible to these patterns. Even imitations of sand-burrowing mole crabs (often called sand fleas) have been concocted that are effective for pompano and whiting in the surf.

The final set of flies necessary for fishing in this area are some topwater patterns. A couple of colors of skipping bugs and popping bugs should suffice. These should be much larger than those used in fresh water, however—sizes 1/0 to 2/0.

The skipping bug has an elongated cork body with a rounded head and hair tail. The shape of its forward end allows it to skip along the surface when retrieved. On the other hand, the popping bug has a shorter, stockier body shape, a feather or hair tail, and a concave front end. When retrieved, it pushes water in front of it to create a popping sound.

Skipping bugs in blue-and-white or red-and-white usually work well, while yellow, red, and orange poppers generally provoke some action. Snook, seatrout, and redfish are most often targeted with these flies, although toothy predators such as bluefish and barracuda are also attracted to them.

Additional Gear

As with almost any pursuit, some pieces of additional gear can make a fishing trip more successful or comfortable.

The first of these is a good pair of polarized sunglasses. While conventional sunglasses simply shade your eyes from bright light, polarized models have a coating that actually cuts down on the amount of glare that reaches your eyes. This is particularly helpful when you look at the surface of the water; without glare, you can see down into the water. As discussed earlier, locating the fish before casting is quite often the linchpin of successful saltwater fly-casting. Thus, anything that makes spotting the fish easier is very important.

It is possible to spend more than $100 on a quality pair of stylish polarized sunglasses. On the other hand, much more moderately priced versions (under $15) are now available in sporting goods departments of chain discount stores.

As with any type of fly-fishing—and particularly when you are wading—you need some way to carry all your tackle. Since the bulk of saltwater fly-casting along the South Atlantic coast is done in hot weather, traditional fly-fishing vests can be quite uncomfortable, thus they are rarely seen along this shore. A better way to store gear is use a pack worn around the waist using an adjustable strap. Often referred to as a fanny pack, this type of storage keeps your gear readily at hand but out of the way of your casting motion.

One rather specialized piece of gear is a stripping basket. This is a plastic basket worn on a strap around your waist, facing forward. Generally, stripping baskets are only used when casting in the surf or from a boat.

When you are stripping the fly after a cast into the surf, and you allow your fly-line simply to drop to the sand or water, the wave action tends to pull or push it in all directions. If you retrieve the line into a stripping basket, however, it stays out of the water. Some stripping-basket designs feature cones sticking up from the bottom. These help keep the coils of line separated, preventing tangling as well.

Stripping baskets are also useful when you are fishing from a boat, particularly for bigger fish. This is also true if the boat does not have an uncluttered deck specifically designed for fly-casting. Without a basket, any retrieved line allowed to fall to the floor of the boat can become snagged on gear or protruding parts of the boat itself. If you hook a big fish that makes a strong run, such a snag ensures that the battle will end quickly with a snapped leader.

When wading under southern saltwater fly-fishing conditions, waders and wading boots are not usually required. Since the climate can be steamy, getting into the water in shorts or lightweight trousers can be refreshing. About the only time waders are necessary is for wintertime excursions, particularly on the Carolina and Georgia coasts. Temperatures do get quite nippy in these areas, so warm neoprene waders are good choices.

While it may be possible to wade barefoot in some areas, this is generally not a good idea. Broken shells, spiny sea urchins, and a host of other objects present dangers to bare feet in salt water. Some type of foot covering is always a good idea. Many anglers simply use old tennis shoes for wading in warmer weather. For summertime wading (or for any season in South Florida), wading booties (or dive boots, if you are also into scuba diving) are a better choice. Their hard-rubber soles protect your feet from shells and coral, while their high tops and snug fit keep sand and other debris from getting inside them.

Most such footwear choices have zippers on the sides, making them easy to put on and off and also making for the snug fit mentioned earlier. This is particularly important if you step into some soft sand or mud. The suction created in pulling your foot loose can often suck a tennis shoe off a foot. With booties, this is not a problem.

There are probably a couple of dozen other accessories that could be mentioned in this discussion, but they do not fall in the category of what I consider necessities. For the experienced or novice saltwater fly-caster, the gear already mentioned is, under ordinary circumstances, all you need to make your fishing simpler and more enjoyable.

Safety

Needless to say, having a sense of security is very important to making any fishing trip an enjoyable adventure. The best time to make sure that you will feel carefree on the water is before you leave home. Being prepared in advance for minor or major emergencies while fishing is much more rewarding than scrambling for solutions once you are faced with a problem far from help.

As with all outdoor pursuits, it is wise to take along a fishing buddy, particularly if you are headed for remote regions. If you have to or choose to go alone, it is imperative to let someone know where you are headed and when you plan to be back. This way, if the worst-case scenario arises, someone will be be looking for you in a timely fashion and will know where to begin the search.

When boating, be familiar with the safety rules and the equipment required by the state in which you are fishing. This information is generally available by making a telephone call to the department that administers coastal resources. Once you know the rules, follow them.

When wading, always take care to know what is ahead of and behind you. Stepping into deeper holes or boat channels on a shallow flat can lead to embarrassing—or life-threatening—situations. Equally dangerous is wading blindly or too deeply into water that has a strong current. Once you lose your footing, getting back to shallow water can cost you some equipment and even prove fatal.

Another danger of wading took me completely by surprise while I was on the South Carolina coast researching this book. I planned to wade the shallow sand flats at the mouth of Pawleys Inlet on a low tide. I barely noticed the sign warning of strong currents, since I would be up on the flats along the edge of the channels and in water no deeper than 18 inches. While wading across one small channel in water less than knee-deep, however, I suddenly sank at least a foot and a half into extremely soft sand. This put the water up to my waist, and the pit of veritable quicksand made it extremely difficult to pull myself free. Had I blundered into this situation during even a moderately rising tide, I shudder to think of the tragic outcome this story might have had.

Arriving back at the parking lot, I saw that the sign actually warned about strong currents *and* soft sand. From that point on, I have kept a keen eye out for warning signs, read them completely, and heeded their advice!

A good piece of equipment to have along whether you are on shore, wading, or in a boat is a whistle. It is a great way to attract attention in emergencies while expending very little effort.

Other items that fall in the category of safety necessities are sunscreen and lip balm. The coastline of the southern states draws millions of visitors each year because of the usually sunny and hot climate. Couple this bright sunshine with its reflection off the water in which you are fishing and you have a prescription for major sunburn and parched lips.

Conventional sunscreens used by swimmers provide adequate protection in many instances, but sunblocks with Sun Protection Factor (SPF) ratings of as high as 45 are available. These block out harmful rays during extended periods of fishing in direct sunlight. Any brand of lip balm will prevent drying, but some can be purchased that also provide protection from sunburn. It is a wise precaution to take both sunscreen and lip balm along on saltwater fishing trips—and use them!

In a similar vein, some saltwater fly-fishing excursions require insect repellents. Fishing on beaches, flats, or open water, breezes are usually prevalent and keep the bugs at bay. On the other hand, if your destination is a backwater bay, a tidal creek, or even a beach during the calm just before dusk, mosquitoes can be a problem. There are plenty of effective repellents on the market that have high deet (short for the scientific name for the diethyl compounds that ward off the bugs) contents, which works to keep mosquitoes away. It is best to stick with those that offer at least 15 percent deet in their composition.

Another denizen of the southern coastline is the sand fly, also known as the sand gnat or no-see-um. When encountered, these minute biting critters can make a fisherman's life miserable. As their nickname implies, sand flies are so small that they are hard to see with the naked eye, but they often attack in swarms and their bites are quite annoying. Even worse, DEET-based repellents have no effect on them. However, Skin-So-Soft Bath Oil (marketed by Avon Products) contains a number of dioctyl compounds that are extremely effective in warding off these pests. The bottles that this oil comes in do refer to its "original woodland" fragrance, but otherwise the manufacturer makes no claims for the product as an insect repellent. Still, it is a necessity when no-see-ums are active.

Skin-So-Soft is not ordinarily available in stores, since Avon distributes its products through sales representatives. In most areas it is easy to locate the local "Avon Lady" and place an order simply by asking around.

Not all the creatures that can cause you pain are swarming in the air. There are also some in the water, where they pose special problems if you are wading. In virtually all the areas where wading is practical, the most frequently encountered of these critters are jellyfish. They can range in size from the diameter of a quarter to more than 7 feet across, and most have stinging cells on their tentacles.

Fortunately, the most common species on the Southeast Coast is the purple jellyfish. Its sting is so mild that most people do not feel it when they come in contact with the tentacles. On the other hand, the Portuguese man-of-war—a larger member of the jellyfish family sometimes found in the surf—can inflict a severe sting. Your best defense against jellyfish is to be vigilant and not wade into any of these pretty but sometimes painful creatures.

Another potentially harmful creature that is fairly often encountered when wading in salt water is the stingray. There are actually a number of species of these fish, which roam near beaches and on tidal flats. These flat-bodied members of the shark family have bony spikes on their whiplike tails. When threatened, they can use these to inflict a painful sting while defending themselves. As with all wild creatures, stingrays strive to keep their distance from people, but they do have one habit that can cause problems: When resting, they often burrow down into the sand with just their eyes protruding from the bottom. Accidentally stepping on one can cause the animal to strike back defensively.

This potential threat has led anglers in South Florida to develop a wading technique called the "stingray shuffle." Essentially, you never raise your feet off the bottom to step; rather, you slide them along the seafloor. This way you spook the ray from its hiding place by touching it, but not pin it to the bottom. As long as the creature can escape, that will be its first reaction.

Finally, among the denizens of the sea, none can trigger our primal fears more than sharks and barracuda. Both are armed with formidable sets of wicked-looking teeth and have developed folklore reputations for ferocity.

Particularly in the case of barracuda, the danger has been greatly exaggerated. Years ago, on my first trip to the Florida Keys, I snorkeled along several of the swimming beaches in Key West and was astounded to find that the water was alive with barracuda of all sizes. Several times I encountered mothers playing in the water with infants or small children, while a 'cuda of 2 to 3 feet in length was very near them. I have no doubt that the bathers would have been running screaming to the beach if they had known they were sharing the water with these fish!

Actually, barracuda pose very little threat to people—as long as the fish realize that we are humans. It is when mistaken identity is possible that trouble can ensue. An angler washing his hand at the gunwale of the boat while wearing a ring or bracelet can be at risk, as can any angler wearing jewelry while wading. 'Cuda are noted for striking shiny spinning lures, such as silver spoons. Obviously, if you kick up some silt while wading, lessening visibility in the water, the chances of a barracuda striking at a shiny piece of metal may increase. If that metal is a wedding band on your finger, the result can be painful.

Sharks pose a similar threat but, because of their potentially larger size, can be even more dangerous. If you wade in salt water, you will at some point find yourself quite near sharks. They do take advantage of feeding opportunities along the beaches and on tidal flats. Atlantic sharpnose, blacktip, and bonnethead sharks are quite plentiful in shallow water along the entire coast, but usually in smaller sizes—less than 3 feet. On the other hand, in South Florida more fearsome bull and lemon sharks, often reaching 6 to 8 feet in length, come up onto shallow flats.

With smaller sharks the same rules apply as with barracuda. As long as they realize what you are, they will keep their distance. Just be a bit more wary of them in turbid waters. I have often waded flats where smaller sharks cruised quite close with no problems.

On the other hand, all sharks of more than 6 feet are large enough to be quite dangerous. Though they, too, are likely to want to avoid you and make a run for it when they recognize your presence, if they do hang around I make it a practice to cede the flat to them.

On one particularly memorable day on the flats at Long Key near Islamorada, Florida, I had a rather unnerving shark encounter in very shallow water. I had noticed several blacktip sharks less than 3 feet long cruising the flat as I waded, looking for tailing bonefish. Several times, when I stripped line from my reel in preparation for casting to what I thought might be pushed wakes of bonefish, I saw the sharks move closer and seem to get agitated, swimming faster. After several such episodes, I realized that the squealing of my reel as I stripped the line was giving off sound vibrations that were attracting the sharks! A couple of quick experiments with the reel made it obvious that this was the case. Since I was stirring up quite a mud trail on the soft flat, I thought it prudent to wade the 100 yards or so back to the beach and find another place to fish. About halfway to the beach, the water at the edge I was heading toward suddenly erupted in a huge swirl as a large fish attacked a school of bait. In the middle of the splashing was a dorsal fin that extended at least a foot or more above the surface. This was a very large shark.

I suddenly lost interest in continuing toward that strip of beach. Instead, I made a beeline for the nearest mangrove shore. It was a muddy mess getting through the mangroves to the nature trail that ran along the shore, but this still seemed the better option. Though that large shark probably posed little threat to me, it never hurts to play it safe with these bigger boys!

Basically, anglers who plan ahead and employ a dose of common sense can spend many days on saltwater bays, rivers, beaches, and creeks without facing serious peril. If you do so, chances are that when trouble does arise, it is more often a nuisance than a disaster.

JIMMY JACOBS

*The lighthouse at Cape Hatteras is the most recognizable landmark
on the North Carolina coast.*

Part II

North Carolina

Due to its position as the northernmost of the states covered in this book and the rather unusual shape of its coastline, North Carolina presents some unique saltwater fishing conditions. To begin with, it is the only state profiled that receives a large migration of cold-water fish species along its shore in the fall and winter months. Also, several major sounds carve deep into the coastline, making for odd mixes of fresh- and saltwater fish. Additionally, just 12 miles offshore of Cape Hatteras, the southern flow of the Virginia Littorde Drift clashes with the Gulf Stream as it moves north. This is as close as the Gulf Stream's warm flow gets to land anywhere north of Central Florida. The semitropical species of fish brought north with the current, coupled with the cooler-water species moving down from New England and the Mid-Atlantic states, provides the greatest variety of quality fishing opportunities on the Atlantic seaboard. This situation has earned the Old North State's Outer Banks the nickname Gamefish Junction.

In all, North Carolina boasts more than 3,000 miles of shoreline along its barrier islands, river estuaries, and major sounds. Unique among the southern states, North Carolina's sounds—such as Albemarle, Pamlico, and Core—form veritable inland saltwater seas that cover an incredible 2,000 square miles! This vast coastline, coupled with a history of settlement more than 300 years old, has led to a large number of shoreside towns, villages, cities, and communities. These stretch from Corona on the Outer Banks in the north to Calabash near the South Carolina border and include such major towns as Wilmington, New Bern, Morehead City, Washington, and Elizabeth City.

In spite of this long history of settlement, however, there are still vast areas of wilderness along these shores. A number of state and federal preserves cover portions of the Outer Banks, Cape Lookout, the Core Banks, and the marshes on the inland side of Pamlico Sound. It is possible to find fishing locations in North Carolina coastal counties that are quite urban or very desolate.

Saltwater fishing from both boats and the shore is very popular in North Carolina. This is reflected in the results of the U.S. Fish and Wildlife Service's 1996 angling survey, which reported that 770,000 saltwater fishermen visited the shores of the Old North State that year—second only to Florida among the South Atlantic states. Of that total, 346,000 were nonresident fishermen.

Fly-casting in the brine has been slower to catch on among Tar Heel anglers. Along most portions of the coast, fly-casters are still rare sights. This can be partially credited to the strong winds and rough waters so often encountered along the various Carolina banks and on the open waters of the sounds. These conditions make fly-casting very difficult. Still, the shallow waters of Albemarle, Pamlico, Core, and Bogue Sounds provide some ideal locations for fly-fishers, though anglers rarely utilize these resources even when the weather permits.

Of course, as is true all along the Southeast Coast, this lack of fly-fishing interest is changing. The opportunities to tangle with striped bass, red drum, spotted seatrout, false albacore, Spanish mackerel, and Atlantic bonito have begun to lure more and more Tar Heels to saltwater fly-casting.

Angling Calendar

As mentioned earlier, the presence of both warm- and coldwater species along the North Carolina coast at various seasons results in a year-round fishery. The species most often available to fly-anglers, regardless of the time of year, are spotted seatrout and juvenile red drum (fish of up to 5 pounds and locally called puppy drum). During the winter months they can be found in the upper reaches of sounds and tidal rivers, even in low-salinity brackish-water areas, but they are more widespread in the warmer months of the year, both in the sounds and around the coast's many inlets.

Red drum in the 5- to 15-pound range show up in numbers in the spring and fall, usually in the sounds and at inlets. At these same times the truly huge bull red drum of up to 50 and 60 pounds begin moving inshore or down from the New England and Mid-Atlantic areas to cruise along the beaches of the Outer Banks, often going as far south as Cape Lookout.

While the bull reds are moving down the coast in the fall, the big bluefish (locally called choppers) are on the move right behind them, usually showing up in many of the same places as the red drum. Fish of up to 20 pounds make these runs, especially when the weather is cold and nasty. The smaller blues of 5 to 15 pounds are more likely to be found along the North Carolina coast in the fall and spring, while in the summer only bluefish of less than 5 pounds are likely to show up. These smallest blues are locally referred to as snappers or Taylor blues. Bluefish are the most often-harvested saltwater species by North Carolina recreational anglers, with the catch ranging from 300,000 to 750,000 fish in recent years.

The striped bass is another glamour species that turns up along the Old North State's coast on a year-round basis. The best season for tangling with big ocean-run stripers is winter, when fish of 35 to 40 pounds are taken. These bruisers, like the larger red drum and bluefish, are nomads making their way south from New England or out of the Chesapeake Bay. They will show up on occasion as far south as the Cape Fear River at Wilmington, but they are much more common to the north along the Outer Banks.

On the other hand, fish of 5 to 10 pounds are common in North Carolina's sounds throughout the year. Their spring spawning runs up the rivers from Albemarle Sound are particularly anticipated events, but stripers are usually found around the area's inlets as well.

A number of other species appear along the North Carolina coast in the spring and summer months, having moved north as the waters warmed. These species are susceptible to fly-casters, though none offers a really extensive fishery. Beginning in March, flounder move inshore all along the coast, followed in the summer by cobia, pompano, Spanish mackerel, and tarpon. From August through November the Carolina coast is invaded by little tunny (false albacore), which offer some truly exciting near-shore fly-casting—but only in limited areas.

State Records

In the case of three of the saltwater species that can be targeted by anglers in the Old North State, the state record is also the currently recognized world record for the species. The world and state records for red drum are held by David G. Deuel for a 94-pound, 2-ounce bull red taken at Hatteras Island in 1984. The dual mark for bluefish is held by a 31-pound, 12-ounce chopper caught by James Hussey in 1972 at Hatteras Inlet. Finally, Robert Cranton's 13-pound Spanish mackerel, hooked at Ocracoke Inlet in 1987, shares the distinction of holding both records.

The North Carolina state record for spotted seatrout is held by John R. Kenyon for a 12-pound, 4-ounce fish taken at Wrightsville Beach in 1961, while the largest flounder on record was caught at Carolina Beach. That fish weighed 20 pounds, 8 ounces and was landed by Harold Auten in 1980.

Among the other fish common on the Carolina coast in the summer are pompano, tarpon, and cobia. The state record for pompano stands at 7 pounds, 13 ounces and was hooked at New River Inlet on Onslow Bay by Arthur Rice in 1981. The largest tarpon on record from North Carolina is the 164-pound fish caught at the Indian Beach Pier on the Bogue Banks in 1978 by John W. Freeman. The standard for cobia was established in 1988 by Tony Moore with a 103-pounder brought in at the Emerald Isle Pier on the Bogue Banks.

North Carolina does not recognize a state record for the striped bass in salt water, since it is considered a freshwater species. The state also does not keep records on false albacore or Atlantic bonito.

Regulations

North Carolina has minimum-size and creel limits for a number of saltwater species, as well as closed seasons for harvesting some fish. These are, however, subject to frequent changes and can vary from area to area, particularly when dealing with striped bass. Since the rules are so prone to change, you should contact the headquarters of the North Carolina Division of Marine Fisheries and request a copy of the most recent regulations covering saltwater species. The address is North Carolina Division of Marine Fisheries, P.O. Box 769, Morehead City, NC 28557.

In the Old North State no license is required to fish in coastal salt water. The state has designated some brackish areas "joint" waters, however. In these bodies of water either fresh- or saltwater species may be present, depending on recent rainfall or other weather conditions. All regulations applying to saltwater and freshwater fishing are enforced on joint waters. When you fish these brackish waters, a North Carolina fishing license is required,

TOM EVANS

*Big red drum are one of the major attractions that draw fly-casters
to North Carolina's Outer Banks.*

regardless of whether you are trying to catch fresh- or saltwater species. In
the following chapters only areas designated coastal saltwater are covered.
Though joint waters sometimes contain saltwater fish that offer fly-casting
options, it is rather hit-or-miss fishing. The saltwater game fish can often be
almost impossible to locate.

For a complete list of the dividing points between the classifications of
water, request a copy of the booklet *North Carolina Coastal-Joint-Inland
Fishing Waters.* The address to contact is North Carolina Wildlife Resources
Commission, 512 North Salisbury Street, Raleigh, NC 27604-1188.

CHAPTER 4

The Outer Banks

MAPS
DeLorme: *North Carolina Atlas* pages 26, 27, 49, 68, 69, 79
NOAA: chart numbers 12207, 12204, 11555, 11544

Whenever saltwater fishing in North Carolina is mentioned, most anglers think immediately of the Outer Banks, which span Currituck, Dare, Hyde, and Carteret Counties. Stretching from the Virginia border southward along Bodie, Hatteras, Ocracoke, and Portsmouth Islands, then along the Core Banks to Cape Lookout, this 170-mile strand of barrier islands offers some of the most highly rated and best-publicized saltwater angling on the eastern seaboard. Whether you are surf-casting, wading shallow flats, or fishing from a boat at inlets, the Outer Banks provide plenty of opportunities for tangling with bull red drum, seatrout, flounder, striped bass, bluefish, and pompano. Although spotting a fly-caster in this area is a rarity, many of the locations with the best fishing are accessible to fly-fishermen.

For anglers used to fishing other portions of the South Atlantic Coast, the Outer Banks do hold some surprises. While most other areas of the coast have palm trees and palmettos along the shore, on the Outer Banks the oceanside vegetation is composed of pine, cedar, and yaupon holly. The miles of windblown sand dunes and beaches on these islands are beautiful, but they are also desolate places. Finding a site to be alone while fishing takes very little effort here, especially to the south of the community of

Nags Head on Bodie Island. South of this point, with the exception of several small villages on Cape Hatteras and Ocracoke Islands, all of the Outer Banks are within the Hatteras or Cape Lookout National Seashore and remain undeveloped. Usually some walking is involved in reaching fishing sites, especially on the beaches. Be aware, however, that crossing the environmentally sensitive sand dunes should only be done at designated walkovers. Violation of this rule can get you a hefty fine anywhere on the Outer Banks.

The only road connecting the Outer Banks is two-lane NC 12, which is carried across Oregon Inlet from Bodie Island to Hatteras Island on the Herbert C. Bonner Bridge. When the road reaches Hatteras Inlet, however, a free state-run automobile ferry is the only connection to the northern end of Ocracoke Island. The ferry covers 5 miles of water and takes 40 minutes to make the crossing.

Once you are in the village of Ocracoke at the southern end of that island, your links back to the mainland are via a couple of toll automobile ferries. One makes $2\frac{1}{4}$-hour crossings to US 264 at Swanquarters on the mainland to the west, while the other runs $2\frac{1}{2}$ hours to the southwest to Cedar Island and the mainland via US 70. Making reservations in advance for either of these is a very good idea, particularly during the summer vacation months. Otherwise, since there are very limited accommodations on this part of the Outer Banks, if the ferries are booked up you could face a very long drive back to the north to get off the islands.

Weather conditions need to be considered when planning a fishing trip to the Outer Banks. From blazing summer heat to frigid northeast gales in the winter, this shoreline is one of extremes. Storm warnings should be heeded here, whether they are for winter gales, tropical squalls in the spring, or late-summer hurricanes. The Outer Banks are no place to be caught off guard by ugly weather!

Obviously, given the inconvenience of travel and problems with the weather, the fact that anglers flock to this part of the Old North State's coast suggests that the fishing must be very good. It is a suggestion that proves to be right on the money!

Although Portsmouth Island and the Core Banks are technically part of the Outer Banks, they are discussed later, in the chapter covering the Crystal Coast. From the standpoint of both fishing opportunities and access, they are more closely tied to that region around Morehead City.

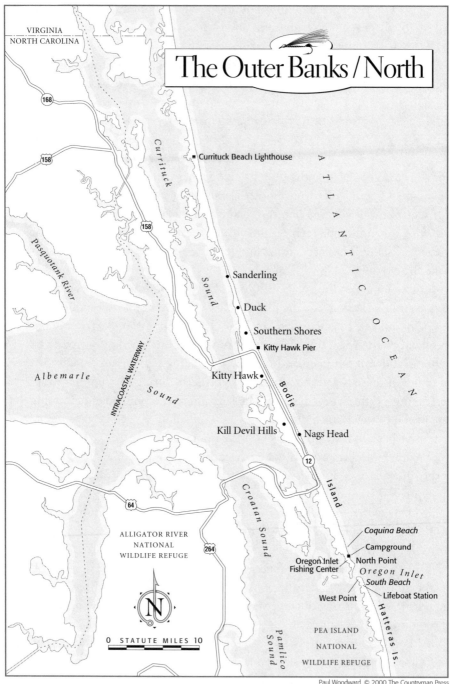

The Outer Banks / North

VIRGINIA
NORTH CAROLINA

Currituck Beach Lighthouse

ATLANTIC OCEAN

Currituck Sound

Pasquotank River

Sanderling

Duck

Southern Shores

Kitty Hawk Pier

Albemarle Sound

INTRACOASTAL WATERWAY

Kitty Hawk

Bodie

Kill Devil Hills

Nags Head

Island

Croatan Sound

ALLIGATOR RIVER
NATIONAL
WILDLIFE REFUGE

Coquina Beach

Campground

Oregon Inlet
Fishing Center

North Point

Oregon Inlet
South Beach

West Point

Lifeboat Station

Hatteras Is.

N

0 STATUTE MILES 10

Pamlico Sound

PEA ISLAND

NATIONAL

WILDLIFE REFUGE

Paul Woodward, © 2000 The Countryman Press

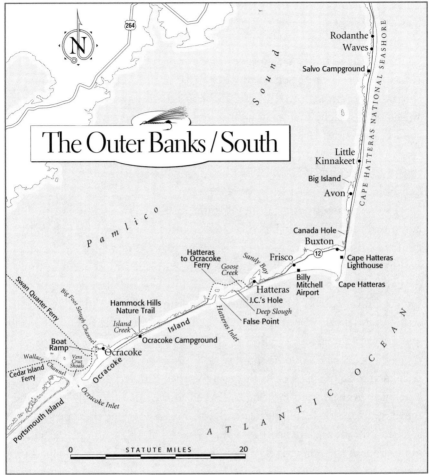

The Outer Banks / South

Paul Woodward, © 2000 The Countryman Press

Bodie Island

Although called an island, this stretch of land is actually a very long, thin peninsula extending south across the state border from the False Cape area of Virginia. Since there is no highway connection up the peninsula to Virginia, however, the only way to reach Bodie Island in North Carolina is via bridges and ferries. This, undoubtedly, has contributed to the local residents' having always referred to and considered Bodie an island.

Bodie Island is by far the most developed and accessible area of the

Outer Banks. Just south of the Virginia border are the communities of Carova Beach and North Swan Beach, but they can be accessed only from Virginia. More than a mile of inaccessible beach in the Swan Island Hunting Club and the Currituck Banks component of the North Carolina National Estuarine Research Reserve separates these communities from Corolla Village to the the south. Farther south the island contains the communities of Whalehead Beach, Monterey Shores, and Ocean Sands in Currituck County, then Sanderling, Duck, Southern Shores, Kitty Hawk, Kill Devil Hills, Nags Head, and Whalebone Cape in Dare County. As mentioned earlier, the southern end of Bodie Island is part of the Cape Hatteras National Seashore.

From the standpoint of the saltwater fly-fisher, the portion of Bodie Island north of Nags Head has very little to offer. On the inland side of the island are the waters of Currituck Sound, which are managed by the state as joint waters. Although saltwater incursions into the sound occur in times of drought, this body of water is ordinarily mildly brackish and far better known for largemouth bass fishing than for holding saltwater species. Though seatrout and puppy drum show up here, fly-casting for them is unpredictable and not very practical.

The beaches of Bodie Island from Corolla south to Nags Head offer a potpourri of saltwater species through the year. Bull red drum make their appearances in the spring months and again in the fall, especially beginning in mid-October. Smaller puppy drum may be found prowling these beaches year-round. Bluefish and striped bass are also seasonal, showing up at around the same times as the bull reds. Through the summer the ocean-run stripers move back up to New England, as do the larger blues. Small Taylor blues remain on these beaches year-round.

Spotted seatrout are possible targets for anglers from spring through fall, as are bottom-feeding flounder and whiting (often called northern kingfish in this area). Weakfish are present in the fall months in deeper sloughs along the beach. Finally, pompano can be found along stretches of the beach that have a lot of broken shells from July through September.

Though the surf and wind both make fly-casting along these beaches difficult, the fish are often found quite close to shore. In many places these beaches incline steeply into the water, and along that first drop is where the fish can often be found. Of course, stout gear in the 9- to 10-weight range is needed to cast because of the wind, and flies need to be weighted when you are fishing for bottom feeders like pompano or flounder. One area of particular interest along this shore is found on either side of the Kitty Hawk Pier. There are deeper holes through here that are quite close to shore and attract many of the species found along the beaches. Other than these holes, good places to try on the northern shore of Bodie Island are wherever you spot obvious feeding activity or tidal washes.

Access to these beaches is rather uneven. At Corolla it is possible to take a four-wheel-drive vehicle onto the beach at the end of NC 12, but there is no off-beach parking for other anglers. Just south of this point the Currituck Beach Lighthouse has a parking area, along with a vehicle ramp and a walkover to the beach. However, the rest of the shore from Corolla to Kitty Hawk is dominated by exclusive residential communities offering very little public beach access. One exception is found 10 miles south of Corolla along NC 12. The Currituck County Public Beach Access has a walkover and very limited parking space at that point.

From Kitty Hawk south to Nags Head, a number of walkovers from the beachfront road are provided at regular intervals for the public. On the other hand, parking space at these points is quite limited. Also be aware that the rules governing driving vehicles on the beaches vary among different communities, with some charging annual or daily fees. Read the posted signs before driving onto the sand, or flag down a local policeman if you are still in doubt.

For the fly-fisherman, the southern portion of Bodie Island holds much more promise. Beginning at Coquina Beach and running south around the end of the island at Oregon Inlet to the sound side near Bodie Island Lighthouse, there are a number of good spots where fly-casting is practical and can be quite successful.

Coquina Beach is located directly across NC 12 from the entrance to the Bodie Island Lighthouse near the southern end of the island. Parking spaces are provided, as is a short walkover from the highway to the beach. Deeper water is quite close to shore, and some local guide services bring their fly-fishing clients here, particularly for striped bass and bluefish in the fall. Though wind can be a problem, at times the breeze comes from the sound side, making the casting quite easy.

The northern side of Oregon Inlet at the southern end of Bodie Island offers some fine prospects to shorebound anglers, while the inlet itself is good for fishing from a boat. Be aware, however, that Oregon Inlet is rather narrow and shallow, and it can be treacherous to navigate. It carries a great volume of water from Pamlico and Albemarle Sounds into the Atlantic Ocean, so it can have quite strong currents. The water in the mouth of the inlet is gener-

A good way to find out about the current fishing hot spots is to check with one of the many bait-and-tackle shops along the Carolina shore.

ally clear during all tide and weather conditions, except when southerly winds occur after heavy rains.

The main species taken at the inlet are bluefish, flounder, red drum, pompano, striped bass, and weakfish. Look for stripers in washed-out troughs in depths of around 12 feet, no more than a couple of hundred yards outside the inlet in the fall and winter. They will move in around the pilings of the Bonner Bridge in the spring as large schools of bait fish begin to congregate at the inlet.

Puppy drum are possible from the beach at the southern tip of Bodie Island, right on around its end into the inlet. In the spring and fall bull reds appear here, too. Flounder and pompano should be targeted at the tip of the island in the summer months. Snapper-sized bluefish are usually around the inlet shore year-round, but show up en masse about the first of September. About a month later larger chopper blues begin filtering in, along with weakfish. Their numbers continue to grow as the weather cools in the fall and winter.

This shore at the southern tip of the island is a beach, but the sand is quite soft. It is possible to reach this area, known as North Point, by running along the beach in a four-wheel-drive vehicle from the access ramp at the National

Park Service's Oregon Inlet Campground, which is immediately north of the inlet on NC 12. Walking to North Point is possible but not practical since the sand on the beach is soft and the trek is a long one. Also, be aware that this is a very popular fishing destination, so there are likely to be quite a number of beach buggies parked on the shore and plenty of live-bait rigs staked out along the beach.

As the shore wraps around the end of the island at the inlet, it is called South Beach. Here the sand drops sharply into the dredged channel of the inlet. Farther around into the inlet is West Point, with channels running through flats and marsh grass. Again, the only practical access to this area is by driving along the beach.

Oregon Inlet is located 8 miles south of the entrance to the Cape Hatteras National Seashore, via NC 12. Across the highway from the campground just north of the Bonner Bridge is the Oregon Inlet Fishing Center, which provides a marina and paved public ramp for boating access. The area immediately in front of the boat ramp is referred to by some as Propeller Slough because of the hole excavated by continual prop wash from boats. At low tide it is a good place for wading the edge and casting to the deep water.

The final accessible fly-fishing destination on this island is the Bodie Island Lighthouse. The lighthouse drive is located 5.7 miles south of the national seashore entrance on the sound side of NC 12. From the end of the visitors center parking area at the lighthouse, a gated dirt road continues to the south. This runs about 0.25 mile to a landing used by a hunt club to access Off Island. The club has a grandfathered lease to use this island and the road. The public cannot drive on the road, but you may travel along it by foot through a pedestrian gate by the entrance.

On the northern side of the landing tiny Long Creek enters the channel between Bodie and Off Islands. A rough path allows access to some of the creek up to the point that an old dam blocks saltwater intrusion. The creek merits a cast or two at high tide, but is virtually dry during the ebb.

The entire eastern shore of the channel between Bodie and Off Islands is wadable on a hard-sand bottom. Most fly-fishers wade along casting into the deeper center of the channel. It is possible to cast almost across the channel here. Another area to target is right along the marsh grass that lines the channel, especially on higher tides.

To the south of the landing you can wade all the way to the end of the channel, where it opens onto Pamlico Sound. In this area there are several marsh-grass islands around which you can fish, never getting into water more than waist-deep. It is also possible to continue fishing along the marsh edge toward Oregon Inlet.

The Bodie Island Lighthouse area is noted for producing speckled trout and smaller schooling striped bass, particularly from April through June, but expect to find some trout here at most times of the year. Puppy drum are also likely to appear at any time in the channels or along the marsh grass.

Hatteras Island

Hatteras Island stretches for roughly 50 miles from Oregon Inlet south to Hatteras Inlet. About 40 miles of that distance lies on a north–south axis, but at Cape Hatteras on the southern end of the island the shore turns sharply to the west. The inland side of the island is lined with miles of hard-sand flats, many of which are accessible from the shore. The flats are only 1 to 4 feet deep, and stretch from 1 to 5 miles out into Pamlico Sound. On the ocean side the shore is lined with undeveloped beaches that provide some of the most productive and popular surf-casting waters along the eastern United States.

The northern third of the island is in the Pea Island National Wildlife Refuge, with the rest in the Cape Hatteras National Seashore. Seven tiny hamlets on the island are not included in the national seashore. From north to south, these are Rodanthe, Waves, Salvo, Avon, Buxton, Frisco, and Hatteras.

The northern end of Hatteras Island at Oregon Inlet offers several options for fly-casting, either from a boat or while wading. The first of these is the point of sand stretching out to the mouth of the southern side of the inlet and the beach immediately south of this point. This is a popular fishing destination—especially in the fall months, when Taylor blues and puppy drum come in quite close to shore. The blues can also be targeted in washed-out sloughs a bit farther off the beach from a boat. Another option is to come up the beach from the south in a four-wheel-drive beach buggy. Unfortunately, if you are fishing on foot, it is a long walk to this spot from the parking area at the southern end of the Bonner Bridge. The designated paved parking area is on the eastern side of NC 12, with beach access through the grounds of the abandoned Oregon Inlet Lifeboat Station. The old station house is slowly disappearing under the encroaching sand dunes.

This parking area is also the jumping-off point for fishing the riprap on the southern shore of the inlet and the old Coast Guard station landing on the eastern side of the Bonner Bridge. Casting from the riprap can be productive for bluefish, flounder, redfish, and weakfish. The deep hole at the

Coast Guard landing has been silting in for years but still offers some good fishing for the same species. The hard-sand bottom slopes out to deeper water, providing good wading possibilities, but you must be careful not to step off into the channel: There is often a strong current coming through the inlet here. Anglers in small boats target the outer edge of the landing's old channel here as well.

The final fishing site at this end of Hatteras Island is found just inside Oregon Inlet. This area has a bottom composed of hard-packed sand for good wading, but a deep channel sweeps close to shore. You can wade out close enough to fish the channel edge, but be aware that the water drops into 40-foot depths. A heavy current runs through the area during changing tides as well.

Still, the abundance of speckled trout and flounder in the summer, plus puppy drum in the spring, makes this area appealing. In the fall the species to target are the spotted seatrout and striped bass that congregate here. Although this area is on the western side of NC 12, use the parking lot on the eastern side of the highway for access. Anywhere on the Outer Banks it is smart to keep your vehicle on paved surfaces unless you have four-wheel-drive. The sand is loose and soft, making it very easy to get a vehicle stuck.

South of Oregon Inlet the beaches of Hatteras Island offer uniformly good surf fishing. The slope of the shore often results in deep-water tidal sloughs right at the beach and close enough to be reached while fly-casting— assuming the wind and surf are not too active. Places to look for are breaks in the whitecaps rolling toward shore. These interruptions indicate sites where water is rushing back out to sea from the deeper sloughs along the beach. These areas of runoff are favorite feeding grounds for red drum and bluefish year-round, plus pompano and flounder in the summer.

The rest of the ocean side of Hatteras Island south to the village of Hatteras offers a number of access points in the form of walkovers from parking areas on the shoulder of NC 12. There are also a few ramps providing vehicle access at the villages. All of these access points are very similar and can be good surf-casting destinations when the fish are present—it simply takes a bit of exploration to determine where to fish on any given day.

On the other hand, the portions of the shore most interesting to fly-fishermen in this area are on the sound side of Hatteras Island. Though some fishing from boats is possible, because of the vast expanses of very shallow flats the sound side is primarily the domain of wading anglers.

Some of the inland side of the Pea Island Refuge is closed to fishing to protect waterfowl and wading bird habitats, with other portions closed to any type of access. These are all marked with signs along NC 12. One exception is found at New Inlet, which is 11.5 miles south of Oregon Inlet. A parking area at this site is on the west side of the road at an unimproved boat ramp. The water at the ramp is quite shallow and suitable for launching only small boats. Some small poles mark the shallow channel that connects the landing with the deeper boat channel out in Pamlico Sound.

The bottom at New Inlet is quite firm and composed of packed sand. Shallow flats extend in both directions from the landing's channel, but the portion to the north offers the most interesting fly-casting options. An old, deteriorating wooden bridge runs out to an island in the sound about 100 yards north of the boat landing. The eastern third of the bridge pilings are close enough to cast to from the shallow flat. This area is particularly noted for holding speckled trout in its boat channel from September through November, but also produces flounder, puppy drum, and small bluefish at other times. Unfortunately, as you wade into waist-deep water near the edge of the boat channel, the bottom becomes softer and unwadable. Anglers in boats also fish this area, but care is needed, since the boat channels are not well marked.

Just to the north of the old bridge are several grass islands. It is possible to wade the flats around these, with the possibility of locating feeding puppy drum. At high tide the water on the flats is only 1 to 3 feet deep.

To the south of the Pea Island Refuge lie the villages of Rodanthe, Waves, and Salvo. Along their shore on the Atlantic, a limited number of walkovers provide access for surf casting.

Also, just south of Salvo on the inland side of the island is the Salvo Day-Use Area. This parklike setting has paved parking, picnic tables overlooking Pamlico Sound, an old cemetery, and a windsurfing area. More important, the shoreline is fronted by a hard-sand flat that is easily waded. As with most of the wadable areas on the sound side of Hatteras Island, the trick for successful fly-fishing is to locate the deeper water. At the Salvo area a deep cut through the flat runs parallel to the bank about 150 yards offshore; it holds drum, trout, and blues.

About 35 miles south of Oregon Inlet lies the village of Avon. It is positioned in the middle of a long stretch of good wading water that runs down the sound side of Hatteras Island. The hard-packed flats on this side of the island are pockmarked with deeper water created when sand was dredged to rebuild storm damage in the past. Now these holes are attractive holding areas for both speckled trout and puppy drum. The best time to fly-fish all these sites is in the morning during the summer. This is when the fish feed most actively and the prevalent southwest wind is most calm. As the day wears on and heats up, the wind increases to 15 to 20 knots on most days, making casting very difficult.

The northern end of the Avon area is marked by the old Little Kinnakeet U.S. Life Saving Service Station. At this point a sand road runs back to the sound side of the island, but it should be tackled only with a four-wheel-drive vehicle or on foot. Along this shore several holes drop down 4 to 6 feet deep; these hold speckled trout during the summer months.

In the village of Avon, a good wading area is located at the northern end of North End Road. This road parallels NC 12 through the village, just to the east of the highway. The best areas to fish are the holes near Big Island. To reach these you must wade across Mill Creek. When the wind is blowing hard from the southwest in the summer months is the best time to fish here, with seatrout and red drum the main targets.

At the southern end of this string of fishing sites lies the Canada Hole windsurfing area. This location is about 1 mile north of the village of Buxton and has a good parking area on the sound side of the highway. In the summer months expect to have to share the water with a number of windsurfers, since this a popular destination for them. Look for the darker-colored water that marks the dredge holes and concentrate on them. But beware of wading too close; the edges of some of the holes drop off sharply. Seatrout are the fish most often encountered here.

At the village of Buxton, Hatteras Island turns sharply to the east, running another 13 miles in that direction to the village of Hatteras. The ocean side of the island along this stretch offers three very good areas for surf casting. The first of these is located on the western end at Cape Hatteras. The Point—as local anglers refer to it—is one of the most popular fishing areas on the East Coast and maybe the best-known destination for red drum in the world. On weekends from the spring through early winter the beach often looks like a parking lot, with dozens of beach buggies and four-wheel-drive trucks lined up along the surf. These vehicles access the Point from the parking area at the Cape Hatteras Lighthouse at Buxton, about a mile to the north. If you are limited to traveling by foot, it is a grueling walk through very soft sand to reach the Point.

Fishing at Cape Hatteras produces striped bass, bull red drum, and chopper bluefish in the spring and fall, while the summer months also yield pompano and Spanish mackerel. The spectacular, world-class fishing for red drum usually occurs from mid-April though May, and again in mid-October through November. Be aware, however, that the wind blows almost constantly here, and fall and winter weather can be nasty. The water is quite rough as well, since Diamond Shoals lie just offshore. This is an area of the sea that has claimed hundreds of ships over the years. For this reason, the Cape Hatteras Lighthouse was built in 1870; today it is the best-known landmark of coastal North Carolina. Towering more than 200 feet above the cape, the entire lighthouse was moved roughly a quarter mile inland during 1999 to protect it from beach erosion.

For fly-casters, the most promise at Cape Hatteras is offered by the water immediately west of the tip of the Point. This water, unlike the steeply inclined sloughs running along the east-facing beach, is rather shallow, allowing for some wading. Smaller bluefish, plus stripers and pompano, are likely to come very near shore here.

The rest of the beach along the southern shore of Hatteras Island to the west of the Point is noted as a good stretch for summertime surf casting. The main species that show up are small bluefish, puppy drum, speckled trout, and pompano. One area of particular note along this coast is found at Beach Ramp 49, just south of the Billy Mitchell Airport near the village of Frisco. Pompano show up in numbers along this portion of the shore from the early summer through early fall.

At the western end of Hatteras Island lies Hatteras Inlet. The tip of the island here is sometimes referred to as False Point to distinguish it from Cape Hatteras. It is another popular surf-fishing destination that requires either a four-wheel-drive vehicle or a long walk in soft sand. The jumping-off point for access is Beach Ramp 55, near the Hatteras-to-Ocracoke ferry landing. All of the summer species mentioned earlier show up here, with the sloughs just inside the inlet being particularly good for pompano. The spring and fall yield red drum, stripers, and bluefish as well.

The sound side of Hatteras Island, as it stretches westward, also has some good fishing locations, which are more accommodating for fly-casters than are the beaches. The best wading sites here are located around the village of Hatteras. Unfortunately, most of the sites are to the southwest of the village and difficult to access.

The only place of note to the east of Hatteras is about a mile from the village on Sandy Bay. There is a turnout for parking on the ocean side of NC 12 at this point. On the sound side of the island, across the road from the turnout, the flats are wadable, with puppy-sized red drum and flounder turning up during the summertime. Some seatrout are also taken here in the warmer months.

The sand road running to the southwest of Hatteras out to False Point is the only land route to the other wading locations on this end of Hatteras Island. Since these sites are 1.5 to 3 miles from Hatteras Village, walking to them in the loose sand is a real trek. They can also be accessed via small boats from the village using the Hatteras-to-Ocracoke ferry channel, then getting out of the boat to wade to the deeper holes surrounded by shallows.

Traveling west along the sound-side shore, the first wading location is Goose Creek—actually just an indentation in the coast of the island. It lies several hundred yards to the west of the boundary between the village and the national seashore property. In the summer the creek yields small red drum, seatrout, and flounder.

The next location is known to some local anglers as J. C.'s Hole. It is roughly 400 yards east of Channel Marker 16 and consists of a stretch of deep water running along the shoreline. This hole attracts numbers of seatrout during the summer.

A bit farther west, Deep Slough lies on the inshore side of Channel Marker 16. This depression in the flats is noted for producing summertime speckled trout, but it is also a place where you can fish streamers deep for at shot at some weakfish.

Finally, a slough runs along the shore between Channel Markers 11 and 13 that yields spotted seatrout during hot weather. This deep trough of water is sometimes referred to as the Power Cable by local fishermen.

As noted, all of these sites on the western end of Hatteras offer better angling in the summer months. The best tactic is to wade near the drop-offs at the edge of the sloughs or holes, then cast to the deeper water.

Ocracoke Island

Running from northeast to southwest and lying just east of Hatteras Island is 16-mile-long Ocracoke Island. The tiny fishing and tourist village of Ocracoke is located on the isle's western end, with the rest of the island contained in the Cape Hatteras National Seashore. The two-lane asphalt strand of NC 12 is the only road running the length of the island. There is a National Park Service campground located on the ocean side of the road at about the midpoint of the island. Traveling along NC 12 you also pass a fenced pasture area

6 miles west of the Hatteras-to-Ocracoke ferry landing. This enclosure is the Ocracoke Pony Pasture and contains a remnant population of the wild horses that have inhabited the island since colonial times.

Adding to the island's lore is the the fact that Edward Teach—better known as the pirate Blackbeard—roamed the surrounding waters. He was captured and beheaded by the British in 1718 in a channel just off the village of Ocracoke. That channel is today known as Teachs Channel.

As you drive along the island highway, the southern side fronts sand dunes, offering occasional vistas of the Atlantic Ocean beaches, while the inland side of the road is lined with salt meadows and marshes. Several small tidal streams cut through the island and under the highway, but for the most part these are too small and shallow to offer any fishing opportunities. A number of vehicle ramps offer access to the beach along NC 12, but all are not always open. It is a good idea to check with the Ocracoke visitors center before venturing onto the beach with a vehicle. Any vehicle you do take to the beach must be a four-wheel drive if you expect to return without getting stuck in the loose sand!

While the beaches of Ocracoke Island are noted for producing plenty of puppy drum and smaller bluefish for surf casters, the truly big reds are rare here. This absence may be attributed to a couple of factors. First, the beaches of Ocracoke are not as steeply inclined as those found on Bodie and Hatteras Islands. These flatter surf areas contain fewer of the sloughs in which big red drum are often found feeding. Also, the number of bait fish found along this shore appears to be smaller than around the islands to the north.

One of the more popular places for surf casting on Ocracoke Island is found 2 miles west of the ferry landing at the eastern end of the island. At this site some old pier pilings extend from the beach out into Hatteras Inlet. Particularly when a northeast wind is prevalent, this spot is noted for producing small drum, seatrout, and flounder. Taylor blues are also possible in any season. After hard rains fall on inland areas, the rip current between the muddy waters flowing out of Pamlico Sound and the clear ocean water is a natural ambush line for predatory game fish.

Though this point holds fish of some kind in all seasons, reaching it can be a chore. If you have a four-wheel-drive beach buggy, access is available from Ramp 59 off NC 12. By foot it is a long trek through soft sand from the walkover on NC 12 that is located about 0.5 mile west of the ferry landing.

One other access point is located on this eastern end of Ocracoke Island. As you travel west from the ferry landing, the first dirt road to your right runs out to a small peninsula on the sound side of the island. This is the only dirt track on the island on which you can safety venture in a regular passenger car (at least in dry weather) without fear of getting stuck. At the end of the road is an unpaved area with room for several vehicles. It borders on a large hard-sand flat that is very wadable. There are several sandbars on the flat that break it up into small channels, especially during lower tides. It is possible to wade across some of the channels during ebb tides as well.

Fishing in the channels during changing tides can produce flounder, red drum, and bluefish. The water is generally only clear enough to see 12 to 15 inches into it, but sight-casting is still sometimes possible by watching for fish breaking the surface, circling gulls, or wakes being pushed by moving fish. Even if none of these is present, try casting streamers into the deeper bends of the channels around the sandbars.

Moving west along the island, the next spot that offers some interesting fly-casting opportunities is the Ocracoke Campground. Ramp 68 provides access to the beach here, with snapper blues and whiting common in the summer surf. In this same area Island Creek cuts into the island from the sound side, flowing under NC 12 beside the campground. This tidal creek offers another angling option; since stretches of its bank are open enough to allow some fly-casting.

Finally, directly across the highway from the campground is Hammock Hills Nature Trail. Though the trail itself does not offer any angling opportunities, at the western end of its parking area is the campground dump station. A dirt road continues from the dump station toward the sound side of the island. This road is quite rough, suited only for four-wheel-drive traffic, but it provides a 0.5-mile walk to the shore. An unimproved landing suitable for launching very small boats is located at the end of the road, while the site also borders on a large expanse of shallow, hard-sand flats that are easily wadable. The major drawback to fishing here is that there is no deep water to key on. Still, flounder and puppy drum can be found scattered through the area in the summer.

Farther west along NC 12, just before the village of Ocracoke, Ramp 72 is situated near the Ocracoke Island Airport. Besides providing beach access, the ramp marks the location of a major slough that often holds bigger red drum, flounder, and seatrout. It can be located by watching for a noticeable break in the dunes behind the beach to the west of the ramp.

Still farther to the west is the tip of the island on Ocracoke Inlet. Another popular spot with surf fishermen, it is accessible only via four-wheel-drive vehicles—unless you can tackle a 2-mile walk through soft sand! The point can be a real hot spot for big drum, flounder, bluefish, seatrout, and weakfish at various seasons. This is especially true when a southwest wind creates a prominent tidal rip just offshore.

For anglers using small boats, the multiple channels of Ocracoke Inlet offer the best bets around the island. Wallace Channel, which drops to 15 feet deep, is the main break between Ocracoke and Portsmouth Islands. It is noted for holding trout, flounder, and even cobia in the warmer months. Cobia may also turn up in Blair Channel, just west of the National Park Service offices; in Big Foot Channel directly in front of the NPS site; or to the east in Big Foot Slough Channel.

There is also a sand spit called Vera Cruz Shoals in the middle of the inlet. You can either fish from a boat or get out and wade the sandbar here if you are fishing in the deeper water along the channel edge. In the spring and fall don't be too surprised if you suddenly spot a huge school of 50-plus-pound red drum swimming just under the surface in front of you!

Regardless of which channel you fish, be aware that the channel edges rise abruptly to shallows of only 1 to 3 feet deep. Care is needed in navigating this area, especially when you stray from the center of the marked channels.

The only public boating access on the island is via the double-lane, paved boat ramp located off NC 12 and adjacent to the ferry dock in the village of Ocracoke.

CHAPTER 5

The Sounds

MAPS
DeLorme: *North Carolina Atlas* pages 26, 27, 46, 47, 48, 49, 66,
67, 68, 69, 78, 79
NOAA: chart numbers 11548, 11555, 12205

The saltwater angling offered by North Carolina's major sounds is rather enigmatic. Viewing a map of the area reveals that Albemarle, Croatan, Currituck, Pamlico, and Roanoke Sounds form a vast complex of salt and brackish water covering almost a million surface acres, with thousands of miles of shoreline. Yet compared to the voluminous information available on the fishing and fisheries of the Outer Banks or Cape Lookout area, relatively little has been reported on this angling resource.

This situation can be partially explained by the very size of these waters, their depth, and the type of bottom found in them. The maximum depth in these sounds is just over 20 feet, with most of the area dropping to only 10 to 12 feet. Along the shore, shallow flats only 1 to 4 feet deep often stretch for a mile or more from the marshy edges. Adding to the problem of finding fish in this huge inland sea is a consistently featureless sand bottom that offers very little in the way of structure to hold fish in specific locations.

Finally, the composition of the water adds more problems. Since there are but three outlets to the sea (Oregon, Hatteras, and Ocracoke Inlets) for this entire drainage, fresh water flowing from the inland rivers takes a long

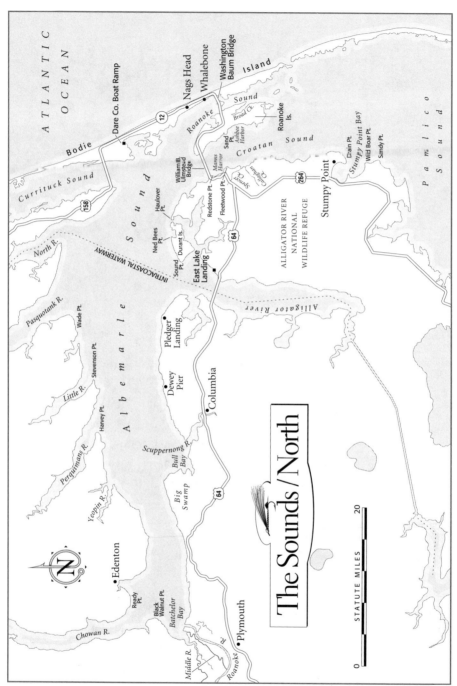

The Sounds/North

STATUTE MILES

0   20

Paul Woodward, © 2000 The Countryman Press

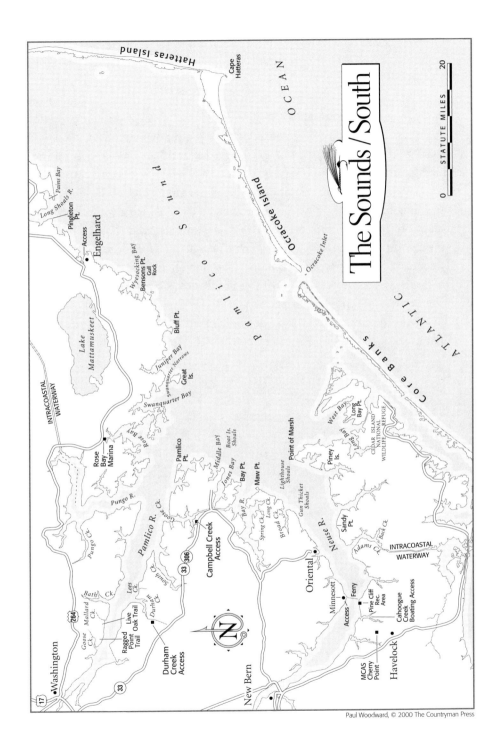

The Sounds/South

STATUTE MILES

0   20

Paul Woodward, © 2000 The Countryman Press

time to mix with the brine, leaving a great deal of the area as brackish water. Consequently, the angling reputation of much of the sound area is based on catching freshwater species of fish.

The most obvious example of this situation is Currituck Sound at the northern end of the complex. At 30 miles long, 4 miles wide, and averaging only 4 feet in depth, it is a sizable body of water but in a remote location with regard to the inlets. During the 1970s and 1980s it had a reputation for producing fantastic largemouth bass fishing. In the late 1980s and early 1990s that changed as drought conditions reduced the inflow of fresh water. The encroaching brine brought with it more saltwater species for a while. Today the balance has again shifted back to freshwater species. And through it all, the entire sound has been managed as joint waters by the North Carolina Wildlife Resources Commission and the North Carolina Division of Marine Fisheries. In keeping with the parameters of this guidebook, Currituck simply does not offer dependable enough prospects for saltwater fly-casting to merit coverage. This same applies to other large portions of the system. Still, the sounds do offer at least some areas that can be considered true saltwater fisheries.

Albemarle Sound

Stretching from the town of Edenton at the mouth of the Chowan River on its western end to the the northern end of Croatan and Roanoke Sounds in the east, Albemarle is the second largest of the Old North State's sounds. It is 55 miles long, averages 8 miles wide, and contains 278,850 acres of water. It runs so far inland that its western banks lose most of the characteristics of saltwater shores. Along many of the rural roads approaching this portion of the sound, you drive through large fields of corn, pass through a thin belt of pine trees, and suddenly find yourself on a narrow sand beach looking out over miles of open water!

On the northern side of Albemarle are the Chowan, Perquimans, Yeopin, Little, Pasquotank, and North Rivers, all of which form sizable bays in their lower reaches. They are, however, all joint waters and predominantly produce freshwater fish. The same is true for the Roanoke, Scuppernong, and Alligator Rivers on the southern side of the sound. For this reason, none of these merits coverage in this book, which instead focuses on the open water of Albemarle Sound. Most of this area is composed of waters 17 to 22 feet deep that offer little bottom structure. Indeed, fly-casters seeking saltwater species usually need only concentrate on the shoreline of Albemarle Sound, especially in its eastern end nearer the ocean outlets. During drier seasons of the year, the western end of the sound can also hold saltwater species that are vulnerable to fly-casting. Unfortunately, virtually all of the angling on Albemarle Sound requires a boat.

Be aware that there are closed seasons, restricted creel limits, plus minimum- and maximum-size regulations in effect for striped bass in Albemarle Sound. There are also minimum-size limits on red drum that differ from other coastal waters. These change frequently, so if you are targeting either of these fish it is imperative to check the latest regulations issued by the Division of Marine Fisheries and the North Carolina Wildlife Resource Commission.

During the midsummer months, all of the open water of Albemarle Sound can hold cruising tarpon. These fish move into the sound in search of schools of forage fish and are found around deeper cuts that have bait fish moving through them. One area of particular note is between Wade Point (on the northern shore of the sound and the western side of the Pasquotank River's mouth) and Dewey Pier on the southern shore of the sound.

Albemarle Sound also hosts a migration of striped bass each year that can produce some exciting action. In March and April stripers congregate in the western end of the sound as they stage for their spawning run up the Roanoke River. These fish are not the giant sea-run striped bass encountered on the Outer Banks, but they do reach up to 30 inches long and weigh up to 10 pounds.

At the mouth of the Roanoke River is Batchelor Bay, which is a good area for ambushing the stripers as they move toward the river in early spring. The water is only 6 to 8 feet deep in the bay, which makes the fish more vulnerable to fly-casting than when they are in deeper water.

Boating access to Batchelor Bay is easiest from the Roanoke River Access. This site is just south of the Zeb Vance Norman Bridge on NC 45, which crosses the Roanoke and Middle Rivers to the northeast of the town of Plymouth. There is a large gravel parking area at this location and a double-lane, paved boat ramp. Running downstream from this landing to the river mouth puts you in Batchelor Bay.

Another area on western Albemarle Sound worth checking out is the mouth of the Chowan River. This river enters the sound from the northwest. Reedy Point on the northern shore and Black Walnut Point to the south often hold stripers in the spring, although the water runs close to 20 feet deep through most of the area. An artificial reef just offshore of Black Walnut Point can be of particular interest.

Boating access to the mouth of the Chowan is best from the Edenhouse Access. Located at the eastern end of the US 17 bridge over the Chowan, the site offers two paved, single-lane boat ramps and a large gravel parking area. It is just upstream of the mouth of the river.

In the midportion of Albemarle Sound there are several places worth targeting for puppy drum, seatrout, and flounder. On the southern shore of the sound Bull Bay is formed at the mouth of the Scuppernong River. The rim of 3- to 6-foot-deep water running around its edges holds some casting opportunities. Also check out the marshy points on the western side of the bay along Big Swamp.

Access to Bull Bay is via the Scuppernong River Access in the town of Columbia. There is a large gravel lot and a two-lane paved boat ramp on a small creek leading into the river. It is located on a gravel drive near the end of Ramp Road, off the northern side of US 64, 1 mile west of the highway bridge over the river. Watch for the sign at the drive entrance on the western side of Ramp Road. Once you are on the water, run downriver to reach the southeastern side of Bull Bay.

Across Albemarle Sound, the northern shore often holds trout and red drum along Harvey Point on the western side of the Perquimans River's mouth. Just east of this location, Stevenson Point at the western side of the Little River's mouth also offers some possibilities for finding fish. Both of these points are accessible by boat from the Shadneck Access on Big Flatty Creek in Camden County. This landing has a single-lane boat ramp that is paved but in very rough condition. There is plenty of parking in a gravel lot.

To reach the landing, travel south from Elizabeth City on NC 34 (Salem Church Road) to its intersection with Soundneck Road. Turn west onto Soundneck Road and drive 0.3 mile, then turn south onto Shadneck Road and continue for 1.5 miles. At the end of the pavement a gravel drive runs off the road to your right, but there is no sign at the intersection indicating the presence of the landing. The ramp is at the end of the gravel drive. Once you are on the water, run south on Big Flatty Creek to Albemarle Sound, then turn west to the mouth of Little River and then the Perquimans confluence.

At the eastern end of Albemarle Sound are additional sites that produce some good fishing. On the northern side of the sound the mouth of the North River is noted for yielding striped bass in both the spring and fall months. The water in the river is 6 to 8 feet deep, but at its mouth the bottom rises up to 4 feet or less. There is, however, a boat channel in the center that offers a thoroughfare for both vessels and stripers. Begin your search for the rockfish around the channel, moving toward either shore until you locate fish.

Stripers can also be found a bit farther east around the Wright Memorial Bridge that spans the junction of Albemarle and Currituck Sounds. The fish around the bridge can run up to 8 pounds and are present from the spring though the fall. Concentrate on the bridge pilings and the deeper channels under the span.

The nearest access point for the North River's mouth and the Wright Memorial Bridge is the Texas Access on Camden Point. This single-lane, paved boat ramp is a rather rough one and offers parking space for only three or four vehicles with trailers. From the village of Camden on US 158, turn southeast onto NC 343. After this road passes through the crossroads of Shiloh it bends due south and is called Texas Road. Beyond the crossroads of Old Trap, Texas Road dead-ends at Camden Point and the boat landing. Once your boat is in the water, travel east along the northern shore of the sound to North River Point and the mouth of the river, or continue east around Powells Point to the Wright Memorial Bridge.

At the southern fringe of Albemarle the best fishing action is in the vicinity of the mouth of the Alligator River. On the western side of the river at Pledger Landing is a shallow flat of 4 feet or less of water. There are also some old trees in the water where the shore is apparently eroding. This area is noted for holding flounder in the spring and summer, with numbers of the fish often concentrated here.

Just east of the Alligator River is Durant Island. The shore of the island facing northwest is a hot spot for spring and fall striped bass action. The area to target is from Sound Point on the west around to Ned Bees Point on the east. A very narrow, shallow flat fronts this side of the island before dropping to depths of around 14 feet. Stripers also show up at the same times of year a bit to the south around the pilings of the Alligator River bridge on US 64.

Finally, just to the east of Durant Island is Haulover Point, at the very northern tip of the Alligator River National Wildlife Refuge. Grass beds along the shore here produce red drum of up to 18 inches in length, as well as spotted seatrout that may weigh from 2 to 5 pounds each.

The easiest access point for all of these locations on the eastern end of Albemarle Sound is the East Lake Landing. This single-lane, paved boat ramp has a large gravel parking area. It is located on the Alligator River near the eastern end of the US 64 bridge. Turn north onto Old Ferry Road to reach the boat ramp, which lies adjacent to the abandoned landing of the old Alligator

River ferry. From the ramp, travel north down the river to Albemarle Sound, turning west to reach Pledger Landing or east for the other fishing sites.

Croatan Sound

The waters of Roanoke and Croatan Sounds that border Roanoke Island offer a number of good options to fly-casters. Though the island's fame rests on having been the site of Sir Walter Raleigh's ill-fated first English settlement in North America in the 1560s, today the island draws adventurers in search of bluefish, flounder, red drum, seatrout, Spanish mackerel, and striped bass. Whether you plan to wade or fish from a boat, these sounds offer plenty of action.

Croatan Sound runs on a north–south axis to the west of Roanoke Island, holding the deepest water found in either of the two sounds. Still, it is only about 9 feet at its maximum depth.

At the northern end is probably the best-known and most popular fishing destination on the sound. The William B. Ulmstead Bridge on US 64 spans Croatan Sound, connecting Redstone Point on the west with Weir Point on Roanoke Island. The area is often referred to by local anglers as Manns Harbor. The main angling attraction at this location is tangling with striped bass in the 18- to 30-inch range that weigh from 2 to 8 pounds. The average size of what anglers consider a good fish here is 5 pounds. A 10-pounder is a monster.

The key to the striper fishing at Manns Harbor is to be on the water when the tide is either rising or falling. When the current is moving, the fish begin feeding around the pilings of the bridge. Often during calm evenings, just before dark, feeding schools of striped bass will appear on the surface. Under ideal conditions, local guides report catching and releasing up to 100 fish per day around the Ulmstead Bridge! A bonus when you are fishing this location is the frequent presence of spotted seatrout.

Although stripers may show up anywhere along the Ulmstead Bridge, most of the boat anglers concentrate on the area of the boat channel at the middle of the sound, or along the western shore near Redstone Point.

The public boating access closest to this area is located on the Outer Banks on Kitty Hawk Bay. The Dare County Boat Ramp is a single-lane, paved facility with plenty of parking in a gravel lot. To reach the ramp, take US 64 east to the Outer Banks, then turn north onto NC 158. In the village of Kitty Hawk turn west onto Kitty Hawk Road. Continue past the inter-

*One way of locating feeding fish on the Old North State's sounds
is to spot the gulls working the surface.*

section with Herbert Perry Road to Bob Perry Road and turn left—the ramp is located on the right side of Bob Perry Road.

Once you are on the water, head west out of Kitty Hawk Bay, then run south along the eastern end of Albemarle Sound. Upon approaching Roanoke Island, head to its western side and the Ulmstead Bridge.

Anglers without boats also have a shot at the striper and seatrout fishing at Manns Harbor. It is possible to park on roadside turnouts on either side of US 64 at the Redstone Point (western) end of the Ulmstead Bridge. At both sides of the span are areas of shallow, wadable, hard-sand flats running out about 100 feet. On the northern side there are some old, small pilings in the sound that can be reached by fly-casting.

For another 0.25 mile north of the bridge you can walk the narrow sand strip along the edge of the marsh grass to fish the sound, with plenty of room for backcasts. The bottom, however, is mucky along here, making wading impractical. The same conditions exist for about 100 yards to the south of the bridge.

Two other sites are noted for producing good spotted seatrout fishing within Croatan Sound. The first is found along the western shore at Fleetwood Point and south past the mouth of Spencer Creek to Callaghan Creek. The marsh grass shores, particularly on the points on either side of the creek's mouth, are the places to target. Almost immediately across the sound on Roanoke Island is the other speckled trout hot spot: Try targeting the shore just off Sand Point, which juts out to the northern side of Ashbee Harbor.

One final spot of interest to fly-casters is the open water at the southern end of Croatan Sound, where it blends into Pamlico Sound. Through here schools of smaller bluefish and Spanish mackerel can be found chasing pods of bait fish on the surface, providing great targets for fly-casting.

These last three Croatan Sound sites are accessible only to anglers in boats. The most convenient public boating access for them is located at Stumpy Point. To reach this access, take US 264 south for 14 miles from Manns Harbor. Turn left onto Bayview Drive (this road shows up as Stumpy Point Road on the DeLorme map) and drive 2.5 miles to the launch site. The ramp is a single-lane, paved one, with a large gravel parking area on the eastern side of the road.

Once your boat is in the water, run south on Stumpy Bay, then east around Drain Point into Pamlico Sound. Running north up Pamlico leads to the southern end of Croatan Sound.

Roanoke Sound

Roanoke Sound lies to the east of Roanoke Island and is bounded on the east by Bodie Island. It is a relatively narrow stretch of sheltered water that contains a profusion of small islands. Roughly midway down the sound the Washington Baum Bridge (also locally called the Manteo Bridge) on US 64 crosses the sound from Roanoke Island, across Cedar Island, to the causeway leading to the village of Whalebone on Bodie Island.

At the northern end of the sound, on the Outer Banks shore at Nags Head, is Jockey Ridge State Park. A 0.25-mile stretch of shoreline in the park's windsurfing area offers a firm-sand bottom. Wading anglers targeting the area at dawn and dusk can hook up with flounder, seatrout, and puppy drum.

This strip of beach cannot be reached via the park's main entrance off NC 158. Rather, you must turn west onto Southside Road from NC 158 at the southern edge of the park. At the end of this road, the parking area for the beach is on the right side of the street.

The area around the Washington Baum Bridge is noted for holding some striped bass in the 2- to 5-pound range. Again, much as with the fishing on Croatan Sound, the time to target these fish is during a moving tide around the bridge pilings.

For spotted seatrout, there are two sites of interest in Roanoke Sound. The first is located between the northern end of Pond Island and the causeway leading to the eastern end of the Baum Bridge. The other is in Broad Creek on the western side of the sound at the southern end of Roanoke Island. As always with seatrout, look for marsh-grass points, shell beds, and feeder-stream intersections to hold the fish at both sites.

On the eastern side of the sound, from the Baum Bridge south to Bells Island, schools of small bluefish can be found chasing bait in the channels between the islands. Also, flounder are usually present on patches of hard-sand bottom all through this area. Some of the flatfish are of doormat size.

All the fishing areas on Roanoke Sound, except for Jockey Ridge, are accessible only by boat. The best public boating access is at the paved Dare County Boat Ramp and parking lot at the western end of the Washington Baum Bridge.

Pamlico Sound

Pamlico is the largest sound located in North Carolina, the second largest estuary on the Atlantic Coast (second only to the Chesapeake Bay), and one of the largest saltwater estuaries in the entire world. From Oregon Inlet to the north, Pamlico Sound stretches for roughly 70 miles in a southwesterly direction to the Cedar Island National Wildlife Refuge. In places it is nearly 30 miles wide. Yet its waters barely reach 20 feet deep at any point in this vast area. On the east the Outer Banks form the shore of Pamlico, with the western edges bounded by the North Carolina mainland. This western side of the sound is fed by its two major tributaries, the Neuse and Pamlico Rivers.

With regard to the finned inhabitants of this vast inland sea, literally all of the inshore saltwater species found along the coast of the Old North State venture into the area. Since fishing destinations along the entire eastern shore of the sound were covered in the chapter on the Outer Banks, here the open waters and western shore are covered. Unlike the shore along Bodie, Hatteras, and Ocracoke Islands on the east, where virtually all of the fishing sites are wadable, the western part of Pamlico is better suited for boat fishing.

Pamlico Sound receives several migrations of fish during the spring and summer months. In general these movements are made by the bigger predators found in these waters. The largest are the tarpon that appear in the late spring through summer. For the most part the fish, which can run to more than 100 pounds, stick to the open water portions of the sound, constantly cruising. The only time to effectively target them with a fly is when you spot them rolling on the surface.

In the same warmer months schools of Spanish mackerel also move into the sound. The most practical way to target these is when they are working a school of bait fish on the surface. Two areas worth particular interest when looking for Spanish are the open waters on the northern end of Pamlico where it meets Croatan Sound, and the waters around Pingleton Shoal. This latter site is to the southeast of Pingleton Point, which lies on the western side of the mouth of the Long Shoals River in Hyde County.

In the late summer the sound is invaded by schools of large red drum, entering through Oregon, Hatteras, and Ocracoke Inlets. Though not giants, these reds are plentiful, in the 15- to 20-pound range, and spread out all through the sound.

Finally, in November and December the sound near Oregon Inlet receives an influx of striped bass in the 18- to 24-inch range, as well as a few larger ones. Though the bulk of these fish stay relatively close to the inlet, some move all the way to the western shore of the sound.

The Pamlico fishery, however, is dependent not on the migratory fish but on its year-round residents: spotted seatrout, puppy drum, smaller bluefish, weakfish, plus flounder. Some local anglers have expressed concerns that the seatrout that are a staple of the fishery have suffered in recent years due to shrimp trawls destroying the grass beds in the sound, and thus these trout nursery areas. Still, though they are on the small side, trout continue to be plentiful in Pamlico.

As is true all along the Southeast Coast, the places to find seatrout, red drum, and flounder in Pamlico are around grass beds, shell bars, and the mouths of tributary streams. Where any of these are found in conjunction with points jutting into the sound, your chances of locating fish are even better.

On the northern end of Pamlico, one of the more dependable locations for intercepting a few fish is at Stumpy Point. The area from Drain Point on the north across the mouth of Stumpy Point Bay to Wild Boar Point on the south is made up of water 6 to 8 feet deep, with a good bit of debris scattered along the bottom. Casting streamers while drifting across this area is a prescription for tangling with seatrout, smaller bluefish, and even some weakfish.

Just south of Stumpy Point Bay, Sandy Point juts out into Pamlico Sound. Off the end of this point the bottom of the sound is very uneven and dotted with holes of up to 12 feet in depth. This creates ideal habitat for attracting and holding spotted seatrout and weakfish.

Both of these sites are best accessed from the public boat ramp at Stumpy Point. A description of the ramp and directions to it were provided in the preceding section on Croatan Sound. Both Drain Point and Sandy Point are south of the boat landing.

Moving southward along the western coast of Pamlico Sound, the next important fishing location is at the mouth of the Long Shoals River. This feeder stream flows south out of the Alligator River National Wildlife Refuge to empty into the sound. The area from Pingleton Point on the west across the mouth of the river to tiny Rawls Island and on across the mouth of Pains Bay is excellent for finding some big seatrout. Also, the Long Shoals River is classified as coastal salt water all the way up to the US 264 bridge over the stream. The mouths of all the feeder streams entering it though that area are worth checking out as well.

Farther south of the mouth of the Long Shoals River is Wyesocking Bay, near the tiny village of Gull Rock. The southern end of the bay is formed by Bensons Point. Just off this point a band of shallow water runs eastward to the submerged Gull Rocks. This area is noted for holding schools of smaller striped bass.

Access to the Long Shoals River and Wyesocking Bay areas is via the public boat ramp at the village of Engelhard. The Engelhard Access has a single-lane, paved ramp with a large gravel parking lot. The site is at the northern edge of the city limits, on Swamp Road to the east of its junction with US 264. The landing is about halfway between the Long Shoals River and Wyesocking Bay.

The Engelhard Access is also one of the few sites on this side of Pamlico Sound that offer any shore access for fly-casting. Roughly 0.25 mile of shore-line around the ramp is open enough for casting. This faces on the sound, wrapping around into the small tidal creek on which the ramp is located. The approach road is paralleled for a short distance by the creek as well.

Once you are around Bensons Point, the shore of Pamlico Sound turns to the east as it approaches the mouth of the Pamlico River. This entire shore to the mouth of the Pungo River can be a hot spot for puppy drum, is good for flounder, and also holds some spotted seatrout. Targeting the flats near the mouths of feeder streams or marsh-grass points along this stretch should put you on some fish. Areas to check out in this region are Bluff Point; Juniper Bay; Swanquarter Narrows, between Great Island and the mainland; Swanquarter Bay; and Rose Bay. In the late summer and early fall expect to find bigger red drum along this coast as well. They tend to show up in the shallower areas in the evening, staying in deeper water during the day.

Boating access to this area is rather difficult. The nearest public ramps are located at the previously described Engelhard Access to the northeast, or at the Belhaven Ramp, far up the Pungo River to the west. There is, however, a commercial ramp that can be accessed for a fee at Rose Bay Marina, off US 264 in the small town of Scranton. This ramp is at the very northern end of Rose Bay.

Pamlico River

The Pamlico River enters the southern end of Pamlico Sound from the west, and to the north of the mouth of the Neuse River. It offers almost 36 miles of saltwater habitat from the city of Washington downstream to Rose Bay, while averaging about 3 miles wide. Although it has a number of tributary streams along its course, among them only Goose Creek, the Pungo River, and the lower half of South Creek are designated coastal waters.

A number of places along the Pamlico yield flounder, seatrout, and puppy drum during the year. The key to finding each of these is to target shallow points along the shore for red drum; deeper water along rocky shore, shell-covered banks, and oyster bars for seatrout; and shallow flats, tight against the shore, for flounder. As a rule of thumb, in the heat of the summer the trout are going to be in water up to 12 to 16 feet deep. The drum and flounder stay in the deeper holes as well during the heat of the day, moving shallower at dawn and dusk. In the spring and fall reds and flatfish may be shallow throughout the day, with the trout joining them early and late. Due to changing levels of salinity in the Pamlico, the game fish tend to move around a lot. It is rare to find them on the same point or bank for more than a day or two, so you need to move around as well until you find hungry fish.

One event that makes fishing on the Pamlico easier in the fall is the run up the river by schools of menhaden. As these bait fish progressively move farther upriver, they are followed by puppy drum, as well as large red drum and striped bass. This run begins in August and continues into November. During this period, the fish may run as far west as the city of Washington at the very head of the saltwater portion of the Pamlico. Similarly, the bait and game fish also run up the Pungo River as far as Belhaven. If you can find the schools of bait at this time of year, catching numbers of puppy drum, in particular, can be fairly easy.

A good location for intercepting some of the fish along the Pamlico is Goose Creek on the southern shore, about 8 miles upstream of the river's mouth. This stream is roughly 4 miles long and 1.25 miles wide, providing plenty of hiding spots for trout, red drum, and flounder.

The best access point for reaching Goose Creek is the Campbell Creek Access. This single-lane, paved ramp is in pretty poor condition but can handle smaller boats. It has a large gravel parking area.

The landing is located on a small feeder stream leading into Campbell Creek, which, in turn, feeds into the upper portion of Goose Creek. At the ramp you are in fresh water and need to run down to Goose Creek to reach the brine. The ramp is located on NC 33 at the eastern end of the bridge over the feeder stream. The landing is on the northern side of the highway.

Directly across the Pamlico, on the northern shore, is its confluence with its largest feeder stream, the Pungo River. The points on either side of the Pungo's mouth are good for flounder, speckled trout, and puppy drum. Farther upstream near Belhaven, Pungo Creek is noted for producing flounder and seatrout in the summer, while, as mentioned earlier, the points on the river hold red drum during the fall menhaden run.

The best access point for the Pungo River and its tributaries is the Belhaven Ramp in the town of the same name. This landing contains a double-lane, paved boat ramp with a large gravel parking area. It is situated at the end of Water Street to the northwest of that street's intersection with the end of Pamlico Street in downtown Belhaven.

The ramp is on Pantego Creek, so you must run just to the southeast to reach the Pungo. Pungo Creek enters the river from the west a little downstream of this point.

Other areas that hold the promise of finding some hungry red drum, seatrout, and flounder are spread all along the Pamlico River's course. Just to the northwest of the mouth of Goose Creek, Indian Island lies in the southern half of the river. Around this small isle is a good spot to try for some puppy drum, particularly in the fall months.

Access to Indian Island is via the Campbell Creek Access, described earlier in the description of Goose Creek. Once you are on Goose Creek, run north to the Pamlico River, then northwest to the island.

Another area to check out is the vicinity of Durham Creek on the southern shore of the Pamlico, along with Bath Creek and the Bayview area directly across the river. On the southern side, the mouth of Durham Creek is 20 miles upstream of Rose Bay, and the points on either side of the mouth are the places to target. Also, a mile to the east is tiny Lees Creek at the Texas Gulf Sulphur mining site. This stream's mouth is noted for holding seatrout.

On the northern shore the points around the mouth of Bath Creek, about a mile west of Durham Creek, are worth casting around as well. Also on this side of the river is AR 291, an artificial reef made of old automobile tires sunk in roughly 15 feet of water in the main river. The reef can hold trout and red drum.

Boating access to this portion of the Pamlico River is easiest from the Durham Creek Access. This single-lane, paved boat ramp has only very limited roadside parking, and the ramp is not marked on the DeLorme map of the area. The landing is near the crossroads of Bonnerton. From NC 33 turn north onto Durham Creek Road, then right onto Bonnerton Road. The ramp is at the bridge over Durham Creek.

The water in the creek at this point is considered fresh, but running downstream brings you to the Pamlico River. Bath Creek's mouth is directly across the river, AR 291 is just to the east on that same shore, while Lees Creek is to the east along the southern bank of the river.

One other place on the Pamlico River deserves mention as a possible fishing destination. Goose Creek State Park, on the northern side of the river, contains about 3.5 miles of shoreline. This river frontage runs from Mallard Creek on the east to the mouth of Goose Creek (sometimes referred to as Upper Goose Creek, to differentiate it from the Goose Creek located near the mouth of the Pamlico) on the west. This area can produce red drum during the menhaden run in the fall, plus flounder and seatrout, particularly in drier seasons when this part of the river is saltier. The flounder are most prevalent around the mouth of Mallard Creek.

The biggest plus for this site for fly-casters, however, is the presence of hard, wadable sand flats along the 0.5 mile of shore on either side of the swimming beach.

This is just west of the mouth of Mallard Creek. The eastern end of the flat is paralleled by the park's Live Oak Trail, while the western end has the Ragged Point Trail running along it. Ordinarily, however, you will not need these trails for access, since it is possible to walk or wade along the shore. Obviously, since the fishing sites straddle the beach, the best fishing conditions are found early and late in the day or during the fall and winter, when fewer swimmers are in the water.

To reach Goose Creek State Park, take NC 264 east from Washington for roughly 7 miles to the intersection with Secondary Road (SR) 1334

(Camp Leach Road). Turn right and proceed to the park entrance on the right side of the road.

Be aware that you need a North Carolina freshwater fishing license to fish in either Mallard or Goose Creeks in the park, but not in the Pamlico River.

Neuse River

The Neuse River is the other major flow emptying into the southern end of Pamlico Sound. Its saltwater portion forms a U-shape as it runs eastward from the city of New Bern for more than 40 miles to its mouth between Pamlico Point on the mainland to the north and Point of Marsh on Piney Island at the southern side. More than 2 miles across for most of this distance, the lower Neuse is a big river. Unlike the Pamlico River to the north, most of the major feeder streams entering the Neuse are designated coastal saltwater habitats, as is the main stem of the river all the way upstream to the US 17 bridge in New Bern. The area from that city down to Wilkinson Point at Minnesott is not very salty—except during drought years, when freshwater inflows are low. For this reason, most of the better saltwater fly-casting destinations are found to the east of the Cherry-Point-to-Minnesott ferry route.

The exception to this rule is during the fall menhaden run that occurs on this river as well. Then the red drum and striped bass pursue bait fish all the way to New Bern. A number of places in the lower reaches of the Neuse, however, are noted for holding puppy drum year-round, and in greater concentrations in the late summer and fall. Seatrout and flounder are also present in the river in fishable numbers in the spring and summer.

As is usually the case, the flats around creek mouths or points are the best places to find fish. A good spot to begin exploring the northern shore of the Neuse at its mouth is Boat Island Shoals, just off Middle Bay and to the north of Sow Island. Here a sand shoal covered by about 6 feet of water runs out into the river, surrounded by depths of up to 18 feet. There are several old shipwrecks on the bottom along the shoals as well.

Just to the southwest of the shoal is the mouth of Jones Bay. Fishing in the deeper water along the drops where the flats end in the bay can yield some dividends in big seatrout.

Moving farther up the Neuse's northern shore, the mouth of the Bay River offers several sites that can be hot spots for puppy drum. Try the flats off Bay Point on the northern side of the Bay's mouth, as well as the shallows around Maw Point on the south. Just inside the mouth of the Bay, the junction of

Spring and Long Creeks forms an inlet that often holds red drum. These enter the Bay River from its southern shore.

Moving upstream, the next area of interest along this shore is around the mouths of Swan and Broad Creeks. Swan is a small feeder stream to the northeast of Broad, which enters the Neuse behind Swan Island. The entire length of Swan Creek, the area around Swan Island, and a shallow flat called Lighthouse Shoals that juts into the river to the south of the creek mouth all hold good fishing prospects for puppy drum. Similarly, the mouth of Broad Creek and Gun Thicket Shoals just south of the creek can be drum hot spots.

Across the Neuse River, the southern shore also offers a number of places that hold good fly-casting possibilities. The mouth of the Neuse on this side is composed of large and small islands interspersed with bays and marshes. The shallow flats around Big Swan and Raccoon Islands are particularly noted for holding puppy drum. These two small isles are just to the northeast of the tip of Piney Island, which holds the Cherry Point Marine Corps Air Station's Point of Marsh Target Range. Point of Marsh, at the northern end of Piney Island, is also surrounded by shallows frequented by drum.

Finally, just to the east of Piney Island lies West Bay. In its southern end, on the eastern side of Long Bay's mouth, is Long Bay Point (sometimes identified at Tump Point). The band of shallow water around this point can be another place to find smaller drum.

Farther upriver, away from the mouth of the Neuse, more sites offer good fishing. On the northern side of the river the bays around the town of Oriental, at the mouths of Greens and Smith Creeks, generally hold flounder.

Just to the west of Oriental is the village of Janerio, at the mouth of Dawson Creek. This site offers one of the rare opportunities on the Neuse for fly-casting access from the shore. For several hundred yards to the east of the mouth of Dawson Creek, the bank of the Neuse is lined with a riprap seawall, fronted by a narrow, hard strip of sand along the shore. This beach wraps around onto the eastern shore of Dawson Creek as well. All of this area is open enough to allow fly-casting and some wading. Janerio Road, which runs west from NC 306 near Minnesott, parallels this stretch of the Neuse's shore.

The final waters of interest on the northern shore of the Neuse are at Wilkinson Point at the village of Minnesott. The shore on either side of the Cherry-Branch-to-Minnesott ferry landing offers good water for finding red drum.

Opposite the Oriental-to-Minnesott portion of the Neuse, the southern shore is practically one continuous stretch of good fishing possibilities. Beginning to the east at Garbacon Shoals (a quite shallow flat that juts into the Neuse almost directly across the river from Oriental, between Cedar Point on the west and Sandy Point on the east), puppy drum may show up anywhere on the shelves of shallows that run as far west as the mouth of Hancock Creek. These fish also cruise up into Hancock as far as its junction with Cahoogue Creek. Places of particular interest along this bank of the Neuse are Adams Creek, upstream to its junction with Back Creek; around Great Neck Point; and the vicinity of Great Island.

One more spot is especially interesting to anglers without a boat. The Pine Cliff Recreation Area in the Croatan National Forest is located just west of the Cherry-Branch-to-Minnesott ferry landing on the southern shore of the Neuse. The sand swimming beach at this location is flanked on both ends by a hard-sand flat that extends several hundred feet out from shore. In all, there is probably 0.5 mile of access to the flat that can be waded and fly-cast.

This U.S. Forest Service facility can be reached by taking Forest Service Road 132 to the west from NC 306, just south of the ferry landing. This gravel road dead-ends in a large gravel parking lot at the beach.

For boating access to the fishing sites along the Neuse River, the best jumping-off point for the mouth of the stream is at Oriental. The Oriental Access is located in the town at the northwestern end of the Robert Scott Bridge on NC 55 (Oriental Road) over the mouth of Greens Creek. Go west one block on Hodge Street from the end of the bridge, then turn south (left) onto Midyette Street. The ramp is at the end of the street. It is a double-lane, paved facility with a large grass and gravel parking lot. Be aware that this is a very busy landing on weekends.

For access farther up the Neuse, there is a single-lane, paved ramp at the Minnesott Beach Access. This is to the east of NC 306, just north of the ferry landing. Follow the signs from the highway to the ramp, a small parking area across the road from it, plus a small picnic area overlooking the river. The approach drive for backing down to this ramp is quite long and narrow.

Also in this area on the southern side of the river is the Cahoogue Creek Boating Access. This is another Forest Service facility, located at the end of Cahoogue Creek Road, 3.4 miles north of NC 101 to the east of the town of Havelock. The approach road is gravel for the last 1.6 miles. The ramp has a single lane that is paved, while the small parking area is gravel. The ramp is at the mouth of Cahoogue Creek on Hancock Creek. You will need to run north (downstream) on Hancock to reach the Neuse River.

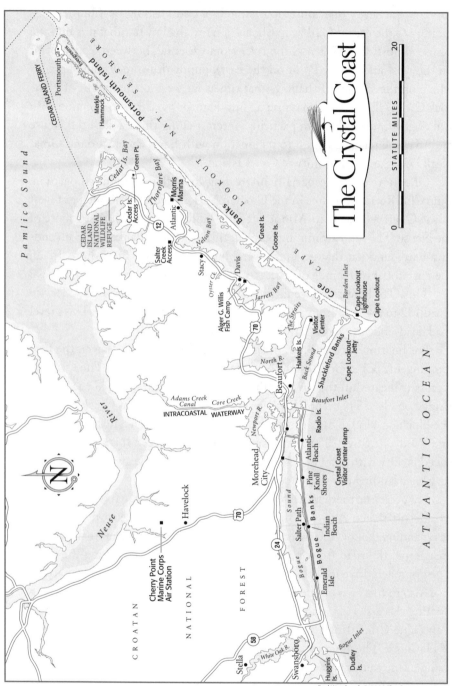

The Crystal Coast

STATUTE MILES

0   20

Paul Woodward, © 2000 The Countryman Press

CHAPTER 6

The Crystal Coast

MAPS
DeLorme: *North Carolina Atlas* pages 68, 78, 79
NOAA: chart numbers 11543, 11544, 11555

Although this chapter takes its name from the Crystal Coast, it actually describes a broader area. *Crystal Coast* is the moniker ordinarily applied to the vicinity of Morehead City and the Bogue Banks beaches, but for purposes of this description, it also includes the Cape Lookout National Seashore to the north. In fact, this chapter deals with the entire coast beginning at Portsmouth Island on the north and including the Core Banks and Sound, Harkers Island, Cape Lookout, the Shackleford Banks, the North River, the Newport River, and finally the Bogue Banks and Sound in the south. Still, this entire stretch of coast is contained in the borders of Carteret County alone.

The reason for lumping the Cape Lookout National Seashore into this chapter is that the northern area of Carteret County is very sparsely populated and includes some extremely desolate areas. While the Portsmouth Island to Cape Lookout shores offer some very good fishing destinations, access to both the barrier islands of the banks and the sound behind them is poor. It is no easy task to reach them, and they are not places for the casual vacationing angler to tackle. For these reasons, they do not merit coverage as an individual destination, but are more appropriately handled in conjunction with the Crystal Coast, which is an area where anglers and vacationers more often find themselves.

Portsmouth Island

There is probably no fishing destination along the Atlantic Coast any farther off the beaten path than Portsmouth Village. Located on the northeastern tip of Portsmouth Island (National Park Service literature usually refers to the island as North Core Banks), across Ocracoke Inlet from the village of Ocracoke, Portsmouth was founded in 1753. For its first 100 years or so, the village thrived as a transfer point where oceangoing ships could off-load cargo onto shallow-draft "lighters" that could cross Pamlico Sound. In 1846, however, a major hurricane opened Hatteras Inlet to the north. This new, deeper inlet soon lured the shipping business away from Portsmouth.

The village continued to survive on commercial fishing until the Civil War, when fear of invasion led the 685 inhabitants to abandon the village. Most never returned, and Portsmouth Village barely managed to struggle into the 20th century. Finally, the last inhabitants left in 1971, when the entire 22-mile island became part of the Cape Lookout National Seashore. Many of the structures in the village are still standing and cared for by the National Park Service.

Portsmouth Island is known as a good spot for surf fishing, and some sources say more puppy drum are caught from its beaches each year than anywhere else in North Carolina. Considering the very small number of anglers who travel to Portsmouth Island, that is a questionable claim. On the other hand, it *is* true that sloughs along the beach hold puppy drum, flounder, and bluefish for most of the year. In September boating anglers target bull red drum just off the beaches, and these fish also enter the near-shore sloughs in October and November. Most of the fishing done here is at the Portsmouth end of the island on southwesterly winds, or at the southwestern end at Drum Inlet during northeast winds.

While it is possible to fly-cast from the beach of Portsmouth Island on many occasions, due to the prevailing along-shore winds this is not a prime destination for fly-fishermen. A commercial vehicle ferry runs from the Morris Marina in the town of Atlantic to the southern end of the island; then you must make a 20-mile beach drive to the village of Portsmouth. Also, commercial day trips are available from the village of Ocracoke for anglers who want to walk the beach. Once on the island, however, you are on your own with the hordes of hungry mosquitoes for which the area is noted. Be aware also that tidal flats separate Portsmouth Village from the beach. Depending on the season and height of the tide these can flood, isolating the beach area from the village. These flats run down the center of Portsmouth Island past the Evergreens and Merkle Hammock areas.

To reach Morris Marina, take US 70 north from the city of Beaufort (pronounced BO-fort) to the road's end in the village of Atlantic. Morris Marina Road is an extension from the end of the highway that leads to the marina parking lot.

The more promising approach to fly-fishing in the vicinity of Portsmouth Island is to use a boat to target the vicinity of Drum Inlet at the island's southwestern tip. This inlet has a rather "mobile" history. Around 1933 a storm first opened the modern site of Drum Inlet. Research, however, has revealed at least five other places where the sea has broken through the islands near this spot in the last couple of centuries. The inlet silted in during the 1950s and was completely closed by a storm back in 1976. In December of that year the Army Corps of Engineers used explosive charges to reopen it, then in 1997 did extensive dredging to create an 11-foot-deep, 75-foot-wide channel through the inlet. Today the inlet has extensive sand flats that remain quite shallow, particularly on its sound side.

The inside flats are usually covered by crystal-clear water that teems with flounder in the summer. In the spring through summer this is also a hot spot for catching puppy drum, while in fall the bull reds show up. Red drum are most prevalent around Dump Island, on the inshore side of Portsmouth Island. Dump Island sits just northeast of the present inlet, offshore of a former break in the island known as Old Drum Inlet. A shallow tidal flat on the southwestern side of Dump Island connects to Portsmouth Island.

The best public landing for fishing Drum Inlet is the Salters Creek Access. This single-lane, paved boat ramp is at the northern end of the Daniel E. Taylor Bridge on US 70 over Nelson Bay. The site offers limited parking in a gravel lot. Once you are on the water, you must run south down the bay to Core Sound, then turn east around Mill Point for the run to Drum Inlet.

Core Sound

Core Sound is the very shallow body of water on the inland side of the Core Banks. Running from Portsmouth Village south for about 45 miles to Cape

Lookout, the sound rarely dips below 8 feet in depth, with most of the area covered by only 1 to 3 feet of water.

Fly-fishing from shore on the Core Banks south of Drum Inlet involves surf casting and standard beach tactics apply. But the difficulty of reaching the banks means the area gets very little fly-fishing pressure. The main species include red drum in the fall, with schools of small bluefish common the rest of the year. The blues may even have some Spanish mackerel mixed in with them in the spring and summer.

Getting to the South Core Banks requires a ferry ride from the mainland. In the midportion of the island a commercial ferry brings four-wheel-drive vehicles across from the village of Davis. Though you can go to the island to travel by foot, the soft sand and long stretches of empty beach discourage most anglers from walking to the fishing. There is also a National Park Service ferry, and a couple of commercial ferries on Harkers Island run to the Cape Lookout Lighthouse area at the southern end of the island. These are discussed later in this chapter.

To reach the ferry landing at Alger G. Willis Fish Camp, take US 70 north from Beaufort to Davis, then turn right onto Community Road. Next, turn onto Willis Road. The fish camp is at the end of this street.

Core Sound offers more fishing options than are found on the banks bordering it, but for the most part they are just as remote and hard to reach. The sound is long, shallow, and a maze of marsh shorelines. The area, however, is known for producing red drum and seatrout on its northern edge around the Cedar Island National Wildlife Refuge on the inland shore. A good access point for fishing this northern fringe of the sound is found within the Cedar Island refuge. Take NC 12 across the causeway to Cedar Island, from its junction just east of the US 70 bridge over Nelson Bay. This road ends at the Cedar-Island-to-Ocracoke ferry landing, but prior to reaching that location, turn right onto Lola Road. This paved road runs to the landing at Green Point (not to be confused with the point of the same name situated slightly to the south in Thorofare Bay). The single-lane, paved ramp is in very poor shape, while offering limited parking space. Still, this is a good site for launching small boats and canoes to fish the shallow flats and marsh islands in the area. For powerboats, Cedar Island Bay to the north of Green Point, along with Barry Bay to the south, are both within reach and are good areas for ambushing some spotted seatrout or puppy drum. Finding channels running through the shallow flats, especially where they are edged with marsh grass or oyster beds, is the key to locating the game fish here.

JIMMY JACOBS

The Core Banks on the Crystal Coast have plenty of coves and grass lines that harbor spotted seatrout.

The Salter Creek Access is another option for getting a boat onto the waters of Core Sound. It is located at the northern end of the Daniel E. Taylor Bridge on US 70 over Nelson Bay. By heading south down Nelson Bay from this single-lane, paved ramp, you can gain access to the midsection of the sound. While there is only limited parking space in the gravel lot at the ramp, the site offers some room for casting from shore around the landing, as well as in the small tidal creek that parallels the approach drive. This is a likely place for hooking either seatrout or puppy drum, as is the entire coast of Nelson Bay to the south. Again, you should be looking for deeper cuts running through marsh grass or shell beds on the flats.

One other area of distinction that can be reached from this ramp requires

Navigating the waters of Core Sound can be a daunting challenge for first-time visitors.

running all the way to the mouth of Nelson Bay, then continuing south across Core Sound. The bay on the opposite shore against the Core Banks, between Great Island (to the northeast) and Goose Island (on the southwest), is a good area for wading for trout and small drum. It may also hold flounder in the summer.

The mainland coast of Core Sound offers a couple of additional options for fly-casting from the shore. A 5-mile stretch of causeway on NC 12 leading out to Cedar Island is lined on both sides by canals. These narrow waterways have mud-flat-type bottoms, while the side opposite the road is lined with marsh grass. Casting into the canals from the highway right-of-way is practical, since traffic is generally very light along this road.

Back to the southwest, a section of US 70 between the village of Stacy on the north and Oyster Creek on the south has a canal running along its eastern side. Another stretch of canals parallels the road from the village of Davis, south along the shore of Jarrett Bay, to the village of Williston. In both instances there are 2 miles of canal at the roadside. The canals have mud bottoms and go almost dry at low tide, but they do offer a possibility of finding cruising puppy drum during higher water levels. Either target the mouths of intersecting ditches, or ride along the road watching for fish tailing, chasing bait, or pushing wakes. All of the canals can be fished from the roadside, and parking turnouts are located periodically along the highway shoulder.

When you fish any of these sites on the road to Cedar Island during the warmer months, be prepared for an onslaught of fierce mosquitoes. These critters show up in hordes and can be maddening unless you come prepared with plenty of insect repellent.

Finally, there is a maze of marsh islands along the southern edge of the sound, along both shores. The flats and waterways between them hold flounder, red drum, and seatrout, but because of the shallow water and difficulty of navigating through them, it is easy to get stranded in this part of the sound. This is not an area appropriate for visiting boat anglers to learn as they go. A better way to learn the area on your first visit is to book a day of fishing with one of the guides working out of the local marinas.

Boating access is available to this end of Core Sound from Harkers Island, just east of the city of Beaufort. Although there is no public boat landing, the southern shore of the island has four commercial marinas with boat ramps. From any of these, head east toward Channel Buoy 2. This takes you to the southern end of Core Sound.

Cape Lookout

Although Cape Lookout is technically part of the Core Banks and is located at their southern tip, it offers enough of a different kind of fishing to merit a description of its own. This end of the Core Banks is dominated by the Cape Lookout Lighthouse. This structure, with its distinctive diamond-patterned paint job, has stood watch over Barden Inlet since 1859. The shoals that run for 2 miles off the southern tip at Cape Point—of which the lighthouse warns ships—also attract hordes of predatory fish. For anglers in seaworthy craft, these shallows offer shots at striped bass, bluefish, red drum, seatrout, weakfish, and false albacore. But this area is often pounded by rough seas.

More tempting fishing options can be found nearby, however, at the rock jetty extending from the western side of Cape Lookout. This site is outside Lookout Bight and south of Power Squadron Spit. The jetty, and Cape Lookout itself, protect the near-shore waters from the northerly winds that are prevalent from fall through spring, making it a year-round fishing possibility. Also, schools of predators migrating along the coast tend to stack up along this rock wall and the shoal just to its west. The jetty, which is submerged and can be dangerous to boats at high tide, is marked by the R-2 Buoy at its western end.

While the jetty is best known as a place to find bluefish throughout the year, weakfish, spotted seatrout, and red drum are other species that flycasters can target along the rocks, especially in the fall. When bluefish are present at this site but reluctant to strike, one trick employed by fly-rodders is to cast large popping bugs but pick them up as soon as they hit the water, creating as much noise as possible. This can sometimes entice the bluefish into a virtual feeding frenzy. Blues of 12 to 15 pounds show up along here.

Probably the most publicized angling on this part of the Old North State's coast in recent years has been the pursuit of false albacore. Though these fish appear all along the North Carolina coast from mid-August until after Thanksgiving each year, they are particularly thick and accessible around Cape Lookout. Schools of fat Alberts can show up slashing through pods of bait fish at the mouth of Barden Inlet, a mile off the coast of Cape Lookout, or at the Shackleford Banks to the west. Due to the usually calmer water, the area inside Lookout Bight in front of Barden Inlet often offers the best sight-fishing opportunities for false albacore. The bight area is sometimes referred to as the Hook by local anglers due to the shape of Cape Lookout and Powerboat Squadron Spit, which surround it.

Local guides and other anglers regularly experience days of hooking 20 to 30 albies that tip the scales in the 15-pound range. The experience of hooking up with one of these fish is consistently described as having your line attached to a runaway freight train! Streamer flies that work for these false albacore in the fall are 2 to 3 inches long and imitate silversides or glass minnows. They should be stripped in using a very rapid retrieve.

The waters of Barden Inlet also offer some angling opportunities to fly-fishermen. The drop-offs into the channel are noted for producing some weakfish, but the most interesting and challenging fishing can be found here in the spring when big cobia cruise its waters. As is usual anywhere these fish are found, targeting buoys and channel markers can be a good tactic. Expect the height of this fishing to be at the end of May, around Memorial Day.

Shorebound anglers find that their only option at Cape Lookout is surf fishing along the beaches. Red drum, seatrout, bluefish and striped bass are the species that ordinarily show up along this shore, but the often harsh and windy conditions can make for difficult fly-casting.

Boating access to the Cape Lookout area is easiest from the commercial marinas along the southern side of Harkers Island, just to the north of Barden Inlet. From any of these, head to the eastern end of the island, then turn south to follow Channel Markers 35 to 20 through an area locally known as the Drain. This 7-mile voyage leads to the inside end of Barden Inlet.

For foot access to the southern end of the Core Banks at Cape Lookout, the National Park Service runs a twice-daily pedestrian ferry from its dock at the national seashore visitors center on the eastern end of Harkers Island. A fee is charged for this ferry service.

Harkers Island

Harkers Island lies inland of Cape Lookout and in the middle of a number of good fishing locations around the city of Beaufort, which is just west of the island. To the east of Harkers lies the southern end of Core Sound, while the southern side of the island is bordered by Back Sound. Across Back Sound are the Shackleford Banks, then the open waters of the Atlantic Ocean. To the west of Harkers Island is the North River and the city of Beaufort. On the north the island is bounded by The Straits (actually a narrow sound) and the mainland of Carteret County.

Throughout this region there are angling honey holes for red drum, bluefish, seatrout, cobia, and flounder. Many of these sites require a boat to reach, but some are available to shorebound anglers, too.

The entire complex of sounds and rivers surrounding Harkers Island is generally very shallow, averaging only 2 to 3 feet deep. There are, however, deeper channels (some marked, some not) crisscrossing the area. This is an area where navigational charts come in handy.

The only access to Harkers Island is via SR 1335 (Harkers Island Road) from the mainland. Where the highway spans The Straits are two bridges. Around these bridges, there are some angling options available. The boat channel under the swing bridge is often a hot spot for spotted seatrout in the daytime for boaters. Also making this area appealing is the access available to wading anglers. The flats on either side of both bridges are composed of hard sand and only a couple of feet deep in most places. It is possible to wade out near the channels or look for trout on the flats near oyster bars on marsh grass edges. A fly pattern whose combination of colors incorporates green is usually good for fishing this area.

Once you are on the island, continue along Harkers Island Road all the way to the eastern end, where the road ends at the Cape Lookout National Seashore Visitors Center. There is a paved parking lot, a picnic area, and several hundred yards of access for fishing from shore. The fishing access stretches from the ferry dock on the eastern end of the island, around Shell Point, to the southern shore facing Back Sound. There are also a couple of rock groins extending into Back Sound along this portion of the shore. The bottom is made up of hard-packed sand, making it easily wadable. Red drum, seatrout, and flounder are the species most likely to be found here.

For boating anglers wanting to target flounder or cobia, the waters of Lighthouse Channel (the Drain) lie just south of the island. From any of the commercial marinas along the southern shore of the island on Harkers Island Road, you can travel east to Channel Marker 35, then turn south toward Barden Inlet. The Drain runs from Marker 35 to Marker 20 along this channel. For cobia, target the channel markers with your casts. Weakfish show up in this deeper channel as well.

Directly south of Harkers Island, across Back Sound, lie the Shackleford Banks. Now deserted, the banks are home to a herd of "Banker Ponies." These wild horses have inhabited the island since the 1500s and get their name from their life on the banks and diminutive size. Prior to 1900 there were five villages on the banks, but hurricanes wiped them out in the late 1800s. Diamond City on the eastern end at Barden Inlet was once the largest settlement on the Outer Banks. This whaling port, which derived its name from the distinctive diamond-patterned paint job on the nearby Cape Lookout Lighthouse, was destroyed in the major hurricane that struck in 1899.

For anglers, the Shackleford Banks still hold some alluring prospects. The shallow flats along the eastern end of the island hold puppy drum and flounder, while marsh grass edges give up seatrout. Toward the western end of the banks the water is deeper, holding small bluefish year-round and cobia during the spring and summer.

To the west of Harkers Island and east of Beaufort flows the North River. Rising in the saltwater marshes north of US 70, all of the North is classified as coastal salt water. The lower end of the river between Beaufort and Harkers Island is noted for holding puppy drum on shallow flats in the North River Marsh and Sheephead Marsh. From the late summer into the fall, look for larger red drum around oyster beds in this area as well. Also of interest is the Middle Marsh area. This group of grass islands and meandering creeks is on the southeastern side of the North River Channel, just southwest of Harkers Island. Middle Marsh can hold seatrout as well as red drum.

Access by boat to this lower portion of the North River is easiest from the Taylor Creek Regional Public Water Access. This facility has a double-lane, paved boat ramp located off Front Street, east of Beaufort in the Lennoxville Community. There is plenty of on-site parking.

Once your boat is in the water, run east along Taylor Creek to its confluence with the North River. It is worth making a few casts to the points on either side of the mouth of Taylor Creek while you are there, since they are both known to hold trout. Middle Marsh is directly south of this junction, across the river channel. A turn to the north leads into the the Sheephead and North River Marshes on the western side of the river channel.

For anglers looking for water to fly-cast from shore or by wading, the causeways on either end of the US 70 bridge across the North River offer possibilities. These shores are lined by shallow sand and mud flats that provide plenty of casting room. There are also some old pilings in the water that are within casting distance of shorebound or wading fishermen. A number of turnouts are available for parking along the roadside. Again, puppy drum and spotted seatrout are the species you are most likely to encounter here.

Bogue Sound

Bogue Sound extends from Beaufort Inlet on the east to Bogue Inlet at its western end, with its southern shore formed by the Bogue Banks. Fishing waters in this area that offer fly-casting options are found on the beaches of the Bogue Banks, in the sound, around Morehead City on the Newport River, and in the White Oak River inside Bogue Inlet. Also located along Bogue Banks are the Crystal Coast communities of Atlantic Beach, Pine Knoll Shores, Salter Path, Indian Beach, and Emerald Isle.

Situated at the eastern end of this region, Beaufort Inlet is well worth exploration by fly-casting anglers. The waters of the inlet are noted for holding schools of bluefish in the fall months, with smaller Taylor blues present year-round. If you are in a boat, watch for gulls diving on bait fish around sandbars in the inlet. Usually the fish chasing the bait to the surface are blues, but Spanish mackerel may be here as well from the spring through the summer. Minnow-imitating streamers cast into the feeding frenzy can take either of these species, but wire leaders are a necessity since both fish have plenty of razor-edged teeth.

Casting around the channel marker buoys in the summer months can lead to hook-ups with cobia in Beaufort Inlet, while fishing deeper channel drops can produce weakfish. The rock jetty extending out from the eastern side of the inlet attracts spotted seatrout in the fall months, too.

Beaufort Inlet also offers good casting options even if you do not have access to a boat. Fort Macon State Park, the site of a Civil War masonry fortification, sits on the eastern end of the Bogue Banks. The park has oceanfront beaches that wrap around the end of the island onto the Morehead City Channel portion of the inlet. Besides the bluefish found in the inlet in most seasons, in the fall months you can find spotted seatrout concentrated along the beach. The fishing in the park is usually best early and late in the day.

To reach Fort Macon State Park from Morehead City, take Morehead Avenue across the Atlantic Beach Causeway to the Bogue Banks. At the intersection with Fort Macon Road (NC 58), turn east and follow the road until it dead-ends in the asphalt parking lot at the fort and beaches.

Just up the Newport River Channel from Beaufort Inlet lies Radio Island. This small isle on the eastern edge of Morehead City offers several opportunities for boating and shorebound fly-casters to locate some hungry fish. The bridge on Radio Island Road from US 70 across to the island is a favorite among local anglers searching for spotted seatrout. Fishing from boats, they target the vicinity of this bridge for trout both at night and during the daylight hours.

On the island itself the Radio Island Beach Access offers a narrow, hard-packed sand beach along the eastern side of the Morehead City Channel (the westernmost of the two channels) of the Newport River. Although the center of the beach near the parking area is likely to be crowded with swimmers and sunbathers on weekends in the spring and summer, there is at least 0.5 mile of beach suitable for wading and fly-casting. Hitting this area early or late in the day, or simply fishing near its ends away from the crowds, is your best bet. Trout, small red drum, bluefish, and flounder are all taken along this part of the Newport River.

To reach Radio Island, take US 70 east from Morehead City. Turn south onto Radio Island Road and follow the signs to the large gravel parking lot and the walkover trails to the beach.

Farther up the Newport River, local anglers target red drum. The biggest fish are in the river in the fall, but puppy drum can be found at most times of the year. As is so often true, the key to this fishing is to locate the fish around oyster beds on shallow flats. The western riverbank, from the Morehead City bridge on US 70 upstream to Newport Marshes, holds some good fishing sites. Also, at the northern extreme of the river check out the flats along Core Creek, which is the route of the Intracoastal Waterway as it cuts through to the Neuse River.

The closest public access by boat to all these locations in Beaufort Inlet and the Newport River is found at the Crystal Coast Visitors Center Ramp. The three-lane ramp and large parking area are both paved. The site has about 100 yards of shore with riprap that faces on Bogue Sound and can be comfortably fly-cast from the seawall along it. The facility is located behind the visitors center off US 70 (Arendell Street) in the suburb of Mansfield, just west of Morehead City. Once your boat is in the water, run east along Bogue Sound, under the Atlantic Beach Causeway bridge, to the Newport River. The Newport River Marshes are north of this junction, Radio Island is to the east, while Beaufort Inlet lies southward.

The beaches of the Bogue Banks west of Morehead City hold the possibility of encounters with puppy drum, flounder, pompano, bluefish, and even Spanish mackerel in the surf. Most of the action is likely to occur during the summer months, around dawn and dusk. In the fall seatrout join the mix along these beaches. As on most beaches, look for the tidal pools and areas where the water runs back out to the surf. Blues and Spanish mackerel often give away their position by feeding on the surface later in the day. The surf around the village of Emerald Isle is a good location to explore for blues and Spanish mackerel during summer evenings just before dark.

Access to the beaches from NC 58 along the Bogue Banks is good, with regional beach access points spread along the shore. At the western end of the banks it is possible to get onto the beach at Bogue Inlet via a walkover beach trail, but no parking spaces are provided. On the sound side of the banks, however, it is a much different story. There is no public access to fishable water from the shore on that side of the Bogue Banks.

The entire length of Bogue Sound offers some interesting options for targeting speckled trout with a fly. The sound is quite shallow, never exceeding 4 feet in depth except in the dredged channel of the Intracoastal Waterway. It is also a veritable maze of shell bars and marsh grass islands that give up trout, some of which tip the scales at 5 pounds or better. This is an area with so much promising water that it pays to check it out at low tide to pinpoint the oyster beds; you can then return to these locations when the water is covering them.

One spot in Bogue Sound that offers a different type of fly-casting is around the Atlantic Beach Causeway bridge. Particularly around the main boat channel, cobia can be located in the spring and summer months. Tossing streamers or crab-patterned flies around the bridge pilings is the best tactic, but rig with heavier-than-usual leaders. Hooked cobia often try to wrap the line around the pilings.

The White Oak River, which flows out of Wolf Swamp, sits at the southwestern end of Bogue Sound. Its West Channel (to the west of Huggins and Dudley Islands) is a good place to look for seatrout on the lower river. Farther upstream there is good access to wadable water above the NC 24 bridge over the river at Swansboro. In fact, the flats around the mouths of feeder creeks all the way up to the head of the estuary at the community of Stella provide wading opportunities for fly-casters. In most cases, though, you need a boat to get to the flats. Puppy drum, flounder, and seatrout are the most common game fish in these waters, with the fall being particularly good for catching numbers of speckled trout.

Public boating access to the eastern end of Bogue Sound is available at the ramps at the Crystal Coast Visitors Center described earlier in this section. To reach the western end of the sound and the White Oak River, the jumping-off point is the Cedar Island Boating Access. This single-lane, paved ramp has a large gravel parking lot located on NC 24, 0.25 mile east of the White Oak River bridge. From the ramp, run your boat east to reach Bogue Sound; the White Oak River is to the west.

CHAPTER 7

Cape Fear

MAPS
DeLorme: *North Carolina Atlas* pages 77, 84, 85, 86, 87
NOAA: chart numbers 11536, 11539, 11543

The most prominent feature and the focus of the saltwater fisheries on the southern third of the North Carolina coast is Cape Fear, just south of the city of Wilmington. Though it is the best-known angling destination in this region, it does not constitute the only area of interest to fly-casters on this part of the Old North State's shore. Still, the other fishing destinations surrounding Cape Fear are not as well known, offer less access to the water, or are a bit off the beaten path. For these reasons, Onslow Bay to the north and Long Bay to the south are lumped with Wilmington and Cape Fear in this chapter.

From Bogue Inlet on the northeastern end of this coast, Onslow Bay stretches along the beaches to New Topsail Inlet at the southwestern end of Topsail Island. Major features of this coastline are Bear Island, Bear Inlet, Browns Inlet, the New River and its inlet, plus Topsail Island. A large portion of the mainland and barrier islands to the north of the New River are contained in the Camp Lejeune Marine Corps Base, which limits shore access to the water.

To the southwest of Topsail Island, the major towns in the Wilmington–Cape Fear area are Wrightsville Beach, Carolina Beach, and Southport. Masonboro Inlet, Mason Inlet, Carolina Beach Inlet, Snows Cut, the

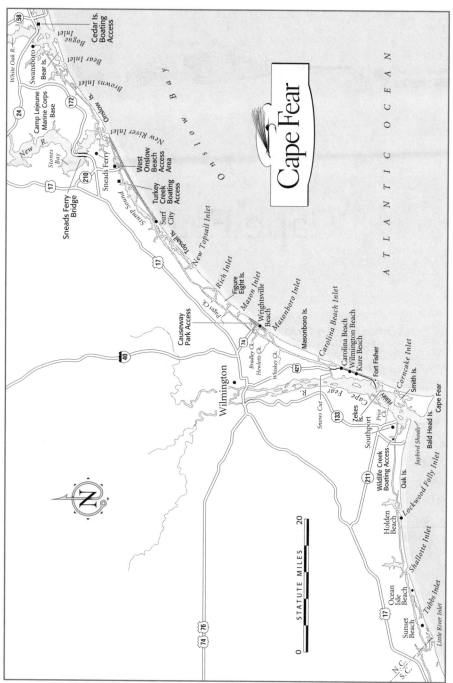

Cape Fear

Cape Fear River, and Bald Head Island are important angling sites on this expanse of shoreline.

From the western side of the Cape Fear River's mouth, Long Bay spans just more than 30 miles of shore to the South Carolina border. Along this stretch are Lockwood Folly, Shallotte and Tubbs Inlets, plus the communities of Oak Island, Holden Beach, Ocean Isle Beach, and Sunset Beach.

One oddity of the fishing through this part of North Carolina was the relative scarcity of red drum along the coast. Between Cape Lookout and Murrells Inlet in South Carolina, for years the only place where these fish showed up in numbers regularly was around Bald Head Island at the mouth of the Cape Fear River in the fall. This situation seems to be changing, possibly because of more restrictive harvest levels for red drum that were instituted in the late 1990s. Puppy drum now can be found in the Cape Fear River, around Masonboro Island and Carolina Inlet.

Onslow Bay

The northern portion of Onslow Bay offers virtually nothing in the way of wading or shore access for fly-fishermen who do not have a boat. The southwestern side of the White Oak River estuary is a maze of grass islands and shallow channels, fronted on the ocean side by Bear Island. This entire barrier island is contained within Hammocks Beach State Park, which can only be reached via a seasonal, toll ferry run by the state park. Though you can reach either Bogue Inlet on the northeastern end of the island, or Bear Inlet to the southwest from the beach at Bear Island, both require long walks on the sand since no vehicles are allowed on the island. This makes surf casting your only reasonable option on Bear Island. Hammock Beach State Park is a place you might want to fly-fish while visiting but not a spot to visit for the fishing alone.

The ferry dock for the park is located east of the town of Swansboro. Take NC 24 west of town, then turn south onto Hammock Beach Road. The ferry landing is 2.1 miles farther, at the end of the road.

Traveling by small boat, you can fish Shacklefoot Channel, located just inside Bear Inlet, or Banks Channel inside Browns Inlet farther south. Both spots hold spotted seatrout, with Banks Channel rated a bit better. Pay special attention to the shell bars separating deeper channels at this latter location.

The nearest public boat ramp to Bear and Browns Inlets is found at the Cedar Island Boating Access, described at the end of the preceding chapter.

It is no easy task to find your way to either of the inlets the first time. To reach Bear Inlet, run south down the White Oak River toward Bogue Inlet, then turn to the southwest to pass behind Bear Island. Proceed with care in this maze of shallow channels and grass islands. At the opposite end of the isle is Bear Inlet. For Browns Inlet, take the Intracoastal Waterway (ICW) to the southwest from the ramp to Banks Channel, then turn south toward the inlet.

The only other angling destination worth mentioning along northern Onslow Bay is even more difficult to reach. A swing bridge across the Intra-coastal Waterway connects Onslow Island to the mainland. There are some very good flats for wading around this bridge, with flounder and speckled trout taken by casting to the boat channel or targeting the grass edges up on the flat. This fishing is hot throughout the fall but at its best in the latter part of the season. Look for the trout where they herd schools of pinfish, lizard-fish, or other bait up against the marsh grass.

What makes this site a bit impractical for fishing, however, is the lack of access. Both shores of the ICW here are within the Marine Corps base. The nearest public boat ramp to the north is at Cedar Island (12.5 miles), while from the other direction the closest ramp is the West Onslow Beach Access Area near Topsail Island (13 miles). This latter facility is described later in this section.

New River Inlet and the river upstream of it offer the next interesting fly-casting locations as you move south along Onslow Bay. When the tide is moving current through this inlet, boating anglers find spotted seatrout, blue-fish, and flounder feeding. Upriver the trout can show up anywhere along the New to the area around the Sneads Ferry Bridge (NC 172). Of particular interest are the deeper holes in Stones Bay above the bridge and Ellis Cove just below it. Trout of up to 10 pounds have been taken in both locations. Also, be sure to direct a few casts to the pilings around the bridge. This is a popular area with local fishermen, however, so be prepared to share it with other anglers on most days.

Access to all of these sites in the New River is best from New River Waterfront Park, which is located at the eastern end of the US 17 bridge in Jacksonville. The double-lane ramp is paved, as is the ample parking lot at the site. From the ramp, run downstream to reach the Sneads Ferry Bridge area.

To the south of the New River Inlet lies Topsail Island. Its beaches and surrounding bays and creeks offer the final good fishing destinations north of the Wilmington area. On the ocean side of the island are a number of regional beach access points. These spread from the northern end at North Topsail Beach, through Surf City, to Topsail Beach at the southern end of the island. Any of these can provide access to some good flounder fishing.

Foot access to the southern side of New River Inlet is available at North Topsail Beach as well. To reach it, take NC 210 across the ICW to the island, then turn northwest onto New River Inlet Road (Old NC 210). Near the end of this road, turn left onto River Drive. There is a limited number of parking spaces at the end of this road. The best time to target this inlet is the first couple of hours after a low tide. The influx of ocean water tends to get the bait fish moving, which attracts hungry predators. Flounder and spotted seatrout are the most promising fish to target.

At the southern end of Topsail Island it is possible to reach New Topsail Inlet by walking down the beach from the last regional access point. It is, however, more than a mile to the inlet. To reach this area, take NC 50 to the southwest from Surf City. This inlet is most noted for yielding flounder.

On the inland side of Topsail Island there are a number of small bays and tidal creeks along the route of the ICW. Of these, the most promising are Alligator Bay near the northern end of the island and Stump Sound near its midsection. Look for channels through the marsh grass where there are shell beds present to find flounder and seatrout.

For boating access to Alligator Bay, launch your boat at the West Onslow Beach Access Area. This single-lane, paved ramp has a gravel lot and is at the western end of the NC 210 bridge and the northern end of Topsail Island. The ramp is on a small canal that leads to the ICW. Running to the northwest up the ICW takes you to Alligator Bay.

To reach Stump Sound, put your boat in the water at the Turkey Creek Boating Access. This facility has a double-lane, paved boat ramp with a gravel parking lot. From NC 210 leading to the northern end of Topsail Island, turn west onto Old Folkstone Road. After 1.6 miles, turn south onto Turkey Point Road (called Harbor Point Road on the DeLorme map). After 1.6 miles, where the pavement ends, run west for another 0.7 mile to the landing. The ramp is on Turkey Creek, which opens onto the ICW just northwest of Stump Sound.

Wilmington–Cape Fear

The Wilmington–Cape Fear region can be broken down into four distinct areas for the purpose of describing its fishing possibilities. These are the waters around Figure Eight Island, the vicinity of Wrightsville Beach, Carolina Beach, and the mouth of the Cape Fear River. From north to south through here the area contains Rich, Mason, Masonboro, Carolina Beach, and Corncake Inlets.

Figure Eight Island is located between Wrightsville Beach to the south and Topsail Island on the north. This island contains a private residential development with controlled access, so there is no public shore access for fishing. For boating anglers, however, there are several fly-casting options along the island shores and in surrounding tidal waters.

At the northern end of Figure Eight Island is Rich Inlet, which is noted for giving up both spotted seatrout and flounder on a regular basis. Your best bet for trout here is to fish the northern side of the channel, immediately outside the inlet. You need a seaworthy boat to tackle this spot, since the inlet can become quite choppy if the wind picks up. Back inside the inlet, drifting and casting to any sandy areas surrounding oyster beds is a good prescription for finding some flounder.

On the mainland side of Figure Eight Island there are a couple of other spots worth checking out. The marsh grass patches and sandbars of Middle Sound along the eastern edge of the ICW are good spots to locate flounder; these fish also show up along the shore in Pages Creek. In these same two spots puppy drum can be found cruising the grass edges at high tide, while during ebb tides they lie around boat docks in Pages Creek. Drifting and casting to the grass edges at high tide works for drum, while targeting your casts to docks at which larger boats are tied works when the water is low. The reason for choosing these docks is that the prop thrust from the bigger boats flushes out deep holes beneath them. Reds lie in these during low tides.

Access by boat to the area around Figure Eight Island is best from the public boat ramp at the Causeway Park Access at Wrightsville Beach. The facility, beneath the eastern end of the US 74/76 bridge to Wrightsville Beach, has a three-lane, paved boat ramp with a large paved parking lot. It is also a very busy access point on weekends.

From the ramp, travel east to the ICW, then turn north and run past Mason Inlet Channel at the southern end of Figure Eight Island. From this point, Middle Sound is east of the ICW; halfway up the shore of Figure Eight, Pages Creek enters from the west. At the northern end of the island, turn east to reach Rich Inlet. Be aware when boating on Middle Sound that most of the water is quite shallow. You must take care to avoid becoming grounded.

To the south of Figure Eight Island across Mason Inlet lies Wrightsville Beach. The area around this island also offers some interesting casting opportunities for both shorebound and boating fly-fishermen.

At the northern end of Wrightsville Beach lies Mason Inlet, where speckled trout are the main species to target. The best places to find the fish are tight against the beach on the southern side of the inlet. A deep channel sweeps right against the shore here, while the beach is hard-packed sand and ideal for wading, especially at low tide.

To reach Mason Inlet, take US 74/76 to Wrightsville Beach, then turn north onto US 74 (Ocean View Boulevard East) when the two routes split. Stay on this road to the parking lot on the beach side near its end. Parking space is very limited here, but it is an easy walk on the beach out to the inlet.

Along the beach at Wrightsville, standard surf-casting conditions exist. Parking and beach access are plentiful, but the parking is not free and there are meters everywhere.

For fly-fishermen exploring Wrightsville Beach, by far the most interesting area is Masonboro Inlet. Located at the southern end of Wrightsville Beach and to the north of Masonboro Island (which is home to the North Carolina National Estuarine Research Reserve), this inlet has rock jetties jutting out from both shores. Bluefish, seatrout, flounder, and Spanish mackerel are often found in the inlet, while red drum congregate here on the falling tide. For flounder, target the sandy bottom parallel to the concrete portion of the jetty along the inlet's southern shore. Also, anywhere in the inlet that sand surrounds oyster beds, you may find flounder burrowed down in the sand waiting to ambush minnows coming off the shell beds.

If you target seatrout in Masonboro Inlet, the places to cast your flies are at either end of the submerged portion of the northern jetty or at the offshore end of the jetty, on the channel side of the rocks. Along the southern jetty, also try the ocean end, but the fish may be on either side of the rocks. Another area to check out is along the bend of the southern jetty at the shore end, where it changes from rock to concrete.

Schools of bluefish (in the fall) or Spanish mackerel (in the spring and summer) may appear anywhere along either jetty. Watch for the fish breaking the surface chasing minnows, or for the gulls that invariably spot the action and dive into the feeding frenzy. Bluefish are most prevalent at the end of a falling tide.

All these fishing sites in Masonboro Inlet require a boat, with the exception of the western end of the submerged portion of the northern jetty; you can cast to this from the beach. Also, the entire end of Wrightsville Beach as it wraps around the southern tip of the island offers good fly-casting prospects for wading or shorebound anglers. The deeper waters of the boat channel swing quite close to this shore, and the spot is especially easy to cast to during lower tide levels. The portion of the beach that offers fly-casting access extends around to the red Channel Marker 10 on the inland side of the island. Access to this area is from the southern end of US 76. Parking spaces (with meters) are provided.

In the fall in particular, large numbers of red drum show up behind Wrightsville Beach along the ICW. From mid-September through October some local anglers find puppy drum concentrated around the mouths of several feeder streams entering the ICW from the west. As mentioned earlier in regard to Pages Creek at Figure Eight Island, the best places to find them are under docks. Especially good are docks at which larger boats are moored. Cast to the deep holes (created by prop wash) directly beneath the boats for the most action.

The mouth of Bradley Creek directly inland from Wrightsville Beach is a good area, as are Hewlett Creek (2 miles south of Bradley) and Whiskey Creek (4 miles to the south of Bradley). Whiskey Creek also has a reputation for producing both flounder and spotted seatrout.

For access to all the sites around Wrightsville Beach, the best public boat landing is at the Causeway Park Access, which was described earlier in this section in the discussion of Figure Eight Island. To reach Masonboro Inlet from the ramp, run south along the channel on the inland side of Wrightsville Beach. This channel empties into the inlet.

To reach the mouths of Bradley, Hewlett, and Whiskey Creeks, travel west from the ramp to the ICW, then turn south. All three creeks empty into the ICW from the west.

To the south of Wrightsville Beach lies the peninsula that separates the Cape Fear River from the Atlantic Ocean. Along this spit of land, from north to south, are Carolina Beach Inlet, Snows Cut, Carolina Beach, Wilmington Beach, Kure Beach, the Fort Fisher State Recreation Area, and Corncake Inlet. The most popular fish species for local anglers through here are bluefish, seatrout, Atlantic bonito, and flounder, all of which can be taken on fly-fishing gear.

At the northern end of the accessible portion of the peninsula is Carolina Beach Inlet, which links the ICW to the open ocean at the tip of Carolina Beach. There is no road access to the inlet, although it is possible to walk the roughly 1 mile of beach to the pass from the end of the road north of Carolina Beach or—more practically—to drive a four-wheel-drive vehicle along the beach. The most frequently encountered species at this inlet are bluefish and red drum, with best conditions for casting to blues occurring during outgoing tides. When you tackle the inlet from a boat, concentrate on fishing across the inlet mouth on the outside of the first buoys.

For boating Carolina Beach Inlet, the most convenient launch site is at Carolina Beach State Park. At the southern end of the US 421 bridge over Snows Cut, follow the signs west to the park entrance, then continue to follow the signs to the marina. A fee is charged to use the double-lane, paved ramp. A large paved parking lot is adjacent to the launch site. An east turn from the boat basin puts you in Snows Cut. At the eastern end of the cut, turn north on the ICW to reach Carolina Beach Inlet.

Snows Cut is a man-made canal carrying the ICW through the Cape Fear peninsula to the Cape Fear River to the west. The cut offers several options for fly-casting along its length.

For the shorebound angler, most of the northern side of the cut can be accessed from Snows Cut Park. This New Hanover County facility runs along the northern side of the cut from the US 421 bridge for 0.25 mile to the west. The park sits up on a bluff, but stairs are provided to the narrow beach below. The beach is interspersed with riprap and spots where the bedrock juts to the surface. It is possible to walk this beach to the west far beyond the edge of the park boundaries—almost to the Cape Fear River outlet. The entire shore is open enough for fly-casting, with flounder, bluefish, red drum, and speckled trout the main species encountered. Just west of the US 421 bridge the cut narrows, and there is exposed bedrock on the northern shore. This is a favorite fishing site for bank anglers.

To reach Snows Cut Park—which has plenty of parking spaces, plus picnic tables on the bluff—turn west off US 421 onto River Road at the northwestern end of the bridge over the cut. The park is on the southern side of River Road.

For boating anglers, the entire length of the cut is fishable, but most of the attention is concentrated on the southern shore that bank fishermen cannot reach. Good boat-launch facilities are located at the western end of Snows Cut at the Carolina Beach State Park marina.

From Carolina Beach south to the Fort Fisher recreation area, the oceanfront through Wilmington Beach and Kure Beach offers only surfcasting, mostly for bluefish, seatrout, whiting, and, possibly, pompano in the summer.

JIMMY JACOBS

*The northern shore of Snows Cut provides casting opportunities
between Carolina Beach Inlet and the Cape Fear River.*

There is good public access to the entire beach along here, but it is crowded
with swimmers in the summer months.

At the Fort Fisher recreation area, erosion has virtually removed the
beach; a riprap shore has replaced it in an attempt to halt the loss of land to
the the sea. This area is sometimes referred to by local anglers as the Monument or the Confederate Monument. Regardless of which name you use, it is
a good place to find speckled trout, especially during the first phase of a
falling summer tide. If you chose to target this area by boat, it needs to be a
very seaworthy craft, since the water can be quite rough, especially when the
surf is pounding heavily on the rocks.

The same can be said for the waters of Corncake Inlet, just south of Fort
Fisher. Here the most popular species are bluefish, which congregate along
the surf line, and spotted seatrout. In August schools of big red drum show
up along the inlet's beaches as well. Expect the beach to be crowded with anglers when the reds are running.

For boaters, the nearest landing is at the end of US 421 near the state's
Southport-to-Fort-Fisher ferry landing. At this location on Federal Point
there is a single-lane, paved public boat ramp. To reach Corncake Inlet from
the ramp, run south, keeping to the east of Zekes Island, until you are 1.5 miles
past that island. At the point where you pass through a hole in the stone riprap

(known locally as the Cribbing), turn east into the inlet. To reach the Fort Fisher rocks, proceed out of the inlet, then turn north along the beach for roughly 3 miles.

The only shore access to Corncake Inlet is from the north, using a four-wheel-drive vehicle along the beach.

The saltwater fishery in the Cape Fear River itself is by far the most diverse on this part of the Carolina coast. Various portions of the 20 miles of the river from Wilmington downstream to the Atlantic Ocean give up red drum, seatrout, small striped bass, and flounder, while the mouth of the river can be a hot spot for bluefish and cobia, along with red drum and striped bass that often run to 40 pounds. At the upstream limit of salt water striped bass can be taken all year long around the pilings of the bridges in Wilmington, but the bulk of the saltwater angling locations on the river are concentrated farther south, roughly from Snows Cut downstream.

The eastern bank of the Cape Fear River below Federal Point offers an unusual opportunity for shorebound anglers in the form of a rock jetty (with sections that have narrow sand beaches along it) that runs from the vicinity of the public boat ramp, to the south along the river to Zekes Island, and beyond to Bald Head Island. Portions of the jetty (known locally as the Rocks) can be walked on by anglers, offering access to an extremely long portion of the shore. In places it is possible to also fish off the western side of the jetty in Buzzard Bay. Flounder, seatrout, red drum, and bluefish are all possible catches along here, especially at gaps in the rocks.

Across the river and slightly downstream is a set of oil docks extending from the western shore, along with mooring posts along the channel. These are just upstream of the Southport-to-Fort-Fisher ferry landing on this side of the river. For boating anglers, these docks offer good possibilities for striped bass in the winter months, with some big sea-run fish showing up. Seatrout are frequently encountered at this location at any time of year, and can also be found at the mouth of Price Creek, near the ferry landing.

At the mouth of the Cape Fear River there are a number of options for a variety of fish. Most of the fishing locations, however, are limited to anglers who have access to a boat. The one exception is found on the waterfront of the historic town of Southport. Positioned on the western bank of the river at its junction with the Intracoastal Waterway, the town's River Walk is fronted by roughly 0.5 mile of narrow beach covered with sand, shells, and rocks. Near the middle of this area is a fishing pier that extends into the river. Though it is too high above the water for fly-fishing, you can cast around its pilings while fishing from the shore or wading. The entire shore on the wa-

TOM EVANS

Spotted seatrout are one of the game-fish species you'll find around the mouth of the Cape Fear River, downstream of Wilmington.

terfront is open enough for fly-casting and holds possibilities for both flounder and seatrout.

Parking spaces are available along the road at the fishing pier. This is a tourist area in the spring and summer, especially on weekends, and probably is more practical as a weekday fishing spot.

For spotted seatrout near the river's mouth, the places to target are the northeastern and northwestern points of Striking Island, plus the mouth of Bay Creek where it enters the Cape Fear from the east on Smith Island. Look for holes and cuts that are slightly deeper than the surrounding water and also near oyster beds.

For big bull red drum, the best time for fishing here is in the late summer, beginning in August. These brutes are found in the surf at this time, particularly on the beaches of Bald Head Island on the eastern side of the Cape Fear River's mouth. The island, however, is a private resort accessible only by boat, so angling in the surf from boats is one way to reach these fish. The other is to rent a room at the resort, which then allows you beach access for fishing.

The open water in the mouth of the river between Oak Island on the west and Bald Head Island to the east is a popular stretch for locating schools of bluefish in the fall. The fish are generally most active during falling tides. Of particular interest are the shallow sand banks on the western side of the river channel, just outside the inlet. These are collectively referred to as Jaybird Shoals and often see marauding bluefish attacking schools of bait fish.

In this same area in the spring and summer it is worth making some casts to the deeper holes near buoys and channel markers. Cobia often patrol these structures, and they can be fooled by well-placed flies.

The most convenient boating access to the lower Cape Fear River is from the Wildlife Creek Boating Access to the west of Southport on the northern side of the ICW. To reach this paved ramp and parking area, take NC 211 west from Southport, then turn south onto NC 133 toward Oak Island. Take a left (east) onto SR 1101 (Fish Factory Road) before reaching the ICW bridge. The ramp is 0.5 mile down this road on your left.

Once you are on the water, run east along the ICW to the Cape Fear River. Striking Island is farther to the east beyond Battery Island, while a turn south leads to the mouth of the river and Bald Head's beaches.

Long Bay

The final stretch of the Old North State's coast consists of Long Bay, from the mouth of the Cape Fear River west to the South Carolina border. This roughly 30-mile strand of shore lies within Brunswick County and takes in Oak Island, plus Holden, Ocean Isle, and Sunset Beaches. Also along here are Lockwood Folly, Shallotte, and Tubbs Inlets.

Oak Island forms the eastern end of Long Bay's coast. The eastern end of the island on the mouth of the Cape Fear River is inaccessible due to its location in a private resort community and the lack of parking or beach access points nearby. In fact, to the east of where NC 133 crosses to the island, there is only one public beach access point. To the west of the NC 133 causeway, beach access on Oak Island is much better from East and West Beach Drives.

The only practical angling sites around this end of the island are limited to access by boat and are basically locations for finding seatrout. The points on either side of the mouth of the Elizabeth River (which runs from the ICW on its northwestern end to the Cape Fear River on the southeast) are noted for holding speckled trout. Also, the mouth of Dutchman Creek on the northern side of the ICW is another good trout drop. In both these locations look for oyster beds along the shore to find the trout.

Boat-launch facilities for the eastern end of Oak Island are found at the Wildlife Creek Boating Access described in the preceding section. Both the Elizabeth River and Dutchman Creek lie just east of the ramp.

At the western end of Oak Island is Lockwood Folly Inlet. The generally clear water in this inlet offers flounder, seatrout, and bluefish to shorebound and boating anglers. The eastern side of the inlet can be reached by foot from the parking area at the end of Oak Island on West Beach Drive. From there it is a short walk down the beach to the inlet. Another option is to take Kings Lynn Drive where it splits off from West Beach to the north. There is a parking area at the end of this road as well, offering access to the inland side of the inlet.

The boat channel through the inlet swings quite close to shore on the tip of the island, putting deeper water within casting range of the beach. Just to the east of the inlet, the shore of the island is lined by a shallow flat with a couple of marsh grass islands. This area has a hard-sand bottom; you can wade around the islands and out to the boat channel.

Across the inlet lies Holden Beach. Lockwood Folly Inlet is also accessible from the end of East Oceanview Boulevard on this island. There is a parking area at the end of the road, and good fishing access from the beach along the inlet.

Boating access to Lockwood Folly Inlet is available at the Holden Beach Access. This single-lane, paved boat ramp with a large gravel parking area is located beneath the southern end of the NC 130 bridge to Holden Beach. From the ramp, run east along the ICW to the inlet.

On the rest of Holden Beach access is available, but parking is very limited. The western end of the island at Shallotte Inlet is inaccessible to vehicles due to a private, limited-access resort at that location.

The western side of Shallotte Inlet on Ocean Isle Beach can be reached on foot along the beach, but it is a rather long walk due to lack of parking and beach access points toward that end of the island. At the dead end of Shallotte Boulevard, however, turn north onto East 2nd Street. This leads to a parking area at the end of the road, from which it is possible to wade around several marsh islands on the inland side of the island. Seatrout are the fish you are most likely to encounter.

The rest of Ocean Isle Beach offers good parking and beach access, but the western tip on Tubbs Inlet cannot be reached due to a gated resort.

One final area remains available to fly-casters before the South Carolina state line. The island of Sunset Beach offers only limited beach access, and what little parking space is available requires a fee. There is also no access to the inlets at either end of the island. There is, however, a shallow flat around marsh grass islands on the western side of the causeway leading to the island. It is a popular stretch among wading anglers, who look for spotted seatrout in the warmer months of spring and summer. There is limited parking space along the causeway, but getting to it from the mainland can take a while. Connecting the island to the mainland is a one-lane drawbridge with traffic lights at either end. Particularly on weekends, the traffic on Sunset Beach Road can back up at this bottleneck.

Murrells Inlet and Wayah Bay are two places where you'll find both puppy drum and seatrout along South Carolina's Grand Strand.

Part III
South Carolina

When it comes to saltwater fly-fishing, the coastal regions of South Carolina have a split personality. The northern portion of the state is one of the few stretches of shore along the South Atlantic Coast not fronted by barrier islands. This region runs from Little River Inlet at the North Carolina border southward to the Pawley Island area and is often referred to as the Grand Strand. Along the Strand, fly-casting opportunities are quite scare.

On the other hand, to the south of the Grand Strand the Palmetto State coast is dominated by the city of Charleston, its harbor, and the nearby coastal islands. Then, anchoring the southern end of the Carolina coast is the low country around the town of Beaufort (pronounced BU-fort). Both of these more southerly regions provide many chances for fly-casters to practice their art on saltwater game fish.

In all, South Carolina has roughly 175 miles of coastline, and these are visited annually by an estimated 190,000 South Carolina anglers. It is also estimated by the U.S. Fish and Wildlife Service that another 192,000 anglers from other states fish in the Palmetto State's salt waters. Among these anglers, red drum, flounder, and seatrout are the most sought-after species. As is true in all the South Atlantic states, the vast majority of anglers use conventional tackle, but fly-fishing is growing in popularity, at least in the regions around Charleston and Beaufort.

Angling Calendar

For fly-casters, the most available species of saltwater game fish in South Carolina are red drum and spotted seatrout. These fish are year-round residents of the Palmetto State's waters. Seatrout are found throughout the state, with the spring and fall being the best times to target them. In the summer they continue to bite but are scattered, rather than in large, easily targeted schools.

Red drum are most prevalent from Murrells Inlet and southward. Puppy drum of 10 pounds or less are the norm in South Carolina, but bigger bull reds of up to 30 pounds appear in the late summer and fall around the inlets and barrier islands. The overall best angling for this species occurs in the milder-weather months of the spring and fall.

During the summer months, several other species of saltwater fish are susceptible to fly-casting along South Carolina's coast. Among these are cobia, jack crevalle, ladyfish, Spanish mackerel, and tarpon. Ladyfish show up in the tidal creeks and rivers of the southern part of the state, while the other three species most commonly appear around inlets during hot weather. Pompano are also present in the northern portion of South Carolina on beaches in the summer; farther south they are more likely to be found around inlets.

Bluefish and striped bass, which are plentiful and popular farther north, become minor saltwater species in South Carolina. Although small bluefish are present year-round and some fish of up to 15 pounds turn up in the cooler months, they make up a relatively small part of the state's recreational saltwater fishery. The same can be said for striped bass in the Palmetto State. Though present in the lower stretches of several coastal saltwater rivers in South Carolina, there is virtually no documentation of the species leaving the estuaries for the bays or open ocean. The best times to fish for stripers are in the spring and fall.

State Records

The South Carolina state record for red drum was posted in 1965 when A. J. Taylor caught one that weighed 75 pounds at Murrells Inlet. Similarly, the state-record spotted seatrout was taken at Murrells Inlet. In 1976 A. Pendergass hooked this fish, which tipped the scales at 11 pounds, 13 ounces.

Still, by far the best place in the Palmetto State for hooking a record-breaker has to be Charleston. No fewer than four records for fish that can be targeted with fly-fishing equipment have come from around that city. A 21-pound bluefish was boated by J. A. Curtis in 1975; J. Benich took a 40-pound, 1-ounce jack crevalle in 1993; a 5-pound, 14-ounce ladyfish was hooked by B. Raver in 1976; and the area also gave up an 8-pound, 12-ounce pompano to C. Mullinax Sr. in 1997.

The state record for striped bass is held by Billy Wayne Chambers. His Combahee River striper pulled the scales down to 46 pounds, 13 ounces back in 1993. The mark for cobia was set in 1976 when H. D. Moon boated an 83-pound, 3-ounce fish from the Broad River. The waters off Myrtle Beach produced a Spanish mackerel that weighed 11 pounds back in 1983 for W. Deas Jr. to set another state record. Finally, the largest tarpon ever taken in the Palmetto State was hooked in 1987 just off Hilton Head Island by S. B. Kiser and weighed 154 pounds, 10 ounces.

Regulations

As with the other states along the South Atlantic Coast, South Carolina has a number of rules applying to the harvest of saltwater game fish. These include creel limits and, in a few instances, closed harvest seasons. Also in common with the other states, the rules are subject to frequent changes. It would be wise to obtain the most recent copy of the booklet *Rules & Regulations for Hunting, Fishing & Wildlife Management Areas in South Carolina.* This is available in many of the places where fishing and hunting licenses are sold. A copy can also be obtained by writing to the South Carolina Department of Natural Resources, Marine Fisheries Division, P.O. Box 12559, Charleston, SC 29422.

As a general rule of thumb, the demarcation line between salt and fresh water in South Carolina is US 17, which runs along the coastal region. There are a few exceptions to the this rule, however. On the Savannah, Wright, Ashepoo, and Edisto Rivers the line is formed by the abandoned Seaboard Railroad track bed, which is very near US 17 on each stream. On the New River on the border of Beaufort County the line is at Cooks Landing, while the confluence of Pepper Dam Creek on the Ashley River north of Charleston is the boundary on that stream. This creek junction is across the river from historic Magnolia Plantation. Finally, on the Cooper River upstream of Charleston, fresh water begins at the confluence of the Black River near Coast Guard Navigational Marker 82.

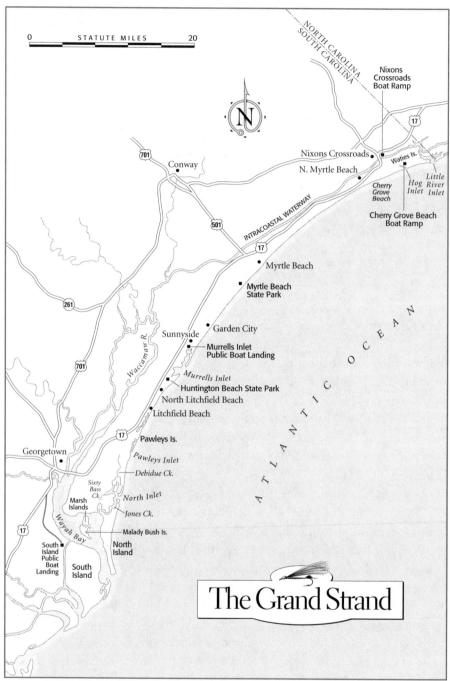

STATUTE MILES

0   20

N

NORTH CAROLINA
SOUTH CAROLINA

Nixons
Crossroads
Boat Ramp

17

701

Conway

Nixons Crossroads

N. Myrtle Beach

Waties Is.

Cherry
Grove
Beach

Hog
Inlet

Little
River
Inlet

Cherry Grove Beach
Boat Ramp

INTRACOASTAL WATERWAY

501

17

Myrtle Beach

Myrtle Beach
State Park

261

A T L A N T I C   O C E A N

Sunnyside

Garden City

Murrells Inlet
Public Boat Landing

Waccamaw R.

701

Murrells Inlet

Huntington Beach State Park

North Litchfield Beach

Litchfield Beach

17

Pawleys Is.

Georgetown

Pawleys Inlet

Debidue Ck.

Sixty
Bass
Ck.

Marsh
Islands

North Inlet

Jones Ck.

Watah Bay

Malady Bush Is.

17

South
Island
Public
Boat
Landing

North
Island

South
Island

South
Island

The Grand Strand

Paul Woodward, © 2000 The Countryman Press

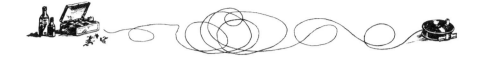

CHAPTER 8

The Grand Strand

MAPS
DeLorme: *South Carolina Atlas* pages 41, 49, 50, 57
NOAA: chart number 11535

The northern portion of the South Carolina coast, stretching from the North Carolina border south through Horry and Georgetown Counties, is regularly referred to as the Grand Strand. This is a family-vacation mecca that centers on beach activities and draws thousands of Carolinians to the shore each spring and summer. In the immediate vicinity of Myrtle Beach there is an almost solid line of hotels, beach houses, restaurants, and probably the heaviest concentration of full-sized and miniature golf courses found anywhere on the eastern seaboard.

Besides Myrtle Beach, the Strand counties contain Little River Inlet, Hog Inlet, North Myrtle Beach, Myrtle Beach State Park, Murrells Inlet, Huntington Beach State Park, Pawleys Island, North Inlet, Georgetown, and Wayah Bay. Unfortunately, the area offers only limited saltwater fishing options, most of which are not conducive to fly-casting. The southern end of the Strand contains the few prime fishing locations found on this part of the coast.

Little River Inlet

Located at the mouth of the Little River right on the North Carolina–South Carolina border, this inlet's jetties are its main attraction for both anglers and fish. These fairly short rock structures are relatively recent additions to South Carolina's list of fishing destinations, having been built to relieve fishermen's concerns that the inlet was being closed by shifting sands. The only access to these jetties is by boat, but it is also possible to beach your vessel and walk out onto the rocks in order to fish them. If you choose this option, however, use extreme care on the slippery boulders.

The best fishing of the year begins in March, when puppy drum show up along the jetties. By April seatrout and flounder join the red drum in chasing bait in the area. During the summer months pompano are also present. Finally, in September bluefish show up in numbers along the rocks. Other species you may encounter here are Spanish mackerel and false albacore.

When targeting any of these fish, local anglers favor the last couple of hours of a falling tide. Look for the red drum to be right up against the rocks, while seatrout will stay several feet off them and along the bottom. Schools of Spanish mackerel or bluefish often give their position away by breaking the surface in pursuit of bait fish. The times to avoid fishing here altogether are on a northeast wind or on days when a winter cold snap is actually moving through the area.

Public boating access to Little River Inlet is available just south in the hamlet of Cherry Grove Beach. The double-lane, paved boat ramp and parking lot are located at the eastern end of 53rd Avenue North, off Ocean Boulevard North in the village. Ocean Boulevard is the main beach road. There are also several hundred yards of creek shore, a fishing pier, and some access to canals along the approach drive to the facility; all offer some fly-casting opportunities at the landing. Puppy drum and seatrout are the species you are most likely to encounter here. To reach Little River Inlet from the landing, head east along the creek, turn south to exit Hog Inlet, then run east along the beach of Waties Island to the jetties at the mouth of the Little River.

In the vicinity of the Cherry Grove Beach Ramp it is possible to park on side streets, walk to the beach, and head east along the sand to access the shore at Hog Inlet. This tiny outlet to the sea offers some opportunities for intercepting several of the species mentioned in relation to fishing at Little River Inlet.

Another way to reach Little River Inlet by boat is to launch at the paved ramp and parking area at the US 17 bridge across the Intracoastal Waterway at Nixons Crossroads. Once you are on the water, run east along the ICW, then follow the Little River to its mouth.

From Cherry Grove Beach south through Myrtle Beach and all the way to Garden City and Murrells Inlet, the only available saltwater fishing is on the beach. There are no barrier islands or river or creek inlets through this stretch of shore, and the Intracoastal Waterway is far inland and considered fresh water. The beach is hard packed for easy walking or wading and can produce Spanish mackerel, puppy drum, trout, and pompano during the year. As noted in the introduction to South Carolina, this area produced an 11-pound Spanish mackerel back in 1983 that still stands as the state record. In the spring through fall these beaches are crowded with swimmers and sunbathers, so fishing early or late in the day is best.

Murrells Inlet

Murrells Inlet is south of Myrtle Beach, between Garden City on the north and North Litchfield Beach to the south. This ocean pass maintains a reputation for being the most intensely fished area along the entire South Carolina coast. The major reason for this popularity is the abundance of forage fish, particularly finger mullet, that show up along the rock jetties on both the northern and southern sides of the inlet. Needless to say, the presence of these bait fish ensures that game fish also visit the area.

Construction of these jetties began back in 1977 and was completed in 1980. At that time the top of the southern jetty was paved with asphalt, creating a perfect casting platform for shorebound fly-casters to reach a lot of good fishing water. The paved jetty stretches about 0.25 mile into the ocean, with the paved portion flanked on both sides with boulders. It is possible to get onto these huge rocks in many places, but take care when attempting it. The boulders have jagged edges, and if wet they can be slippery. The jetty on the northern side of the inlet does not connect to the beach, is not paved, cannot be reached by foot due to a private development on that shore, and is accessible only to boating anglers.

Seatrout fishing usually begins heating up at Murrells Inlet in March. The inlet produced the state-record trout, an 11-pound, 13-ounce monster, in 1977, as well as having yielded the previous state record for this species. The major problem with targeting trout from the jetty is that they tend to

JIMMY JACOBS

*One of the species to target from the Murrells Inlet jetty in
the summer is Spanish mackerel.*

hold in deeper water near the bottom, just off the inlet side of the rocks.
Since much of the action for all species takes place here during the last couple
of hours of falling tides, strong currents can make it hard to get a fly down
to where these fish hold.

By April channel bass begin to show up in force along the Murrells Inlet
jetties as well. While most of these fish run in the 3- to 5-pound range and
hug the edge along the entire length of the stone structures, bigger bull reds
can sometimes be found at the very end of the rocks. These red drum often
tip the scales at up to 25 pounds each, but the state-record 75-pounder was
also caught here in 1965. The best time for fishing this area is on a northeast
wind that has surf crashing on the rocks. At these times, target the side in
the protected lee of the jetty. The worst times for fishing here are days when
cold snaps are moving through in the fall, or when the water coming out of
the inlet is running exceptionally clear. The angling for both trout and red
drum holds up around the jetties to as late as December each year.

In the summer months pompano and Spanish mackerel begin appearing
around Murrells Inlet. The surf line to the south of the inlet is your best bet
for the pompano, while mackerel often show up just off the rocks. In fact,
schools of Spanish mackerel can sometimes be found chasing pods of bait
fish just a fly-cast away from the jetty. If they are pushing the forage along
the rocks, it is possible to simply walk the top of the jetty following them as

they feed. In September and October false albacore and bluefish occasionally get within casting range of the rocks as well.

Although flounder are present around Murrells Inlet, you are much more likely to encounter them inside the pass than around the rocks. There are a number of marsh grass islands on a sandy, wadable flat to the south of the inlet. Besides flounder, red drum and seatrout are also found around the grass. This is another area that holds a lot of bait fish and crustaceans that attract game fish. As the flat nears deeper channels of water, the bottom becomes muddier, making wading less practical. If you prefer to keep your feet dry, a sand spit extending from the inland end of the southern jetty offers casting access to a tidal creek entering the salt marsh, which wraps around behind the rock barrier.

Do not expect the angling on the jetty or in the marsh to be very crowded. Most of the pressure comes from fishermen in boats. Reaching the jetty requires a long walk along the hard-packed sand beach from Huntington Beach State Park to the south. Although park literature says the facility is 3 miles south of Murrells Inlet, the walk is actually more like 1 mile if you use the northern parking lot. The prospect of making this trek discourages many bait-fishermen, who generally prefer not to carry all their gear that far. The park is located on US 17 just south of the inlet. A fee is charged to enter the facility.

To reach Murrells Inlet by boat, the best public access is Murrells Inlet Public Boat Landing. This is located on the eastern side of US 17 in the hamlet of Sunny Side to the north of the inlet. It has a triple-lane, paved boat ramp; a large parking lot is located across the highway from the launch site. From the landing, running south along the creek leads to Murrells Inlet.

To the south of Huntington Beach State Park there is very limited public access or parking for surf fishing at North Litchfield Beach, while Litchfield Beach itself offers no public beach access or parking.

Pawleys Island

Pawleys Island lies just south of Litchfield Beach and roughly 13 miles south of Murrells Inlet. The island offers good options for several species, with the most accessible fishing at its southern end. Here the waters of Main Creek flow around the end of the island into Pawleys Inlet. While the inlet is passable for small boats at high tide, during ebb levels it is composed of several shallow channels separated by sand flats that have depressions and washouts on them. Most of this inlet area is wadable at low tide and contains plenty of

JIMMY JACOBS

The warnings about soft sand in Pawleys Inlet should definitely be heeded!

bait fish. Signs at the parking area warn of strong currents and soft sand in the inlet, and these should be heeded. This is not a place where you want to get stranded on a sandbar during a rising tide or go blindly rushing across a channel. Step into an area of soft sand and you can find yourself in big trouble. Once upstream of the sand flats at the inlet mouth, Main Creek is navigable by small boats during all tide levels.

If you prefer to stay on the beach to cast, you can cover the area from the first private dock up in Main Creek all the way around the end of the island to several rock and timber groins that extend out from the beach on the ocean side. These groins are particularly good places to target during rising tides.

There is a large, unpaved parking lot on the southern end of Pawleys Island from which you can access both the groins on the beach and the mouth of Main Creek.

The same cannot be said of the northern end of the island. There is no practical access from shore to Midway Inlet to the north of Pawleys Island. This inlet, along with the marsh grass shores lined with oyster beds on Main Creek behind the island, can be fished from small boats.

Spotted seatrout can be found in Main Creek and around both inlets during most of the year, while small puppy drum appear in the same areas in the spring and again in the fall months. Red drum and flounder are also noted for showing up around the groins on the southern beach.

To reach Pawleys Inlet, take Myrtle Street south along the beach to its dead end at Pritchard Street. Turn left onto Pritchard and proceed to its end at Spring Street. Turn right to reach the parking area at the end of this street.

Although there are three paved, single-lane public boat ramps on Pawleys Island, none has room for parking vehicles and trailers! All three ramps are on Main Creek. The ramp on the southern end of the island is reached by going south on Myrtle Street to its junction with Pritchard Street and turning right. The ramp is at the end of Pritchard. On the northern end of the island there are ramps at the ends of 3rd and 4th Streets, which are on the western side of Atlantic Avenue. Atlantic is the main beach road at that end of the island.

Wayah Bay

Anchoring the southern end of the Grand Strand is the city of Georgetown at the head of Wayah Bay. The waters of the bay, its mouth on the Atlantic Ocean, and the creeks connecting it to North Inlet generally hold red drum year-round, although they are not noted for producing bull reds. Spotted seatrout are present in numbers from July though early March each year, while May through November are the months to find flounder. One additional species that shows up with regularity is the tarpon. These silver kings can be found around the mouth of the bay or near North Inlet from late July through October.

Virtually all the fly-casting in this vicinity is limited to fishing from boats. Most of Wayah Bay is surrounded by marshes, and the US 17 bridge at Georgetown is the demarcation line between salt and fresh water. The only practical wading or shore access is on the beaches of North and South Islands, but these can also be reached only by boat.

The best areas for seatrout are around Marsh and Malady Bush Islands in the lower portion of Wayah Bay. This area is dotted with shoals and oyster bars. Two other good spots are Debidue Creek and the mouth of Sixty Bass

ZANE JACOBS

Speckled trout are low-country favorites among South Carolina fly-casters.

Creek, both just inside North Inlet. Red drum usually are found around the submerged jetties at the mouth of Wayah Bay, or along the surf line on North Island and South Island, on either side of the mouth of the bay.

To fish the Wayah Bay area, the best public boating access is from the South Island Public Boat Landing. This double-lane, paved ramp has plenty of parking and is adjacent to the South Island Ferry Landing on South Island Road at the Intracoastal Waterway. To reach the landing, take US 17 south from Georgetown, crossing the Sampit River bridge. When US 17 bears to the southwest, take South Island Road (Secondary State Road 18) to the south and continue to the ramp at the ferry landing.

Once you are on the water, run northeast along the ICW to Wayah Bay. Marsh and Malady Bush Islands are directly in front of the waterway's mouth. Turn east and follow the bay as it turns south to reach its mouth and the jetties on the Atlantic. From here you can run either northeast for North Island's beaches or to the southwest to reach the beach of South Island.

To access North Inlet, Debidue Creek, and Sixty Bass Creek, run due east from the mouth of the ICW to North Island. Head north along this island's inland shore to the mouth of Jones Creek, then follow this stream to North Inlet. When you reach the inlet, Sixty Bass Creek is to the west, while Debidue is straight ahead to the north of the inlet.

CHAPTER 9

Charleston

MAPS
DeLorme: *South Carolina Atlas* pages 56, 57, 60, 61
NOAA: chart number 11513

Lying on the central portion of the Palmetto State's coastline, the city of Charleston and its harbor are a hotbed of saltwater fishing activity on a year-round basis. The angling, however, is not confined to the harbor. In fact, all of Charleston County from the Santee River delta on the north to the mouth of the Edisto River to the south is loaded with good places for pursuing game fish in the brine with fly tackle.

The shore of Charleston County, from north to south, begins with the North and South Santee Rivers flowing on either side of Cedar Island. These are followed by the Cape Romain National Wildlife Refuge's Cape Island, McClellanville, Bull Bay, Bull Island, Price Inlet, Capers Island, Capers Inlet, and Dewees Inlet; then comes the Charleston Harbor vicinity with the Isle of Palms, Breech Inlet, Sullivan Island, the harbor itself, plus the Wando, Cooper, and Ashley Rivers. The shore finishes with the stretch of coast from Charleston Harbor to the Edisto River, which includes Folly Island, Folly Inlet, Kiawah Island, the North Edisto River, Edisto Island and Beach, and finally the South Edisto River.

A generalized fishing calendar for this area promises anglers a shot at red drum all year long, with speckled trout showing up in the spring months of

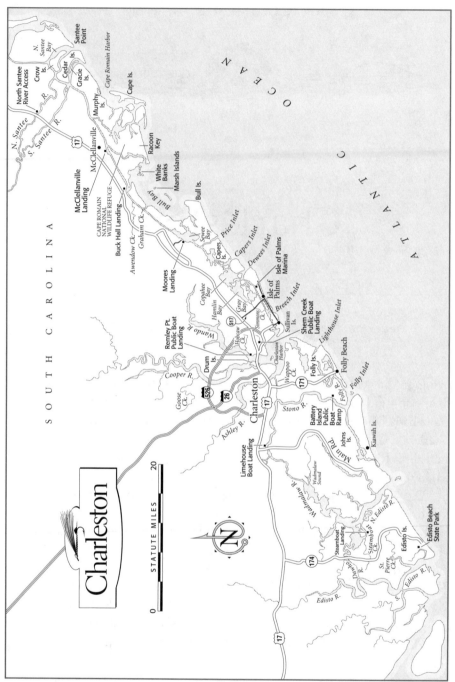

Charleston

STATUTE MILES

0   20

N

SOUTH CAROLINA

ATLANTIC OCEAN

North Santee
River Access

N. Santee R.

S. Santee R.

N. Santee Bay

Crow Is.

Cedar Is.

Gracie Is.

Santee Point

Murphy Is.

Cape Romain Harbor

Cape Is.

McClellanville

McClellanville Landing

CAPE ROMAIN
NATIONAL
WILDLIFE REFUGE

Buck Hall Landing

Racoon Key

White Banks

Marsh Islands

Bull Is.

Bull Bay

Awendaw Ck.

Graham Ck.

Sewee Bay

Price Inlet

Capers Is.

Capers Inlet

Mooees
Landing

Copahee Bay

Dewees Inlet

Isle of Palms Marina

Hamlin Bay

Gray Bay

Isle of Palms

Breech Inlet

Wando R.

Remley Pt.
Public Boat
Landing

Simmons Ck.

17

Hobcaw Ck.

Sullivan Is.

Shem Creek
Public Boat
Landing

Lighthouse Inlet

Drum Is.

Charleston Harbor

Folly Is.

Folly Beach

Cooper R.

Goose Ck.

526

26

Charleston

Wappoo Ck.

Folly Inlet

17

Stono R.

171

Folly R.

Ashley R.

Battery
Island
Public
Boat
Ramp

Kiawah Is.

Limehouse
Boat Landing

Main Rd.

Johns Is.

Wadmalaw R.

Wadmalaw Sound

174

Steamboat Landing

Steamboat Ck.

Edisto Is.

N. Edisto R.

Edisto Beach
State Park

Toogoodoo Ck.

Dawho R.

St. Pierre Ck.

S. Edisto R.

Edisto R.

17

Edisto R.

March through May and again in October through December. Bluefish are present in numbers from April through November, while flounder are slightly less available, inhabiting these waters from May through November. Spanish mackerel and ladyfish, which appear in June, are joined by tarpon and jack crevalle in July. All four of these species generally remain in the area until the end of September.

Santee River

The twin flows of the North and South Santee Rivers form the northern boundary of this chapter's coverage of the Charleston area. The border of Charleston County actually runs along the middle of the South Santee, leaving Cedar Island and the confluence of the North Santee in Georgetown County.

The Santee flows out of the famed Santee-Cooper chain of reservoirs to the north and, in fact, carries virtually all of the flow coming from these lakes. The Cooper River, which runs into Charleston Harbor, is also dammed to create these freshwater lakes, but only a trickle of water is released into its drainage. As a result, the nutrient-rich flow from the reservoirs ends up in the Santee. This situation makes the inlets at the twin mouths of this river a haven for bait fish.

Red drum and trout are both plentiful in the lower stretches of the rivers, particularly around shell bars and marsh grass islands. The area around Santee Point on the northwestern bank of the North Santee's mouth, and the shores of Cedar and Murphy Islands are noted as hot spots for bluefish, while Spanish mackerel are possible in the inlets' mouths. Both of these fish are summer targets for fly-casters. Look for them especially anywhere that schools of menhaden are present. The brackish waters of the lower North and South Santee Rivers also hold striped bass from October through March, with the best places to look for them around and just below the US 17 bridge. They are most practical as fly-casting targets when they are chasing bait-fish pods on the surface.

All of the fly-fishing on the Santee Rivers is accessible only to boating anglers. The best place to access these waters is the South Santee River Access. In one of those geographic oddities that seem to occur, the landing is actually on the North Santee River, where US 17 spans the waterway. This double-lane, paved ramp has a large parking area as well. To reach Cedar and Murphy Islands, run downstream to the mouth of the river and turn southwest. The South Santee River can be reached by turning to the southwest and running behind Murphy Island on the Intracoastal Waterway, just upstream of Crow Island.

Cape Romain National Wildlife Refuge

This 29,000-acre federal refuge stretches from Cape Romain Harbor on the north to Price Creek at the southern end of Bull Island and presents a veritable wonderland of great fishing opportunities. On the other hand, it is a bit off the beaten path and requires some local knowledge to navigate. At its northern end, between the village of McClellanville on the mainland and Cape Island and Raccoon Key to seaward, there is a maze of creeks, marsh islands, and small isolated bays. The central portion of the refuge is composed of the open waters of Bull Bay, but also contains the White Banks and Marsh Islands, all of which are waterbird rookeries and off limits to entry. In the south there is another maze of small islands and creeks stretching from Moores Landing on the inland side to Bull and Capers Islands on the ocean side. The only practical fishing from shore is offered on the beaches of the barrier islands in the refuge, but you still need a boat to reach these areas. The bottom line is that when venturing into this region for the first time, you probably need to hire a guide or share a boat with someone who knows the waters.

Having stated that cautionary note, there are some locations in the Cape Romain area that merit highlighting. Suffice it to say that the myriad channels behind Cape Island and Raccoon Key are year-round homes to both puppy drum and spotted seatrout. By targeting creek intersections and shell bars, you can find enough hot spots to keep you busy for years. The inland side of Cape Romain Harbor is particularly good for trout in the winter months. Any places that sandy bottoms occur through here are likely to hold flounder during the warmer months. Additionally, the beach side of Cape Island is noted for holding huge bull red drum in the surf line during the spring. Beginning in late April these fish of up to 30 pounds are prowling the shoreline in search of bait fish. They can be targeted from boats or from the beach, but the only access to this island is via private boats.

The closest public access point is at the McClellanville Landing. Located in the sleepy fishing village of McClellanville, the facility is at the end of Pinckney Street, 1.5 miles east of US 17. The two-lane, paved ramp is a bit rough, while the unpaved lot provides plenty of room for parking. The landing is immediately behind the Village Museum.

Traveling south from the ramp quickly puts you on the Intracoastal Waterway, but to the southeast of the ICW the maze of islands and channels begins and there is no direct way to reach Cape Island. As mentioned earlier, this is an area where you want to be with an experienced navigator.

The broad expanse of Bull Bay is a good place to find tarpon rolling on the surface during the summer months, while trout and puppy-sized red drum are plentiful on its inland side. During the winter months, concentrate your casting efforts on the deeper channels along the ICW on the northwestern edge of the bay for reds and speckled trout. You also encounter some weakfish in these drops.

Access by boat to Bull Bay is easiest from the Buck Hall Landing. This U.S. Forest Service facility is located just to the southeast of US 17 near the mouth of Awendaw Creek at the crossroads of Buck Hall. The boat ramp is at the end of Forest Service Road 242. A parking fee of $5 is charged at the landing.

Once you are on the water, motor out to the ICW, then run southwest along it to Graham Creek. Follow this stream to the south to reach Bull Bay.

On the southern flank of the Cape Romain refuge the creeks and bays behind Capers and Bull Islands are places to target puppy drum and seatrout. Again, finding oyster bars and casting to them during falling tides will produce fish. If the bars are at creek intersections, they can be even better hot spots. The sandy areas of Capers and Price Inlets at either end of Capers Island produce flounder during the summer months, too.

The best-known fishery in this part of the refuge is found on the seaward side of Capers and Bull Islands. On both of these barrier isles there are trees lying on the beaches—victims of erosion—as well as stumps protruding from the sand. During higher tides, when these are inundated, red drum move in to feed around them. It is possible to fish around this cover from boats or by wading the beach. Again, however, there are no bridges to the islands, so you need a boat for access.

A federally operated day ferry makes the 30-minute run to Bull Island from Moores Landing near the refuge's Sewee Visitors Center. This service is not offered every day of the week even in the summer, and only on Saturday from December through February, so you need to contact the visitors center for an updated schedule. Carry all the supplies you need for a day of fishing, since there are no facilities on Bull Island.

Besides the ferry dock, there is also a boat ramp at Moores Landing. The single-lane paved ramp has a steep drop-off at the end of the launch pad and can be used only for two hours on either side of a high tide. There is adequate parking at the site, but the whole facility is enclosed in a fence that has an automated gate. It opens at 6 AM and closes at 9 PM.

To reach Moores Landing, take Sewee Road (SSR 584) to the east of US 17. Turn south onto Bull Island Road (SSR 1170). The landing is at the end of the road. Again, the maze of creek channels to the southeast of the ICW and Sewee Bay requires local knowledge to navigate.

Isle of Palms

The Isle of Palms lies just north of Charleston Harbor, and the waters around it offer several options for catching fish on a fly. Although there is access to the beach on the island, this is a very popular swimming area in the warmer months when the fishing is best. Early and late in the day it is possible to encounter puppy drum, bluefish, and pompano along here.

One spot that attracts a lot of angling attention is Breech Inlet at the southwestern end of the island. Here a bridge with a catwalk spans the inlet to the shore of Sullivan Island. While the catwalk offers no fly-fishing opportunities, you can cast to the pilings of the bridge from the beach at either end—though the number of bait-fishermen dangling lines in the water may be a casting hazard. It is also possible to cast from the narrow sand beaches that run on either side of the inlet all the way out to the points on the Isle of Palms and Sullivan Island. Though the shores look wadable, signs posted here prohibit wading due to strong currents and a sharp drop-off into the boat channel.

Flounder and red drum usually move into this area in May, when baitfish schools begin appearing in concentrations. Reds of up to 15 pounds are often hooked at this location.

For anglers with boats, the inland side of the Isle of Palms holds even more promise. The Intracoastal Waterway runs through here, flanked on both sides by winding creeks, marsh islands, and mounds of oyster shells. These provide terrific habitat for red drum and seatrout. Additionally, the relatively shallow water of the area makes fly-casting for the two species very practical.

For seatrout, which are much more prevalent here in the spring and fall, Simmons Creek is a fertile fishing ground. This tidal stream runs north off the ICW just southwest of the Ben Sayer Bridge on SC 517. The creek runs to the northwest, passing under SC 517 to connect to Hamlin Sound. Targeting the shell beds along its shore yields trout, but red drum also are possible.

JIMMY JACOBS

Huge oyster-shell bars fill the sound to the inland side of the Isle of Palms, creating great channel bass habitat.

Virtually the same conditions apply on the small creek that wraps around the southern end of Goat Island in the same general vicinity. If you are traveling northwest on the ICW, as soon as you pass under the SC 517 bridge this stream is the next tidal creek on your left. If it has a name, it does not appear on any chart I have seen. The creek meanders to the north, eventually connecting to Gray Bay. Again, seatrout inhabit its waters, along with puppy drum.

To the north of SC 517 and inland of the Isle of Palms are (from south to north) Gray, Hamlin, and Copahee Bays, which contain an outstanding sight-casting fishery for red drum. The fish are found here virtually year-round, with the fall through spring being the best time to locate them. The waters of these bays are relatively clear and shallow. They are filled with oyster-shell mounds that are inches beneath the surface at high tide but exposed during an ebb. These shell flats are crisscrossed by narrow channels that run 6 to 7 feet deep at low tide. Navigating these channels is easy at low tide but can be much harder when the shell beds are underwater. Local anglers have marked some channels with sticks topped by soft-drink bottles painted red or green to mark their port and starboard sides.

The best fishing at these locations is during low tides early and late in the day. At these times schools of red drum can be spotted pushing wakes, tailing, or chasing bait anywhere on the flats. Anglers often drift the area, watching for signs of the schools, then slowly and quietly move to within casting range. The flats here are composed of "puff" mud that sends up mud clouds when disturbed. Although much of the area is firm enough to wade, there is no shore access, there are softer spots, and—since you have to have a boat to get to the area anyway—fishing from the vessel makes more sense.

At the southern end of this area the SC 703 bridge over the ICW connects the mainland to Sullivan Island. The pilings of the bridge and surrounding marshes can provide action for puppy drum, seatrout, and bluefish. The area is also known for holding a lot of ladyfish during the warmer months of the year.

The closest boat-launch facility to the fisheries at the Isle of Palms is the Isle of Palms Marina. This marina and a double-lane, paved ramp are at the end of 41st Street to the northwest off Palm Boulevard (the main beachfront road). Though this is an excellent facility with plenty of parking, a hefty $10 launch fee is charged.

The nearest public ramp is the Shem Creek Public Boat Landing on Charleston Harbor. Located at the end of Live Oak Drive, it is on the northern side of SC 703 and Shem Creek in the town of Mount Pleasant. This is a single-lane, paved ramp with a good parking area, but it gets very busy on weekends.

Once your boat is in the water, run down Shem Creek to Charleston Harbor, then turn southeast to the entrance of the ICW behind Sullivan Island. Run northeast up the ICW past the SC 703 bridge and continue to the Isle of Palms and the SC 517 bridge.

Charleston Harbor

The waters of Charleston Harbor actually present two challenges to fly-casters hoping to identify the better locations for targeting game fish. The area is so well known for producing saltwater fishing action that many anglers can readily list several honey holes around the harbor that give up a variety of species. For this reason, the twin challenges are to cite the good fly-fishing locations—and to explain why the better-known fishing holes are not on the list.

The jetties at the mouth of Charleston Harbor actually fit into both of these categories. At times in the summer when tarpon are rolling on the surface or bluefish and Spanish mackerel are busting pods of bait fish along the rocks, fly-fishermen in boats have a shot at hooking these fish. On the other hand, considering that this area is one of the most celebrated saltwater an-

JIMMY JACOBS

The area around Fort Sumter at the mouth of Charleston Harbor holds both seatrout and red drum, but it is best for nighttime fishing.

gling locations on the South Carolina coast, it does not offer fly-casters a very dependable fishery. While huge red drum and just about every other inshore and offshore species are likely to show up along these 2-mile-long rock piles, the currents are strong, wind is usually a consideration, and most of the water is quite deep. All these factors apply particularly to the seaward tips of the jetties and Dynamite Hole in the southern jetty—a gap in the rocks that was, by some accounts, created to allow shrimp boats easier access to near-shore waters.

In a similar vein, the riprap around Fort Sumter at the harbor entrance is noted for holding both red drum and seatrout. Yet this island, which is most famous as the scene of the opening shots of the Civil War, is mainly a night-fishing destination.

Finally, at the northern side of the entrance to the harbor, the rocky bottom known as the Grillage and the waters around Buoy 22 are fabled locations for big red drum, black drum, and even king mackerel. But again, the water here is deep and currents are swift, making fly-casting very difficult.

Having mentioned the better-known locations on the harbor that do not measure up, let's turn to the actual fly-casting destinations here. All are situated in the inner portion of the harbor. Let's start on the northeastern side of the area.

The first of the harbor hot spots is the Crab Bank. This is a small marsh island that sits just offshore of the town of Mount Pleasant, immediately east of the mouth of Shem Creek. While catching red drum and seatrout is possible year-round at this site, the summer months offer a wider variety of fish. Schools of bluefish, Spanish mackerel, and ladyfish also appear. This is also the northernmost spot where jack crevalle are common inshore on the Southeast Coast. Tossing big popping bugs in front of cruising pods of crevalle can entice savage strikes and extremely rugged battles, since fish are often in the 20-pound range.

If you are targeting the Crab Bank in the summer, the best times to fish are early in the morning and late in the evening, when the sun is not beaming directly on the water—or on you! Also, the always heavy boat traffic will be at its lightest on the harbor, making fishing easier.

Directly east between the Crab Bank and the city of Charleston lies Shutes Folly Island. Also known locally as Castle Pinckney Island, it is the site of the Castle Pinckney National Monument. You can find casting opportunities along its shoreline for speckled trout, red drum, bluefish, jack crevalle, and flounder.

To the east of Castle Pinckney on the waterfront of downtown Charleston lies the Battery. This stone wall protects the older portion of the city from flooding, but has also provided good fishing conditions. Local anglers toss baited hooks from the seawall for flounder that often reach doormat (larger than 6 pounds) proportions. Spottail bass are sometimes encountered here as well. Though the fishing at this site has been reported to be rather slow recently, it still merits checking out.

Another location worth some investigation is Drum Island in the mouth of the Cooper River to the north of Castle Pinckney. The island is crossed by US 17, and the bridge pilings on either side traditionally produce channel bass and seatrout. Also check out the northern tip of the island for schools of feeding bluefish in the summer months.

The Cooper River—which flows into Charleston Harbor from the north, on the eastern side of the city—is noted for holding seatrout, red drum, and some striped bass. The best places to look for trout and red drum are around points on the riverbank or at feeder creek mouths where shell beds are present. The southern end of Daniel Island (where the Wando River enters from the east) is a good location for channel bass and trout, as is the mouth of Clouter Creek on the eastern side of the Cooper. In fact, any shell bed on the river all the way up to the freshwater demarcation line at Goose Creek is a possible trout or red drum hot spot.

Finding striped bass in the lower Cooper River saltwater areas is a wintertime occurrence. Although they sometimes show up around the docks of

POLLY DEAN

The water around Castle Pinckney in Charleston Harbor gives up hefty jack crevalle in the summer.

the Charleston Navy Base on the western side of the river upstream of the city, they are usually present in numbers only after dark. On the other hand, targeting feeder stream mouths on falling tides or concentrating on the channel drops along the river up to Goose Creek can yield some stripers in the colder months.

The final fishing area on the northeastern side of Charleston Harbor is the Wando River and its tributaries. This flow is a good place to ambush some red drum, but even more so to hook seatrout. Although both species are present year-round, red drum are more active in the winter, while trout bite best in the spring and fall. Trout of up to 5 pounds are taken regularly from the Wando's waters.

When you are looking for reds on the river, concentrate on shell beds—though the fish will push all the way up to the edge of the marsh grass, especially on a high tide. Look for trout on the first drop out from the shore. In the winter months the trout are going to be in water from 6 to 18 feet deep, so fishing weighted flies very slowly is the key to success.

Hobcaw Creek is the first major tributary entering the Wando from the east upstream of the junction of the Wando and Cooper Rivers. This tidal stream winds behind the Wando Terminal of the Port of Charleston. Just inside the mouth of Hobcaw there is a marina on the right-hand bank. The shore opposite the marina docks is a steep mud bank lined with shell beds.

These are in depths of 4 to 8 feet at high tide, but exposed during ebb flows. During any tide level, this is a good shoreline for targeting seatrout.

Another location on the Wando to check out is the mouth of Nowell Creek, which connects the Wando to the Cooper River. The confluence of the creek on the western side of the Wando is near the green Channel Marker 17 on the river. Cast very tight against the marsh grass on the northern point of the creek's mouth during higher tides for red drum, but come back out to the first channel drop for trout. As always, spots where there are oyster beds are the most promising.

There is no practical access to any of these harbor areas for fly-casting from the shore. Boating anglers can reach them from a couple of public landings. For Crab Bank, Castle Pinckney, and the Battery, the Shem Creek Public Boat Landing in Mount Pleasant (described earlier in the Isle of Palms section) is the most convenient. Traveling southeast from the mouth of Shem Creek leads you to Crab Bank, while Castle Pinckney and the Battery are due east of the creek.

For the fishing sites in the Cooper and Wando Rivers, the Remley Point Public Boat Landing is the best jumping-off point. Located on 3rd Street off Mathis Ferry Road in Mount Pleasant, the landing is just upstream of the Old Cooper River Bridge (US 17) and at the mouth of the Wando. There is a large paved parking lot, and the double-lane, paved boat ramp is situated inside an artificial boat basin jutting out into the river.

Once you are on the river, Drum Island is due east in the middle of the Cooper. The fishing sites on the Cooper are upstream of this island. Running west up the Wando from the landing leads you to Hobcaw and Nowell Creeks.

The southwestern shore of Charleston Harbor gets less publicity than the northeastern—and for good reason. About the only areas of interest on this side of the harbor are up in the Ashley River. The mouths of the Ashley's tributaries are the places to try, with the confluence of Orange Grove Creek and its large shell beds among the best. Also, check out the part of the river just upstream of the Mark Clark Expressway Bridge, up to the freshwater demarcation line at Pepper Dam Creek and Magnolia Plantation. Again, the mouths of feeder streams and shell beds offer the most promising places for some action. All of these Ashley River sites hold red drum and spotted seatrout, while the ones upriver from the expressway bridge also hold striped bass in the winter months.

The best boating access to the Ashley River is via the Wappoo Cut Public Boat Landing. From US 17 in Charleston, take SC 171 south toward

Folly Beach. The landing is at the SC 171 bridge over Wappoo Creek. This double-lane, paved ramp has a large paved parking area. It is also possible to cast to the bridge pilings from the shore in the public area here. Be aware that this is a very busy ramp on weekends. Once you are on the water, run east along Wappoo Creek to its mouth on the Ashley River, then turn north for the fishing sites on the Ashley.

Folly Island

Morris, Folly, and Kiawah Islands form the beachfront to the south of Charleston Harbor, providing a range of fly-casting possibilities. For the most part, however, Kiawah Island is off limits unless you are a guest at the island resort. Morris Island is mostly marsh and beach with no access from the mainland, although its beaches are noted for giving up red drum. This leaves Folly Island as the focus of the public fishing in this area.

The oceanfront beaches of Folly Island are lined with rock and wooden groins designed to prevent beach erosion. A fringe benefit of these is that they attract game fish, particularly during high tides. From the fishing pier on the beach near the end of SC 171, the groins to the east are in good shape but do not offer much in the way of a casting platform. For anglers, they are simply structures to attract fish. Toward the western end of the island some of the groins are deteriorating, while others that are in good condition have wooden piling walls that offer good casting platforms. There is plenty of beach access east of the fishing pier off East Arctic Street, while West Ashley Street provides the beach access points along the western portion of the island. Along this beach puppy drum, seatrout, flounder, and bluefish are all possibilities for surf casting.

The eastern end of Folly Island does not come to a sharp point like most barrier isles, but rather has a blunt end facing on Lighthouse Inlet. The Charleston County Parks and Recreation Department controls a patch of undeveloped land on this tip of the island. The property is gated, with only foot access allowed along the old road section at the end of East Arctic Street. Another possibility for access is to walk down the beach from the end of East Arctic. This has the added advantage of sending you past two stone groins on this portion of the beach.

Along the blunt eastern end of Folly Island, the surf is quite calm, since it breaks up on the shoals around the lighthouse sitting out in the inlet. Ordinarily, however, the wind is pretty heavy on this unprotected shore.

As you walk north around the end of Folly Island a sand spit extends for about 0.5 mile up Lighthouse Creek, ending in a marsh grass tidal flat. Some wading and casting around the mouth of the Folly River (which wraps around behind Folly Island) is possible, but closer to the mouth of the inlet are signs warning against wading due to heavy currents. The entire expanse of Lighthouse Inlet is noted for producing good seatrout fishing.

The western end of Folly Island is occupied by Folly Beach County Park ($4 entrance fee), which offers beach access and a 1-mile walk to Folly Inlet at the tip of the island. Near the end of the island, a substratum of black clay juts through the beach sand in several places, with heavy currents and washouts present in front of these.

A sandy beach wraps around the end of the island onto the Folly River and continues for another 0.5 mile. Near the end of the beach access, a channel marker pole sits right against the low-tide beach line with a water gauge attached. The gauge indicates a sharp drop into 4 to 6 feet of water.

About 100 yards before the pole you will find an area of oyster shells in a small indentation or cove on the beach that is only inches deep at low tide. During flood tides the bed is 50 feet offshore in 4 to 5 feet of water, offering an excellent place to cast for puppy drum or seatrout.

Just past the marker pole on the beach, the sand comes to an abrupt end at a small tidal creek. It is possible to follow this creek upstream for several bends during all tide levels. Its far shore at its mouth on the river is lined with oyster beds, and bait fish are generally present in the creek—all of which indicates that this is another good place to cast for red drum and seatrout.

If the county park is closed (it does not open until 8 AM), you can leave your vehicle at the last public beach access on West Ashley Street, which makes the walk to the end of the island a 1.25-mile trek.

On the inland side of Folly Island, the Folly River forms a 450-foot-wide sound to the west of the SC 171 bridge to the island. The waters of this sound drop to 22 feet and hold virtually every saltwater fish native to this part of the coast. To the east of the SC 171 bridge, the river narrows considerably. To the north of the river at both ends of the island are mazes of salt marshes and tidal creeks. These marsh areas are full of reefs of oyster shells that make them a perfect habitat for spottail bass and speckled trout. One area of particular interest is marked as Clark Sound on maps, but locals often refer to it as James Island Sound. In all these tidal marshes the falling tide is usually the best time to target the shell beds.

Boating access to the Folly River and inland marshes is available at the

JIMMY JACOBS

The lighthouse in the Folly Inlet guards the entrance to Lighthouse Creek on the north end of Folly Island.

Folly Beach Public Boat Ramp on the southwestern end of the SC 171 bridge onto the island. It has a double-lane, paved ramp with plenty of paved parking. Access to the inland salt marshes is possible all along the northern side of the Folly River via a number of small creeks.

The main stream entering Folly Inlet from the inland side is the Stono River. This flow offers several good options for encountering both channel bass and seatrout. In its lower reaches near the inlet the trout fishing is best in the fall and winter months. Target shell beds along here that are in 6 to 8 feet of water. Farther upstream, the riprap where Wappoo Creek enters from the east is a good spot for finding red drum. Virtually any feeder stream mouth or shell bar on the upper Stono can also hold trout or red drum, up to the point where it joins Wadmalaw Sound and thus the Wadmalaw River.

Access by boat to the lower Stono River is best at the Battery Island

Public Boat Ramp. This landing, which is not shown on the DeLorme map, is at the end of Sol Legare Road (SSR 632), 2.5 miles west of SC 171 at the tip of Sol Legare Island. The landing has a double-lane, paved boat ramp with plenty of room for parking. Public access to the upper Stono River is best at the Limehouse Boat Landing. This site is on Johns Island to the southeast of US 17, via Main Road (SSR 20). The landing is at the southern end of the John F. Limehouse Memorial Bridge over the river. There is no sign identifying the entrance to the facility. A two-lane, paved boat ramp and large unpaved parking area are provided.

Edisto Island

Edisto Island lies at the southwestern end of Charleston County, but back in 1975 the town of Edisto Beach, on the southwestern tip of the island, was annexed to Colleton County. Regardless of who claims the area, the waters around the island add a few more possibilities to the region's angling inventory. At the eastern end of the island the North Edisto River empties into the Atlantic, while the South Edisto River sweeps past Bay Point at the other end of the isle. Both of these flows are noted for holding puppy drum year-round while also attracting tarpon to their mouths in the summer. The North Edisto has a large number of feeder creeks entering it from both sides, all of which provide good possibilities for speckled trout.

Access via boat to the North Edisto is provided at the Steamboat Landing. This facility is located to the north of SC 174 on Steamboat Landing Road. The ramp is at the end of the road, the last 0.5 mile of which is unpaved. The single-lane ramp is paved, but the parking area is not. A stretch of tidal creek along the approach road leading to the landing can be cast from the roadside. This stream can hold seatrout and red drum, and it offers one of the few bank-fishing accesses in this part of the coast. Once you are in your boat, head east along Steamboat Creek to the North Edisto River.

The South Edisto River is known for producing mainly red drum and flounder. The flounder are most often found in the mouth and up into St. Pierre Creek—the first major tributary upstream of Edisto Beach on the eastern side of the river.

A very good spot for finding red drum or flounder is at the inshore artificial reef that South Carolina fisheries managers have created on the South Edisto. This structure is marked by several mooring buoys in the river, about 1.7 miles upstream from the mouth of St. Pierre Creek.

ZANE JACOBS

*The tidal creeks around Steamboat Landing north of Edisto Beach
offer easy access for fly-casting.*

The best access to the South Edisto River is from the Live Oak Boat Landing, which is not shown on the DeLorme map. This facility is located north off SC 174 at Edisto Beach, via Palmetto Road. The last 0.75 mile of the approach road is unpaved. The single-lane ramp on Big Bay Creek is paved, but the large parking area is not. Once you are on the water, head west on the creek to its mouth on the South Edisto, then turn north for St. Pierre Creek and the artificial reef.

The final possibility for fly-casting in this area is in the town of Edisto Beach. From the point at which SC 174 reaches the shore and turns west, you will find 4 miles of beach to Bay Point at the South Edisto River. There is limited public access and parking along this entire stretch, which is lined with private residences and beach houses. Rock, timber, and concrete groins are found on the beach, with most near the western end. There are, however, a couple on the eastern end near the entrance to Edisto Beach State Park. These make good casting platforms for fishing beyond the breakers during rising tides.

At the western end of the island the beach wraps around into the South Edisto, while the area east of SC 174 (in the state park) has a very steep beach that should provide some action for pompano in the summer months.

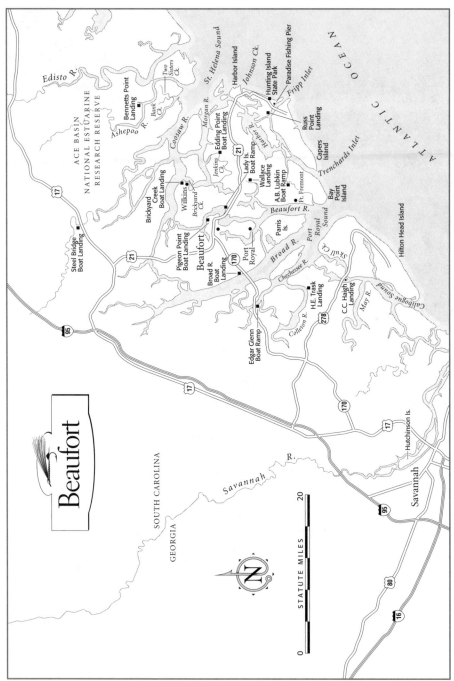

Paul Woodward, © 2000 The Countryman Press

CHAPTER 10

Beaufort

MAPS
DeLorme: *South Carolina Atlas* pages 59, 60, 62, 63
NOAA: chart number 11509

The southernmost portion of the Palmetto State coast spans the area around the city of Beaufort, stretching from Colleton County in the northeast, across Beaufort and Jasper Counties, to end at the Georgia border on the Savannah River in the southwest. Along this shore are the Ace Basin National Estuarine Research Reserve, St. Helena Sound, Hunting Island State Park, Trenchards Inlet, Port Royal Sound, the cities of Beaufort and Port Royal, Hilton Head Island, and Calibogue Sound. The major rivers flowing through the area are the Ashepoo, Coosaw, Morgan, Beaufort, Broad, and May.

Fly-casters venturing onto this portion of the South Carolina coast find red drum and seatrout in the creeks, rivers, and sounds on a year-round basis. Flounder are also found in large numbers in the spring and summer through here. Additionally, this is the part of the Palmetto State shore where tarpon fishing is most available and the pursuit of these huge fish with fly-casting gear has been most popular. The silver kings show up along here in late June and cruise the inlets until the early fall.

Ace Basin

The Ace Basin National Estuarine Research Reserve stretches across a very large expanse of Carolina low country in southwestern Charleston County and southeastern Colleton County. The many marsh islands and tidal streams of the basin that border on St. Helena Sound are the most interesting to saltwater fly-fishermen. As with the rest of the Palmetto State's coastal regions, the best places to target red drum and trout throughout this basin are spots where tidal creeks join and cover submerged oyster beds.

Though such habitat is spread throughout the Ace Basin, the area around Hutchinson Island particularly stands out. This island lies just northeast of St. Helena Sound. It is bounded on the east and south by the Ashepoo River and to the west by Rock Creek. Accessible only by boat, this area's best places to fish require that boat to have a very shallow draft. Bank and Two Sister Creeks, small streams that meander through Hutchinson Island, are shallow and filled with shell beds—and hot spots for channel bass and trout.

One other feature of the Ace area is the presence of striped bass in some of the more inland waterways in the fall and winter. Where the Ashepoo and Combahee Rivers pass under US 17, the bridge pilings are recognized spots for casting for linesiders. One spot less often mentioned is found 12 miles nearer the coast where Secondary State Road 26 crosses the Ashepoo. Locally this spot was referred to for many years as the Brickyard Landing (not to be confused with the official Brickyard Landing at the end of SC 802 north of the city of Beaufort), but its actual designation is the Frank E. Baldwin Jr. Bridge Access. In general terms, the angling for stripers begins at Thanksgiving in all these areas.

The most convenient boating access for Hutchinson Island is the Bennetts Point Landing. This two-lane, paved boat ramp with a dirt parking lot is on Bennetts Point Road off SSR 26. The ramp is on a small creek; once you are in the water, run downstream to the Ashepoo River. Hutchinson Island is directly across the river. Unfortunately, to reach the interior creeks of the island, you must run around to the other side of the island. This is easiest to do by rounding the southern end on the Ashepoo.

For boating access to the striper fishing on the Ashepoo River, there is a narrow, single-lane, paved ramp at the Baldwin Bridge Access, with a small dirt parking lot on site. Besides providing fishing access at the Baldwin

Bridge, this is the jumping-off point for boating up the Ashepoo to the US 17 bridge, although that is a long and winding run on the river.

For fishing the Combahee River bridge on US 17, the ramp to use is the Steel Bridge Boat Landing. This single-lane ramp with a large dirt parking lot is located just upstream of the bridge on the western side of the river and the northern side of the highway.

St. Helena Sound

The major feature of the fishing in St. Helena Sound is the presence of tarpon, which move in each June. These fish often push the 100-pound mark, and though they range all over the sound, the mouth of the inlet is the most dependable place to intercept them.

Because of the sediment load of the water coming out of the rivers, the sound is quite murky. For this reason, targeting the tarpon is difficult. You have to find the fish giving away their position by rolling on the surface to have a chance of a hook-up. They are most active on incoming and high tides around sandbars that are swept by strong currents. The area around the A Buoy is good for this kind of fishing.

Two boat landings offer easy access to St. Helena Sound. The Brickyard Creek Boat Landing is a single-lane, paved ramp with a large parking lot at the village of Wilkins. The facility is on Brickyard Creek Road off Sams Point Road (SC 802), to the north of Beaufort. Once you are on the water, run north out of Brickyard Creek into the Coosaw River. Turn to the southeast and run downriver into St. Helena Sound.

The other option is to launch at the Edding Point Boat Landing on St. Helena Island. This single-lane ramp is paved and has a good parking area. It is located on SSR 74 to the north of US 21. The ramp is on Jenkins Creek. After launching, run north down Jenkins Creek to the Morgan River, then turn southeast for the run to St. Helena Sound.

Hunting Island State Park

Hunting Island State Park has some of the best shore access to fly-casting opportunities found on the southern end of the Palmetto State's coast. The island has been a state-owned playground since 1938, boasting more than 200 campsites, 15 cabins, and a host of other amenities. For fly-casters, the options of wading or casting from shore on the beach, in the inlets, or into

The lagoon in Hunting Island State Park is one of the most heavily fished saltwater locations on the Palmetto State shore.

the Lagoon in the interior of the island are the attractions of this state park. The waters around the park give up red drum, seatrout, and flounder, with bluefish, ladyfish, jack crevalle, and even Spanish mackerel possible on the ocean side.

This 5,000-acre island stretches for 4 miles from Johnson Creek on the northern end to the Story River on Fripp Inlet at the southern shore. The park can be reached by taking US 21 east from the city of Beaufort. The road turns south upon reaching the island and runs down the entire length of its center.

The beachfront on the island is accessible from parking areas within the park. North Beach offers the standard surf-casting possibilities. The beach has enough incline to provide fairly deep water close to shore, unlike barrier island beaches farther south. At the inlet where Johnson Creek enters the Atlantic, a shallow sand flat extends out into the pass. It is possible to wade for several hundred feet out into the inlet at high tide, and even farther during an ebb. Additionally, the beach wraps around into Johnson Creek, offering shore- and wade-fishing opportunities in the stream, too.

On the southern end of the island the beach is eroding, providing a different kind of surf casting. Here the beach is covered with trees that have

ZANE JACOBS

The South Beach of Hunting Island State Park is covered with downed trees that attract game fish on the rising tide.

toppled onto the sand as their roots have become exposed. Tide action has washed out holes around them, which provide good casting targets when the tide has risen enough to cover the trees and depressions in the sand.

It is also possible to access Fripp Inlet by walking down the hard-packed sand beach to the southeastern end of the isle. Here deeper water along the mouth of the Story River is within casting range for several hundred yards. This stretch of beach is noted for giving up some good flounder in the summer.

At the western end of this beach on the river, the Lagoon juts northward into the interior of the island. The bottom is hard sand in the mouth of the Lagoon as well, allowing wading and making it possible to fly-cast all the way across this body of water. This is a good place to intercept channel bass, trout, or flounder leaving the Lagoon during falling tides or staging to enter it just prior to the flood stage. Directly inside the entrance to the Lagoon on its eastern shore a tiny tidal creek enters, surrounded by shell beds. Again, this is a good place for casting. Beyond the creek mouth, the shore becomes marsh grass and the water gets deeper.

The upper end of the Lagoon is accessible from both sides via park roads. The bottom of the Lagoon is covered with a sticky black mud that is firm enough for wading but quite slippery. This body of water receives some of the heaviest shore-fishing pressure on the South Carolina coast. On weekends its banks can be elbow to elbow, with virtually all the anglers being bait-tossers. At low tide a number of mud bars appear out in the Lagoon, particularly toward its southern end. Even at low tide it is possible to run smaller boats up into the Lagoon, though slow and careful navigation is required. In all, the Lagoon runs well over a mile into the heart of Hunting Island. The species most commonly caught here are seatrout, red drum, and whiting.

On the western side of the Lagoon inlet, the Hunting Island–Paradise Fishing Pier juts out at an angle into Fripp Inlet. While it does not offer a fly-casting site, it is worth noting that at 1,120 feet, it is touted as the longest freestanding fishing pier on the Atlantic.

The shores of the Story River inland of the fishing pier are lined with marsh grasses, as are the Harbor River and Johnson Creek to the west of Hunting Island. Where shell beds are present along the banks, red drum and speckled trout are often found.

Boating access to Hunting Island's waters is available at the Russ Point Landing, which is in the state park. Not shown on the DeLorme map, it is found on the Story River inside Fripp Inlet. It can be reached via a rough dirt road running west off US 21 just before the highway crosses the bridge to Fripp Island. The ramp is single lane, with only a small parking area. Once you are on the water, you can run east to the mouth of the Lagoon or turn west to reach the Harbor River and Johnson Creek.

Port Royal Sound

Located south of the cities of Beaufort and Port Royal and to the northeast of the resort island of Hilton Head, the vicinity of Port Royal Sound offers several options for fly-casting. Unfortunately, from Hunting Island south through this area to the Georgia border there are only very limited opportunities for shore or wade fishing for fly-casters. The area is more suited to fly-fishing from a boat.

Slightly to the northeast of the mouth of Port Royal Sound is Trenchards Inlet, between Capers Island to the east and St. Phillips Island on the west. This pass to the ocean is noted for giving up numbers of flounder in the summer as well as holding some trout, red drum, and bluefish. The inlet is wide and deep, so target the shallower, sandy shores for flatfish. The other species are likely to be found around the many secondary creeks entering the inlet.

Boating access to Trenchards Inlet is easiest from the A. B. Lubkin Boat Ramp. While this facility is not on the DeLorme map, it is located at the end of Station Creek Drive, just northwest of the intersection of Seaside Drive (SSR 77) and the Carolina Causeway in the Longwood community on St. Helena Island. It is on the southeastern side of the island, on the waters of Station Creek. A single-lane, paved ramp is provided, along with a paved parking area.

Additionally, there are canals on both sides of the drive as it approaches the ramp. These canals and the area around the ramp provide a couple of hundred yards of casting possibilities. The canal to the northeast of the road originates in a culvert at the edge of the parking lot and holds a lot of bait fish and crustaceans, making it likely to be visited by game fish as well.

Once your boat is launched, head northeast along Station Creek. It then turns east to connect to the northern end of Trenchards Inlet.

In the main body of Port Royal Sound several types of fishing are available, but the most popular are for tarpon in the summer and red drum on a year-round basis. Tarpon are most often found in the sound during rising tides; they cruise the sandbars along the northeastern shore from the tip of Bay Point Island up the Beaufort River to Fort Fremont. Look for these fish rolling in areas of strong current over the bars as the tide rises.

The most convenient boating access to this part of the sound is from the Wallace Landing. It is located at the end of Martin Luther King Jr. Drive (SSR 45) on St. Helena Island in the Fort Fremont community. The single-lane, paved ramp has only limited parking space. Once you are on the water, the tarpon grounds stretch from the ramp south to the mouth of the sound.

Angling for channel bass in Port Royal Sound is dependent both on the tides and on being able to sight the fish. Local fishermen target puppy drum during rising tides, especially in the morning. An added advantage of fishing at this time of day is that the dominant southeast winds, which can make fly-casting difficult, are not as prevalent as in the afternoon. The key to this fishing is sighting the spottails cruising or tailing over shell bars as the tide submerges the oyster beds. Also, the clearer the water, the better since the fish do not bite as well in murky or muddy conditions. The best action comes when the red drum are in $2\frac{1}{2}$ to $3\frac{1}{2}$ feet of water. As the tide rises, it is possible to follow them right up onto the shell beds to the marsh grass line that rings most of the sound.

Specific areas on which to concentrate your efforts are the shores of Parris Island, which holds the U.S. Marine Corps Recruitment Depot, and Daws Island. This latter site is a marsh island and state heritage preserve on the southeastern side of the Broad River between Parris and Hilton Head Islands. The Chechessee River separates Daws from Hilton Head. Simply start at the downriver end of these islands and work your way up the shoreline, moving with the rising tide until you spot some feeding reds.

Similarly, Moss Island Creek behind Bay Point Island at the northern side of the entrance to Port Royal Sound holds channel bass during rising tides. Here it is possible to follow the fish upstream as the tide floods. Another place to find the same kind of conditions is in the Beaufort River, which enters the sound directly from the north. Of particular interest in this stream are the marsh islands and shell mounds on either side of the US 21 bridge over the river in the city of Beaufort.

One final option is to try some casts around the pilings of the SC 170 bridge that spans the Broad River between Lemon and Port Royal Islands at the head of Port Royal Sound. Fishing here is keyed to getting a fly into the water when the tide is moving and schools of bait fish are active. Besides red drum and seatrout, flounder and tarpon are likely to be present in the summer months.

Boating access to the fishing on Port Royal Sound is possible from a number of landings. For the Parris Island shoreline the closest is the Wallace Landing, described earlier in this section. For Daws Island, the H. E. Trask Landing, southwest of Colleton Neck on the Colleton River, is one option. This double-lane, paved ramp has plenty of parking and lies at the end of Sawmill Creek Road (SSR 744) to the north of US 278 as that highway heads to Hilton Head. From the ramp, run north on the Colleton River to its mouth on the Chechessee River beside Daws Island.

Another place to launch for fishing the southeastern side of Daws is up the Chechessee at the SC 170 bridge over this river. The Edgar Glenn Boat Landing has two paved lanes with plenty of parking. Additionally, about 100 yards of packed-sand beach lies between the boat ramp and the pilings of the highway bridge, offering some casting room from shore. Channel bass, trout, and flounder are all likely to be in this area at various times of the year. From the ramp, run downstream on the Chechessee River to reach Daws Island.

A good launch point for fishing around the SC 170 bridge on the Broad River—as well as the northeastern side of Daws Island and southeastern shore of Parris—is the Broad River Boat Landing. This facility is on the

TOM EVANS

The marshes around Hilton Head Island and Port Royal Sound
hold plenty of hungry red drum.

173

northwestern side of the river at the end of the SC 170 bridge. Other than a two-lane boat ramp and parking lot, this site has a fishing pier and about 200 yards of casting room to the northeast from the dock pilings around a tiny point and into the mouth of a small tidal creek. Once you are on the water, Daws and Parris Islands are downstream of the landing.

For fishing the area around the US 21 bridge in downtown Beaufort, the Lady Island Boat Ramp on the southern side of the town is convenient. Although it is not on the DeLorme map, this facility has a four-lane ramp. Parking is limited. The marsh islands and shell beds on the eastern side of the highway bridge are right in front of the landing.

On the northern side of Beaufort is the Pigeon Point Boat Landing. This single-lane, paved ramp is at the end of Pigeon Point Road, off US 21 directly north of town. It does, however, have only very limited parking space for vehicles and trailers. The US 21 bridge is downstream on the Beaufort River from this site.

The final sites around Port Royal Sound that merit coverage are found along the shores of Hilton Head Island's elite resort communities. This island lies just southeast of the mouth of the sound and is bounded on its other end by Calibogue Sound. Although there is some public access to the island's beaches, their very gently sloped shores are not conducive to attracting game fish in close to the sand.

On the other hand, the waters of Port Royal Sound off the island's northwestern end and those of Calibogue Sound, at the opposite end, are both noted for producing tarpon—in many cases very big tarpon. A fish boated, photographed, and released in September of 1998 was measured at 86 inches long with a 44-inch girth, which would put a fair estimate of its weight at more than 200 pounds! A 194-pounder was recorded back in the summer of 1996 as well.

As with most tarpon fishing in South Carolina, however, the murky waters around Hilton Head limit the sight-casting possibilities with fly gear. Still, when the fish are rolling or attacking bait fish on the surface, they become vulnerable. Target them over sandbars during rising tides in June through the first of October off either end of the island.

The other fly-casting option around Hilton Head is for red drum in the tidal creeks and marshes on the inland side of the island. The May and Cooper Rivers, Calibogue Sound, and Skull Creek all have some good areas, with shell-bed concentrations the places to target during rising tides. Some spotted seatrout are likely to be present in these spots, too.

The best boating access to Hilton Head's tarpon fishing on the north-eastern end of the island is from the Wallace Landing at Fort Fremont, which was described earlier in this section. From this landing, run southeast across the mouth of Port Royal Sound to reach Hilton Head.

For fishing Calibogue Sound, the May and Cooper Rivers, or Skull Creek, use the C. C. Haigh Landing. It is located at the US 278 bridge over the Intracoastal Waterway. The site has a paved, double-lane boat ramp with an enormous parking lot.

As you run south from the ramp, Skull Creek enters from the east, then the May River from the west. After you enter Calibogue Sound, the Cooper River confluence is on the western shore.

*Around Savannah, and all along the southeast coast, red drum
more than 27 inches long must be released.*

PART IV
Georgia

O f all the states on the southern Atlantic seaboard, Georgia is probably the least associated with saltwater angling. There are many reasons for the situation, but one of the most obvious is that the Peach State has very little seashore. From the Savannah River on the South Carolina border south to the St. Marys River at the northern rim of Florida, the coastline of Georgia stretches barely 100 miles.

Along the coast there are only four "water" towns or cities—Savannah, Darien, Brunswick, and St. Marys—plus three major island communities on Tybee, St. Simons, and Jekyll Islands. The rest of the coast is made up of a string of barely inhabited barrier islands covered with Spanish-moss-decked live oaks and palmettos, backed by salt marshes filled with spartina grass. This lack of sea access has resulted in Georgia's anglers focusing more on inland fisheries than those on the coast. It also helps that the freshwater fishery consists of 300,000 acres of reservoirs, 200,000 acres of farm ponds, and 16,000 miles of streams and rivers.

On the other hand, while the saltwater fisheries along the Georgia coast may have been overlooked, they are very good. This short stretch actually extends for more than 1,000 miles when measured along the edges of the maze of marshes, islands, creeks, and rivers. The 475,000 acres of salt marsh, which have remained virtually untouched by development, now provide the largest single nursery for shrimp, fish, and other marine life on the East Coast. Finally, the state has never allowed inshore gillnetting, so fish stocks have not been subjected to the drastic depletions that have occurred in other coastal areas.

Of course, such a good thing cannot go unnoticed indefinitely. The Coastal Resources Division of the Georgia Department of Natural Resources estimates that since the late 1980s, the number of saltwater anglers in the state has more than tripled. Yet they very much remain a "visiting or vacationing" population, since 77 percent of the estimated 80,000 anglers reside in inland counties, with most living more than 100 miles from the salt. According to 1996 U.S. Fish and Wildlife Service figures, another 57,000 anglers visit the Peach State coast from other states. In spite of the growth, Georgia still has the smallest saltwater angling population of the states covered in this book.

Fly-casting has also been quite slow to catch on in Georgia's waters. Probably the most important obstacle to the development of fly-fishing interest is the very meager opportunities that exist for wading and sight-casting. A great deal of Georgia's coastal waters are marshes with very soft, mud bottoms, thus wading is difficult to impossible. In fact, even walking along the edge of the water in the spartina grass usually is not practical. If you cannot get to the water, you obviously do not fish!

Georgia's coastal waters, which originate from nutrient-laden marshes and river estuaries, are often murky, adding another difficulty. Sighting fish in such water requires that the fish actually break the surface even to be noticed. Once you do locate fish, you must virtually hit them on the head with a fly to get their attention. All in all, these are not the best circumstances for fly-casting.

Angling Calendar

Having noted all the negatives of fly-fishing the Peach State coast, there are still plenty of opportunities for tangling with predatory species in these waters. As a rule, fishing in Georgia's salt water is best in the fall, when lack of rain makes for clearer water in the estuaries and sounds. The other good fishing period is in the spring and summer, when the number of cooperative species in these waters is highest.

Red drum (often called spottail or channel bass) and spotted seatrout (known locally as speckled trout) offer the most dependable and abundant targets to which you can fly-cast in Georgia waters. Both are present year-round in creeks, rivers, sounds, and along beaches. Small bluefish also show up all year long, but they tend to be more prevalent in the spring as schools of them migrate along the beaches and sounds. Other fish that offer fly-casting possibilities are striped bass, tarpon, ladyfish, Spanish mackerel, and jack crevalle.

In the spring the fishing for red drum, seatrout, bluefish, Spanish mackerel, and striped bass is very good. Stripers, however, are found in very limited portions of the Peach State.

Once the heat of summer arrives, the stripers move up freshwater rivers looking for thermal refuges to wait out the blistering southern summer. This hot weather may drive the stripers inland, but it also heralds the arrival of tarpon, jack crevalle, and ladyfish. The ladyfish congregate in the same locations that attract trout and reds, while tarpon hang around inlets or just off beaches. Jack crevalle are ordinarily found along jetties and in inlet mouths, often in the same places that hold bluefish and Spanish mackerel.

In the fall red drum, trout, and striped bass are again the main fish to target with a fly-rod; indeed, this is the time when all three species offer the best fishing of the year in Georgia. Although bluefish hang around, tarpon, Spanish mackerel, jack crevalle, and ladyfish begin moving south by October.

During the winter months, the fishing slows considerably along the Peach State coast. Weather conditions make angling difficult, especially outside inlets, so what activity there is takes place in sounds, rivers, and creeks. Channel bass and seatrout are the only really dependable species during these months.

State Records

The Georgia state record for red drum stands at 47 pounds, 7 ounces and was taken from the KC Reef by Richard Price in November 1986. The standard for spotted seatrout is 9 pounds, 7 ounces and was caught in Christmas Creek on Cumberland Island. That catch was made by Tommy Hill in July 1976. The largest bluefish recorded in the state was taken in April 1980 from the G Reef by Gary Altman and weighed 17 pounds, 12 ounces. Georgia's largest tarpon was caught in July 1995 by Christopher Edwards while fishing in Buttermilk Sound on the Altamaha River. That fish tipped the scales at 161 pounds.

The largest ladyfish recorded in Georgia was most appropriately caught by a woman. Marjorie Neighbert was fishing near Cumberland Island in August 1978 when she boated the 5-pounder. The record for jack crevalle is 36 pounds and was caught by Byron Williams in Wassaw Sound in June 1996. As for Spanish mackerel, the standard-bearer is an 8-pound, 4-ounce fish hooked in May 1991 by Hal Waters Jr. while fishing 5 miles east of the YS Buoy.

Georgia does not recognize a state record for striped bass in salt water, since this is considered a freshwater species. Still, the state record for the species is 63 pounds. That striper was taken far up the Oconee River near the town of Dublin in May 1967 by Ward Kelly. Because there are no dams downstream of that point on the river system, it is likely that the record fish inhabited the brine at some period of its life.

Regulations

There are special open seasons on a number of saltwater fish species in Georgia, as well as creel and minimum- or maximum-size limits in effect. These, however, are subject to frequent change. To fish in fresh or salt water in Georgia requires a resident or nonresident fishing license. For up-to-date information on the regulations and license requirements, pick up a copy of the current *Georgia Sport Fishing Regulations* booklet wherever fishing licenses are sold in the state, or contact the Georgia Department of Natural Resources, Coastal Resources Division, One Conservation Way, Suite 300, Brunswick, GA 31520-8687.

The Coastal Resources Division also publishes a free publication titled *Angler's Guide to Georgia Saltwater Fishing Access Sites*. This 62-page booklet provides information on and directions to boat ramps, fishing piers, and bank-accessed fishing sites in all of Georgia's coastal counties. A copy can be obtained by mail from the address above.

CHAPTER 11

Savannah

MAPS
DeLorme: *Georgia Atlas* pages 39, 55
NOAA: chart number 11509

The saltwater fishery in the vicinity of Georgia's largest coastal city encompasses all of Chatham County, in which metropolitan Savannah is located. As is the case on most of the Peach State's coast, the shore around its oldest and most historic town is a mixture of river estuaries, sounds, barrier islands, and tidal marshes. These stretch from the Savannah River on the city's northern rim; southward along Tybee, Little Tybee, Wassaw, and Ossabaw Islands; to the Medway River and St. Catherines Sound. Also found within this range are Wassaw and Ossabaw Sounds, plus the Wilmington and Ogeechee River drainages.

The Savannah area offers good seasonal opportunities to encounter all seven species of fish that provide practical targets for fly-rodders in Georgia. It also has a wealth of accommodations, restaurants, marinas, and historic attractions to entertain visiting anglers during the hours not spent on the water.

Savannah River

The Savannah River forms the border between Georgia and South Carolina, as well as the northern boundary of the city of Savannah. Along its lower

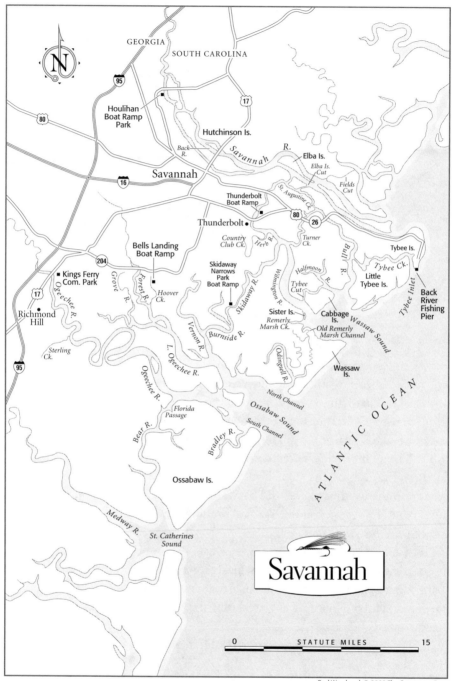

GEORGIA
SOUTH CAROLINA

Houlihan
Boat Ramp
Park

Hutchinson Is.

Back R.

Savannah R.

Elba Is.
Elba Is. Cut

Savannah

St. Augustine Ck.

Fields Cut

Thunderbolt
Boat Ramp

Thunderbolt

Country Club Ck.

Herb R.

Turner Ck.

Tybee Is.

Tybee Ck.

Bells Landing
Boat Ramp

Skidaway
Narrows
Park
Boat Ramp

Halfmoon R.

Bull R.

Little Tybee Is.

Tybee Inlet

Kings Ferry
Com. Park

Grove R.

Forest R.

Hoover Ck.

Skidaway R.

Wilmington R.

Tybee Cut

Back
River
Fishing
Pier

Richmond
Hill

Ogeechee R.

Vernon R.

Burnside R.

Sister Is.
Remerly Marsh Ck.

Cabbage
Is.

Old Remerly Marsh Channel

Wassaw Sound

Sterling Ck.

L. Ogeechee R.

Ogeechee R.

Florida Passage

Bear R.

Bradley R.

Oatland R.

North Channel

Wassaw
Is.

Ossabaw Sound

South Channel

A T L A N T I C   O C E A N

Ossabaw Is.

Medway R.

St. Catherines
Sound

Savannah

0   STATUTE MILES   15

Paul Woodward, © 2000 The Countryman Press

reaches, where it contains salt water, the Savannah is dominated by its shipping channel and port facilities. It does, however, offer a couple of fishing sites of interest to fly-fishers.

The first is on the Back River, a side channel of the Savannah on the northern side of Hutchinson Island. An abandoned tide-gate structure is located on this channel about 1 mile east of the US 17 bridge over the Back River. The gate was built to control silting in the Port of Savannah, but instead destroyed salt marshes and very nearly wiped out the striped bass fishery on the river. A couple of legacies of this tide-gate experiment are the stockings of striped bass that have taken place in the river since the late 1970s, and a ban on harvesting stripers from the river.

Now stripers in the 2- to 10-pound range are taken regularly from around the old gate, as are channel bass of the same size. The standard tactic is to cast streamers to the gate structure. Any other rocky structures, such as jetties and riprap, in this area may hold stripers as well.

The most convenient location for launching a boat near the tide gate is Houlihan Boat Ramp Park. The park is to the north of the city at the eastern end of the Houlihan Bridge (GA 25) over the Savannah River. The park is on the southern side of the highway. The ramp is a double-lane, paved facility with plenty of parking; it is located on the Front River channel of the Savannah. To reach the tide gate, travel downstream through the Rhodes Cut and turn left into the mouth of the Middle River. Proceed around the northern end of Hutchinson Island, then run southwest into the Back River and past the US 17 bridge to the gate.

The other area of the Savannah River noted for producing stripers and red drum is at the mouth of Fields Cut on the northern side of the stream. Fields Cut is located roughly 15 miles downstream from Savannah. The cut is the route of the Intracoastal Waterway (ICW) north from the Savannah to the Wright River. The shores of the Savannah on either side of the mouth of Fields Cut, as well as the first few hundred yards up into the cut, generally hold stripers. Again, any rocky structure you can find may attract fish.

The best jumping-off point for boating to Fields Cut is the F. W. Spencer Community Park Boat Ramp on the Wilmington River. The park has a double-lane, paved ramp with a large parking area. Spencer Park is located just east of downtown Savannah, where the Island Expressway to Tybee Island crosses the river. The park is on the northern side of the highway.

From the ramp, run north up the Wilmington River. Turn right into St. Augustine Creek, then left into the Elba Island Cut. After crossing the South

Channel of the Savannah River, continue through the cut between Elba Island on the west and Long Island to the east. When you reach the main channel of the Savannah, Fields Cut will be directly across the stream. This entire route is on the Intracoastal Waterway, so simply follow the ICW channel markers.

Tybee Island

As is the case all along the Georgia coast, locations where shorebound anglers can reach good fly-casting waters are rare around Savannah. In fact, the only real opportunity is found on Tybee Island (also sometimes known as Savannah Beach). At the southern end of the island the waters of Tybee Inlet and Tybee Creek provide some casting for red drum, bluefish, and seatrout, with added summer opportunities for encounters with Spanish mackerel, ladyfish, and jack crevalle.

About 0.5 mile up the northern shore of Tybee Creek from the inlet mouth is the Back River Fishing Pier, owned and maintained by the Georgia Coastal Resources Division. Although the pier itself offers no fly-fishing possibilities, it does provide an access point for the creek's shore. Wading or casting from shore is possible from the pier to the southern tip of Tybee Island. Besides casting to the pilings of the pier (unless the pier is in heavy use by bait-fishermen), try targeting the many abandoned pilings, groins, shell beds, and old pipes on the flat that extends out to the boat channel. As the tide covers these structures, they attract both bait and game fish. Along here the bottom is gently sloped and composed of hard sand. As you approach the point of Tybee Island, the water in the inlet becomes much deeper very close to shore, but you also find a number of pilings and other debris on the bottom. This entire stretch can be waded and fished—except at high tide, when the water reaches the riprap seawall.

On the actual point of the island the conflicting currents of the creek meeting the surf create a tidal rip, which washes out depressions in the shallow sand flat. There are several stone groins on the beach here as well. As the tide comes in, they are inundated and offer new casting targets. This area usually holds plenty of bait fish and can be waded during all water levels except high tide. In the spring and summer this is a good area to find some bluefish, jack crevalle, or Spanish mackerel in the surf.

If you wade the waters off the point, be aware that the tide comes in quickly; losing track of its progress can leave you stranded on a sand spit with deep water and heavy currents between you and the shore.

*Debris on the flats of the Back River at the south end of Tybee Island provides
a good casting target when the flood tide comes in.*

The rest of the beaches on Tybee can be fished with standard surf tactics. Look for tidal washes or fish chasing bait in the surf, and target these areas. All the species mentioned earlier are possibilities along the island's oceanfront.

Tybee Island can be reached by taking US 80 east from Savannah. Once you are on Tybee, turn right onto Jones Avenue and continue 1.6 miles to Chatham Avenue. Turn right again and travel 0.1 mile to Alley Way 2 on your left. The Back River Fishing Pier is at the end of the alley. There are a number of places to access the oceanfront beaches all along Tybee as well.

Wilmington River

The Wilmington River flows along the eastern edge of the city of Savannah, passing by the suburban fishing village of Thunderbolt. This river is noted for the number of good trout and channel bass drops along its course. These are good spots to fish at any time of year for these species and are likely to hold ladyfish as well in the summer.

The first of these drops are just downstream and to the east of Thunderbolt. They are on the northern side of the river, directly across from the mouth of the Herb River. A series of four small tidal creeks enters the Wilmington along here, and any of them can hold trout or red drum.

Another stretch of good water is located on the Wilmington's tributary, the Herb River, where it makes a sharp U-turn around the southern end of Sullivan Island. From the point where the river turns west to start around the island, speckled trout and spottail bass are often found on the outside of the river bend to midway up the other side of Sullivan Island. From there to the mouth of Country Club Creek on the northern side of the river, trout and reds frequent both shores.

Another Wilmington feeder stream, Turner Creek, can also be a hot spot for red drum or speckled trout. Virtually any outside bend of the stream, as well as its mouth, is likely to hold fish at any time of year. To reach Turner Creek, head downstream on the Wilmington River from Thunderbolt, passing the mouths of the Herb and Skidaway Rivers on the southern shore. The next major feeder stream entering from the northwest is Turner Creek.

The best access to the Wilmington River is from the Thunderbolt Boat Ramp. It is located at the end of Macceo Drive, 0.4 mile north of US 80, just east of that highway's bridge over the Wilmington.

Wassaw Sound

Wassaw Sound is located between Little Tybee Island on the north and Wassaw Island to the south. The waters of the Bull, Halfmoon, and Wilmington Rivers all flow into the sound.

To the northeast of the Wilmington's mouth is Cabbage Island. The waters to concentrate on at this site are along the island's southeastern shore, especially from the mouth of Cabbage Creek to the northeastern corner of the isle at the confluence of the Halfmoon River. The side of the island facing northeast on the Halfmoon has some good spots as well, particularly at the mouth of Tybee Cut. All these drops are productive for seatrout, reds, and ladyfish at various times.

To the southwest of the mouth of the Wilmington, the shore from the northern end of Sister Island, to the mouth of Remerly Marsh Creek, and on to the Salt Pond Shoals area along the northeastern shore of Wassaw Island is loaded with good water for trout and red drum. Through here, the mouth of Old Remerly Marsh Channel and any of the tidal creeks emptying directly into the sound can be especially productive. These two sites can best be reached by boat from the public landing in Thunderbolt, which was described in the previous Wilmington River section.

Little Ogeechee River

Flowing into the northern portion of Ossabaw Sound, the Little Ogeechee River and its feeder streams, the Burnside, Grove, Forest, Moon, and Vernon Rivers, contain opportunities for tangling with a number of fish. Not only does this area hold drops for channel bass, trout, and ladyfish, but striped bass are also present in the spring and fall.

The upper reaches of the Little Ogeechee River in southern Chatham County are the areas that can hold stripers. Rockfish Creek, a tributary of the Little Ogeechee via the Grove River, is especially noted for holding striped bass. It enters the Grove on the southwestern side of Middle Marsh Island. Stripers also show up around Middle Marsh Island in the Grove, as well as in the Forest River on the northwestern side of the island. Also, the northwestern shore—where the two river channels split at the northern end of the island—can hold some fish. In all these sites the mouths of small feeder creeks with moving current are the most productive places to target.

The best spot to launch a boat to fish these portions of the upper Little Ogeechee drainage is the Bells Landing Boat Ramp. This double-lane, paved ramp has ample parking spaces and is located 7.1 miles east of I-95 via GA 204. At Apache Avenue turn south and travel 0.6 mile to the ramp, which sits on Hoover Creek.

Once you are on the water, head south down Hoover Creek to its junction with the Forest River at the midsection of the northwestern side of Middle Marsh Island. Turn either direction to go around the island. Rockfish Creek is the only major creek entering the Grove River on the opposite side of the island.

Farther downstream to the east on the Little Ogeechee drainage are a number of good places to find trout, red drum, and ladyfish. The first is located where the Moon River makes a sharp bend around the western end of Pigeon Island. Several small tidal creeks that enter the river from the southwestern side of the island should be checked out thoroughly. Once you are around the western end of Pigeon Island, shift your focus to the other side of the river, which faces the isle's northwestern shore. Again, the confluences of tidal feeder streams are the places to target.

A good jumping-off point for this area is the Skidaway Narrows Park

Boat Ramp. Skidaway Narrows connects the Skidaway River on the north to the Moon River to the south. To reach Skidaway Narrows Park from I-95, take GA 204 east for 10.4 miles to Montgomery Cross Road. Turn right and travel 1.2 miles to Waters Avenue, then take another right. After 3.9 miles, the park is on your right just before the drawbridge to Skidaway Island. The park has two triple-lane, paved ramps with plenty of parking. From the ramp, travel southwest through the narrows to the Moon River. A right turn into the Moon puts the southwestern shore of Pigeon Island on your right.

Another option for trout and channel bass can be reached by exiting Skidaway Narrows into the Moon, but turning left to enter the Burnside River. The last 0.5 mile of the northern shore of that river, as it approaches Possum Point at its junction with the Vernon River, has several feeder streams that enter the main flow. All are worth checking out, as is the first 0.5 mile of the Vernon's eastern bank to the north of Possum Point.

Ogeechee River

The Ogeechee River runs into the southern end of Ossabaw Sound and, upstream from its junction with the Intracoastal Waterway (at the Florida Passage), forms the boundary between Chatham County on the north and Bryan County to the south.

Of particular interest to fly-casters on the Ogeechee is the stretch of water just downstream of the town of Richmond Hill. From the city limits downstream past Ford Island to the mouth of Sterling Creek on the southwestern side of the river is where striped bass generally show up. The mouths of small feeder streams and outside bends of the river channel hold the most promise. As usual, red drum are likely to be encountered in these locations as well.

It is also worth venturing up Sterling Creek as far as the Ford Plantation, since the fish often are found in this tributary. The plantation overlooking the creek at Sterling Bluff was owned and visited by Henry Ford from 1925 to 1947. It is presently operated as an exclusive resort.

The best launch site for reaching this striper water is at Kings Ferry Community Park on the Chatham County side of the Ogeechee River at the US 17 bridge. This site is upstream of Richmond Hill. The park has a double-lane, paved ramp with a large parking lot. Once you are on the water, Ford Island is a short run downriver.

Ossabaw Sound

Ossabaw Sound is wedged between Wassaw Island on the north and Ossabaw Island to the south. It is fed by the Ogeechee River on the south and the Little Ogeechee River to the north. The waters of the Little Ogeechee flow through Green Island Sound before emptying into Ossabaw Sound.

One area of Ossabaw Sound merits particular attention if you are looking for seatrout or red drum. On the south side of the sound the Bradley River snakes into the interior of Ossabaw Island. The mouths of secondary streams entering the entire length of the Bradley from the marshes offer good fishing for trout and red drum.

Ossabaw Sound also offers a couple of options for finding tarpon in the summer months. The big silver kings can often be seen rolling on the points on either side of the sound's inlet to the ocean.

The first of these tarpon sites is on the southern tip of Wassaw Island. Here the waters of the North Channel of Ossabaw Sound sweep past the point of the island in an area where sandbars in 2 to 6 feet of water drop sharply off into depths of up to 40 feet. The fishing stretches from the mouth of the Odingsell River on the back side of Wassaw around to the beach area on the island's oceanfront.

The other tarpon spot is across the sound to the south, on the northern end of Ossabaw Island. On this end of the island, at Bradley Point, the water is only 1 to 2 feet deep along the beach that faces due east As the shore turns to the northwest along the blunt end of the island, the South Channel of Ossabaw Sound drops swiftly to 20- to 25-foot depths. On the other side of the channel, out in the middle of the sound, the water over submerged sandbars is again only 1 to 2 feet deep. Both the edges and the open waters of the South Channel can hold tarpon in this area.

All of these Ossabaw Sound destinations can be accessed from the Skidaway Narrows Park Boat Ramp, which was described earlier in the Little Ogeechee River section. From the boat ramp, travel south to the Moon River, then run via the Burnside and Vernon Rivers to the Little Ogeechee. Turn east to pass though Green Island Sound and then into Ossabaw Sound.

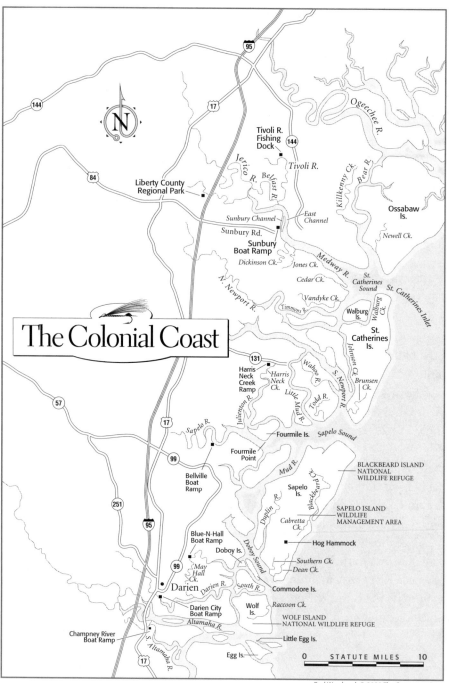

The Colonial Coast

95

144

N

17

144

Tivoli R.
Fishing
Dock

Tivoli R.

Ogeechee R.

Jerico R.

Belfast R.

Killkenny Ck.

Bear R.

84

Liberty County
Regional Park

East
Channel

Ossabaw
Is.

Sunbury Channel

Sunbury Rd.

Sunbury
Boat Ramp

Dickinson Ck.

Jones Ck.

Medway R.

Newell Ck.

St.
Catherines
Sound

St. Catherines Inlet

N. Newport R.

Cedar Ck.

Vandyke Ck.

Timmons R.

Walburg
Is.

Walburg
Ck.

St.
Catherines
Is.

57

131

Harris
Neck
Creek
Ramp

Harris
Neck
Ck.

Wahoo R.

Johnson Ck.

S. Newport R.

Brunsen
Ck.

Julienton R.

Little Mud R.

Todd R.

17

Sapelo R.

Fourmile Is.

Sapelo Sound

99

Fourmile
Point

Mud R.

251

Bellville
Boat
Ramp

Sapelo
Is.

Duplin R.

Blackbeard Ck.

BLACKBEARD ISLAND
NATIONAL
WILDLIFE REFUGE

SAPELO ISLAND
WILDLIFE
MANAGEMENT AREA

95

Blue-N-Hall
Boat Ramp

Doboy Is.

Cabretta
Ck.

Hog Hammock

99

May
Hall
Ck.

Doboy Sound

Southern Ck.

Dean Ck.

Darien

Darien R.

South R.

Commodore Is.

Darien City
Boat Ramp

Wolf
Is.

Raccoon Ck.

Champney River
Boat Ramp

Altamaha R.

WOLF ISLAND
NATIONAL WILDLIFE REFUGE

S. Altamaha R.

Little Egg Is.

17

Egg Is.

0   STATUTE MILES   10

Paul Woodward, © 2000 The Countryman Press

CHAPTER 12

The Colonial Coast

MAPS
DeLorme: *Georgia Atlas* pages 55, 63
NOAA: chart numbers 11502, 11509

The midsection of the Georgia coast is a rather isolated area that defies easy categorizing. The reason for calling it the Colonial Coast is the presence of the now abandoned colonial seaport of Sunbury on the Medway River at its northern end and Darien—another former port city dating from colonial times—on the Altamaha River at the area's southern fringe.

Between these two sites this coast stretches across Bryan, Liberty, and McIntosh Counties, taking in Doboy, Sapelo, and St. Catherine Sounds. The oceanfront is formed, from north to south, by St. Catherines, Blackbeard, Sapelo, and Wolf Islands. None of these isles is connected to the mainland by a bridge or ferry, and all are very sparsely populated. Blackbeard and Wolf Islands are both national wildlife refuges, with U.S. Fish and Wildlife personnel making up the only year-round inhabitants. St. Catherines is privately owned, used for endangered species research, and off limits to most visitors. Much of Sapelo Island is state owned and operated as a wildlife management area, but the small community of Hog Hammock does have a number of year-round residents.

Entwined in and around these sounds and islands is a maze of tidal rivers, creeks, and marshes that stretch from the Bear River on Bryan County's northern border to the Altamaha at McIntosh County's southern edge.

In bygone days Darien was a major seaport and center of the lumber industry, but today activity centers on fishing, shrimping, and tourism. Though the selection is limited, the town offers your best opportunities for accommodations and eateries in the area, as well as some interesting historical sites.

As is true all along the Georgia coast, red drum and trout are the main targets of fly-casters, but striped bass, tarpon, ladyfish, bluefish, jack crevalle and Spanish mackerel are also good possibilities.

St. Catherines Sound

St. Catherines Sound is located between its namesake island on the south and Ossabaw Island to the north. The sound's main feeder rivers are the Bear River, entering on the north from behind Ossabaw; the North Newport River, which joins from the south from behind St. Catherines Island; and the Medway River, emptying from the west. The entire sound is loaded with good spots to find seatrout, red drum, ladyfish, and flounder.

The southern tip of Ossabaw Island on the sound has a shallow shelf with water 3 to 4 feet deep wrapping around it. This shelf extends all the way up the Bear River to the mouth of Newell Creek. The entire shore, plus all of Newell Creek, can hold concentrations of trout and drum.

Across the Bear River, on its southwestern shore, there are a number of other trout and channel bass drops just upstream of the river's mouth onto the sound. The area to concentrate on is from the first marsh creek entering that side of the river upstream to the mouth of Kilkenny Creek. The mouths of the feeders and any shell beds along the shore are the places to target.

On the southern side of St. Catherines Sound you will find an area that holds a vast number of likely spots to tangle with red drum or seatrout, along with flounder and ladyfish in the summer. Where the North Newport River enters the sound from the south, its eastern side is dotted with shell bars that can hold fish, as do both ends of Walburg Creek (which flows around Walburg Island) and the northern outlet of Johnson Creek. In this same area the western shore of the North Newport is entered by Cedar and Vandyke Creeks, plus the Timmons River. The points on either side of all these tributary mouths, as well as any secondary feeders entering them, also are places to check out. Just hitting all the likely-looking spots in this area can provide multiple days of angling challenge.

If tangling with a tarpon is your goal, the main channel of St. Catherines Sound deserves some attention. At the mouth of the Medway River, the deepest water (35 to 40 feet) sweeps along the southern shore and across the mouth of the North Newport River. The spot where this deep channel meets the shallows of the Medway Spit out in the middle of the stream is where the tarpon generally patrol. Here the water drops off quickly from 2 feet on top of the spit to 6 feet or more. This fishing area extends to just inside the inlet's mouth.

Located on the outside of the inlet is a deeper hole about 0.5 to 1 mile wide that runs more than 3 miles offshore. This water is up to 40 feet deep and completely surrounded by depths of only 6 to 10 feet. Tarpon may be found rolling on the surface anywhere in this area but often favor moving along the contoured edges of the hole.

The nearest public boat-launch facility for all these St. Catherines Sound locations is on the Medway River at the Sunbury Boat Ramp. Located in Liberty County, the ramp is at the site of the once-thriving port of Sunbury, which today is just a ghost of its colonial glory. Only the remains of the Revolutionary War–era Fort Morris hint at the area's past importance.

The launch facility has one double-lane, paved boat ramp with plenty of space for parking vehicles. To reach the site, take GA 38 east from I-95 for 4.5 miles to Fort Morris Road. After a left turn, proceed 3 miles to Stevens Road and turn right. After 0.3 mile, the ramp is at the end of the road on the Medway River.

Once you are on the water, you have a run of approximately 6.5 miles down the Medway to St. Catherines Sound. Bear in mind that both the inshore and ocean sides of St. Catherines Inlet are big, open-water areas. Having the proper-sized and -styled boat is necessary to fish this area.

Medway River

The Medway River is the largest of the three that feed into St. Catherines Sound and offers some interesting fishing situations of its own. There are a number of trout and red drum drops on the main river, just downstream of Sunbury. Immediately downstream of the old town site, at the end of the marsh island that separates the Sunbury Channel from the East Channel of the Medway, the river begins bending to the east. This outside bend is worth inspecting, including the mouths of Dickinson and Jones Creeks. There are also several small marsh islands directly across the river in the mouth of Demeries Creek. The multiple outlets these create often hold fish as well.

As mentioned earlier, this part of the Georgia coast is the most inacces-

*The estuaries along the central part of the Georgia coast
are nurseries for hordes of small channel bass.*

sible stretch. One result of this situation is a lack of access sites where shore-bound anglers can reach any major fly-fishing spots. There are, however, two locations in the Medway River drainage worth checking if you are already nearby. On the other hand, neither merits making a trip of any appreciable distance to sample the fishing.

The first of these is the Tivoli River Fishing Docks in Bryan County. The Tivoli is a feeder stream that joins the Belfast River just at the point where they both dump into the northern side of the Medway River.

These two docks merit mention because they are on either side of the Belfast-Keller Road bridge over the Tivoli and both are low to the water; each has low handrails. Thus you can fly-cast from either dock to the pilings of the highway bridge. Also, since the stream is relatively small, you can cast to a fairly wide area of the marsh shores. This is a location in which to target channel bass and speckled trout. The downside of the fishing docks is that it does not take many bait-fishermen with lines out to make them crowded sites for fly-casting.

To reach the Tivoli River Fishing Docks, exit I-95 to the east on GA 144 near the town of Richmond Hill. Drive 10 miles to the intersection with Belfast-Keller Road and turn right. After 2 miles, the road crosses the Tivoli River. The parking area for the docks is on the left side of the road, just before it crosses the bridge.

The second shore access point is located at the Liberty County Regional

Park Boat Ramp (signs at the site identify the park as the Jones Creek Recreation Area). The park has a very narrow and rough boat ramp that is suitable only for small-boat or canoe launching. On either side of the ramp the shore is clear enough for fly-casting for a few hundred feet. The water in front of the ramp is on a lagoon off a bend in Jones Creek, which eventually feeds into the Medway via the Jerico River. The park has plenty of room to accommodate parked vehicles, along with picnic areas on the water. The site is excellent for launching a johnboat or canoe for fishing this portion of Jones Creek. Again, trout and red drum are the species on which to key.

Access to the park from I-95 is easiest by taking GA 38 west for 1.5 miles to Isle of Wight Road. Turn right and go 2 miles. The park entrance is on your right just before you cross the bridge over Jones Creek.

St. Catherines Island

A couple of angling sites on St. Catherines Island are usually worth the effort to reach. The first is McQueen Inlet, at the mouth of Cracker Tom Creek, halfway down the ocean side of St. Catherines Island. The inlet separates the island's middle and southern beaches. Just to the southwest of the inlet and 1,000 yards offshore, the water drops abruptly from about 1 or 2 feet down to 7- to 9-foot depths. The edge of this flat is especially noted as a good place to intercept feeding tarpon. On the other hand, as is true with most of the secondary inlets on the barrier islands, it is not unusual to find trout, red drum, Spanish mackerel, bluefish, ladyfish, or flounder also hanging around the area.

The Sunbury Boat Ramp described in the St. Catherines Sound section is also the best jumping-off point for fishing McQueen Inlet. Once you are out of the mouth of St. Catherines Sound, head south about 6 miles to the inlet.

The very southern tip of St. Catherines Island also has a number of drops along its shore for trout and red drum, as well as some opportunities for encountering tarpon. The last 2 miles of the island's beachfront and the shore wrapping around its southern end to just past the mouth of Brunsen Creek are good places to look for tarpon. Through here there is a series of sandbars in 7 to 9 feet of water, alternating with troughs that drop to 15 to 20 feet. The current sweeping in and out of the South Newport River with the changing tides washes over this area, while clashing with the surf to create breakers.

For trout and spottail bass, there are a number of good drops along the southern coast of St. Catherines Island. Beginning at the extreme tip of the island and moving to the northwest along the shore, you will encounter a couple of small tidal cuts as well as the mouth of Brunsen Creek. These outlets should be targeted all the way up to the southern confluence of Johnson Creek.

The most convenient boat-launch facility for the southern end of St. Catherines Island is found at the Harris Neck National Wildlife Refuge. There are two launch sites in the refuge, but the Barbour River Landing is the one to use. To reach this landing from I-95, go south on US 17. After 1 mile turn turn left onto GA 131 (Harris Neck Road). Travel 7.1 miles to the end of the road and turn left into the Harris Neck National Wildlife Refuge on Barbour Landing Road. After 0.5 mile the parking lot and a steep, single-lane, paved ramp are on the right side of the road. Unfortunately, this ramp is closed during the wood stork breeding season from March 1 through August 31 each year.

Although the Harris Neck Creek Ramp is nearby as the crow flies, it is not a very good alternate launch site. Its location on Harris Neck Creek, which empties into the Sapelo River via the Julienton River, makes for a long and twisting course down to St. Catherines. A better alternate launch point for the spring and summer months is the Bellville Boat Ramp. To locate this single-lane, paved ramp, take GA 99 east from I-95 for 5 miles to Bellville Road, then turn north (left). After 1.6 miles, turn left into the ramp's driveway.

The ramp is positioned on the Sapelo River, so traveling downstream to the east leads to Sapelo Sound and the southern end of St. Catherines Island. It is roughly a 12-mile run down the Sapelo River to the sound.

Sapelo Sound

Sapelo Sound is located between the southern end of St. Catherines Island and the northern tip of Sapelo Island. It is fed by three rivers—the South Newport entering from the north, the Sapelo from the west, and the Mud River from the south. The sound holds possibilities for catching trout and red drum year-round, as well as tarpon, ladyfish, and flounder in the summer months.

Of special note on the northern side of the sound is the shallow submerged bar extending between the channel of the Intracoastal Waterway (coming through Johnson Creek) on the east and the channel of the South Newport River on the west. This spot is noted for producing reds during all tidal stages, with the fish likely to turn up on either side of the bar or even on top of it.

To the west of this site is a long stretch of the northern shore of Sapelo

Sound that holds a large number of trout and redfish drops. Beginning up in the South Newport River at the mouth of the Wahoo River and continuing west, the Todd, Barbour (also called the Swain River on some maps), Little Mud, and Julienton Rivers enter this side of the sound before you reach Four Mile Point on the southern tip of Four Mile Island. The points on both sides of all these confluences can hold fish, as can the secondary tidal streams entering from Four Mile Island. The best spots have oyster beds along the marsh.

Across Sapelo Sound to the south is an area noted for its red drum fishing. All along the stretch from the northern tip of Blackbeard Island to the point that Blackbeard Creek (which separates Blackbeard from Sapelo Island) emerges from the marsh, the creek channel hugs the shore and is 7 to 8 feet deep. On the northwestern side of the channel there is a shallow flat covered with only 1 to 3 feet of water. The island-side shore of the channel ordinarily holds the fish, but drum are prone to move up onto the flat during high tides.

In this same vicinity, at the very northern tip of Blackbeard Island the water is up to 45 feet deep right along the shore and carries the current coming out the Sapelo River. This area often holds tarpon during the summer months and is worth a look if you are targeting the silver kings.

To access this area, use the Barbour River Landing in the fall and winter (it is closed during the warmer months) or the Bellville Boat Ramp. Both of these ramps were previously described in the St. Catherines Island section. From the Barbour River Landing, simply run south on the stream until it empties into Sapelo Sound. From the Bellville ramp, travel east on the Sapelo River to just past the mouth of the Broad River on the northern shore. Four Mile Point is immediately east of the Broad River.

Sapelo Island

Another spot for some possible tarpon action is Cabretta Inlet between Blackbeard and Sapelo Islands. This small inlet is approximately 6 miles south of Sapelo Sound. Here the tarpon sometimes congregate on a 4- to 5-foot-deep flat in front of and on both sides of the inlet. Additionally, the fish move up into both Cabretta Creek (to the south) and Blackbeard Creek (to the north) inside the inlet. It is not uncommon to run into schools of trout, red drum, flounder, or ladyfish inside the inlet, while bluefish and Spanish mackerel are possibilities outside.

This inlet can also be reached by launching at the Barbour River Landing or Bellville Boat Ramp, as described in the St. Catherines Island section. A run along Blackbeard Island's oceanfront is required to reach this area from Sapelo Sound, so a seaworthy boat is necessary.

Doboy Sound

Doboy Sound lies between Sapelo Island's southern shore and the northern tip of Wolf Island. The Carnigan River enters the sound from the northwest, while the Darien River breaks up into the North, Back, and South Rivers as it enters the sound from the west around Commodore and Doboy Islands. Both sides of the sound offer some good fly-casting possibilities.

On the northern shore of the sound, the spots to check out for trout and red drum are the mouths of Dean and South End Creeks, as well as the smaller unnamed tidal flows entering the sound from Sapelo Island. These extend all the way up to the mouth of the Duplin River.

On the southern side, target the mouths of Raccoon Creek and the South River on Wolf Island. Farther up the sound the mouths of the Back and North Rivers around Doboy and Commodore Islands offer more possibilities for trout and channel bass.

To reach the Doboy Sound drops, use the public landing at the Blue-N-Hall Boat Ramp. From I-95, follow GA 251 for 1.2 miles east to US 17. Turn south and travel 1 mile to the GA 99 intersection. Turn left and continue 4.5 miles to the sign for the boat landing. Make a right turn; the ramp is at the end of the road.

Once you are out of the creek on which the ramp is located, run south to the North River. Turn east, and that stream enters the sound at Doboy and Commodore Islands.

Darien River

The waters of the Darien River and its tributaries near the town of Darien in southern McIntosh County hold several sites noted for producing red drum and, on occasion, striped bass. Specifically, there are two creeks—both of which enter the Darien River on the northern side—just downstream from town. The first of these is Black Island Creek. Reds and stripers are ordinarily found around its mouth, as well as back in the creek to upstream of the early colonial historic site at Fort King George.

JIMMY JACOBS

The waterfront in the village of Darien is a good launch point for finding channel bass and striped bass in the Darien River.

Farther to the east, past the area of the Darien River known as Long Reach, May Hall Creek enters the flow from the north. Fishing around its mouth or at the first big bend where this creek turns sharply north can produce some striper and channel bass action.

The best access point for both these sites is the Darien City Boat Ramp on the town's waterfront, just off US 17. This is a single-lane, paved ramp, but it does not have a very big parking area. Across the drive from the ramp are some old tabby walls (a building material composed of shell, lime, sand, and water, used extensively in colonial times in Georgia). These are the remains of warehouses that were burned in 1863 by the 54th Massachusetts Infantry, which was featured in the motion picture *Glory*. From the city dock, the creek runs downstream to Black Island and May Hall Creeks, which are 1.5 and 4 miles, respectively.

Altamaha River

Besides being the largest river emptying into the Atlantic Ocean along Georgia's coast, the Altamaha also provides fly-casters some of this coast's best and most varied fishing possibilities. Not only does it have trout and channel bass drops, but it is also noted for some of the most dependable

JIMMY JACOBS

*The Two Way Fish Camp on the lower Altamaha River lies
at the heart of the best tarpon waters on the Georgia Coast.*

tarpon fishing on the Peach State coast, plus the possibility of tangling with striped bass a bit farther inland.

The area for tarpon fishing in the Altamaha is a good one—and a big one! The entire course of the river, from Altamaha Sound upstream to the mouth of the Butler River above Rabbit Island, can hold fish. This upstream point is directly south of the town of Darien and a full 10 miles from the ocean. Along this course the river's several channels spread out to almost 2 miles at their widest point.

Midway along this course the southern side of the Altamaha is bordered by Buttermilk Sound, which connects the river's main channel with the South Altamaha River. It was near the northern end of Buttermilk Sound that Christopher Edwards boated his state-record tarpon back in 1995. This fish tipped the scales at 161 pounds.

Still, the most consistent tarpon action is likely to be found at the very mouth of the river, just outside the inlet at Altamaha Sound. A couple of hundred yards out, very shallow flats give way to 4- to 6-foot depths. This break line often attracts feeding tarpon.

There is an exceptional drop for spottail bass located at the mouth of the Altamaha as well. This site, between Egg and Little Egg Islands—both of which are part of the Wolf Island National Wildlife Refuge—is noted for producing big red drum in the 20- to 30-pound range. The deeper channels between Wolf, Egg, and Little Egg hold fish most of the time, but the oyster mounds between Egg and Little Egg attract red drum into shallower water where fly-casters can get to them. All three of these islands lie on the southern side of the river.

Farther up the river, around the US 17 bridges over the Altamaha and the South Altamaha are some places to try for striped bass in the spring and fall. As usual with these fish, target spots where you find rocks or other structures such as pilings in the water. Dent Creek, which is the first downstream tributary of the South Altamaha on its southern shore, is another place to look for striped bass.

The best place for launching a boat to fish the Altamaha or South Altamaha is the Champney River Boat Ramp. To reach this site, take GA 251 south from I-95. After 1.2 miles, turn south onto US 17 and proceed 3.3 miles to the Champney River Bridge. The parking area for the ramp is on your left, just across the bridge.

Once your boat is in the water, run eastward downstream to where the Butler River enters from the north. The tarpon ground continues from this point all the way to the Atlantic Ocean.

To reach the South Altamaha and Dent Creek, run downstream and turn south into the Wood Cut. This cut enters the South Altamaha just below the US 17 bridge. Turn east into the river to reach the mouth of Dent Creek.

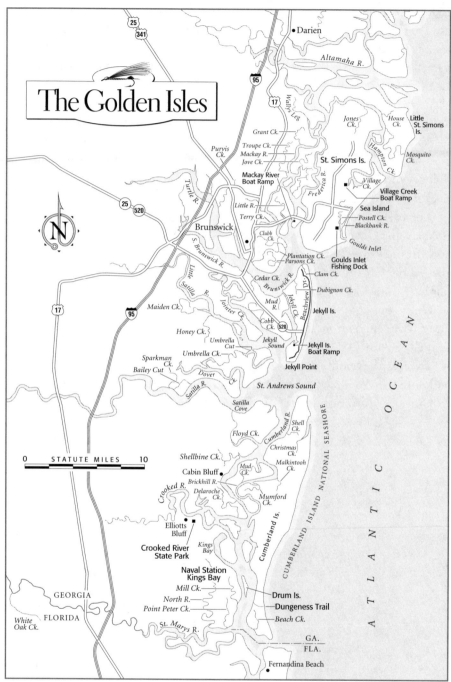

The Golden Isles

CHAPTER 13

The Golden Isles

MAPS
DeLorme: *Georgia Atlas* pages 63, 71
NOAA: chart number 11502

The Golden Isles along Georgia's southernmost coast have drawn visitors for hundreds of years. As early as the 16th century, Spanish missions were founded on the barrier islands, followed by English settlements in the 1700s. In the late 19th century this was the playground of America's wealthiest tycoons. Then, after World War II, these isles began attracting the vacationing masses. The resorts, history, and island life of St. Simons; the luxury of Sea Island; the parklike beaches and golf courses on Jekyll Island; the wilderness and national seashore of Cumberland Island; and the industry and artist colonies of the city of Brunswick continue to call visitors to this coast.

Of course, many visitors have found time to drop a line into the waters around the Golden Isles, but fishing has in general been something you did while on the coast, rather than a reason for going there. Although this is to some extent changing, the saltwater fishing—and fly-fishing in particular—along this stretch of shore remains largely undiscovered.

Bounded on the north by the mouth of the Altamaha River, the area of the Golden Isles spans Glynn and Camden Counties, covering Little St. Simons, St. Simons, Sea, Jekyll, Little Cumberland, and Cumberland Islands before ending at the quaint and historic town of St. Marys on the Florida border. Also found on this shore are the island town of St. Simons Island and the U.S. Navy's massive Kings Bay Nuclear Submarine Base. St. Simons, St. Andrews, and Cumberland Sounds provide the outlets that release the waters of the Satilla and St. Marys Rivers to the sea.

Little St. Simons and Little Cumberland Islands are both privately owned, with no public access or roads connecting them to the mainland, although the former is managed as an exclusive vacation hideaway. Sea Island is also private but has a causeway and is home to the Cloister, an exclusive (and expensive) resort complex open to the public. St. Simons Island is basically a residential area connected to the mainland by the Torras Causeway (a toll road), but it does have commercial and resort areas, along with public beaches. Jekyll Island has private residences and a causeway but is mostly publicly owned; it is managed as a park by a state authority, and a parking fee is charged for each vehicle coming onto the island. Finally, Cumberland Island makes up the Cumberland Island National Seashore, and though it is not connected by road to the mainland, the National Park Service runs regular shuttle ferries to the island.

Since the Golden Isles provide the best access to Georgia's barrier islands and beaches, it is not surprising that this part of the coast also offers the best access for shorebound anglers. This is especially true on St. Simons and Jekyll Islands, but also to a lesser extent on Cumberland Island and in the vicinity of St. Marys.

Hampton River

The Hampton River is the flow that separates Sea and St. Simons Islands from Little St. Simons Island, which lies to their north. Along its course from the Mackay River on the west to its mouth on the Atlantic Ocean, the Hampton has more trout and redfish drops than any comparably sized stretch of water in the Golden Isles region. This is particularly true of the portion of the river lying to the east of the mouth of Jones Creek. Through this area the mouths of House, Mosquito, and Village Creeks all offer good fishing sites, as do most of the other smaller nameless secondary tributaries entering the Hampton River. It is also worth exploring the secondary stream mouths that empty into the lower portion of Village Creek. These drops continue eastward on the Hampton to the northern tip of Sea Island, where the river joins the ocean. As always, when you are targeting reds and trout, look for shell beds for the most consistent action.

The most convenient public boat-launch facility for the Hampton River is at the Village Creek Boat Ramp. This single-lane, paved ramp is situated on a small tributary of Village Creek. The water in this feeder stream can be quite shallow at the ramp during low tides, so use caution.

To reach the Village Creek Boat Ramp, take the Torras Causeway to St. Simons Island, then turn left onto Sea Island Road and go 3.1 miles to its intersection with Frederica Road. Turn left again and proceed 1.7 miles to Harrington Drive. Make a right turn and go 1 mile to the end of the road. The ramp is located on the right side of Harrington Road.

Once you are on Village Creek, run north to the point at which it makes a sharp turn to the east. From this bend downstream to the Hampton River is where to find the creek's fishing hot spots. Where Village Creek joins the Hampton River, turn left and run upstream for most of this river's fishing drops.

Mackay River

The Mackay River is the main stream that separates St. Simons Island from the Georgia mainland. Though this section bears the stream's name, very few of the fishing drops mentioned are actually on the river. Rather, it is the headwaters of a number of tributaries that hold the fish, with the common denominator being that they all flow into the Mackay. In fact, the two spots on the main river that merit mention are at its junction on the north with the Frederica River and on the south where the Back River splits off the Mackay. The points formed at both locations are worth exploring for spotted seatrout.

Between these two locations, the Mackay is fed by four streams that provide a number of good fishing sites. In each case these drops are found in the upper end of the creeks, where they begin to break up into a number of secondary channels. The mouths of these feeders generally hold trout and channel bass.

The first of these creeks is Wallys Leg, which empties into the Mackay from the west at the point where the Frederica River branches off the eastern side of the main river. Farther south, Grant Creek enters the Mackay from the west as well, providing more angling options. Finally, at the point where the Back River splits off the Mackay, Troupe Creek enters from the west, while Jove Creek's mouth is on the eastern shore. Both of these creeks also provide good drops in their headwaters.

The best public landing for accessing the fishing along the Mackay River is the Mackay River Boat Ramp. This double-lane, paved ramp with its large parking lot is positioned on the river at the Mackay River Bridge on the Torras Causeway. The drive for the ramp is located 0.3 mile east of the bridge, on the southern side of the highway. Once you are in the boat, head north up the Mackay River to its junctions with Troupe Creek, Jove Creek, and the Back River.

St. Simons Island

St. Simons Island lies northeast of the city of Brunswick and is tied to the mainland by the Torras Causeway. A great deal of the northern and western portions of the island are in private hands and offer little access to the water. On the other hand, the oceanside beaches do provide some opportunities for anglers to reach saltwater fish from the bank, even with a fly-rod.

There is one very good area on St. Simons where shorebound anglers can get to some productive fishing water, plus a couple of others that offer lesser options for casting to fish. The best access for wading fly-casters on this island is found at Goulds Inlet, where Postell Creek and the Blackbank River empty into the pass separating St. Simons from Sea Island.

During lower tide levels the St. Simons Island's shore on the southern side of Goulds Inlet is made up of a deep channel that drops quickly to 6 to 7 feet of water right at the beach. In the breakers at the mouth of this channel, however, the water is only 1 to 2 feet deep, making it possible to wade across easily. Beyond the channel is a hard-sand flat that becomes completely dry at ebb tide. A couple of other smaller, shifting channels also cut through this bar. The result is a patchwork of tidal washouts and channels that can all be fished by wading anglers.

Farther back into the inlet, the St. Simons shore is lined by a riprap wall composed of large stones. At the western end of this wall the Goulds Inlet Fishing Dock runs out into a deeper basin. Although the pier itself is not conducive to fly-casting, it is possible to fish around the dock pilings from the shore. Also, if you proceed carefully it is practical to fish from the riprap during all tide levels. Just remember to watch where you plant your feet, especially when the rocks are wet at times of higher tidal flows. During lower tides you can wade around almost the entire edge of the basin, casting from virtually any direction.

Expect to share the basin in front of the dock with some boating anglers, even at low tide. Because of the shallow water in the mouth of the inlet, these boats come through the Blackbank River from the island's inland side. What draws them to the area is the frequent presence of red drum, spotted seatrout, and flounder. In the summer tarpon may also show up here. A former state-record tarpon was taken back in 1986 just off Goulds Inlet by Wendy Mead. It tipped the scales at 139 pounds!

Another area to keep an eye on at Goulds Inlet is the crosscurrents of the tidal rip at the mouth of the southern channel. Again, lower tide levels are probably most promising for fishing this area. In the spring and fall smaller bluefish are a possibility in this turbulent water.

To reach the Goulds Inlet Fishing Dock parking lot and access to the inlet, take the Torras Causeway from Brunswick to St. Simons Island. After 4.4 miles, turn right onto New Sea Island Drive. Proceed 0.2 mile and turn left onto Kings Way Drive. Continue 3.8 miles on this street, which will change names to Ocean Boulevard along the way. At First Street, turn right and go another 0.1 mile to Bruce Drive. Turn left onto Bruce Drive, then travel another 0.7 mile to the end of the road and the dock parking area.

On St. Simons it is also possible to fly-cast to some deeper water near the St. Simons Island Pier in the heart of the old business district. During all but high tide levels a sandy, hard-packed beach is exposed in front of the riprap seawall on both sides of the fishing pier. This beach extends for more than a mile on the northern side of the structure. Since the pier sits on the southern end of the island on St. Simons Sound, the Brunswick shipping channel comes close to shore, with water depths of 20 to 60 feet. A number of species of fish are likely to emerge from these depths up onto the narrow shelf of beach along here.

To reach the St. Simons Island Pier, take the Torras Causeway to the island. After 4.4 miles, turn left onto New Sea Island Drive. Then, at 0.2 mile, make a right turn onto King's Way Drive. Go another 2.2 miles to Mallory Street and turn right. The pier and parking lot are at the end of this road.

The final possibility for some shorebound fly-casting on St. Simons Island is found along the Blackbank River. Where the river is running parallel to and on the northern side of the Sea Island Causeway (Sea Island Road), it can be reached from the shore. Still, access is not particularly easy here. You have to walk across a sand and marsh grass flat to get to the river from the causeway, but paths made by fishermen are fairly easily seen toward the western end of the causeway. Wearing boots is a good idea when tackling this site, and it is advisable to watch your step. Footing can be slippery, and encountering soft mud is a possibility all along this stretch. Again, seatrout and red drum are the species most likely to be hooked.

To reach this part of the Blackbank River, take the Torras Causeway for 4.4 miles to Sea Island Road and turn left. Stay on this road until it becomes a causeway headed to Sea Island. The river is on the northern side of the road.

St. Simons Sound

St. Simons Sound is located at the southern end of St. Simons Island, to the north of Jekyll Island, and carries the main shipping channel leading to the Port of Brunswick. For this reason, it holds a lot of deeper water, plus plenty of ship and boat traffic. The sound is fed from the north by the Back, Mackay, and Frederica Rivers, while the Brunswick River enters from the west.

From the standpoint of fishing, the sound can be broken down into northern and southern halves. The northern half of the fishing water is made up of the marsh grass and shell bed points formed between the mouths of the Back and Mackay Rivers, plus the points on either side of the mouth of Plantation Creek to the south of these rivers' juncture. Expect to encounter trout and spottail bass at these points, with flounder and ladyfish present in the summer as well. Also, it is worth checking out the Back River up to the point formed where the Little River joins it from the east. Fishing back up into Plantation Creek to the cut where it opens onto Clubb Creek can be productive, too.

Although the southern portion of St. Simons Sound has some good trout and channel bass drops at the mouth of Parsons Creek (on the northern shore) and at the mouths of the Mud River and Cedar and Dubignon Creeks (on the southern side), the rest of the story on this side of the sound, unfortunately, is not a good one.

The Coastal Resources and Environmental Protection Divisions of the Georgia Department of Natural Resources (DNR) have issued several fish consumption advisories for the Turtle River and Terry Creek drainages, which feed the Brunswick River and affect part of the sound. In the case of the Turtle River these are based on the presence of polychlorinated biphenyls (PCBs) and mercury found in some samples of fish taken in the watershed. The now banned PCBs are the residue of industrial activities in the 1950s and 1960s. They will eventually disappear from the environment here, but the process takes many decades. The mercury can be attributed to industrial activity in many cases, too, but it is also found naturally in the environment.

JIMMY JACOBS

*The mouth of Jekyll Island's Clam Creek is a good spot
for casting on a falling tide.*

It is thus more difficult to filter out of the ecosystem.

Be aware, however, that these warnings are based on a 150-pound person consuming 4 to 8 ounces of the affected fish species for a period of 30 years. Such a diet would make that individual a 1 in 10,000 risk for health problems. The guidelines are obviously quite conservative, and the Georgia DNR states that they are, in most cases, not designed to discourage anglers from eating their catch.

It is recommended that no seafood be consumed that is taken from either Purvis or Gibson Creeks. Both feed into the Turtle River near the GA 303 bridge in Brunswick. Upriver of this bridge it is recommended that no more than one meal per week of red drum, flounder, or blue crab be consumed. Also, no more than one meal per month of spotted seatrout or croaker is advised. Finally, no clams, mussels, oysters, or black drum from this vicinity should be eaten.

From the GA 303 bridge downstream to Channel Marker 9 at the mouth of the South Brunswick River, only one meal per week of flounder is recommended, while red and black drum, spotted seatrout, croaker, and blue crab should be limited to one meal per month. Again, no shellfish from this area should be eaten.

From Channel Marker 9 downriver to the mouths of Parsons and Dubignon Creeks, the advisories recommend eating no more than one meal per week of croaker and blue crab, while black drum and spotted seatrout should be limited to once per month. No shellfish from this stretch of river should be eaten.

On Terry Creek the warnings are prompted by the presence of toxaphene and the disturbance of contaminated sediments that have resulted from ongoing cleanup operations. To the south of the Torras Causeway, consumption of yellowtail (silver perch) should be limited to one meal per week, while clams, mussels, and oysters should be avoided altogether. To the north of the causeway in Terry and Dupree Creeks, no fishing or swimming at all is advisable due to the cleanup.

For updated information on fish consumption advisories in Georgia, pick up a copy of the current *Georgia Sport Fishing Regulations,* available wherever fishing licenses are sold.

Jekyll Island

Jekyll Island lies to the south of St. Simons Island and is the most accessible of the barrier islands on the Peach State coast. As mentioned earlier, much of this isle is publicly owned and managed by an authority through the Georgia Department of Natural Resources. As a result, the entire Jekyll beachfront is available to anglers, but the water is quite shallow all along it. Surf action is generally light, and the bottom is made up of gently sloping, hard-packed sand. This makes for easy wading and casting, but difficulty in identifying fish-holding areas.

There are several other areas on the island, however, that offer better prospects for fly-casters. The first of these is at the northern end of Jekyll. The Jekyll Island Pier extends out to the deep water of the shipping channel in St. Simons Sound. While the pier offers no fly-fishing possibilities, the riprap under it and extending along the shore to the west can be fished. Depths of up to 17 or 18 feet are found quite close to this bank.

To the east of the pier is an even more interesting situation. A shallow mud flat extends from the pier to the mouth of Clam Creek, a distance of about 200 yards. At low tide this area it is practically dry, but it is covered by a couple of feet of water at flood tide. Though too soft to wade, a bicycle trail runs along it, offering easy shore access. The trail crosses a bridge over the mouth of Clam Creek, allowing access to the other side of the stream as well. On this eastern side of the creek a sand beach (with some mucky spots) provides a good casting location for working the bridge pilings and the mouth

JIMMY JACOBS

The public boat ramp and adjacent beach on a small tidal creek on Jekyll Island are good places to cast on a falling tide.

of the stream. This is a particularly good area to try on the last half of the falling tide, as the water flushes from the marsh to the south. The current from the creek sweeps around the end of the point on this side of the creek, and during lower tide levels it is possible to cast very close to the fishing pier.

Another option is to fish back up into Clam Creek for a short way by walking up a very lightly used trail at the edge of the stream's western side. The trail is quite muddy and, at especially high tide, may be under a couple of inches of water. Additionally, the road that runs out to the fishing pier has a couple of picnic areas along it positioned on bends in Clam Creek. Each of these offers a short stretch of stream that can be fished from the bank, assuming you can keep your casts low and under the live oak branches.

Speckled trout, channel bass, and flounder all show up in this area. In fact, the state-record flounder—15 pounds, 10 ounces—was taken from the Jekyll Island Pier back in 1990.

To reach this area, take the Jekyll Island Causeway (GA 50) from the mainland. Stay on the road until it dead-ends into Beachview Drive. Turn left and drive 4.3 miles to Calm Creek Road. Turn right and proceed to the end of the road at the Jekyll Island Pier.

Another lesser-known area that provides some shoreline fly-casting room is located at the Jekyll Island Boat Ramp. This site is on the inland side of the island on Jekyll Creek, to the south of the causeway. On either side of

The St. Simons Lighthouse provides the backdrop for fly-casting from the beach near the Jekyll Island Pier.

the public boat landing there is some access for shorebound anglers. To the south of the ramp, a tidal creek extends into the island in the area behind the nearby water park. It is possible to cast to the mouth of this creek from the riprap beside the boat ramp or the hard-sand and shell beach that is exposed during lower tides.

On the northern side of the ramp it is possible to walk along the exposed sand at low tide, or along a trail at the marsh's edge during higher levels. This shore is composed of sand with a number of oyster beds. Access is possible for about 100 yards, to the spot where a tiny tidal tributary enters Jekyll Creek. The green Channel Marker 23 is directly in front of the mouth of this feeder creek, and you can make long casts out to the marker. This entire area around the boat ramp can hold seatrout or red drum, plus other species such as ladyfish and whiting.

You can access the Jekyll Island Boat Ramp by crossing the causeway onto the island and making a right turn onto Riverview Drive. After 0.6 mile, turn right into a dirt drive. If you get to the entrance to the water park, you have missed the turn. The boat ramp is at the end of the 0.5-mile drive.

One final spot for some shoreline fly-casting action is Jekyll Point, on the extreme southern end of the island facing St. Andrews Sound. Here the current coming out of the sound during falling tides conflicts with the waves rolling in from the ocean. The resulting tidal rips wash out holes along the beach and create churning surf where predatory game fish ambush their prey. Also, sticking up out of the water about 50 yards offshore is the mast of a 45-foot shrimp boat that sank in 1995. At flood tide the mast is in about 8 feet of water, but the rate of sand deposition on this end of the island is so great that the rest of the boat has been completely covered. This mast makes an obvious casting target during higher tides, but stands high and dry at ebb tide. This site can hold red drum, speckled trout, bluefish, Spanish mackerel, or jack crevalle in various seasons.

To the east of Jekyll Point, the beach wraps around the end of the island into Jekyll Sound. For about 0.5 mile, to the St. Andrews Recreation Area, the beach is fronted by a gently sloped, hard-sand flat. There is plenty of casting room along the shore during lower tides. At high tide the water reaches the driftwood and fallen trees that lie along the shore, making moving along the beach or casting from it more difficult.

To the north of the St. Andrews Recreation Area the beach reaches to a small tidal creek with marshes stretching beyond. It is possible to cast around the mouth of this feeder creek from the end of the beach.

The parking area at the St. Andrews Recreation Area provides the best access to the beach and Jekyll Point. To reach this area, travel south from the causeway on Riverview Drive past the water park. Toward the end of the island, the recreation area is on the right side of the road at the end of a short, paved drive.

Jekyll Sound

Jekyll Sound is the body of water just behind the southern tip of Jekyll Island. At its southern end this sound opens onto the larger St. Andrews Sound, which in turn drains into the Atlantic Ocean. On the north Jekyll Sound is fed by the waters of Jointer Creek, while Jekyll Creek empties into it from the east. The western side of the sound is fed by the Little Satilla River on the north and Umbrella Creek to the south.

The major area for targeting trout and reds in the sound itself is found on the points of the spartina marsh islands located between the mouths of Jointer Creek and the Little Satilla. These are particularly good for trout during high tides, but where oyster beds are present, they can hold other fish as well during any tide stage. Back up in Jointer Creek the two outlets along the northeastern shore that connect to Cobb Creek can also be good holding areas for trout or red drum.

In the Little Satilla River there are a number of trout and channel bass drops located at the point where Maiden and Honey Creeks join the river from its southwestern side. Also, for about a mile upstream from this point, the area where the shallow shelf jutting out from the southwestern shore drops into the river channel is worth checking out for the same species.

Umbrella Creek offers a large number of trout drops along its course through the spartina grass. Virtually all of the places where feeder streams join it are likely to hold fish at some point in the tidal cycle. Of special note is Umbrella Cut, where a gap in the creek's northern shore opens into the Little Satilla River. Fishing the points on either side of the cut can be productive.

Access to the Jekyll Sound fishing destinations is easy from Jekyll Island Boat Ramp. Directions to the boat ramp can be found in the previous section on Jekyll Island. Once you are on the water, run south down Jekyll Creek to its mouth on Jekyll Sound. Turn west to reach the mouths of Jointer Creek, the Little Satilla River, and Umbrella Creek.

St. Andrews Sound

St. Andrews Sound is made up of the waters between Jekyll and Cumberland Islands. Its major tributaries are Jekyll Sound on the north, the Satilla River from the west, and the Cumberland River to the south. A major strand of shallow water called Horseshoe Shoal separates the channels of the Satilla and Cumberland Rivers in the middle portion of the sound.

St. Andrews contains a major fishing ground for summer tarpon that stretches from outside the inlet almost to the mouth of Shell Creek on the Cumberland River, as well as up the Satilla River as far as the mouth of Dover Creek. Although the water—which is 5 to 7 feet deep at the inlet mouth—sometimes holds fish, most of the area where they are found is composed of the deep (15 to 25 feet) main river channels. In the case of the Satilla River, the area of interest stays north of the Horseshoe Shoal.

On the southern side of the sound all the mouths of small tributaries should be probed with a cast or two when you are looking for seatrout, red drum, and the other more seasonably available fish. These feeders stretch from the mouth of the Cumberland River up the Satilla, through the area known as Satilla Cove, to the mouth of Floyd Cut. Across the river from this point, the mouth of Dover Creek is also a likely spot to tangle with some trout or red drum. In fact, all of Dover Creek, which flows parallel to the Satilla before emptying into the river, offers many such trout and red drum

JIMMY JACOBS

*The Umbrella Cut on the south side of the Satilla River is a good place
for intercepting speckled trout and ladyfish in the summer months.*

drops. In the creek concentrate on the intersections with cuts from the river
or from Umbrella Creek to the north. The mouths of these connecting channels usually attract fish.

The best jumping-off point for the fishing around the edges of St. Andrews Sound is the Jekyll Island Boat Ramp. Directions to the ramp can be
found in the previous section on Jekyll Island. Once your boat is launched,
head south on Jekyll Creek to Jekyll Sound, then continue south into St. Andrews Sound.

Satilla River

Upstream of the mouth of Dover Creek, the Satilla River continues to offer a
variety of fishing options. Approximately 3 miles west of Dover Creek's
mouth, a cut on the northern shore of the Satilla connects it and Dover
Creek. Around the mouth of the cut is a good place to prospect for channel
bass and seatrout.

Also, from this point upstream for about 2 miles to the mouth of Bailey
Cut on the river's northern shore is a good area for locating tarpon during
the summer months. Through here the river makes a turn, with the deeper
water of the outside bend along its northern bank. This deep channel drops
to more than 20 feet quite close to shore and is where the tarpon tend to
show up.

Above this tarpon area, the mouths of Bailey Cut, Sparkman Creek, and White Oak Creek all offer more chances to locate feeding trout and channel bass.

To reach the Satilla River, the closest public boat-launch facility is the Jekyll Island Boat Ramp. The directions for this site are found in the earlier Jekyll Island section. From the ramp, run south down Jekyll Creek, through Jekyll Sound, and into St. Andrews Sound. A westward turn into this sound will point your boat into the Satilla River's mouth.

Cumberland River

The Cumberland River flows on the inshore side of Cumberland Island, with its entire length confined to Camden County. On the north it opens into St. Andrews Sound, while on the southern end it joins the Crooked River at the point where they both empty into Cumberland Sound.

All the fly-fishing destinations along this flow are spots where seatrout and red drum are likely to be encountered, with flounder and ladyfish possible in the summer. Besides the drops in the main river, the Brickhill River (which branches off the Cumberland to the east) and Shellbine Creek (which feeds in from the west) also have a number of good sites.

The outside bend on the western side of the Cumberland River where it passes the community of Cabin Bluff holds the river's greatest concentration of trout and channel bass drops. A narrow shelf of shallow water along the shore drops off into the river channel's 15- to 35-foot depths. When the fish are up on this shelf, they are most vulnerable to fly-casting. This shore should be checked out as far south as the mouth of Delaroche Creek.

Shellbine Creek, which enters the Cumberland to the north of Cabin Bluff, is worth checking out back into the stream to the point at which it begins breaking up into a maze of small feeders. Of particular interest are its outside bends.

On the Brickhill River, which forms the inland shore of the northern half of Cumberland Island, the places to target are the feeder streams from the island or from the marshes to the west. Pay special attention to the mouths of Mud, Malkintooh, and Mumford Creeks. The point where the southern end of the Brickhill rejoins the Cumberland River should also be checked out on both shores.

The final area on the Brickhill deserving notice is the outside bend where its eastern side sweeps by the dock at Plum Orchard on Cumberland

Island. Plum Orchard is one of the Carnegie family's mansions from the early 20th century; it has been restored by the National Park Service. The Park Service ferry calls at the dock several times per day, but other than this, the shore should offer some undisturbed prospects for trout and red drum.

The best public launch site for the Cumberland River's fishing is at Crooked River State Park. Directions to the ramp can be found in the following section on the Crooked River. Once you are on the river, travel east from the ramp to Cumberland Sound. At the sound turn north and run approximately 0.5 mile to the southern junction of the Brickhill and Cumberland Rivers. The Brickhill is on the east, while the larger Cumberland is the western fork.

Cumberland Island

Virtually all of Cumberland Island is contained in the Cumberland Island National Seashore. Although the island is accessible only by boat, the National Park Service runs daily scheduled ferries from its dock in the town of St. Marys. Be aware, however, that once you are on the island you will be traveling by foot. There is one commercial hostelry on the island, the Greyfield Inn, which has a grandfather clause allowing it to bring vehicles to Cumberland on its private ferry; all other visitors must walk.

The entire beach on Cumberland is open to public use and is especially noted for producing speckled trout in the spring and red drum in the fall months. The island, however, is about 15 miles long, which makes for a long stretch of beach to scout by foot.

One area particularly worth targeting is the southern tip of Cumberland Island, where the waters of Cumberland Sound flow to the ocean through the inlet. Because this inlet is used by nuclear-powered submarines heading to and from the Kings Bay Naval Base, a long jetty composed of large boulders has been placed on the beach and extends about 3 miles out to sea. Casting from the shore to the washed-out holes in the sand along the nearshore part of the jetty—especially as the tide ebbs and flows over these holes—can be productive for channel bass, trout, flounder, bluefish, whiting, or Spanish mackerel at various times of the year. Needless to say, approaching the jetty with a boat can provide even better fishing access.

You can also walk along the beach around the end of the island as far as the mouth of Beach Creek. This tidal stream drains the island's southern marshes, and its mouth is noted as a productive drop for speckled trout and flounder.

Reaching the jetty area requires a walk of a couple of miles down the beach from where the Dungeness Trail crosses the island from the Park Service dock. Just before you get to the jetty, a trail also cuts across the island toward the mouth of Beach Creek.

To reach this same area by boat, the St. Marys City Boat Ramp is the best jumping-off point. This first-rate facility has two single-lane, paved ramps with plenty of adjacent parking. From I-95, go east on GA 40 for 9.3 miles to the point at which it dead-ends into St. Marys Street. Turn right and go 0.1 mile to the ramp on the left side of the road.

After launching your boat, head east down the St. Marys River to its mouth on Cumberland Sound. Continue east in the sound to the ocean inlet. The southern end of Cumberland Island and the jetty make up the inlet's northern shore.

For the angler with a boat, Cumberland Island offers one other promising site. The mouth of Christmas Creek opens onto the Atlantic Ocean between Little Cumberland Island and the northern end of Cumberland Island. This is one of the most celebrated fishing sites anywhere on the Peach State's coast. A shallow sandbar running parallel to the shore, a couple of hundred yards off the beach, guards the entrance to the creek. Around the bar is a good place to find tarpon, seatrout, bluefish, jack crevalle, ladyfish, red drum, flounder, and Spanish mackerel. Almost any species of inshore fish is liable to show up here! Anchoring just off the outside of the bar and casting to its breakers is the usual fishing technique, but keep an eye open for schools of fish breaking the surface as they work over pods of bait. Also, gulls congregate over this type of action, so watch for circling and diving birds.

Additionally, it is possible to run up into Christmas Creek. Be aware, however, that you can get stranded in the creek during low tides. The entrance to the inlet can be very shallow at ebb tide. Still, trout and red drum favor the creek, while ladyfish and big tarpon can often be found in it during the summer.

The Jekyll Island Boat Ramp, described earlier in the section on Jekyll Island, is the most convenient place to launch when you are heading for Christmas Creek. Once your boat is on the water, run south down Jekyll Creek into Jekyll Sound, then continue into St. Andrews Sound. Next, turn east through the inlet to the open ocean. Turning south, hug the shore of Little Cumberland Island until the mouth of Christmas Creek appears.

Cumberland Sound

Cumberland Sound is formed on its northern end by the waters of the Brickhill, Crooked, and Cumberland Rivers. The Brickhill and Cumberland join just at the northern tip of the sound, while the Crooked River empties in from the northwest. On the southern end of the sound, the St. Marys River adds its waters from the west. Also on the western side of the sound is Kings Bay, which is off limits to anglers due to the presence of a nuclear-submarine base.

To the west Cumberland Sound is bounded by the Georgia mainland, while the eastern border is formed by Cumberland Island. In its central portion the sound is split into two channels by Drum Island.

Tarpon fishing is the main attraction on Cumberland Sound in the summer months, with fish roaming a large area of it. From the southern tip of Cumberland Island back up the sound to roughly halfway up the western side of Drum Island is the area in which the silver kings tend to show up. Basically the fish travel in the main channel of the sound, where depths of 15 to 65 feet of water are found.

Additionally, there are a limited number of trout and channel bass drops along the shores of Cumberland Sound. Places to try when fly-casting for these species are either shore at the southern end of the channel between Drum and Cumberland Islands, the mouth of Point Peter Creek on the western side of the sound, and the mouth of Mill Creek on the western shore across from Drum Island. Also, the first two major outside bends of the stream up in Mill Creek are worth checking out.

The best public launch site for fishing Cumberland Sound is the St. Marys City Boat Ramp, which was described earlier in the section on Cumberland Island. After putting your boat in the water, head down the St. Marys River to the east. The river opens onto Cumberland Sound.

Crooked River

The main attraction of the Crooked River for fly-casters is the presence of Crooked River State Park on its southern shore. Located just north of the town of St. Marys, the park perches on the heights of Elliotts Bluff overlooking the river.

The bluff's sheer drop of 30 or more feet to the beach and water makes

JIMMY JACOBS

The colonial-era seaport of St. Marys is now just a village that offers boating access to the St. Marys River and Cumberland Sound.

access for fishing impossible in most of the park, except near the boat ramp. Positioned at the western end of the park, the ramp has a floating dock that offers a casting platform for fishing back toward shore (assuming there are not too many other fisherman already on the dock).

To the east of the dock there is 0.25 mile of hard-packed sand beach beneath the bluff that can be accessed. This is on an outside bend of the river, so the current sweeps along the shore. The beach is littered with downed trees, broken picnic tables, and other debris that has fallen from the eroding bluff. All this structure makes good cover for the fish as the river rises with the tide. Still, this stretch of shore is open enough for fly-casting most of the time. Unfortunately, at high tide when all of the structure is flooded, the beach almost disappears. Only about 100 yards of it near the boat ramp is out of the water and provides a place from which to cast.

Along this beach, erosion has also exposed patches of black substratum clay. This harder ground is riddled with the holes of fiddler crabs. Additionally, the eddies along the shore, especially the big one created by the fishing dock and ramp, are usually infested with schools of bait fish, making the shore a prime place to look for game fish. Spotted seatrout and red drum are the species you are most likely to encounter.

To get to Crooked River State Park from I-95, travel east for 3.6 miles on GA 40. Turn left onto Kings Bay Road and continue for 2.1 miles to GA Spur 40. Take another left and drive 4.2 miles to the end of this road, which dead-ends in the park at the boat ramp. A daily parking fee is charged in the park.

St. Marys River

The St. Marys River forms the border between Georgia and Florida along much of its course between the Okefenokee Swamp and Cumberland Sound. The area of interest to saltwater fly-casters, however, extends inland only to the US 17 and I-95 bridges. Downstream of these crossings the river sweeps past the once-flourishing seaport of St. Marys, which now thrives on tourism and fishing.

Just east of town the North River enters the St. Marys from the north, and the junction of the two rivers holds several good drops for reds and trout. These are found along either side of the North's mouth and at the first couple of outside bends back up in that stream. Also, the outside bend on the southern side of the St. Marys, just upstream of the North River's mouth, has a number of good drops. As is often the case, the shallow shelf of water between the main river channel and the shore is the place to look for fish.

The final sites on the river worth checking out are the pilings of the I-95 and US 17 bridges. In the spring and fall striped bass often show up around these structures, and it is not uncommon to find a few channel bass mixed in with the stripers as well. Also, try fishing around the small island immediately upstream of the I-95 bridge and the mouths of the twin feeder creeks entering from the north just downstream of the bridge.

The best access to these areas is offered by the St. Marys City Boat Ramp described earlier in the Cumberland Island section. Once you are on the water, head eastward downriver to the mouth of the North River, or turn west and run upriver to the highway bridges.

Sebastian, Fort Pierce, and St. Lucie Inlets provide some of the best fishing for big snook found on Florida's east coast.

Part V

Florida

When it comes to saltwater fishing, Florida is the foremost state in the nation for several reasons. It has, by far, the longest coastline of any state on the eastern seaboard, stretching from the St. Marys River at the Georgia border around the peninsula to the Perdido River at the Alabama state line. Though the straight-line distance between these points is barely 350 miles, if instead you trace the contours of the coast, Florida's shores cover more than 8,000 miles! A quick look at a map of the state reveals that a little over 40 percent of its coast—or more than 3,200 miles—are located between Fernandina Beach and Key West along the east coast of the Florida peninsula.

In terms of saltwater anglers, the Sunshine State also has more fishermen casting into the brine annually than any other state. The 1996 U.S. Fish and Wildlife Service surveys place the number of Florida saltwater anglers at 1,436,000. Added to this figure are 819,000 nonresidents who test the state's salt waters each year. In fact, Florida's resident saltwater fishermen outnumber the 1,289,000 resident and nonresident anglers in Georgia, North Carolina, and South Carolina combined. More nonresidents cast into Florida's waters than the 770,000 total saltwater anglers found in the number-two state on the southeastern seaboard, North Carolina.

Additionally, having been discovered in 1513 by Juan Ponce de León and first settled in 1565 by Pedro Menéndez de Avilés at St. Augustine, the Sunshine State has had a long history since the arrival of the first Europeans.

This has allowed plenty of time for discovery of its fishing honey holes and development of a bank of knowledge concerning its saltwater fisheries.

Finally, due to the Sunshine State's geographic location, its waters teem with a variety of tropical and semitropical game fish, some of which are found in none of the other states in the nation. Bonefish, mangrove snapper, permit, and snook are a quartet of such fish that can be targeted exclusively in Florida waters, while jack crevalle, ladyfish, Spanish mackerel, and tarpon are also available virtually on a year-round basis. Additionally, the temperate weather conditions experienced by the peninsula mean that some of these fish are likely to be feeding along the shore during any month of the year.

Angling Calendar

As mentioned, saltwater fishing in Florida has no dead months. Even in the middle of winter, extreme southern Florida generally holds game fish in shallow water where fly-casters can reach them. During rare cold snaps, fishing may be slow for a few days, but it quickly recovers when temperatures return to normal. Even more important, however, is the fact that when winter weather conditions are in the average range, the entire eastern shore of the Sunshine State experiences mild temperatures and feeding fish. Conversely, the scorching heat of summer actually makes the fishing better for some of the species like jack crevalle, ladyfish, and barracuda. In short, it is a rare time when nothing is biting in Florida's inshore waters.

In order to describe the annual movements of inshore saltwater species in Florida, it is necessary to break the state down into northern and southern zones. The north can be arbitrarily described as Fernandina down to Cape Canaveral, with the south stretching from the Cape to Key West. In both zones the spring and fall are the hot seasons for sport fishing, with most of the species present and hungry.

On the other hand, the northern portion of the coast has enough of a winter to drive some species south. Fish that are found along this coast in warm weather but disappear in the winter are jack crevalle, ladyfish, pompano, Spanish mackerel, snook, and tarpon. The mainstays of the fishery through here are the year-round resident redfish and seatrout. Bluefish and weakfish reverse this schedule and are found along the shoreline in the fall through spring, but less commonly in the summer months.

In South Florida, the spring through fall months are times to target all of the fish except the blues. These cool-water fish do show up as far south as Miami in the winter, but are virtually absent except during the colder months. The fishing for bonefish, permit, and tarpon slows appreciably in the winter, but the fish are present and can be caught even then.

The Florida Keys do present a different picture, however, since they are actually quite tropical. Flounder, redfish, seatrout, and snook show up on the northern portions of this string of islands, particularly on the western side in Florida Bay, but they are not nearly as important angling targets as they are farther north. Here barracuda, bonefish, mangrove snapper, permit, and tarpon are the species most often encountered year-round.

State Records

Three of Florida's state records for fish that present some inshore fly-casting opportunities also enjoy the status of being world records. On May 5, 1995, Craig F. Carson was fishing in the Indian River at Fort Pierce when he boated a 17-pound, 7-ounce spotted seatrout to claim both the Sunshine State and the world record for this popular species. At the northern end of the state, Chester E. Dietrick also claimed dual titles when he caught an 8-pound, 1-ounce Florida pompano at Flagler Beach on March 19, 1984. Another world and state record holder is Thomas Sebestyen, who took a 58-pound, 2-ounce permit at Fort Lauderdale on June 30, 1997. Finally, Michael Baz tied the world record and set the state mark for ladyfish when he caught a 6-pounder from the Loxahatchee River in Jupiter on December 20, 1997.

With 13 other species of saltwater fish that commonly cross paths with fly-casters in Florida, it presents a problem to know where to start in covering the rest of the state records. Simply as an organizational tool, the rest of the fish are listed in alphabetical order.

The Florida record for barracuda is held by Harold K. Goodstone for the 67-pounder he boated at Islamorada in the Keys on January 29, 1949. For bluefish, the record is a 22-pound, 2-ounce chopper caught at Jensen Beach on March 3, 1978, by Liz Yates. The bonefish mark was set on December 1, 1977, in Islamorada by Peter Costanzo for a 15-pound, 6-ounce bone. The western coast of Florida produced the biggest cobia on record. John P. Whibbs boated this fish, which weighed 114 pounds, 8 ounces on April 10, 1994, at Pensacola.

The state record for flounder is held by Larenza W. Mungin. While fishing in Nassau County in North Florida, he caught a flatfish that tipped the scales at 20 pounds, 9 ounces. He made the catch on December 23, 1983.

The next record came from the waters of Jupiter Inlet. Gerald J. Washburn took his 57-pound jack crevalle on May 18, 1993, while Joshua L. Becker caught a 4-pound, 10-ounce ladyfish from the same waters on March

27, 1992. The state-record Spanish mackerel was taken nearby as well. John F. Colligan boated a 12-pounder at Fort Pierce on November 17, 1984.

The standard for mangrove snapper (also known as gray snapper) was set at Port Canaveral on June 14, 1992, by Steve Maddox, who caught a 17-pounder.

The record for red drum (more often called redfish in Florida) is held by Terry L. Parsons for the 51-pound, 8-ounce monster red he hooked in Sebastian Inlet on August 29, 1983. This record is one that is unlikely to be challenged anytime in the near future, barring a change in the regulations. All redfish larger than 27 inches long must now be released immediately. Thus it is presently illegal to break the Florida record for the species!

For snook, the record stands at 44 pounds, 3 ounces for a fish caught at Fort Myers by Robert De Cosmo on April 25, 1984. The largest tarpon on record came from Key West on February 17, 1975. Gus Bell was the angler who boated the 243-pound monster. Finally, the record for weakfish in Florida is owned by George R. Mizell Jr. for his 10-pounder taken at Port Canaveral on December 30, 1987.

Regulations

In the Sunshine State anglers, with some exceptions, must possess a saltwater fishing license. Resident anglers who are fishing from the shore or a dock attached to shore are exempt, as are all resident anglers over 64 years of age and state-certified disabled anglers. All anglers under 16 years old are also exempt.

Resident anglers fishing from a boat must have a license, as must all nonresident anglers, whether they are fishing from a boat, dock, or shore.

Like the other states along the southeastern seaboard, Florida has a number of creel and minimum- or maximum-size limits in effect for various saltwater game fish. It also has closed seasons for the harvest of several species. Of special interest is the rule requiring a $50 tag for harvesting a tarpon and a $2.50 permit for the keeping of snook. The tag and permit are in addition to the regular state saltwater fishing license and must be purchased prior to catching the fish.

One other nebulous area of the regulations needs to be covered. There is no clearly delineated line between salt water and fresh water on Florida's creeks and rivers running from the interior to the sea. At present it is a judgment call on the part of wildlife officers or officers of the marine patrol as to which of the licenses an angler must have. This is due to situations such as those found

The Sunshine State coast is a study in contrasts, offering both great natural beauty and commercial development.

on the St. Johns River in the northeastern part of the state and in suburban Miami. In times of little rainfall, saltwater fish may be found up the St. Johns to Orange Park, but when heavy rains fall the fish do not venture upstream of the city of Jacksonville. Adding to this problem is that redfish commonly turn up in Lake George, more than 60 miles above Orange Park! At the other extreme, there are places in Miami where fresh water from canals passes through locks into saltwater areas no more than 100 yards from Biscayne Bay.

As a result of this wide variation, there is a gray area along the coast where it falls to the state officers to decide whether you are fishing for salt- or freshwater species when they check your license. If you do choose to venture up creeks or rivers that change from fresh to salt water, your best bet is to pick up a copy of the freshwater fishing regulation booklet where licenses are sold, get from it the telephone number of the nearest office of the Florida Fish and Wildlife Conservation Commission (FWCC), and call for clarification regarding the stream you intend to fish. Your other options are to buy both a fresh- and a saltwater license, or to limit your casting to bodies of water that are entirely salt.

The regulations covering saltwater fishing are subject to frequent changes, so it is best to also obtain a copy of *Fishing Lines,* the newsletter of the FWCC, Division of Marine Fisheries. This publication is updated regularly with the current saltwater fishing regulations. It is available wherever saltwater fishing licenses are sold, or by writing to the Division of Marine Fisheries, 620 South Meridian Street, Tallahassee, FL 32399-1600.

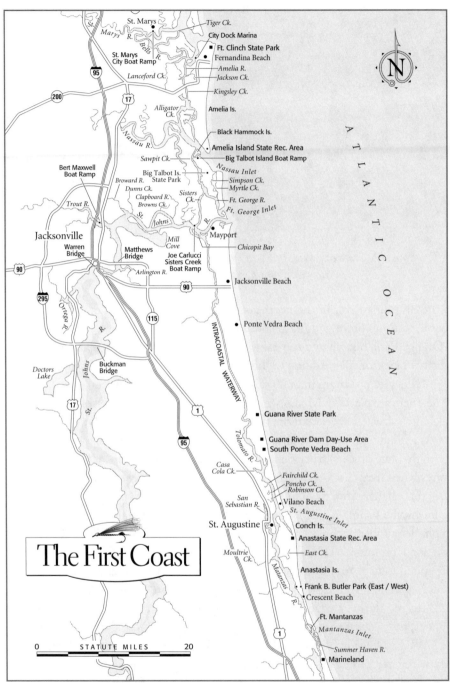

N

St. Marys
Tiger Ck.
City Dock Marina
Ft. Clinch State Park
St. Marys
City Boat Ramp
Fernandina Beach
Amelia R.
Jackson Ck.
Lanceford Ck.
Kingsley Ck.

Alligator
Ck.
Amelia Is.

Nassau R.
Black Hammock Is.
Amelia Island State Rec. Area
Sawpit Ck.
Big Talbot Island Boat Ramp

Bert Maxwell
Boat Ramp
Big Talbot Is.
State Park
Nassau Inlet
Broward R.
Simpson Ck.
Dunns Ck.
Myrtle Ck.
Clapboard R.
Sisters
Ck.
Trout R.
Browns Ck.
Ft. George R.
Ft. George Inlet
St.
Johns

Jacksonville
Mill
Cove
Mayport
Warren
Bridge
Matthews
Bridge
Chicopit Bay
Joe Carlucci
Sisters Creek
Boat Ramp
Arlington R.

Jacksonville Beach

Ponte Vedra Beach

INTRACOASTAL WATERWAY

Ortega R.

Buckman
Bridge

Doctors
Lake
Johns
St.

Guana River State Park

Guana River Dam Day-Use Area
South Ponte Vedra Beach

Casa
Cola Ck.
Tolomato R.
Fairchild Ck.
Poncho Ck.
Robinson Ck.
San
Sebastian R.
Vilano Beach
St. Augustine Inlet

St. Augustine
Conch Is.
Anastasia State Rec. Area
Moultrie
Ck.
East Ck.

Anastasia Is.

Frank B. Butler Park (East / West)
Crescent Beach

Ft. Mantanzas
Mantanzas Inlet
Summer Haven R.
Marineland

ATLANTIC OCEAN

The First Coast

0   STATUTE MILES   20

Paul Woodward, © 2000 The Countryman Press

CHAPTER 14

The First Coast

MAPS
DeLorme: *Florida Atlas* pages 41, 58, 68
NOAA: chart numbers 11486, 11488

The northeastern coast of the Florida peninsula is referred to as the First Coast, since it was the first portion of the state settled by European adventurers. Stretching from the Georgia border on the St. Marys River to Marineland, just south of Matanzas Inlet, this coast takes in the major towns of Fernandina Beach, Jacksonville, and St. Augustine in Nassau, Duval, and St. Johns Counties. Also along the shore are the mouth of the St. Marys and St. Johns Rivers, plus Nassau, Fort George, St. Augustine, and Matanzas Inlets. Amelia, Big Talbot, Little Talbot, Conch, and Anastasia Islands make up the rest of the important features for fly-casting anglers.

Several ecological features of this region are also important when you are picking a time and place to fish with fly-casting gear. This is the region that experiences the greatest range of tides in the Sunshine State. The difference between the flood and ebb tides here can be as much as 6 feet. Not only does this affect where the fish are, but it means that anglers in boats need to be careful when entering shallow creeks, sounds, or bays. The tide can fall right out from under a boat, leaving you stranded for up to six hours while awaiting the return of the waters! Similarly, anglers on foot need to be careful when wading out across channels to sandbars or flats. The rising tide can leave you with a harrowing wade in strong currents, or even the need to swim ashore if you are not paying close-enough attention to the movement of the water.

The fact that the water in the rivers and creeks of northeastern Florida is draining out of nutrient-rich spartina grass marshes makes them very dark colored in comparison to the water found in the central to southern parts of the state. Thus, sight-casting is usually difficult—as is wading, since most of the shallow flats are covered with soft black mud and sediment. The fish love this environment and the abundant food supply it provides; this type of bottom also tends to hold heat longer when the sun shines on it during the winter. But of course, it is virtually impossible to wade. As a result, there are some very good shallow flats in this part of the state that are almost unfishable either from a boat or afoot during low tides.

Finally, the fact this area experiences some cold weather in the fall and winter makes its marine fish population very changeable. It holds year-round residents like red drum, seatrout, and flounder. During the summer cobia, tarpon, snook, ladyfish, jack crevalle, pompano, and Spanish mackerel are common. In the fall and winter bluefish and weakfish show up along the beaches and inlets, while striped bass drop down the rivers into the saltwater estuaries as well.

Amelia Island

Situated at the northern end of the First Coast, Amelia Island is fronted by the Atlantic Ocean; is bounded on the north by the St. Marys River; to the west by the Amelia River, the South Amelia River, and Kingsley Creek, which connects them; and on the south by Nassau Sound and the Nassau River. The entire island is located in Nassau County. Though far better known for its historic sites around Fernandina Beach and its exclusive beach and golf resorts, Amelia Island's surrounding waters also offer some very good fly-casting options.

The St. Marys River holds a wide variety of angling possibilities for both shorebound and boating fly-fishermen at the northern end of Amelia Island. If you are on foot, the place to start your search is in Fort Clinch State Park at the northern tip of the island. This park contains a Civil War–era brick fort, but more important to anglers are the beaches, groins, and jetties on the southern side of the St. Marys River. The old fort is at the northeastern corner of the island, and the beach running west toward the mouth of the Amelia River has several rock groins extending out into the river. These make

JIMMY JACOBS

The flats to the west of the Fernandina Beach's Fort Clinch
go completely dry on a low tide.

good casting perches during high tides, but be very careful when walking on them. When wet, they can be hazardously slippery. Between these groins are shallow sand or mud flats that hold flounder, redfish, or trout when flooded. At low tide, however, they are dry, and the places to cast are off the ends of the groins.

To the east of Fort Clinch out to the mouth of the inlet, deeper water cuts close to shore and the beach is steeper, with a lot of broken shells. This is a place to look for some pompano during the summer months, casting small mole crab imitations. At the mouth of the inlet a jetty extends out into the ocean adjacent to the deep inlet channel. This jetty has a narrow concrete wall running down its center, with huge boulders on either side. It is possible to walk the wall to its end and even continue (with care) out onto the boulders beyond.

An additional unique feature of this inlet is the presence of a fishing pier on the inlet side of the jetty, which parallels the rock structure for well over half its length. Though the pier itself offers no fly-casting opportunities, its pilings are barely 20 to 50 feet from the jetty, depending on the level of the tide. At low tide it is possible to walk a very narrow strip of sand along the jetty and cast to the pier supports. During higher tides, casting from the jetty rocks is practical.

The water on the inlet side of the jetty is deep, particularly at the end of the fishing pier, but on the beach side it varies. Near the beach the water is fairly deep and steeply slanted; the sand contains a lot of broken shells, indicating another good area to check out for pompano. Farther out along the jetty is a shallower sandbar roughly even with the end of the fishing pier. There are turbulent currents across this sand flat during moving tides, and usually plenty of bait fish as well. Much of it is within casting range of the rocks and worth checking out, particularly for bluefish in the fall and winter, or Spanish mackerel in the summer.

When you are targeting redfish at this jetty, the first of the incoming tide is the time to fish the ocean side of the rocks; as the water rises, look for the fish on the other side moving into the inlet. Once the tide is full, the best spot to target is the very end of the jetty, which probably is more practical with a boat. The reds are ordinarily very close to the rocks at this time. Once the tide starts falling, they will remain close to the boulders but move up both sides of the rocks. The redfish can run from 15 to 30 pounds each here and are generally present from May until November.

Farther back in the St. Marys River are a number of spots along the southern side of the flow for finding redfish, seatrout, and ladyfish in the summer, with some tarpon as well. In the fall and winter, schools of small bluefish are out in the river, while even striped bass appear upstream of Amelia Island.

The feeder streams draining spartina grass marshes to the south of the St. Marys and west of the Amelia River are good places to find redfish cruising the mud flats or joining seatrout to hang around oyster bars at channel drops. Be aware of the fact, however, that many of these creeks and rivers have very shallow flats at their entrances. Get caught in them at low tide and you will probably have a bar of ankle-deep water with a muddy bottom blocking your way back out. The streams to check out around Tiger and Little Tiger Islands, off the St. Marys, are Tiger Creek and the Jolly River. Tiger Basin is a square mile of shallow water filled with marsh grass islands, mud flats, and shell mounds that connects the Jolly River on the north and the Bells River to the south. It is also noted for holding redfish at almost any tide and any time of the year.

To the west of the Amelia River, the streams to try at the northern end of Amelia Island are St. Joseph and Jackson Creeks and the Bells River. Take note of the mud and oyster bar flats extending into the Bells near its mouth from the northern shore on Little Tiger Island. Off the Bells, Lanceford

Creek also merits some attention. Another body of water to try is Soap Creek, which is actually a shallow slough connecting Lanceford Creek to the Amelia River to the south. This stream is deep at either end, but contains shallow shell and mud flats in its midsection.

Finally, the upper reaches of the St. Marys River from the I-95 bridge downstream to the vicinity of the Jolly River's mouth can hold striped bass in January and February. These fish tend to congregate around bridge pilings or off small points that cause the water to swirl.

Boating access to all these areas on the St. Marys end of Amelia Island can best be gained from the City Dock Marina in downtown Fernandina Beach. Another alternative, particularly for upriver areas, is the St. Marys City Boat Ramp on the Georgia side of the river. This facility has two single-lane, paved boat ramps with plenty of paved parking. From I-95, go east on GA 40 for 9.3 miles to the point at which it dead-ends into St. Marys Street. Turn right and go 0.1 mile to the ramp on the left side of the road.

After launching your boat, head east down the river to its mouth, or head upstream for the I-95 bridge. On the St. Marys River there is a reciprocal agreement in effect between Florida and Georgia. Anglers from either state may fish anywhere on the main stem of the river with a fishing license from either state. If you venture up a tributary on the northern side, a Georgia license is required, while heading into feeder streams on the southern side of the river requires a Florida saltwater license.

Along the ocean side of Amelia Island, there is good access to the beach from FL A1A via walkovers and parking areas on the northern half of the island in the city of Fernandina Beach. Also, in the city vehicles are allowed on portions of the beach. Along the southern portion of the island, Nassau County parks provide beach access.

The entire beach on Amelia Island is characteristic of barrier island shores. The sand is hard packed, but the incline of the beach is quite gentle, making the water rather shallow all along the shore. The beach does, however, provide standard surf-casting options to tidal pools and runouts.

At the point that the FL A1A bridge crosses Kingsley Creek onto Amelia Island, there is room to park on Creekside Drive on the northern side of the highway and eastern end of the bridge. From here there is foot access to several hundred yards of the eastern shore of Kingsley Creek (Intracoastal Waterway) to the south, to the point where a small feeder stream enters from Amelia Island. This stretch is open enough for backcasting and offers the possibility of redfish and trout, plus jacks, tarpon, and ladyfish in the summer.

Between the FL A1A bridge and the southern end of the island, a number of feeder streams run through the marshes along the South Amelia River. Any may hold fish at various times, but the most often targeted is Alligator Creek, which enters from the west. It offers a 9- to 12-foot-deep channel with oyster beds along the shore, making it good for trout in particular. It is at its best as a fishing hole during the last hour of a falling tide.

The southern end of Amelia Island offers one last location to intercept a few game fish with a fly-rod. This entire tip of the island is contained in the Amelia Island State Recreation Area. At the northern end of the FL A1A bridge leaving the island, a parking lot (fee charged) is provided on the eastern side of the road. From this point, there is 0.5 mile of beach to the east to the point of the island where Nassau Sound meets the Atlantic Ocean. On this point the conflicting currents of the waves and the river cause tidal rips and wash out depressions in the sand. Bait fish congregate here, providing a situation that attracts redfish, trout, bluefish, and even Spanish mackerel very close to shore.

The old bridge across Nassau Sound to the west of the present highway bridge is now used as a fishing pier. Though it is not practical for fly-fishing, its pilings (and those of the new bridge) can be cast to from shore. To the west of the bridges a 0.25-mile hard-sand flat along the shore to the first private docks on the river. In this area a small tidal creek enters from the north. This can be waded at high tide, though it is virtually dry during ebb levels. This flat is a good spot for finding seatrout, redfish, and flounder.

It is legal to drive vehicles onto the beach to the east of the FL A1A bridge, but four-wheel drive is recommended. Also, from April 1 through August 31, vehicles are not allowed more than 0.25 mile east of the highway in order to protect shorebird nesting areas. If you choose to fish this area, expect plenty of company, especially near the bridge on weekends. It is a popular fishing site, for good reason. Nassau Sound is well known for holding large schools of bait fish through most of the year. The sound is filled with undulating but constantly shifting sandbars that attract the pods of bait, which in turn are pursued by flounder, bluefish, redfish, Spanish mackerel, tarpon, and cobia.

For boating access to Nassau Sound, the best launch site is in Big Talbot State Park. A description of this facility is in the following section on Talbot Islands Parks.

Talbot Islands Parks

To the south of Nassau Sound and Inlet lie Big Talbot and Little Talbot State Parks, along with Fort George Island, which contains the county-owned Huguenot Memorial Park. These three islands in Duval County are surrounded by the Nassau and Fort George Rivers, several smaller creeks, plus the Atlantic Ocean beaches. Together they provide a variety of saltwater angling sites for fly-fishermen.

Connected to Amelia Island by the FL A1A highway bridge, Big Talbot Island is positioned at the northern end of the string of island parks. Although the island is 4 miles long, only about a third of this distance is made up of beaches on the Atlantic Ocean. The rest of the island—its southern end—lies along Simpson Creek, inland of Little Talbot Island. All of the beach is accessible for surf fishing via the main park entrance 0.7 mile south of the island's northern tip; 0.7 mile farther south at the Black Rock (or Blackrock) Trail; or another 1.6 miles south at the Big Pine Trail. All these spots have parking areas off FL A1A and paths that lead to the beach, where standard surf-fishing possibilities are available.

At the northern tip of Big Talbot is the most interesting site for shorebound anglers in this area. Where the FL A1A highway crosses to the island, you will find a parking lot on the western side of the road for a single-lane, paved boat ramp. The ramp is actually on Sawpit Creek, which carries the Intracoastal Waterway to the west of the island. The parking area is more than 100 yards from the boat ramp via a paved drive. A fee is charged for launching a boat in the park, as well as a small fee for using the parking area if you are not putting a boat in the water. The ramp is the best jumping-off point for fishing Nassau Sound by boat, while also providing several options for shore or wade fishing.

At the boat ramp a small tidal stream enters Sawpit Creek just west of the launch site. It is possible to cast all around the mouth of this feeder and the marsh grass point on its western side from the bank near the ramp. Also, a small pier at the ramp makes it possible to cast to the grass and shell bank between the launch site and creek mouth. This is a good place for redfish and speckled trout, particularly for a couple of hours on either side of a high tide.

From the parking area for the boat ramp, foot access is also available to the old FL A1A bridge that lies to the west of the present span. By walking north on it, you can gain access to the eastern end of Black Hammock Island. This tip of the island is cut off from its larger western portion by the ICW, which was dredged through the isle. Where the bridge leaves the northern end of Big Talbot, you can get onto the narrow sand beach that runs along the mouth of Sawpit Creek and, to the east, along Nassau Sound toward the ocean. Both of these beach sections are open enough for casting. Also, access is available to the northern side of the Sawpit Creek's mouth on the southern shore of Black Hammock Island. Here a small tidal creek enters Sawpit on the western side of the old highway. At its mouth there is a small sand flat spreading off its channel that can be waded during higher tide levels, though it goes virtually dry at ebb tide. The feeder creek's channel can be fished from the shore for a couple of bends upstream as well. Additionally, at the mouth of the creek a short stretch of Sawpit Creek is fishable by wading along the shore. These sites are good for reds, trout, and flounder.

From the old bridge at this point you can also walk the beach around the eastern end of Black Hammock Island. This beach has a lot of rubble and flooded grass beds, which make good casting targets during higher tide levels. Finally, at the southern end of the old bridge on the northern side of Black Hammock Island, the shore of the Nassau River is available for casting from a narrow sand beach. This open shore runs east all the way to the ICW cut through Black Hammock.

At the southern end of Big Talbot Island, FL A1A crosses Simpson Creek to tiny Long Island, then Myrtle Creek to Little Talbot Island. There is limited access for casting on Simpson Creek along here. It is possible to park on the highway right-of-way to fish around the bridge, while to the south of the crossing Simpson Creek parallels the highway for a short distance. Along here casting access is available at several points on the shore, as well as for a distance via a foot trail along the creek after it turns away from the road. It is possible to wade portions of Simpson Creek along the road, too. Reds, trout, and flounder are the species to target.

On Little Talbot Island the fishing access is a bit more limited. The entire island offers surf fishing on the Atlantic Ocean from fee parking areas in the state park. Also, at the southern end of the island, just before the FL A1A bridge to Fort George Island, there is a free parking area on the shore of the Fort George River. To the east along the shore of the river, foot access is available via a trail (or a narrow sand beach at low tide) for up to 0.5 mile of shoreline on the Fort George River. A lot of bait is generally present in tiny coves and feeder ditches along here. Trout and redfish are the most likely species along this shore, all of which is castable.

Finally, across the river on Fort George Island, Huguenot Memorial Park is located to the east of the highway. A fee is charged for entering this Duval County facility, which offers beach access to the southern side of Fort George Inlet. Fly-casting is possible along this beach, although it is also used for swimming in the warmer months.

St. Johns River

To the south of the Talbot Islands parks lie the city of Jacksonville and the mouth of the St. Johns River. This stream is by far the largest river in the Sunshine State and offers very big water for angling. Though it narrows some toward its mouth, the St. Johns is more than a mile wide where the Buckman Bridge (I-295) crosses it. And for the most part, this is angling water that is accessible only by boat.

Some fishing takes place along the southern jetty at the mouth of the St. Johns for bluefish, jack crevalle and Spanish mackerel in warmer weather, plus huge 15- to 30-pound redfish in May through November, but this is not an area for small boats. The shipping channel is used by major ocean-going freighters as well as aircraft carriers of the U.S. Navy's Atlantic fleet from the Mayport naval facilities, so wakes can be substantial along these rocks.

Of more interest to fly-casters are the upriver areas of the St. Johns, which give up redfish and seatrout year-round and huge tarpon in the summer while holding schools of marauding bluefish in April through June. To find tarpon, look for fish rolling on the surface in Mill Cove, downstream of the city of Jacksonville. For bluefish, the places to watch are the mouths of feeder creeks from the city's downtown bridges north to the ocean. These blues are easiest to locate and catch when they are busting bait-fish pods on the surface. Redfish are likely to be back up in the many feeder streams, cruising along shell mounds and bars, often in areas so shallow that they can be reached only with small johnboats.

Though all the fish mentioned so far on the St. Johns offer great sport at some time of the year, the most available and dependable species is the spotted seatrout. This is especially true in the spring from March through May, when these fish are spawning. The trout move into the river and concentrate in areas that hold bait fish. Look for seatrout around the mouths of feeder streams. If there are dock or bridge pilings in these spots, the largest "gator" trout are likely to be hiding around them. Fish such locations during falling tides for the most action.

Just how far up the St. Johns the trout range depends on recent weather trends that influence the salinity of the river's water. During periods of little rain the brine pushes upriver, carrying with it bait fish and seatrout as far as Mandarin Point and the mouth of Doctors Lake at Orange Park. The trout also enter major tributaries like the Ortega and Arlington Rivers during these conditions.

On the other hand, with more normal rainfall levels the trout rarely travel upstream beyond the area around the Warren Bridge on US 17 in downtown Jacksonville. It is then time to look for fish in the lower reaches of the Arlington River, plus Pottsburg and Little Pottsburg Creeks (all feeding the St. Johns from the east) in the middle of the city. Also check out the spoil islands (created from the residue, or spoil, from channel dredging) in the main river south of the Warren Bridge, and the pilings at the southern side of the Matthews Bridge on US Alt 90.

To the north of the city, the mouths of the Trout and Broward Rivers; Browns, Clapboard, Dunns, and Sisters Creeks; as well as Mill Cove and Chicopit Bay all hold trout in the spring. In the case of Dunns Creek the water is shallow during all tide levels and requires very careful navigation to avoid shoals of oyster shells. In Mill Cove and Chicopit Bay the same is true during low tides. The easiest boating is in Clapboard Creek and the Trout River. In the case of Clapboard and Sisters Creeks, redfish are also present during lower tide levels.

It is worth noting that the FL 105 (Heckscher Drive) causeway and bridge at the mouth of Dunns Creek offer one of the few areas in metro Jacksonville where fly-casting from shore is practical. At the bridge and to the west along the causeway are a number of parking turnouts with foot access to the creek and the St. Johns's shores.

For boating access to the lower St. Johns, Chicopit Bay, plus Browns, Clapboard, and Sisters Creeks, Joe Carlucci Sisters Creek Boat Ramp is most convenient. This double-lane, paved facility has plenty of parking and is located at the end of McKenna Drive to the south of Heckscher Drive. The ramp is at the mouth of Sisters Creek on the northern shore of the St. Johns. The park has a riprap shore on the St. Johns shipping channel, while just to the west (and outside the park boundaries) the southern side of McKenna Drive offers a couple of hundred yards of castable and wadable sand shore.

From the ramp, run north into Sisters Creek, south across the St. Johns shipping channel to Chicopit Bay, or west to Browns and Clapboard Creeks.

Launch facilities for the downtown bridges; the Arlington, Trout, and Broward Rivers; Mill Cove; plus Dunns and the Pottsburg Creeks are best at the Bert Maxwell Boat Ramp on the Trout River next to the I-95 bridge. This site has a large paved parking area with a double-lane, paved ramp. It is located at the end of Maxwell Road to the southwest of Broward Road. If you are traveling north on I-95, exit at Broward Road, then make the first left turn onto Maxwell.

The park at the ramp has a concrete seawall running several hundred yards along the northern shore of the Trout River, from which casting is possible. This wall also wraps around into a tidal creek to the west of the ramp. At either end of the wall there are grass beds within casting distance. The marked boat channel coming into the ramp also offers some deeper water to target with casts from the seawall. Finally, there is a fishing pier in the park that runs out parallel to the I-95 bridge pilings. Because this structure is built low to the water and has very low railings, it is possible to cast from it to the adjacent bridge pilings.

From the ramp, run east out of the Trout River and continue east on the St. Johns for the Broward River and Dunns Creek on the northern side of the river, or Mill Cove on the southern shore. To reach the Arlington River, Little Pottsburg and Pottsburg Creeks, or the city bridges, turn south on the St. Johns. The Arlington River enters the main flow from the east just past the first bridge (Matthews Bridge on US Alt 90). The Pottsburg creeks are tributaries on the southern side of the Arlington.

To the south of the St. Johns River's mouth, the only real fishing of note down to St. Augustine is surf casting along the beach. Through here the beach fishing yields pompano, whiting, and bluefish. Inland, the Intracoastal Waterway is mostly confined to a dredged channel from Jacksonville Beach to south of Ponte Vedra Beach; there is virtually no public access.

St. Augustine

Roughly 30 miles south of Jacksonville lies Florida's and the nation's oldest city—St. Augustine. Founded in 1565, the town sits just inside St. Augustine Inlet, fronted by Anastasia and Conch Islands. Besides a wealth of historical sites and attractions, the town and its environs also hold some very interesting fishing destinations for boating and wading fly-fishers.

The first of these is to the north of the city, near South Ponte Vedra Beach at Guana River State Park. The Guana River has an earthen dam at the southern end of the park; the lake behind it is considered fresh water, although it does hold a population of resident redfish. To the south of the dam down to the mouth of the Guana on the Tolomato River, the stream is a good place to intercept summer redfish chasing bait along the shell-lined shores during rising tides beginning in mid-June. When the water nears the flood stage, larger reds of 20 to 30 pounds join the smaller fish in the river. During lower tide levels, the fish drop back down into the Tolomato. Also, at low tide the boating channel in the Guana River is only 4 to 6 feet wide, so it is easy to run aground.

One point of shore access exists for this fishing as well. The Guana River Dam Day-Use Area (which has a daily parking fee in effect) is located on the western side of FL A1A in South Ponte Vedra Beach and provides an unimproved sand launch ramp just below the dam. The area around this ramp also offers some shoreline casting opportunities. At the eastern end of the dam a sand drive leads south to a parking area on a small lagoon off the main river. A narrow sand beach offers casting room along this part of the lagoon's shore as well.

At the mouth of the Guana on the Tolomato River, which carries the Intracoastal Waterway through here, there is water in the 14- to 19-foot-deep range. Speckled trout can be found here at ebb tide as they wait to enter the Guana with the rising water. Also of interest is a spot just north of both the Guana's mouth and Channel Marker 37 on the eastern shore of the ICW. Directly out from the sandy point near the marker, a freshwater spring bubbles up from the bottom in about 8 feet of water. To the south of this spring, a 16- to 20-foot-deep hole has washed out that often holds seatrout and huge black drum of up to 90 pounds.

Also north of St. Augustine are a number of small feeder creeks draining into the Tolomato from the west. These are known for producing lots of small seatrout in the spring and fall, but also for giving up some fish of more than 5 pounds. When you locate schools of trout on shell bars in these places, look for the bigger single fish to be separated from the schoolies on nearby shell-covered bottom.

In the backs of some of these creeks are deeper depressions holding $1\frac{1}{2}$ to 2 feet of water at low tide, separated from the stream's mouth by hundreds of yards of ankle-deep water. This slightly deeper water often holds numbers of redfish of up to 30 inches, as well as some bigger trout. Of course, these fish are very difficult to get to, since the bottom is too soft for wading and the water is so shallow for boating. Casa Cola Creek, which enters the river from the west just south of the Guana River's mouth, holds this type of situation and is also known for giving up a lot of winter flounder. To the south of Casa Cola, Fairchild, Pancho, and Robinson Creeks are also on the western side of the Tolomato and are good trout-fishing destinations.

Boating access for these sites north of St. Augustine is most convenient at the Vilano Boat Basin (identified on some maps as the Vilano Beach Boat Ramp). This paved, double-lane ramp with a parking area is located off Vilano Road (FL A1A) at the western end of the Vilano Beach Bridge between St. Augustine and Vilano Beach. From the ramp, run north up the Tolomato River for Robinson, Pancho, Fairchild, and Casa Cola Creeks on the western shore then, after 6 miles, the Guana River on the eastern side.

In town the areas to the east and south of downtown St. Augustine also provide some interesting and varied fly-fishing possibilities. Most of these are centered on Anastasia State Recreation Area and its Salt Run. From the gate at the recreation area (a fee is charged to enter), vehicle access is available to the Salt Run, which is a shallow lagoon stretching south from St. Augustine Inlet behind Conch Island. This body of water often gives up redfish and flounder but is best known for producing spotted seatrout in the summer months. Unfortunately, this is also the time when windsurfers and folks on personal watercraft are most active, making fishing difficult. For this reason, it is a good site to try early in the morning at first light. Flood tides are better fishing times on the Salt Run, although it can hold fish during any water level. In its deeper northern end, boating anglers do well by targeting docks and deeper channels. At the other end of the lagoon to the south of the recreation area picnic sites, the Salt Run can be easily waded from shore even at high tide. The bottom, which appears mucky when exposed at low tide, is mostly firm sand covered with a thin veneer of soft mud and sprinkled with shells. Small depressions in the bottom are not deep but can cause you to trip, so wade carefully. The best point of access for wading is just south of the concession area where canoes and kayaks are rented.

Once you are in the water, concentrate on the marsh grass shoreline during higher tides, especially where schools of bait fish are moving along the grass line. During lower levels, look for any signs of game fish tailing, pushing wakes, or chasing bait in the open water.

The other option for casting in the Anastasia State Recreation Area is from the beach or at Cape Francis on St. Augustine Inlet. Access is available to vehicles through the recreation area for driving on the beach north to the cape. From there, foot access is possible to the rock jetty on the southern side of the inlet. Be careful, however, since the top of this jetty is not paved. The jetty gives up redfish in the fall, some running up to 30 pounds. The beach to the south along Conch Island provides angling for pompano, bluefish, and whiting. Farther south, the beach along Anastasia Island to Matanzas Inlet has similar surf-casting opportunities, with good access from FL A1A.

The Matanzas River flowing through St. Augustine offer several possibilities for finding seatrout and redfish.

Boating access to the Salt Run or the inlet is easiest from Light House Park on Anastasia Island. This county park contains a 19th-century lighthouse that is open to the public, but—more important—it has a double-lane, paved boat ramp with plenty of parking spaces. Located near the northern end of the Salt Run, the entrance to the ramp is off Red Cox Drive 0.3 mile east of FL A1A. Once your boat is in the water, you can begin fishing the Salt Run or motor north to reach St. Augustine Inlet.

Matanzas River and Inlet

Stretching south for roughly 15 miles from St. Augustine to Matanzas Inlet, the Matanzas River has traditionally been the back door to that city, since in past centuries it was the route pirates used to raid colonial St. Augustine. Today, as a fishery, it continues to be an overlooked secondary waterway in this area. Yet it holds a number of possibilities for fly-casting anglers.

From the 17th-century Castillo de San Marco coquina fortification (made of a limestone rock composed of fossilized shells) just north of the Bridge of Lions on FL A1A in St. Augustine, and south to the mouth of East Creek on Anastasia Island, the waterway is lined with docks and holds shallow oyster beds. These two types of cover attract seatrout to the river year-round, but the spring and fall are the best times of year for hooking these fish.

Also, it is worth checking out the mouth of the San Sebastian River, which enters the Matanzas from the west, just south of the city. Another place to target is the back of East Creek, which lies on the eastern side of the river opposite Lewis Point on the mainland. This stream has a shallow flat in its mouth but slightly deeper water farther inland on Anastasia Island. Besides trout, redfish also are known to cruise the mud flat in the upper creek.

Finally, across the Matanzas from the mouth of East Creek and to the south of Lewis Point is Moultrie Creek. This is another site to investigate for redfish during falling and low tides.

Boating access to the Matanzas and San Sebastian Rivers in St. Augustine is best from the Vilano Boat Basin, described earlier in the section on the city. From the ramp, run south on the Matanzas past the Castillo and the old city waterfront to reach the mouth of the San Sebastian.

For boat access to East Creek and the midsection of the Matanzas, launch your vessel at Frank B. Butler Park (West). This St. Johns County facility is located at the end of Riverside Boulevard to the west of FL A1A, just north of Crescent Beach. Butler Park (East) is on the other side of the highway and offers only beach access.

The boat ramp has plenty of space for parking trailers, with a single, paved lane. It is, however, in rather rough shape and in need of resurfacing. The site is located at the mouth of a small tidal creek that empties into the river. A couple of hundred yards of the creek can be covered with casts from the park's shore, but at low tide it is almost dry. Still, even then bait fish crowd into the part of the stream near the river. In front of the boat ramp and lining the channel out to the Matanzas River, marsh grass islands and shell beds cover mud flats, offering a good spot to look for trout and redfish from a canoe or small flat-bottomed boat. Once you are launched, head north on the Matanzas for about 3.5 miles to the mouth of East Creek on, of course, the eastern shore.

At the southern end of the First Coast lies Matanzas Inlet. The name *Matanzas* originates from the Spanish word for "slaughter," for it was at the inlet that Pedro Menéndez de Avilés put French explorer Jean Ribault and several hundred of his shipwrecked Huguenot followers to the sword in 1565 to secure Spain's control of Florida. Today the coquina watchtower built on Rattlesnake Island in 1740 by the Spanish to guard St. Augustine's back door bears the name *Fort Matanzas* and continues to overlook the inlet.

This pass to the ocean is well known as an angling hot spot, but mostly for bait-fishermen setting out their lines from the FL A1A bridge over the inlet. On the other hand, it does have some possibilities for fly-casting. There is plenty of paved parking space at the northern end of the bridge and easy access to this shore of the inlet.

As a rule, the water in the inlet and lower Matanzas River is clear. A wadable, hard-sand flat extends along the northern shore of the inlet, all the way up the riverbank to the National Park Service ferry dock for Fort Matanzas. Some grass beds are present along this shore, just inside the inlet mouth.

As current rushes into or out of the inlet with the tide, the water can become quite turbulent very near shore. This provides a good location for game fish to ambush helpless bait fish caught in the rush. It obviously is also a good place for fly-casters to ambush the game fish. Several old pilings are in the water within casting range of the northern shore, just west of the inlet bridge. The pilings of the bridge provide a similar opportunity. On the point at the northern side of the inlet to the east of the bridge, crosscurrents of the river and surf create tidal rips, plus constantly changing sandbars and holes. This is another place where predators lie in wait for passing bait. The inlet fishing is usually best during falling tides.

The southern side of the inlet in the community of Summer Haven does not provide as convenient access to the inlet's shore. Still, the beach at the mouth of the inlet and to the south can be reached from a parking area along the abandoned stub of old FL A1A fronting the ocean. This strip of sand is noted for holding schools of 15- to 30-pound red drum in the surf during the fall months. Other fish commonly encountered at Matanzas Inlet are smaller redfish, trout, flounder, snook, and pompano. During the mullet run in the fall tarpon of better than 100 pounds also appear in the inlet!

One other nearby option for fly-casting is found along roughly 2 miles of FL A1A south of the inlet. The Matanzas River (also referred to as the Summer Haven River here) runs under the road just south of the inlet, then parallels the eastern side of the highway. The waters of the Intracoastal Waterway run down the highway's western side. Both of these are accessible at several points along the highway right-of-way. Casting from shore is possible, as is wading around the marsh islands on the western side of the road. At high tide much of this area is covered by only thigh- to waist-deep water. Turnouts along the roadway provide parking for anglers.

Boating access to the lower Matanzas River and Inlet is easiest from the Frank B. Butler (West) Park at Crescent Beach, which was described earlier in this section. From the ramp, run south on the river until you sight the inlet.

CHAPTER 15

Daytona Beach

MAPS
DeLorme: *Florida Atlas* pages 68, 74, 75, 81
NOAA: chart numbers 11484, 11486

Although this chapter is named for the beach resort city that lies at the center of this portion of the East Florida coastline, this title is mostly a response to the individualistic nature of the communities along here. While the rest of the Sunshine State's Atlantic seaboard is neatly packaged into various coasts, this area has resisted that urge. Instead, Flagler Beach in the north bills itself as "The Quiet Side of Florida," while Daytona is "The World's Most Famous Beach," and New Smyrna on the south is the "World's Safest Beach." For the sake of organization, I have lumped them together as the Daytona Beach area.

This part of the coast stretches from Pellicer Creek at the Flagler County border on the north, through Volusia County, to the Brevard County border on Mosquito Lagoon in the south. Along the way it takes in the towns of Marineland, Flagler Beach, Ormond Beach, Daytona Beach, and New Smyrna Beach. The only pass here is at Ponce de León Inlet (usually referred to simply as Ponce Inlet) between Daytona Beach and New Smyrna Beach. Other bodies of water, besides Pellicer Creek and Mosquito Lagoon, are the southern Matanzas River, the Tomoka River and Basin, Bulow Creek, the Halifax River, and the Indian River North.

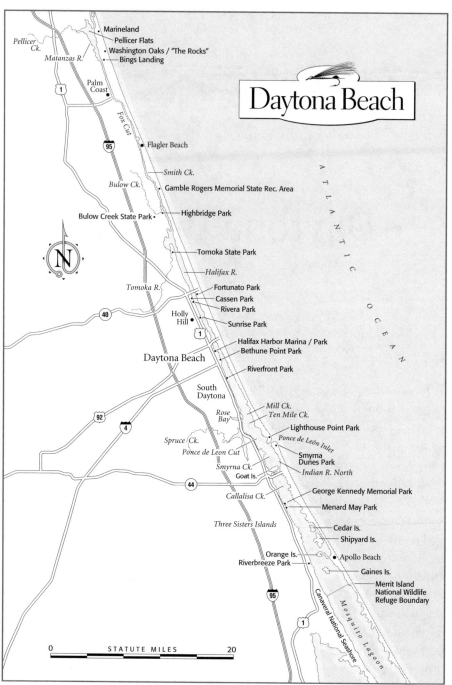

Daytona Beach

Pellicer Ck.

Marineland
Pellicer Flats
Washington Oaks / "The Rocks"
Bings Landing

Matanzas R.

Palm Coast

Fox Cut

Flagler Beach

Smith Ck.

Bulow Ck.

Gamble Rogers Memorial State Rec. Area

Highbridge Park

Bulow Creek State Park

Tomoka State Park

Halifax R.

Tomoka R.

Fortunato Park
Cassen Park
Rivera Park

Holly Hill

Sunrise Park

Halifax Harbor Marina / Park
Bethune Point Park

Daytona Beach

Riverfront Park

South Daytona

Mill Ck.
Ten Mile Ck.

Rose Bay

Lighthouse Point Park

Spruce Ck.

Ponce de León Inlet

Ponce de Leon Cut

Smyrna Dunes Park

Smyrna Ck.

Indian R. North

Goat Is.

George Kennedy Memorial Park

Callalisa Ck.

Menard May Park

Three Sisters Islands

Cedar Is.
Shipyard Is.

Orange Is.
Riverbreeze Park

Apollo Beach

Gaines Is.

Merrit Island National Wildlife Refuge Boundary

Mosquito Lagoon

Canaveral National Seashore

ATLANTIC OCEAN

0   STATUTE MILES   20

Paul Woodward, © 2000 The Countryman Press

Southern Matanzas River

From the boundary separating St. Johns County from Flagler County to the south, the Matanzas River continues beyond Marineland all the way to the exclusive and self-contained resort community of Palm Coast. Its major tributary along this course is Pellicer Creek, which actually forms the border between the two counties to well west of I-95. This highway, however, marks the upstream limit of interest for fly-casters looking for saltwater species of fish. Some redfish or snook venture farther up the creek, but it is much more of a freshwater fishery in its headwaters. When the stream does enter the Matanzas River, it is in a broad bay called Pellicer Flats.

In its upstream areas Pellicer Creek is a meandering, tannin-stained stream surrounded by spartina grass marshes. From I-95 downstream to the US 1 bridge the creek often holds some tarpon in the summer months, with fish of up to 50 pounds possible. Along with the silver kings, snook occasionally appear here in the summer, while redfish and trout are year-round residents of the creek. Below the US 1 crossing look for trout and reds to be hanging around the many boat docks along the shore or cruising the mouths of the frequent tidal feeder ditches during falling tides.

Though Pellicer Creek contains some deep water, care is needed to navigate it even in small boats. There are shallow mud bars all along its course and, due to the dark color of the water and mud, they are hard to spot. Since the single public boat ramp on the creek can handle only small craft and Pellicer Flats at the mouth is extremely shallow, a large boat is not a valid option for fishing the creek anyway.

The shallow waters on Pellicer Flats are full of oyster beds and more mud bars. Although game fish sometimes give away their positions by chasing bait or pushing wakes, much of the angling on these flats is blind-casting. Trout and redfish inhabit these waters from fall through spring, but the area can suffer from a couple of problems that kill the summer fishing. First, the water on the flats gets so hot under the summer sun that it holds fish only at first light. The other problem, which can also occur at other times of the year, is that heavy rains inland can empty so much fresh water into the creek and flats that the saltwater fish abandon them.

To the south of Pellicer Flats, the Matanzas River is broken into smaller creeks and channels on its western side by marsh islands, while the eastern edge carries the Intracoastal Waterway along a string of spoil islands. The deeper channels in here are where the reds and trout take refuge when they leave the flats.

On the eastern shore of the Matanzas south of Pellicer Flats lie Washington Oaks State Gardens. While the name may belie the facts, this park facility offers a couple of good fly-fishing options to anglers. The 400-acre tract stretches from the river eastward to the beach, contains ornamental gardens and natural areas, but also provides access to wadable stretches of the Matanzas River and exposed coquina rock formations on the ocean beach. The surf around these rocks is noted for holding big redfish in the fall while giving up bluefish, pompano, and whiting at other times. A parking area for the beach is located on the eastern side of FL A1A in the gardens' boundaries.

On the riverfront, smaller redfish, flounder, and seatrout are the main species you will encounter. The Mala Compra Nature Trail in the park runs parallel to the river from the picnic area to the visitors center, offering several side trails to the water. The best of these is at a boardwalk over a tidal pool leading to the wading bird viewing area. At the end of each side trail the shore is composed of an easily wadable shelf of hard-packed sand and shells. This gets you far enough out from the shoreline vegetation to cast into the deeper water toward the ICW channel. At the northern end of the Mala Compra Trail (roughly 0.5 mile long) behind the visitors center, a concrete seawall lines the shore for 100 yards or so. Here the ICW channel is no more than 50 or 60 feet from shore and the green Channel Marker 105 is within easy casting distance of the seawall. To the north of the seawall's end, the wadable sand shelf continues for several hundred more yards.

No parking is allowed behind the visitors center, so walking the trail from the picnic area is your only way to access this fishing. A fee is charged for entering the gardens. Washington Oaks State Gardens are located 4 miles north of St. Joe Road (the Palm Coast toll road) via FL A1A.

At 1.2 miles south of Washington Oaks, Bings Landing is also located on the western side of FL A1A. This Flagler County park offers shore anglers the opportunity to cast from a couple of hundred yards of seawall to the very southern end of the Matanzas River, just before it disappears into Fox Cut on the Intracoastal Waterway. There is a fishing pier on site, and its pilings are good casting targets from the seawall as well. Also, the boat basin at this location has riprap shores at its entrance and eastern side to which you can cast. Besides reds and trout, the area surprisingly gives up some small barracuda to fly-casters in spite of its north-central position on the coast.

Of even more importance than its shore access, Bings Landing has a double-lane, paved boat ramp with a large paved parking area. This is the best public ramp for launching a fishing trip on the southern end of the Matanzas River or for Pellicer Flats. Once you are on the water, run north up the Matanzas for the deeper channels around the spoil and marsh islands. Just north of these lie the waters of Pellicer Flats on the western side of the river.

The other boating access point for this part of the river is located on Pellicer Creek in Faver-Dykes State Park. Positioned halfway between I-95 and Pellicer Flats, the park has a steep, single-lane, paved boat ramp suitable for putting small craft into Pellicer Creek. A fee is charged for entering the park, which offers no good fly-fishing access from the shore. To reach the state park, take Faver-Dykes Road east from US 1, just south of its intersection with I-95 in St. Johns County.

Tomoka Basin

From the Palm Coast area south to Flagler Beach, your only real fishing option is surf casting along the beaches for red drum, bluefish, pompano, and whiting. The ICW runs first through Fox Cut inland of Palm Coast, then through Smith Creek, with very little access at Flagler Beach. Finally, south of this area and down to Ormond Beach, the waters draining into Tomoka Basin become the dominant fishing resource.

The one good point of entry to Smith Creek is the Gamble Rogers Memorial State Recreation Area just south of the town of Flagler Beach. A fee is charged for entering the park. This facility straddles FL A1A and provides beach access and a boat basin to the west off the ICW. The concrete seawall along its western and northern sides provides casting possibilities along the basin, out to its mouth on Smith Creek. Flounder, redfish, trout, and small barracuda are encountered in the boat basin at various times.

There is a single-lane, paved boat ramp at the basin with a large sand parking area. Before you head out to the creek, it is worth casting along the marsh grass southern shore, which sometimes holds smaller red drum.

A few miles south of the Gamble Rogers recreation area, Bulow Creek State Park takes in a large expanse of tidal marsh and hardwood hammocks to the west of FL A1A. A west turn onto Highbridge Road leads to Highbridge Park, which is a Volusia County facility at the bridge over Smith Creek and the ICW. To the west of the bridge, Bulow Creek parallels first Highbridge Road, then Walter Bordman Lane to the Bulow Creek bridge. A number of side channels run right along the roadside for 1.5 miles to the

*The west side of Tomoka Basin gives up some smaller snook
in the summer months.*

bridge, offering turnouts and some casting room on this tidal creek. The area
through here is known as Mound Grove; it was formerly a citrus-growing
and -packing area but is now quite popular for its scenic bicycle tour route.
Watch for riders while driving the road or making a backcast at roadside. The
species of game fish you are most likely to encounter in Bulow Creek are redfish and seatrout, with the summer possibility of hooking a snook.

Boating access to Bulow Creek is via the boat ramp at the Knox Bridge at Highbridge Park. This double-lane, paved ramp with large sand and gravel parking area is located at the southeastern corner of the bridge on the ICW. There is limited casting space in the park, especially to the pilings of the fishing pier under the bridge. The mouth of Bulow Creek is just south of the bridge on the western side of the ICW.

Between the Mound Grove area and Ormond Beach to the south, Smith Creek empties the waters of the ICW into the eastern edge of Tomoka Basin. This large, shallow bay is at the mouth of the Tomoka River, which drains the Hull Cypress Swamp to the west. The basin's dark, brackish waters average only 2 to 3 feet deep, although deeper channels and holes are found in it. The shoreline is rimmed with marsh grass and mud banks, while oyster beds are common throughout.

The eastern side of the basin is dominated by the deep water and spoil islands of the ICW, which passes through it, while the major feature of the western shore is a maze of mosquito-control canals crisscrossing the bordering marsh. These canals are quite shallow, but their mouths offer good places to find game fish during changing tides. The small waterways parallel both sides of the Old Dixie Highway (FL 5A) to the north of its bridge over the Tomoka River, with some roadside casting access. The bottoms of these canals are made up of very soft, sticky black muck and not suitable for wading.

The most common species in the basin is the red drum. These fish are here year-round, with single fish of up to 10 pounds scattered through the basin in the summer months. In the fall, however, schools of 6- to 8-pounders cruise much of the basin. Of course, seatrout are found here as well, and even snook show up in limited numbers in the summer. One place to give special attention is the cable crossing at the southern end of the property line for Tomoka State Park on the western shore. Here a band of rocks extends 150 yards out into the basin. Also, on the eastern side of the basin, cast to the spoil islands along the ICW.

The presence of Tomoka State Park on the basin makes access easy. The park has a boat basin to the south of the Old Dixie Highway bridge, with a single-lane, paved boat ramp and a large paved parking lot (a fee is charged for entering the park, which does not open until 8 AM). Also, the park runs a canoe rental concession. These craft are ideal for getting back into the shallow canals that lie just across the mouth of the Tomoka River from the boat basin.

Additionally, just south of the boat basin a tiny sand island parallels the shoreline. The northern side of this isle has a very shallow, hard-sand flat extending out from it. On its southern side is a much deeper channel. By beaching a canoe on the island, it is possible to cover almost this entire channel with casts from the narrow strip of sand beach.

Just across the flat to the north of the island, a sign on a marsh grass point warns that this is a manatee area. From the sign eastward, the entire bottom is made up of oyster shells that are just beneath the surface during low tide. It is worth checking out this area during high tide levels.

For boating access to Tomoka Basin before 8 o'clock in the morning, use the ramp at Highbridge Park (described earlier in this section). Once you are on the ICW, head south to the red Channel Marker 36, then follow the marked channel west into Tomoka Basin.

Halifax River

From Tomoka State Park south, the Halifax River carries the Intracoastal Waterway for 15 miles through the towns of Ormond Beach, Daytona Beach, and New Smyrna Beach. To the east of the river, the beaches of these three communities have for years had national reputations of one kind or another. At Ormond the beach was the site of the establishment of the first land speed records by automobiles shortly after the turn of the 20th century, earning the town the title, "Birthplace of Speed." Daytona's beach is acclaimed simply for being famous, thus the "World's Most Famous Beach." New Smyrna's beach is shielded by offshore rock ledges that sap the Atlantic surf of power, making it the "World's Safest Beach" for swimmers. But none of these beaches is noted for its fishing. In fact, they all slope so gently that they resemble the barrier island beaches of Georgia and South Carolina. Such conditions simply do not attract game fish to the surf, so the angling on these shores is usually not very productive. The only exceptions are the beach at the mouth of Ponce de León Inlet between Daytona and New Smyrna, as well as Apollo Beach to the south of the latter city.

On the other hand, the Halifax River from Tomoka State Park down to the river community of Port Orange does offer some fly-fishing possibilities. The most consistent of these takes the form of night casting to lighted docks along the shore of the river. Ladyfish, snook, and seatrout are the fish most often encountered after dark around these structures. The only noted daytime option is casting for trout around the spoil islands or submerged spoil piles at the edge of the ICW. Of course, as with any sizable stretch of water in this part of the Sunshine State, seatrout, redfish, snook, jack crevalle, la-dyfish, and tarpon are active in the Halifax at various times of the year and during different tide phases. There just are not a lot of situations along the river that consistently hold them in one place with regularity. The result is that any of the few fishing access points can provide some action, but none is predictable.

One of these shore access opportunities is at the upper end of the Hal-ifax, around the Granada Boulevard Bridge (FL 40) in Ormond Beach. At the eastern end of the bridge Fortunato Park offers about 200 yards of castable shore running north along the riverbank. On the western end of that same span is Cassen Park, to the south of the bridge. This facility offers a seawall under the bridge from which you can cast to the pilings of both the bridge and the park fishing pier. Additionally, Cassen Park provides boating access to the upper Halifax. A double-lane, paved boat ramp with a large gravel parking area is located on the river here.

Slightly to the south along South Beach Street is Rivera Park, which holds 0.2 mile of castable seawall on the river. All three of these facilities are Ormond Beach city parks, and together their proximity makes them a desti-nation where a fly-fisherman can reach enough water to spend several hours.

Continuing south on South Beach Street along the western side of the Halifax, Sunrise Park in the town of Holly Hill provides boating access to the river's midsection. Here a single-lane, paved boat ramp with a small parking lot is on the eastern edge of South Beach Street.

To the south of the old riverfront business district in Daytona Beach, three more parks provide boat ramps and limited casting room along the shores of the Halifax. The largest of these is Halifax Harbor Park, which is immediately south of the US 92 bridge over the river and on the eastern side of Halifax Harbor Marina off South Beach Street. A large paved parking lot is located next to an eight-lane, paved boat-launch facility. Additionally, a concrete seawall in the park offers a 0.25-mile of casting to the river.

Continuing south, Bethune Point Park is at the end of Bellevue Avenue to the east of South Beach Street. It features a single-lane, paved ramp with a paved parking lot but only a very short strip of waterfront for casting.

Finally, at Riverfront Park in South Daytona a double-lane, paved ramp is provided. Paved parking lots are also on site, situated on both sides of Pal-metto Avenue. This facility lies to the east of US 1 via Big Tree Road. At the intersection of Big Tree and Palmetto, turn north; the park will be on the right side of the road.

Ponce de León Inlet

Ponce de León Inlet and the waters inside the pass on the Halifax and North Indian Rivers provide some of the best fly-casting options along this part of the coast.

Beginning at the FL A1A bridge in the town of Port Orange, the fishing in the Halifax gets more interesting as the river takes on a different character. First, in the town of Port Orange there is a large, wadable flat located on the river's western side. It is immediately behind the bowling alley on US 1, but finding a place to park is a problem. This shallow water is noted for holding tarpon of up to 50 pounds during the warmer months of summer.

South of Port Orange the river is broken up into many small, winding side channels by mangrove islands, sandbars, and oyster banks. These tidal creeks are great places to locate hungry seatrout from early fall all the way into the following spring months. The mouths of Mill and Ten Mile Creeks, where they empty the water from Rose Bay into the western side of the Halifax, are good places to target during falling tides, as is the mouth of Spruce Creek a bit to their south. Also, Spruce Creek can be waded from parking turnouts along US 1 where that highway crosses the stream. Shallows extend up the creek around oyster beds and small islands to the Florida East Coast Railway bridge. Jack crevalle, seatrout, redfish, snook, and small tarpon all frequent these waters.

Running south from Spruce Creek and carrying the ICW is Ponce de León Cut. Where the cut turns to the southeast just inside Ponce Inlet, Smyrna Creek runs to the southwest, then continues south under the North Causeway (FL 44) to join the Indian River North beside Chicken Island. Both Ponce de León Cut and Smyrna Creek are great trout-fishing areas during falling tides in the fall through spring months. To the south of the South Causeway (FL A1A) in New Smyrna, Callalisa Creek meanders through marshes on the western side of the Indian River North and provides the same type of seatrout action. When you are navigating any of these creeks, slow is the proper speed. There are a lot of no-wake zones, but the frequent sandbars and oyster beds make moving slowly a necessity anyway.

To the east of the junction of the Halifax River and Indian River North lies Ponce Inlet. There are Volusia County parks on both sides—Lighthouse Point Park on the north and Smyrna Dunes Park on the south. A fee is charged for entering these facilities, but one fee is good for day use of both sites.

JIMMY JACOBS

The north jetty at Ponce de León Inlet offers some casting options beyond the surf.

From the parks, you can gain access to the beaches on both sides of the inlet as well as the strips of sand wrapping around into the inlet. Additionally, there are rock jetties on both sides of the inlet. The one on the south is short—it is just a pile of huge rocks running off the beach. It is possible to walk out on this one, but a great deal of care is needed in moving along the potentially slippery surfaces. On the northern jetty the center is made up of a paved concrete walkway with guardrails, but you can also get out onto the boulders that line both sides of it. Finally, the shores of the inlet are composed of hard-packed sand that is wadable just inside the inlet.

The fish most often found around and in the inlet are whiting, seatrout, and redfish. During the fall mullet run, tarpon, jack crevalle, and bluefish feed here as well. Snook, ladyfish, and Spanish mackerel are other species sometimes encountered.

To reach Lighthouse Point Park and the northern jetty, take FL A1A south from the western end of the Port Orange bridge over the Halifax River. Then follow the signs from the end of the the road.

Boating access for Smyrna Creek, Callalisa Creek, Ponce de León Cut, Ponce Inlet, Spruce Creek, and Rose Bay is best from the ramps on either side of the creek running under the western end of the North Causeway (FL 44) bridge in New Smyrna Beach. There are four-lane, paved boat ramps on both sides of the stream. The one on the west provides paved parking, while to the east the lot is sand.

From the ramp, run east out into the Indian River North, which is running east–west at this point. Continue east on the river to Goat Island, where Smyrna Creek enters the main stream from the northwest. Just past Goat Island, Callalisa Creek's mouth is on the southern side of the river. After the river turns back to the north, Ponce de León Cut enters from the west, just south of Ponce Inlet. Follow the ICW through the cut to Rockhouse Creek and turn east to the inlet. Continue north on Ponce de León Cut to its northern end, where Spruce Creek is on the western shore. To reach Ten Mile and Mill Creeks, which provide access to Rose Bay, head north from this point on the Halifax River (the same stream as the Indian River North, but the name changes at Ponce Inlet). These creeks empty into the river roughly 3.5 miles north of the inlet.

North Mosquito Lagoon

Mosquito Lagoon is one of the legendary saltwater angling destinations on the east coast of the Florida peninsula. Its expansive hard-sand flats covered with sea grass beds are noted for holding hordes of mega-sized redfish and many other game fish species. While those conditions do occur to a certain extent in the northern reaches of the lagoon, there is a different fishery here as well. From the town of Edgewater on the western shore of the lagoon, south to the northern boundary of the Merritt Island National Wildlife Refuge at the village Oak Hill, the northern lagoon's fishing conditions are akin to those found around New Smyrna. This change of conditions runs roughly along a line from Oak Hill on the west, through Gaines Island, to Eldora on the eastern shore. There are marsh grass and mangrove islands dotting its waters, which are broken up into small channels filled with oyster beds and bars. This part of Mosquito Lagoon is more noted for producing great seatrout fishing in the fall through spring than for its red drum action.

In this area the spots to target are the drop-offs along oyster beds in 4 to 10 feet of water. The best time is when falling tides are moving along the shores of the mangroves and marsh grass, where the bars of oysters are usually found. Look for these conditions to the south of the Three Sisters Islands area, where the old channel of the ICW turns southeast from its present course. Of particular interest are the bays, creeks, and cuts around Cedar Island. Though many of these hold plenty of trout on oyster shell beds, the tide can play nasty tricks on unwary anglers here. When it starts falling, it drops in a hurry and can leave you stranded on mud very quickly. If you venture into this region, the fishing can be great, but do not let it distract you from watching the water level.

Access for boating the mangrove channels at the northern end of North Mosquito Lagoon down to the Three Sisters area is easiest from George Kennedy Memorial Park in Edgewater. This Volusia County park has a four-lane, paved boat ramp with a small parking lot. A seawall around the point on which it sits offers casting to marsh grass along the shore or open water for a couple of hundred yards.

To reach the park, take US 1 south to the town of Edgewater. At the traffic light at the intersection with Park Avenue, turn east and continue for two blocks. This street dead-ends into South Riverside Drive. The park entrance is immediately north of this intersection.

A bit south of Kennedy Park on South Riverside Drive is Menard May Park. Though this site has just a single-lane, sand boat-launch area that can handle only small boats, it does offer a strip of shoreline that can be cast from shore or waded. The sand bottom along the bank at the park is hard packed. From US 1, take East Ocean Avenue to its dead end on South Riverside Drive and Menard May Park.

For access to Cedar Island, use the double-lane boat ramp and paved parking area just inside the northern entrance to the Canaveral National Seashore on FL A1A. This is to the south of the western end of New Smyrna's South Causeway. Cedar Island is immediately east of this landing.

For boat access to the southern end of North Mosquito Lagoon, the jumping-off point is Riverbreeze Park, 2 miles north of Oak Hill. This Volusia County facility has a four-lane ramp with a huge paved parking area. It is 0.4 mile east of US 1 via H. H. Burch Road.

When you are boating North Mosquito Lagoon, be aware that no-wake speeds are the norm, and the winding channels can be quite confusing. You want to be with an experienced navigator on your first venture or two here. This is not an area for novice boatmen to challenge.

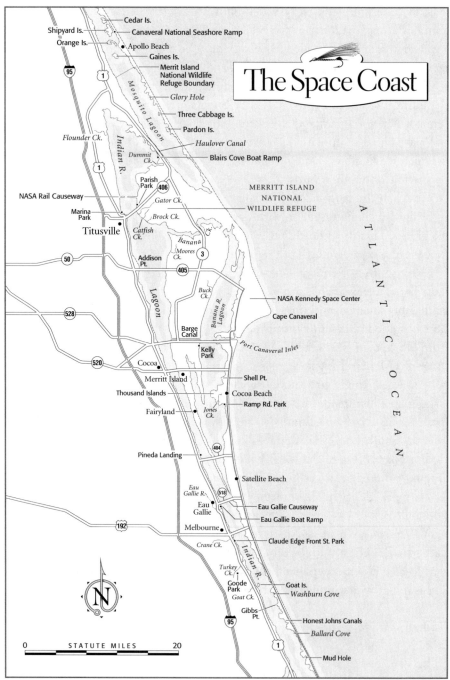

The Space Coast

Cedar Is.
Shipyard Is.
Canaveral National Seashore Ramp
Orange Is.
Apollo Beach
Gaines Is.
Merritt Island National Wildlife Refuge Boundary
Glory Hole
Three Cabbage Is.
Pardon Is.
Flounder Ck.
Haulover Canal
Dummit Ck.
Blairs Cove Boat Ramp
Parish Park
406
NASA Rail Causeway
Gator Ck.
MERRITT ISLAND NATIONAL WILDLIFE REFUGE
Marina Park
Brock Ck.
Titusville
Catfish Ck.
Banana Moores Ck.
3
Addison Pt.
405
50
Buck Ck.
NASA Kennedy Space Center
528
Cape Canaveral
Banana R. Lagoon
Barge Canal
Kelly Park
Port Canaveral Inlet
520
Cocoa
Merritt Island
Shell Pt.
Thousand Islands
Cocoa Beach
Fairyland
Jones Ck.
Ramp Rd. Park
Pineda Landing
404
Satellite Beach
Eau Gallie R.
518
Eau Gallie
Eau Gallie Causeway
Eau Gallie Boat Ramp
Melbourne
192
Crane Ck.
Claude Edge Front St. Park
Turkey Ck.
Goode Park
Goat Is.
Goat Ck.
Washburn Cove
Gibbs Pt.
95
Honest Johns Canals
Ballard Cove
1
Mud Hole

Mosquito Lagoon
Indian R.
Lagoon
ATLANTIC OCEAN
Indian R.

N

0   STATUTE MILES   20

Paul Woodward, © 2000 The Countryman Press

CHAPTER 16

The Space Coast

MAPS
DeLorme: *Florida Atlas* pages 81, 82, 87, 88
NOAA: chart numbers 11476, 11484

Florida's Space Coast is located along the east-central portion of the Atlantic side of the peninsula and takes its name from the presence of the National Aeronautic and Space Administration's (NASA) Kennedy Space Center on Cape Canaveral, which lies in the middle of the region. This entire coast, however, is contained within the boundaries of Brevard County alone. For the purposes of describing the fishing, a small portion of the extreme northern end of Indian River Lagoon and the midsection of Mosquito Lagoon that are in southern Volusia County are included in this chapter. Their angling resources are very similar to those described here.

From north to south, the Space Coast takes in south Mosquito Lagoon, the northern and southern sections of Indian River Lagoon, Banana River Lagoon, and the northern Indian River. Along these shores are the Canaveral National Seashore's northern and southern sections and the Merritt Island National Wildlife Refuge. The U.S. military and NASA also control a large segment of the shore through here in the Cape Canaveral Air Force Station and Patrick Air Force Base, as well as the Kennedy Space Center. The Space Coast runs from the village of Oak Hill on the western shore of Mosquito Lagoon south to the Indian River County line, just north of Sebastian Inlet.

*The launch towers of Kennedy Space Center loom over
the fishing grounds of the Mosquito Lagoon.*

Along this coast are found the towns of Titusville, Cocoa, Merritt Island, Cocoa Beach, Satellite Beach, Eau Gallie, and Melbourne. There is only one ocean pass on this coast, Port Canaveral, which is located north of Cocoa Beach and is a major port for Caribbean-bound cruise ships. Although not a true inlet, the Haulover Canal that connects the Intracoastal Waterway between North Indian River and Mosquito Lagoons has many of the same features as one of those passes and is an angling focal point.

Huge expanses of all three of the lagoons and portions of the Indian River are made up of shallow, hard-packed sand flats that are covered with sea grass beds. Virtually all of these are wadable, with the only limiting factor being access. Many are cut off from shore by the ICW or boat channels running through the lagoons, others by the presence of private property or military areas with restricted access along the shore. Nature also provides some barriers in the form of muddy marshes and mangrove thickets that block anglers on foot from the water. In spite of these obstacles, Banana River, Indian River, and Mosquito Lagoons—along with the Indian River itself—offer a great deal of accessible wading water and great fishing. In fact, the area is second in these categories only to the Florida Keys among all portions of the coast south of the Virginia border.

Spotted seatrout, jack crevalle, black drum, pompano, ladyfish, tarpon, and snook are all present in portions of the lagoons at various seasons, often providing frenzied fishing action. Yet it is the red drum here that offer the premier fishery. Unlike other areas where bull reds move offshore to deeper water as they mature, truly huge red drum spend all their time cruising, tailing, or chasing bait in these shallow lagoons. Schools of up to 200 fish are sometimes encountered, made up of red drum in the 36- to 50-inch length range and weighing 20 to 40 pounds each! Fishing for these brutes is a sight-casting sport, since the water is shallow and quite clear. Anglers either wading or in boats watch for the pushed wakes of these herds of redfish on the flats. If the weather is too windy for this type of sight-fishing, it is still possible to find the schools where they are tailing along the shores in sea grass beds. During particularly rainy periods, the culverts, ditches, and feeder creeks emptying into the lagoons become great places to find redfish looking for easy meals. And do not be surprised to find concentrations of snook at the same locations.

Mosquito Lagoon

Trying to pinpoint the fly-fishing hot spots in Mosquito Lagoon presents a bit of problem. I can almost simply point at the water. The lagoon is 17 miles long from north to south, varies from 15 to 25 miles wide east to west, and composed almost entirely of hard-packed sand covered with sea grass. Fully a third of this vast area is covered by water only 12 to 18 inches deep. This is a wade fisherman's paradise. Additionally, the lagoon is so far from ocean inlets that changes in water depth because of the tides are virtually nonexistent.

As mentioned earlier, redfish are the stars of the fly-fishing follies on Mosquito Lagoon, and their schools tend to be quite mobile. They feed on a flat for several days, then move on in search of more forage. For flats anglers, and particularly those who are wading, this fishing is a matter of finding access to the water, then hoping to cross paths with the fish. The best time of the year for finding reds on the flats in Mosquito Lagoon begins in March to early April and runs all the way through November or December. Then chilly temperatures will send the fish looking for the deeper-water haunts within the lagoon.

If you choose to tackle these waters in the spring through fall, come well prepared with insect repellent and sunscreen. Otherwise you will get very miserable on these flats and marshes.

A few places of note keep popping up in conversations with anglers about Mosquito Lagoon; here redfish are regularly ambushed in the shallows.

On the eastern shore of the lagoon, just north of the Haulover Canal, the stretch of shore from Pardon Island north to Three Cabbage Island is good, as is the vicinity of Bird Island another 2 miles to the northwest. Just to the east of Bird Island is a small bay called Glory Hole, which has a reputation for holding schools of reds. Both of these locations are lightly fished, probably because of the difficulty of navigating their sand shoals. If you are targeting the grass beds in these spots—or, for that matter, anywhere in the lagoon—those that extend all the way to shore are best. Reds are more often found feeding over grass beds than over bare sand bottoms.

Of course, there are other species of game fish to be hooked in the lagoon, but they are less likely to be found on the very shallow flats than are redfish. The lagoon does have a few deeper areas that hold these other fish—if for no other reason, then simply because they are deeper. The first of these is around the mouth and channel leading out of the Haulover Canal that connects Mosquito Lagoon to Indian River Lagoon. The channel of the Intracoastal Waterway running east from the canal provides a sudden and steep drop from the flats into deep water, and game fish regularly hang on the edge of the channel. Besides redfish in cooler weather, the channel harbors seatrout, snook, flounder, black drum, and even grouper at other times. Another area local anglers mention is The Klinkers—small spoil islands made of material dredged from the ICW channel. They run in a line for more than 5 miles from the mouth of the Haulover Canal to the northwest, along the western side of the ICW channel. The waters around them regularly give up smaller redfish and some very big seatrout.

Another deep-water option is offered by two flats located on the lagoon under water that is 5 to 6 feet deep. One of these is Deep Tiger Basin, which lies to the east of Channel Marker 19 on the ICW. The center of this flat is crossed by a line of pilings marking the northern boundary of the Merritt Island National Wildlife Refuge. To the south and east the flat is bounded by Tiger Shoals, while to the north Georges Bank runs along it. In this area anglers often use the feeding activity of gulls to tell them where redfish, trout, or other game fish are attacking pods of bait. Especially in cooler weather, fishing the drop from the Georges Bank into the basin is very good for redfish. In all, Deep Tiger Basin covers about 1 square mile of the lagoon.

The other deep flat is located along the eastern side of the ICW, beginning at Channel Marker 27 and continuing south to Marker 35. Again, this can be a good place for fall or winter, cool-weather fishing.

The final bit of structure in Mosquito Lagoon to key on is one that can

JIMMY JACOBS

There are some good reasons to stay on the Indian River Lagoon flats and not stray into the canals of Merritt Island!

work for boaters, waders, or bank casters. Back in the 1950s, when the space program began to change the face of the Cape Canaveral area, many dikes were constructed along the lagoons to flood saltwater marshes and thus control the reproduction of salt marsh mosquitoes. Unfortunately, this also had a detrimental effect on the entire marsh ecosystem, so today measures have been taken to repair the damage. The cure has involved building culverts under the dikes to allow water to flow into and out of these marshes. The mouths of these culverts (there are more than 700 scattered along Indian River, Mosquito, and Banana River Lagoons) can be hot spots for trout, redfish, and snook, especially when water is flowing from the canals behind the dikes into the lagoon. On Mosquito Lagoon the culverts are found to the south of the Haulover Canal, along the western shore.

On the back side of the dikes—which are topped by dirt roads—are canals where fill dirt was dredged to make embankments. The bottoms of these canals are composed of very soft, black muck where wading is impossible and dangerous. You can become trapped in this mire. Also, the brackish waters on this side of the dikes support a healthy population of alligators, some of which are quite big. It is a good idea to keep an eye out for them when you are walking the dike roads as well.

Access to the dikes and culverts from shore is available from Mosquito Lagoon Road, which runs east off FL 3 (Kennedy Parkway) 2.3 miles south of the Haulover Canal. The entrance to this dirt road is immediately north of the Atmospheric Science Field Laboratory building (the only structure on FL 3 in the Merritt Island refuge). After 0.3 mile the road reaches the lagoon, then turns south along it all the way to County Road (CR) 402, just inside the southern entrance to the Canaveral National Seashore. Along the dike road are a number of culverts, bordered by long stretches of wadable flats. Be aware, however, that the road is gated, and the gates are locked during duck hunting season in the winter months. Even then, foot access along it is possible. The road is rough, but it is passable to passenger cars when driven carefully.

Boating access to Mosquito Lagoon is available at several locations. At the northern end of the lagoon there is a double-lane, paved ramp with a good parking area in the North District of the Canaveral National Seashore. Although the ramp and much of this section of the national seashore on the eastern side of the lagoon lie in Volusia County, they are included in the Space Coast because this side of Mosquito Lagoon more closely resembles the southern portion than it does the part near Edgewater. Here the shore is lined by shallow sand flats with grass beds. There are no appreciable oyster beds.

To reach the North District of the national seashore, take FL A1A south from the eastern end of the South Causeway in New Smyrna Beach. The seashore entrance gate is on FL A1A.

Along the western side of the lagoon you find a sand boat ramp and unpaved parking area at the end of a dirt road 0.7 mile east of FL 3. The landing is best used by small boats only. This road lies 3.9 miles north of the Haulover Canal. Wading is possible along here, but the line of Klinkers is just offshore and, beyond them, the deep channel of the ICW.

At 1.4 miles north of Haulover Canal another dirt road runs 0.4 mile east from FL 3 to Mosquito Lagoon. Here there is a single-lane, paved boat ramp, but it is in very poor repair. The small parking area at the site is unpaved. This is another landing that cannot handle very large boats. The shore is accessible here for wade fishing, but the line of dredged Klinkers lies very close to shore, limiting the size of the wading area.

At the Haulover Canal you can use the Bairs Cove Boat Ramp to access the midsection of Mosquito Lagoon. The landing is located on a small boat basin on the southern side of the canal, to the west of FL 3. This is a single-lane, paved ramp with a large dirt parking area. Once you are on the water, run east through the Haulover Canal to reach Mosquito Lagoon.

The final boat ramp on Mosquito Lagoon is found in the South District of the Canaveral National Seashore at Eddy Creek, just south of the seashore's Parking Area 8. The parking lot is paved at the landing, but the ramp is sand and has a single lane. It is possible to wade both north and south of the ramp area at the lagoon, with the flats to the north being particularly noted for holding redfish.

There are a number of other spots within the Canaveral National Seashore where wading is possible. One of these is in the South District at Parking Area 12. A trail at the northern end of the parking lot leads to the shores of Mosquito Lagoon and a hard-sand flat.

To reach the South District of the national seashore, take CR 406 east across the Max Brewer Memorial Parkway Causeway from Titusville to Merritt Island. Turn right onto CR 402 for the entrance gate of the South District and Playalinda Beach. The parking areas, including Parking Area 12, are along the beach road.

In the North District of the Canaveral National Seashore are a number of places where you can reach the shores of Mosquito Lagoon for wade fishing. All of these have hard-packed sand bottoms covered with sea grass.

As you travel south from the entrance gate, the first is at Turtle Mound, which is a prehistoric shell midden left behind by early Native American inhabitants of the area. At the southern end of the parking area is a gated dirt road that leads about 100 yards to a picnic area on the shores of the lagoon. The seashore visitors center lies a bit farther south and its picnic area also offers access to the water.

On Eldora Road, which is a one-way paved track running west of FL A1A to the abandoned site of the old town of Eldora, Parking Areas 6, 7, and 8 all provide shoreline openings to the wading flats.

Farther south on FL A1A, Parking Area 3 offers a 0.5-mile trail to the east through a hardwood hammock to the Wind Castle area on the lagoon. There is a single picnic table on the shore here, along with an opening in the shoreline vegetation for wading out onto the flats.

The final point of access is Parking Area 5 at the southern end of the road access to the North District of the seashore. A drive drops down the dunes to the east of the parking area, where you will find a rough, single-lane boat landing. On either side of the ramp it is possible to wade out onto the lagoon's sand and sea grass flats. Additionally, a sand road runs south; it is closed to vehicle traffic but does provide foot access to Mosquito Lagoon to the south.

North Indian River Lagoon

Indian River Lagoon is a very large body of salt water almost unaffected by tidal changes because of its more or less landlocked position. Water has to filter from Mosquito Lagoon through the Haulover Canal to reach it in the north, while at its other end the nearest ocean pass is at Sebastian Inlet, more than 60 miles south of the canal. The lagoon is generally referred to as running from the vicinity of the Volusia County–Brevard County line north of the community of Scottsmoor, southward to the point that it and Banana River Lagoon join to form the Indian River just north of the Eau Gallie Causeway (CR 518). For the purposes of describing the fishing in Indian River Lagoon, I will define the north section as all the water north of the Max Brewer Memorial Parkway Causeway on CR 406 and west of the Haulover Canal.

The entire shoreline that lies to the north of the CR 406 causeway is edged with shallow, wadable sea grass flats noted for holding schools of redfish and, in a few instances, seatrout. For wading fly-casters, it is simply a matter of finding the places that are accessible from shore in order to reach the fishing. There are also many flats that are much better reached by boat, along with some sites in the lagoon that hold deeper water where boating anglers can locate fish.

In the extreme northern end of the lagoon near Scottsmoor (on the western shore) redfish schools regularly congregate over the grass flats along the western shore between the town and Flounder Creek to the south. Directly east across the lagoon from the mouth of Flounder Creek is a protrusion from the shore known as Grassy Point. At this spot you will encounter some of North Indian River Lagoon's rare mangrove islands and shoreline. Fishing around them can produce both redfish and spotted seatrout.

There is a very rough, dirt boat landing at Scottsmoor. It is, however, fit only for launching small johnboats.

Also farther south on the western shore of the lagoon are grass flats that attract redfish. These are located offshore of the Wiley community near the village of Mims. These shallows line the shore to the north of the spot where the ICW channel coming west from the Haulover Canal turns south to parallel the lagoon coast.

This part of the shore can be accessed via small boats by using the sand ramp at Wiley. From US 1 at Mims, head east onto Wiley Road. After 1.2

miles, this road dead-ends. Turn north onto Hammock Road (dirt) and go 0.2 mile to a dirt road on your right (which has no street sign identifying it). Turn onto this road, crossing the Florida East Coast Railway tracks. The ramp is at the end of this road, 0.1 mile east of Hammock Road. The redfish flats are north of this access point.

Almost directly in front of the Wiley ramp and running northeast to the Haulover Canal is the channel of the Intracoastal Waterway. Along the northern side of the channel are more of the dredge-debris islands. Tossing flies around these klinkers can produce seatrout, ladyfish, and jack crevalle. Concentrate especially on the islands between the green Channel Markers 13 and 19. Also try the drop-off located along a sandbar a little west of the red Channel Marker 12 for redfish and trout at any time of the year.

At the eastern end of the ICW channel across Indian River Lagoon lies the Haulover Canal. Casting flies to the shoreline of this deep cut can yield jack crevalle, snook, flounder, ladyfish, trout, and redfish.

To the north of the Haulover Canal and all the way to the end of the lagoon, the western shore has culverts under dike roads connecting the lagoon to the salt marshes. All of these offer fish-holding possibilities, although you must ordinarily get out of your boat and wade the very shallow water to get near them. For the footbound fly-caster, these culverts can be reached at a couple of places from dike roads. The first of these is 1.1 miles north of the Haulover Canal via FL 3. A dirt road marked with a WATERFOWL HUNTING ACCESS sign runs to the west from the paved highway. Where it reaches the lagoon, the water is wadable; there is also access to the north along a dike road with culverts.

Farther north, at 2.2 miles from the Haulover Canal, Sawmill Creek Road runs to the west of FL 3. After 0.1 mile, you should bear to the right at a fork. When the road reaches the lagoon, it turns north to run 10 miles along a dike with culverts at the shoreline. The road emerges onto US 1 immediately to the east of this road's bridge over the Florida East Coast Railway tracks at the northern end of the lagoon. Sawmill Creek Road leaves the lagoon for 1.8 miles before reaching US 1. When you are traveling east on US 1, it is very easy to miss the entrance to Sawmill Creek Road. It is marked with a small PUBLIC ACCESS ROUTE sign.

To the south of the Haulover Canal, three places along Indian River Lagoon's western shore offer more fly-casting options to boating anglers. The first of these is located on the extreme eastern edge of the northern portion of lagoon and is known as Dummit Cove. A small tidal stream on Merritt

Island here is named Dummit Creek as well. This corner of the lagoon has lush grass flats and is most noted for producing seatrout during the early-morning hours.

This site is also accessible to shorebound anglers via Dummit Creek Road, a dike road that runs off FL 3 about 100 yards south of the Atmospheric Science Field Laboratory. This is roughly 2.4 miles south of the Haulover Canal. The road has a WATERFOWL HUNTER ACCESS sign at its entrance but is otherwise unmarked. From the highway, it rambles west to the edge of Dummit Creek and Cove to eventually connect with the Black Point Wildlife Drive near its end on CR 406. Because the wildlife drive is a one-way road, Dummit Creek Road should be entered from the east; otherwise you have to drive the entire 7 miles of the Black Point Wildlife Drive (which offers no access to the lagoon's waters) just to reach the western end of Dummit Creek Road.

Once it strikes the lagoon, Dummit Creek Road travels along a dike that has a number of culverts running under it. The shore is wadable, though the bottom is not as firm as you find at other sites on Indian River and Mosquito Lagoons. Also, be aware that this dike road is closed to vehicle traffic along the lagoon during the winter duck hunting season.

The other two boating locations on North Indian River Lagoon are found to the north of Black Point and at Marsh Bay Point, immediately west of Dummit Cove. Here there are deep flats that hold seatrout and redfish. Casting along the area where the shallows drop into the deeper water is most productive.

For boating access to the fishing locations on the eastern side of Indian River Lagoon, the Bairs Cove Boat Ramp on the Haulover Canal is your best jumping-off point. From the boat basin on the canal, run west out of the canal, then turn north for Grassy Point and the culverts along Sawmill Creek Road. From Haulover run south for Dummit Cove, Marsh Bay Point, and then Black Point. This is also a good place for launching to run west across the lagoon to the Wiley and Scottsmoor vicinities, if your boat is too large to use the ramps in these areas. Additionally, the western side of the parking area at the Bairs Cove Boat Ramp has a hard-sand shoreline where wading is possible. Bairs Cove is at the southern end of the Haulover Canal bridge on the western side of FL 3. It has a single-lane, paved ramp with a large dirt parking lot.

One other point of boating access for the southern end of this region is found on the CR 406 causeway at Titusville. Parrish Park is on the eastern portion of the causeway and offers a triple-lane, paved ramp with a large paved parking area. To reach the fishing grounds described earlier, run north up Indian River Lagoon past the NASA railway causeway, then bear east for Black Point or west for Wiley.

To the east of the boat ramp in Parrish Park there is 0.4 mile of shore access at both sides of the causeway for casting from shore or wading.

Finally, just north of the CR 406 causeway is a long stretch of shoreline in Titusville's Marina Park that offers casting room. This bank runs from the mouth of the boat basin at the marina south to the causeway. Both here and in Parrish Park redfish and seatrout provide the most productive fishing. Trout are most commonly found near the mouth of the marina's basin.

South Indian River Lagoon

The southern section of Indian River Lagoon runs from the Max Brewer Memorial Parkway Causeway on CR 406 in Titusville south to the Eau Gallie Causeway, where it joins Banana River Lagoon at the northern end of the Indian River. As you travel south along this portion of the waterway it becomes narrower, and its shores grow more civilized.

Before the eastern shore leaves the Merritt Island refuge, however, one portion of the lagoon's eastern bank merits description. Half a mile after you cross the CR 406 causeway heading east you find a small parking lot on your right with a station for picking up information about the refuge. At the western end of this parking area Peacock Pocket Road (dirt) runs south. This dike road continues along the eastern shore of Indian River Lagoon, weaving for 12 miles around Gator, Catfish, and Brock Creeks to Peacock Pocket, which is near the mouth of Banana Creek. It is worth noting that Banana Creek itself is on the Kennedy Space Center grounds and is a restricted, no-entry area. From Peacock Pocket, the road winds back to CR 402, but a spur reconnects it with CR 406 about 0.5 mile past the information station on CR 406.

Along most of its route Peacock Pocket Road runs along the top of dikes, with many culverts passing under it. All of these are potential fishing hot spots. Near its entrance the road is rather rough from heavy use, but farther along it becomes a smoother, grass-covered roadway. It is passable even to passenger automobiles if you take your time and drive with care.

Though snook and trout can show up around the culverts on Peacock Pocket Road, the flats that front them are usually the haunts of schools of tailing redfish. These flats are hard sand and wadable. On the other hand, Gator, Catfish, and Brock Creeks have pockets and fingers with rather mucky bottoms. Be sure you are on the lagoon's shore before charging into the water!

South of Banana Creek's mouth all the way down to the Hubert Humphrey Bridge on CR 520 in the town of Merritt Island, neither the access nor the quality of the fly-fishing opportunities is as good as in the northern lagoon. All of the eastern shore to the Bennett Causeway Bridge on FL A1A is in the Kennedy Space Center restricted area, providing no shore access. Though grass flats occur along here, the only two spots noted for holding fish on a regular basis are the mouth of Moores Creek and the flats immediately north of the dredge channel that parallels the eastern end of the NASA Causeway (CR 405). Trout and snook hang around the mouth of Moores Creek, while the seatrout is the species to target to the north of the causeway. On the causeway itself no parking is allowed; NASA has a checkpoint gate here, so there is no fishing access at all from the bank. Just south of the eastern end is another flat good for seatrout that is covered with sea grass and provides good wading. Unfortunately, it is also accessible only by boat.

Along Indian River Lagoon's western shore through this same area there is little in the way of noted fly-casting hot spots. Immediately south of the Brewer Causeway in Titusville lie several deeper cuts leading to marina docks. These often hold schools of speckled trout, as does a deep dredge hole on the northern side of the NASA Causeway's western end, south of Addison Point. Though the water under the bridge on the causeway just east of this point also attracts trout and redfish, it is deep and fish are usually on the bottom, making them tough to reach with a fly.

The best places for consistent fly-casting action in this part of the lagoon are on the western shore on either side of the Port St. John area. To the north lies the Orlando Utilities Commission's electric power plant, while the Florida Power and Light Company's Cape Canaveral plant is to the south. The outflow of warm water from these plants creates a super fishery for big jack crevalle and ladyfish throughout the winter months. The flat just off the Cape Canaveral plant is the most wadable. Additionally, the intake canals at both locations are noted for holding snook and small tarpon in the summer months. All of these can be accessed by boat, but wading from public access points on shore to the north of the Cape Canaveral plant is also possible.

One final spot to check out is located north of the Barge Canal, which runs along the eastern end of the Bennett Causeway Bridge over Indian River

Lagoon. There are spoil islands here that were created with the dredge material from the canal. Try casting the flats surrounding these isles for seatrout.

Of course, along the entire stretch of the lagoon from Titusville down to Merritt Island schools of redfish can show up anywhere—and often do in the fall through spring. Still, there are no sites through here known for holding them on a regular basis.

Two other options exist for fly-casting in the lagoon through here, and in fact continue all the way south to the Eau Gallie Causeway on CR 518. There are small spoil islands and submerged debris humps on the eastern side of the channel of the Intracoastal Waterway as it runs down the entire southern portion of Indian River Lagoon. Any one of these can be a speckled trout honey hole on any given day. All are worth exploring when you are in their vicinity.

Additionally, when you are on the lagoon watch for schools of pompano. They can sometimes be spotted skipping across the surface of the water. When you see this, dropping small shrimp imitation flies into the school can provoke strikes and some interesting fishing action. This phenomenon can occur virtually anywhere in the southern portion of the lagoon.

Access points for boating this part of Indian River Lagoon are found at three locations. For the northern end, use the ramps at Parrish Park on the Brewer Causeway, which were described earlier in the section on North Indian River Lagoon.

In the midportion the Port St. John Boat Ramp offers a two-lane, paved ramp with a large parking lot on the western shore off US 1. It is positioned just north of the Cape Canaveral power plant between the two electric generating facilities. Besides boat access, this ramp offers several hundred yards of shore access to the north into Brevard County's Nicol Park. Some of this shore is open enough for casting, while limited wading access is available, particularly to the south toward the warm-water discharge area of the Canaveral plant.

At the southern end of this stretch Lee Wemmer Park is located on the waterfront of the town of Cocoa, immediately south of the western end of the Hubert Humphrey Bridge. It has a four-lane, paved boat-launch facility with a large dirt parking lot. There is also access here for casting around the pilings under the bridge and several hundred yards of shoreline to the east of the park's boardwalk along the causeway.

The rest of Indian River Lagoon offers a fairly standard set of targets for fly-casting. Along its eastern and western shores the places to try are boat docks and the mouths of man-made canals or natural creeks. All of these hold seatrout from time to time and are mostly accessible only by boat.

At the western end of the Pineda Causeway on CR 404 there is shore and seawall access to the water on both sides of the highway. There are pull-offs on both sides of the road for parking on the causeway as well. Additionally, to the north of the road the shore is accessible, as is a wadable flat, all the way up to Pineda Landing. This county park has a single-lane, paved boat ramp with limited parking space just off US 1, north of its intersection with CR 404. The flats from the ramp to the causeway attract both trout and redfish.

The final point of access to Indian River Lagoon is at the Eau Gallie Causeway on CR 518, which has a double-lane, paved boat ramp on its eastern end, to the south of the highway. There is also a large sand and gravel parking lot. Here you will find shore access for casting or wading on both sides of the road, from the main channel bridge to the span over a smaller secondary channel to the east. In all, this accessible area runs for 0.3 mile along the causeway. Also, if you look north, Dragon Point is visible near the eastern side of the river. This is the spot where Indian River and Banana River Lagoons join to form the Indian River. It is also notable for the huge, lime green, plaster dragon that the landowner has constructed on the tip of the point!

Banana River Lagoon

Banana River Lagoon is the third of the major landlocked bodies of water that make up the Space Coast fishery. Positioned to the east of Indian River Lagoon and south of Mosquito Lagoon, it stretches from the confines of the Kennedy Space Center on the north down to just north of the Eau Gallie Causeway, where it joins Indian River Lagoon to form the Indian River.

The entire lagoon is noted for holding seatrout, baby tarpon, snook, and jack crevalle. But it is the huge redfish—up to 50 inches long and weighing 40 pounds—and black drum of up to 50 pounds on which these waters have built their reputation. While the fishing in Banana River Lagoon is at least as good as, if not better than, that found in the other two lagoons, it has been less explored by anglers. There are two reasons for this. First of all, the northern half of the lagoon's shores are located in the restricted-access areas of the Kennedy Space Center, so they cannot be reached for bank or wade fishing from the land. As for the waters in this part of the lagoon, they are contained in the Banana River Marine Sanctuary, which is a manatee refuge. To the north of the power line that parallels the northern side of the Bennett

Causeway (FL A1A), motorized vessels are not allowed. This means a body of water that is about 3.5 miles wide and 12 miles long, covering 13,800 acres, can be entered only by canoes and kayaks. The limits this puts on exploring its fishing are obvious.

Still, some portions of the sanctuary are known for giving up fish to hardy anglers who paddle in. In what should come as no great surprise, all of these locations are in the southern part of the sanctuary, to the south of the NASA Causeway (CR 405) and in paddling range of the boundary of the manatee refuge.

Once you are in the refuge you can get out of the canoe to wade the flats, but be aware that the area has a very healthy population of curious alligators. Some are large enough that you should think twice about getting anywhere near them, even in a canoe or kayak!

The northernmost point where anglers regularly tangle with redfish and trout is on the grass flats along the western shore of the lagoon, south of the NASA Causeway and down to the mouth of Buck Creek. While redfish are often found tailing in these waters, from March through November do not be surprised to find big black drum tailing in the shallows as well! Working a Clouser Minnow or crab pattern in tan, brown, or black color combinations very slowly along the bottom to these fish can lead to hook-ups, followed by long and tough battles with black drum that often top 20 pounds each.

Farther down the western shore, more grass flats hold reds, trout, and black drum to the south of Duck Point. Directly east and offshore of these shallows are some submerged debris piles that were created when the main boat channel was dredged down the lagoon. These also attract fish.

Be aware that during the summer months, baby tarpon of up to 40 pounds are likely to be encountered on the grass flats along the entire western shore of Banana River Lagoon. When these fish are rolling on the surface in this skinny water, approaching them by leaving the canoe to wade is about the only way to get within casting distance without spooking them.

Another similar area of flats that holds fish is located at the dredged channel to the Kennedy Space Center on the eastern shore of the lagoon. There is a string of dredge-debris islands along the channel; the flat is to the south of these, just off Peterson Point and Quarterman Cove.

Yet another fishing location to the north of the Bennett Causeway is on the eastern shore between Duck Pond and the shore paralleled by CR 401 (Cape Road) leading into the Cape Canaveral Air Force Station. Here again, the bottom is carpeted with sea grass and holds trout, reds, and black drum.

JIMMY JACOBS

Dragon Point at the junction of the Indian River and Banana River Lagoons is pretty hard to miss!

Finally, the area around the locks connecting the Port Canaveral West Turning Basin to the lagoon can be a hot spot for jack crevalle in the warmer months. The site is immediately north of the Bennett Causeway's eastern end.

The best access point for all of these destinations to the north of the Bennett Causeway is on CR 401 on the lagoon's eastern side and immediately west of the air force station gate. On the northern side of the road is an open shoreline where canoes and kayaks can be launched.

To the south of the Bennett Causeway, motors are allowed on boats, so access and information on the fishing are both in greater supply. By far the most common fish targeted by fly-casters in the lower portion of Banana River Lagoon are redfish and trout. There is no shortage of flats on which they can be found. Places where both species are likely to be encountered in situations conducive to fly-casting include the eastern end of the Merritt Island Causeway (CR 520). On the northern side of the road, to the west of the Cape Canaveral Hospital, is a wadable flat accessible from the shore. The fish are generally found near this flat's edge, where the water drops into a deeper channel. On the southern side of the causeway a huge wadable grass flat also is good for fishing, but it is separated from the shore by a boat channel. Only the narrower band of shallow water between the channel and the roadway can be reached by wading from the parking lot of Constitutional Bicentennial Park on the southern side of the causeway. The park also has a single-lane, paved boat ramp and a parking area that provide boating access to the midsection of the lagoon.

The other convenient public boat landing for this area sits just south of the eastern end of the Bennett Causeway. Kelly Park is a Brevard County facility located on North Banana River Road. It has a double-lane, paved ramp with a paved parking area. The park also has several hundred yards of shoreline offering casting room on its boat basin and the lagoon's shore.

The entire Bennett Causeway to the east of the park is accessible for fishing from the shore or seawalls on both sides of the highway, as well as having some areas that can be waded. The northern side of the causeway has a couple of small islands and stone wave barriers that are close enough to the bank to reach with a fly-cast.

To the south of the causeway, toward its eastern end, a large shallow flat is separated from the shore by a boat channel. On the western side of this flat a shallow sandbar juts up along its rim. This bar is noted for often attracting schools of redfish. Unfortunately, it is a spot that can be reached only by boat.

The Thousand Islands area on the eastern side of the Banana River Lagoon at the southern edge of the town of Cocoa Beach holds several options for catching various species of game fish. To begin with, the canals running east toward FL A1A, just south of Shell Point, are good for snook, tarpon, trout, ladyfish, and jack crevalle. Though these canals have a lot of shore, all are designed to provide boating access to residential neighborhoods, so the land along them is private property. They offer no shore access for fishing.

The large grass flat lying to the south of Houseboat Cut is another Thousand Island site noted for giving up numbers of seatrout, while redfish show up on the flat to the northwest of Jones Creek's mouth in an adjacent area. Just south of Jones Creek and east of Sprig Point the channel running out from Ramp Road Park is also good for both redfish and trout.

Boating access for all of these Thousand Islands sites is easiest from the Ramp Road Park in Cocoa Beach. This city park has a single-lane, paved ramp with plenty of parking. Channel markers lead south from the ramp to Banana River Lagoon. To reach the ramp requires overcoming the one-way street situation in Cocoa Beach. South Atlantic Avenue is one-way headed north. To the east is South Orlando Avenue, running as a one-way street going south. Together these thoroughfares carry FL A1A parallel to the lagoon and the ocean.

From either of the roads, head west on South 5th Street. At its intersection with South Brevard Avenue, turn south and continue to Ramp Road. Turn east on this street; the park is at its end.

The mouth of Newfound Harbor is directly west of the Thousand Islands, on the opposite side of the lagoon. A shoal and tiny islands jut out from Buck Point, which is at the tip of the spit of land known as Horti Point on the eastern side of Newfound Harbor, separating the harbor from the lagoon to the east. These provide a good spot to prospect for seatrout, as do the boat docks on the western side of the harbor's mouth.

Moving south along the western side of Banana River Lagoon, two small islands sit just offshore of the Fairyland community. These are to the east of Honeymoon Lake. The flats around the isles are accessible by boat and hold reds and seatrout. Two miles farther south the grass flats off the community of Lotus are firm and wadable; they attract redfish and seatrout as well. The shore along here, however, is privately owned, so there is no easy access to parking or the water from the road.

At the western end of the Pineda Causeway on Merritt Island you find wadable flats on both the northern and southern sides of the highway (CR 404) near its intersection with FL 3 (Tropical Trail). These are more good places to encounter seatrout and red drum.

Finally, where Banana River Lagoon narrows just before emptying into the Indian River at Dragon Point, the docks along both shores are places to expend a few casts for seatrout. To the east of this area and joined to the lagoon by cuts is the Grand Canal in Satellite Beach. This waterway is protected from the wind in most directions, making it a good place to cast for small snook under almost any conditions. It is also a hot spot for tarpon during the early spring, beginning in March.

Boating access to the southern reaches of Banana River Lagoon is most practical from the boat ramp on the southern side of the Eau Gallie Causeway (CR 518), just south of the lagoon's mouth on the Indian River. This facility was described earlier in the section on South Indian River Lagoon. Run north from the ramp, passing to the east of the giant plaster dragon sitting on Dragon Point at the junction of Indian River and Banana River Lagoons.

It is worth mentioning before leaving the Banana River area that the ocean along here also offers some interesting casting options. On the north, at the jetties protecting both sides of Port Canaveral Inlet, bluefish, flounder, ladyfish, and snook frequently show up, as do schools of redfish along the adjacent beach to the south. This Cape Canaveral area is also well known for the bluefish action it provides in the surf during the winter months. Pompano and whiting are targets for summer casting from the sand, and snook cruise the beach in the spring months. All of the beach from Port Canaveral south to Sebastian Inlet has good access, with the exception of the stretch that falls within the Patrick Air Force Base between Cocoa Beach and Satellite Beach.

Indian River

The final section of the Space Coast fishery is composed of the waters at the northern end of the Indian River. Through here the river is narrower than the lagoons to the north; given the proximity of several inlets, there is more obvious tidal influence on water levels as well.

At the northern end of the river, on the western shore and immediately south of the Eau Gallie Causeway, the Eau Gallie River enters from the west. The mouth of this feeder stream is a good place to target trout in the winter months. Farther up the river, tarpon and jack crevalle are usually present. An additional benefit of fishing in the Eau Gallie is that it is generally sheltered from the prevailing winds. The boat ramp on the Eau Gallie Causeway, which was described earlier in the section on the South Indian River Lagoon, is very convenient for launching a boat to fish this tributary river.

The next area of major interest to fly-casters is a complex of facilities at the Melbourne Causeway on US 192. At the eastern end of the main bridge lies a wadable flat on the southern side of the road. This stretches east to a couple of smaller channels and has a hard-sand bottom. Smaller seatrout are the game fish most often encountered here.

At the western end and southern side of the bridge lies Kiwanis Park at Geiger Point. This county facility offers some shore access and wading possibilities around the mangrove restoration project going on in the adjacent cove.

The Claude Edge Front Street Park in Melbourne is immediately south of the causeway on the western shore, providing boating access to this part of the river. It has a four-lane, paved boat ramp with plenty of paved parking. It does not, however, have any shore access for fly-casting.

Finally, just south of Front Street Park is the mouth of Crane Creek. The points on either side of the creek mouth often hold seatrout in the winter months. Running up the creek past the US 1 bridge, you find a marina basin on the creek. It is a place to encounter jack crevalle and tarpon out in the open water, while casting to the numerous docks can produce snook.

A little less than 3 miles south of Crane Creek on the western shore is a very similar fishing situation at Turkey Creek. Winter trout congregate around its mouth, and it also has a marina basin to the west of US 1. It is noted for giving up snook and tarpon to fly-casting anglers. There is a public boat ramp in Goode Park on the southern side of Turkey Creek, just upstream from the marina basin.

Rather than trying to list them in great detail, let's simply say that there are a great many man-made channels and canals on both shores of the Indian River all the way down to Sebastian Inlet. In cooler weather these deeper bits of water are refuges for seatrout. Virtually all hold fish from time to time, so when weather conditions dictate, any of them is worth probing with a streamer. The same can be said for the spoil islands that line the Intracoastal Waterway along the western side of the river. The drops along their shores hold cool-weather trout, too.

Traveling south along the Indian River, the next location of interest to fly-fishers is at Goat Creek and Goat Island on the western shore. This is one of the few sites on this part of the river with good shore access for wading in an area noted for holding fish. Just south of the US 1 bridge over Goat Creek, there are parking turnouts on the highway right-of-way along the river's shore. The bottom here is hard-packed sand and grass flats that are easily waded, particularly to the north toward the creek mouth. Seatrout, jack crevalle, and ladyfish are the species usually found here.

Some care is needed in wading this location, however. Signs at the shore warn of deep holes on the flats. These depressions are fairly obvious, if you are paying attention, and can be avoided.

Directly across the river on the eastern side is Hog Point. From this location south to Sebastian Inlet, all the really interesting fly-casting sites are located on this eastern shore. Hog Point is a protrusion into the river lined with mangroves and surrounded by grass flats. It can be a real hot spot for snook, but you usually have to get the fly right next to the root system of the plants to interest the fish. Of course, when you hook one of these battlers, the problem becomes getting it back out of the mangroves! In fact, from this spot south, snook become more and more of a factor as fly-casting targets on the Indian River.

A bit farther down the eastern shore of the river, at the opposite end of Washburn Cove from Hog Point, lies Gibbs Point. This is adjacent to the community of Melbourne Shores. The point is another site covered with mangroves that the snook find quite appealing.

Roughly 1.75 miles south of Gibbs Point is the entrance to Mullet Creek and a group of residential canals running off to the east of the creek. These are often referred to as Honest Johns Canals (actually they are in the Evans Pines community) because of the presence of Honest Johns Fish Camp on Mullet Creek. These canals have given up several line- and tippet-class world-record spotted seatrout, and the area is famed as a winter hot spot for this species. Tarpon are also often found in these canals. The places to look for both the silver kings and the big trout are toward the eastern end of the man-made channels, anywhere that the water drops to about 10 feet deep. At its southern end Mullet Creek opens onto Ballard Cove, which is lined with private boat docks where seatrout and redfish often lurk.

All the fishing sites from Hog Point to Ballard Cove are restricted to fishing from a boat, or require a boat to reach even if they are wadable. The best jumping-off point for investigating them is John Jorgensen's Landing. This Brevard County facility is located on US 1 on the western side of the Indian River, about 1 mile north of the community of Grant. It has a two-lane, paved boat ramp with a large sand parking lot. Hog and Gibbs Points are north of this ramp, while Mullet Creek's northern mouth is slightly to the south, with Ballard Cove farther in that direction.

The final fishing site at the southern end of the Space Coast is located in Brevard County's Long Point Park on the eastern side of the river and just north of Sebastian Inlet. This park has a double-lane, paved boat ramp with plenty of paved parking. A fee is charged for both parking and launching a boat. There are a couple of mangrove-lined islands in front of the boat ramp, then a huge grass flat on the river. Some wading is possible around these. The grass flat is quite shallow but often holds seatrout. The channel coming into the park from the north is called Mud Hole. The cove running off to the east of it is noted as a good place to tangle with snook in the summer months.

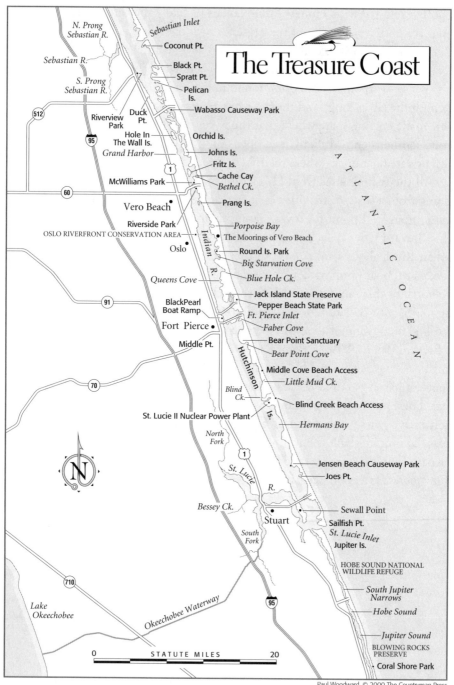

The Treasure Coast

N. Prong Sebastian R.
Sebastian R.
S. Prong Sebastian R.
512
Riverview Park
Duck Pt.
Hole In The Wall Is.
Grand Harbor
McWilliams Park
95
1
60
Vero Beach
Riverside Park
OSLO RIVERFRONT CONSERVATION AREA
Oslo
Queens Cove
91
BlackPearl Boat Ramp
Fort Pierce
Middle Pt.
70
St. Lucie II Nuclear Power Plant
710
Lake Okeechobee

Sebastian Inlet
Coconut Pt.
Black Pt.
Spratt Pt.
Pelican Is.
Wabasso Causeway Park
Orchid Is.
Johns Is.
Fritz Is.
Cache Cay
Bethel Ck.
Prang Is.
Porpoise Bay
The Moorings of Vero Beach
Round Is. Park
Big Starvation Cove
Blue Hole Ck.
Jack Island State Preserve
Pepper Beach State Park
Ft. Pierce Inlet
Faber Cove
Bear Point Sanctuary
Bear Point Cove
Middle Cove Beach Access
Little Mud Ck.
Blind Ck.
Blind Creek Beach Access
Hermans Bay
North Fork
1
St. Lucie
R.
Jensen Beach Causeway Park
Joes Pt.
Bessey Ck.
Sewall Point
Stuart
Sailfish Pt.
South Fork
St. Lucie Inlet
Jupiter Is.

Indian R.
Hutchinson Is.

ATLANTIC OCEAN

HOBE SOUND NATIONAL WILDLIFE REFUGE
South Jupiter Narrows
95
Okeechobee Waterway
Hobe Sound
Jupiter Sound
BLOWING ROCKS PRESERVE
Coral Shore Park

N

0   STATUTE MILES   20

CHAPTER 17

The Treasure Coast

MAPS
DeLorme: *Florida Atlas* pages 96, 97, 103, 109
NOAA: chart numbers 11474, 11476

The name *Treasure Coast* has its roots in the period that began with the exploration and exploitation of Central and South America by Spanish conquistadores. Much of the gold, silver, and other wealth looted from the Aztec and Inca empires, or mined through slave labor in the following centuries, was sent back to Spain via the New Spain treasure fleet, which made periodic runs across the Atlantic loaded with riches. These wooden galleons would come up through the Straits of Florida, riding the northerly currents of the Gulf Stream to Cape Canaveral, then turn east for Europe. Unfortunately, more than once these fleets were met by fierce hurricanes, which smashed many of the vessels and littered the seafloor with plundered loot. The profusion of such shipwrecks along this shore, and the fact that for years coins have washed ashore to be picked up on beaches, led to the area's moniker.

For fly-casters, however, it could be called the Treasure Coast because of all the fishing destinations it holds that are real gems. Stretching across Indian River, St. Lucie, and Martin Counties, the region is bounded on the north by the Sebastian River and Inlet, while running all the way to the Palm Beach County line, just north of Jupiter Inlet. Through this area it takes in the major towns of Vero Beach, Fort Pierce, and Stuart, plus a host of smaller beach and river communities. Inlets are located at Sebastian, Fort Pierce, and St. Lucie, while most of the coast is fronted by three barrier islands. From north to south they are Orchid, Hutchinson, and Jupiter Islands. Behind these islands is the Indian River as far south as St. Lucie Inlet. From there to the southern boundary of the Treasure Coast, the Intracoastal Waterway runs through Great Pocket, Peck Lake, South Jupiter Narrows, Hobe Sound, and Jupiter Sound to the Palm Beach County line.

Along this way portions of the coast are in the Indian River Aquatic Preserve, Jensen Beach to Jupiter Inlet Aquatic Preserve, Pelican Island National Wildlife Refuge (the first such refuge ever established), Hobe Sound National Wildlife Refuge, and many state, county, and city parks. In all, the Treasure Coast stretches for more than 60 miles along the Florida peninsula's shores and—with the exception of striped bass—offers every species of saltwater game fish pursued by fly-fishermen on the Southeast Coast!

When it comes to the Indian River fly-fishing opportunities along this coast, it is not possible to pinpoint every location on the river where seatrout hang out around the mouths of man-made canals and feeder streams, or along the deep edges of channels around dredge-debris islands on the ICW. I can only note that every one of these situations between Sebastian and Jupiter Inlets is a potential honey hole for this species. Particularly during cooler weather, all merit a few exploratory casts.

Orchid Island

Orchid Island, the barrier between the Indian River and the Atlantic Ocean, runs from Sebastian Inlet on the north to Fort Pierce Inlet to the south. It stretches for just shy of 28 miles along the Atlantic. Vero Beach is its only heavily developed portion.

At the northern end of Orchid Island, entering the Indian River from the west, is the St. Sebastian River (though virtually everyone shortens the name to simply the Sebastian). This stream offers a number of good options for fly-casting to saltwater game fish. The water under the US 1 bridge across the river's mouth is infested in the spring and summer with seatrout, redfish, and snook, while the sand flats to the west of the bridge are famous for giving up huge flounder in the fall months.

As the river turns south, just inside its mouth you'll find an outside bend along the northern shore with a number of docks sticking out into the stream. Redfish, trout, snook, and jack crevalle hide around these structures.

About a mile farther up, the tracks of the Florida East Coast Railway cross the river. Not only is this generally considered the boundary between fresh and salt water on the river, but it is also a good spot to find snook feeding in the summer months. Just upstream of the rail bridge the river is joined by its South and North Prongs. Though the water is brackish and, after heavy rains, mostly fresh, in the spring silver kings can be found rolling in the South Prong of the Sebastian, while the North Prong is noted for containing these fish in the summer months.

All these locations require a boat for easy fishing, but getting to them is slow because the entire river system is a manatee zone; powerboats must maintain no-wake speeds. There is a public boat ramp on the South Prong, but it is actually easier to launch at Riverview Park on the Indian River and run north on the ICW to the mouth of the Sebastian River. This park has a double-lane, paved boat ramp. There is limited parking at the ramps but more on the opposite side of the road. The facility is next to the Sebastian Yacht Club building on Indian River Drive, where County Road (CR) 512 (Fellsmere Road) intersects it.

Across the Indian River from the mouth of the Sebastian River lies Sebastian Inlet, one of the premier angling destinations on this part of Florida's coast. This is an area where you can virtually pick your own poison. It has a great variety of species available at different times of the year. From February through April seatrout are present and biting, joined in that last month by flounder. In May snook fishing turns on and lasts until July. In June and July the snook are joined in the feeding frenzy by barracuda, redfish, tarpon, mangrove snapper, and even permit. The permit hang around the inlet until August, but the snapper stay on into September. October is a golden month at Sebastian, with snook, reds, trout, and tarpon all active. The trout action continues into the winter, when flounder, and pompano get into the act as well. As you can see, this is a very hot area for fishing.

Although Sebastian Inlet is easily reached via the Sebastian Inlet State Recreation Area, not all of the access points are practical for fly-casting. There are jetties on both sides of the inlet's mouth, along with catwalks under both sides of the FL A1A bridge. All of these allow fishing, but they are high above the water and currents are quite strong along them. Along the inside of the inlet, to the west of the FL A1A bridge on the southern shore, you find an area of the bank where casting into the inlet waters is possible. On the northern shore, also inside the inlet, is a shallow lagoon that is wadable during high tides, but goes dry on the ebb.

There is a double-lane, paved boat ramp and parking lot in the recreation area on the southern shore of the inlet. The ramp actually faces south on the Indian River. This provides access for boat fishing in the inlet, which is best on a north or west wind; when the breezes are blowing from the south or southeast, the inlet becomes too choppy for small craft. This is also a good launch site for running across the Indian River to the mouth of the Sebastian River.

To the west of the boat ramp out to Coconut Point, there is bank access for casting in the Indian River. To the east of the ramp the bottom is hard-packed sand, offering some wading possibilities.

The Sebastian Inlet State Recreation Area has entrance drives and parking areas on both sides of the inlet. An entrance fee is charged, but it admits you to both sections of the park.

Immediately south of Sebastian Inlet on the eastern shore of the Indian River lies News Cut. This long cove is right at the side of FL A1A, with plenty of parking along the highway. The bottom here is hard sand with sea grass. It is an excellent place to wade fish for snook, reds, and trout. News Cut stretches for almost 4 miles along this shore, ending at Black Point. At the southern end near the point, besides reds and trout, the water holds schools of roaming jack crevalle in the spring through fall.

To the south of Black Point and across the river from the town of Sebastian lies Sprat Point in the Pelican Island National Wildlife Refuge. The flats running from the western edge of the point south to the eastern side of Pelican Island are good spots for encountering redfish in the shallows, as well as an occasional seatrout.

Just south of Sebastian on the western shore of the river, tiny Duck Point juts into the Indian River. The flats on its eastern border are good for red drum and speckled trout.

The most convenient boating access for all these locations south of Sebastian Inlet is Riverview Park in Sebastian, which was described earlier in this section. The ramp is almost directly across the river from Black Point.

The next area of interest to fly-fishermen along Orchid Island's shores is at the Wabasso Causeway (CR 510) and Wabasso Island, which it crosses. The entire western shore of Wabasso Island provides good wading and fishing for reds, while its southern shore also gives up snook and trout. The best access to these flats is by boat, but it is possible to work along the shore on foot from the causeway.

Wabasso Causeway Park has a double-lane, paved boat ramp with plenty of dirt parking spaces on its southern side. The entire shoreline of the causeway is accessible from seawalls or the shore. To the east of the ramp are flats with hard-sand bottoms that extend to a small channel separating the causeway from Wabasso Island. It is possible to wade most of this flat, covering the water in the small channel and out to the offshore boat channel as well.

At the western end of the causeway, the shore running south is a good place for boating anglers to prospect for redfish. Target the area directly west of the southern end of Wabasso Island.

It is also worth noting that the Atlantic Ocean beach at Wabasso is excellent for catching pompano from the surf in November through March. This rather rocky section of coast is best fished on a light wind from the west when the water is clear and the surf calm—all of which make for ideal fly-casting conditions.

The next spot on which to concentrate some casting attention is around Hole in the Wall Island. This island is in the Indian River to the west of the beach community of Indian River Shores. The western shore of the Indian River just north of the island is good for redfish, and these same schools of reds also feed along the oyster bars that lie on the western side of Hole in the Wall. To the east of Hole in the Wall Island, the sides of the channel between it and Pine Island are worth checking out, since they both give up smaller snook.

The best public boating access for Hole in the Wall Island is at Wabasso Causeway Park, which was described earlier in this section.

Continuing down the Indian River along Orchid Island, the next fishing site is on this river's western shore, directly across from Johns Island. The shore is lined with oyster bars to the north of the Grand Harbor community, and these are regularly patrolled by redfish. The two canals that lead into a complex of residential waterways at Grand Harbor are good places to encounter some hungry snook.

The vicinity of the city of Vero Beach is one of the few places along the Treasure Coast not known for good fishing. The number of access points and regularly producing hot spots through this portion of the Indian River are quite small.

Boating anglers have a few options for finding fish in places conducive to fly-casting. To the north of the FL 60 bridge, at the northern end of Fritz Island, lies Bethel Creek on the river's eastern shore. The mouth of this creek is a good place to find snook in the spring months, while back up the creek to the east of Cache Cay is patrolled by tarpon during the heat of the summer.

The best launch site for reaching this area, along with other Indian River fishing sites south of Hole in the Wall Island, is McWilliams Park. This Vero

Beach city park is located north of the FL 60 bridge's eastern end. It has a four-lane, paved boat ramp on a basin off the main river, along with plenty of paved parking. Limited casting from shore to the boat basin is also available in the park. Once your boat is in the river, run north, staying to the east of Fritz Island, to reach the mouth of Bethel Creek.

South of the 17th Street Bridge in Vero Beach, the only spot of note for fly-casting is on the eastern shore of the river in the channel behind Prang Island. This cut often produces spotted seatrout during moving tides.

Riverside Park, south of FL 60 at the eastern end of its bridge over the Indian River, provides the closest public boat ramp for fishing Prang Island. The park has a boat basin with a double-lane, paved ramp and plenty of paved parking. Also, a pedestrian walkway out to an island in front of the parking area allows limited casting to the boat basin and the Indian River along the shore and from the island.

As if to make up for the lack of fishing options in downtown Vero Beach, just 2 miles south the eastern side of the Indian River from Porpoise Point to Round Island provides a continuous variety of species and fishing holes. The cove on the northern side of Porpoise Point is noted for giving up numbers of seatrout. South of the point, Porpoise Bay allows access to the residential canals of The Moorings of Vero Beach on its southern shore. These deep waterways have a reputation for giving up big tarpon in the winter months, along with snook and seatrout. The open waters to the south, called Moorings Flats, are the scene of great summertime action for redfish and trout in shallow water.

Across the Indian River from The Moorings lies an excellent hard-sand flat that is accessible from shore for wading in pursuit of redfish and trout. The shore along the flat is a tangle of mangrove roots that should also hold snook.

To reach this flat, take US 1 south from Vero Beach. At Oslo Road turn east, passing the Oslo Riverfront Conservation Area. The last 0.4 mile of the road before it reaches a boat landing on the river is unpaved. The ramp is single lane and paved, with a small dirt parking area. It is possible to wade onto the flats to either side of the narrow boat channel leading out from the ramp.

Back on the eastern shore of the river, south of The Moorings lies Round Island Park. This Indian River County facility offers several species of fish and ways to get to them. The park contains a boat landing, canoe landing, mangrove islands, deep channels, and adjoining grass flats on the river. Tarpon gang up in the deep runs and the boat basin, while snook hide along the island's mangroves. The nearby grass flats often hold trout and red drum.

Places to target in the park's vicinity include Big Starvation Cove to the south for trout and reds; the outflow of mosquito-control culverts along the cove's northern shore; Lost Bay, which connects the boat basin to Big Starvation Cove, for redfish on its flats and snook in the surrounding mangroves; and the grass flats in the Indian River off Round Island's western shore for seatrout.

Though not a part of the park waters proper, the western shore of the Indian River directly across from Big Starvation Cove is noted for holding numbers of redfish and snook on wadable grass flats. These flats run along about 1.5 miles of the shore to the south. Unfortunately, the shore access is not good on that side of the river; you need a boat to reach the fishing.

The park has a double-lane, paved boat ramp with parking area. Once you are on the water, follow the marked channel to reach the Indian River. This is also a good jumping-off point for boating to the fishing destinations around The Moorings and Porpoise Point, just to the north, or across the Indian River to the opposite shore's grass flats. Though very little shore access exists, there is a canoe-launch area, and such a craft can easily put you in casting distance of fish without involving inordinate amounts of paddling time.

To reach Round Island Park, take FL A1A north from Fort Pierce. The park entrance is on the western side of the road about 5.5 miles north of town.

Between Round Island Park and Fort Pierce Inlet are two more fishing sites that merit mention. Blue Hole Creek and the residential canals of Queens Cove are on the eastern side of the river and hold snook most of the year. These can be reached from the boat ramp at Round Island Park as well.

The southern end of Orchid Island at Fort Pierce Inlet offers a few more places for fly-fishermen to try their hands, though all but one of them require a boat. Access to the northern side of the inlet requires a long walk on the beach, since no parking areas are nearby. Once you are there, the northern jetty is inaccessible from shore, but it is possible to cast near it from shore. In all, however, the trek to the inlet isn't worth it from a fishing standpoint.

The Jack Island State Preserve, just north of the inlet, provides foot access to Jack Island. Unfortunately, though it looks promising on a map, it does not offer a viable shore fishery either.

On the other hand, there *is* one strip of beach known for exceptional fishing just north of the inlet. The Radar Hole is immediately north of Pepper Beach State Park. This depression on the beach side of the offshore sandbar holds pompano in the fall through spring months.

For boating anglers, the places to hit include the channel between Orchid and Coon Islands leading into Tucker Cove on the the northern side of the inlet. This is good water for finding trout and snook. You can also locate snook around Jim Island, which the North Beach Causeway (FL A1A) crosses, and in Fort Pierce Cut leading into Wildcat Cove. Additionally, the grass flats west of Jack Island can be a seatrout hot spot.

Boating access to all of these sites is easiest from the four-lane, paved boat ramp on Jim Island, on the North A1A Causeway. It is located on the northern side of the highway and has a paved parking area.

Hutchinson Island

Hutchinson Island serves as a barrier between the Indian River and the Atlantic Ocean for just short of 22 miles between Fort Pierce Inlet on the north and St. Lucie Inlet at Stuart in the south. While each end of the island has seen some major development, much of Hutchinson remains in a wild state. The St. Lucie II Nuclear Power Plant is located very near the midpoint of the island, while the waters of the river to the west are in the Jensen Beach to Jupiter Inlet Aquatic Preserve.

The entire beachfront on Hutchinson Island offers good surf-fishing possibilities. Also, St. Lucie and Martin Counties both have a number of parks and access points that make it easy to reach the beach. The last of an incoming tide through the first half of an outgoing flow is usually best time for fishing from the sand. In the spring snook show up along the breakers, while pompano are there from fall through spring. Whiting are found in the troughs near the shore all year long. The best time for fly-casting the surf is on southerly or easterly winds, just at dawn or dusk.

Surprisingly, the beach on Hutchinson Island is not all the same: A distinct change occurs right at the border between St. Lucie and Martin Counties. A dredging project in Martin County some years back caused the depressions close to shore to fill in with sand, creating a wider, more sloping beach. To the north in St. Lucie County the beach is narrower, and there is a noticeable sandbar about 40 yards offshore with a trough running parallel to the beach west of it. Obviously, the St. Lucie County beaches offer the better surf casting.

At the very northern end of Hutchinson Island is Fort Pierce Inlet, which offers a potpourri of fish species. During the summer and early fall big snook invade this inlet, joined by equally large jack crevalle that hang around the signs and channel markers inside the inlet. The rest of the year seatrout,

The dike roads along the shore of the Indian River to the south of Fort Pierce offer foot access to both mosquito canals and flats on the river.

smaller snook, and some redfish are the main targets. In the winter months some bluefish will also appear around the inlet mouth.

Access to the Hutchinson Island side of Fort Pierce Inlet is quite good from South Jetty Park. This facility offers beach access as well as a paved fishing pier atop the jetty. Rather than being just a straight rock pile running out into the ocean, this jetty has a smaller pier running south from its main arm, creating more casting room. You can cast from the paved surface or climb out onto the rocks to fish. Watch your backcasts, however, since the jetty is lighted for night fishing and has power lines strung overhead. This jetty is also crowded with anglers, especially on weekends. A good paved parking area is provided for fishermen.

Back to the west toward the city of Fort Pierce, the park containing the St. Lucie County Historical Museum sits on the South A1A Causeway, to the east of the bridge over the Indian River. This park is on the northern side of the highway and has a double-lane, paved boat ramp and hard-sand parking area. Also, along the northern side of the causeway is a 0.25 mile of wadable beach flats. Trout, snook, and jack crevalle are the most likely species here.

The waters under the bridge on the South A1A Causeway are good for snook, as are the marina docks to the north along the river's western shore. At the western end of the bridge on this northern side is the Black Pearl Boat Ramp, a double-lane, paved ramp with a large parking area off North Indian

River Drive. Obviously, it is very convenient place for launching a fishing boat to try for the snook in the surrounding waters.

South of the western end of the causeway bridge lies the Fort Pierce Riverwalk. Most of this paved walkway along the waterfront has a high railing that makes fly-casting impractical. However, near its northern end behind the Fort Pierce Community Center the seawall is fronted by several hundred yards of a narrow sand and rock beach, where casting is possible. This stretch runs from the marina north to the causeway. Expect to encounter snook, trout, and jack crevalle along here.

Directly across the Indian River from the Riverwalk area of Fort Pierce lie Thumb Point and Faber Cove. The many docks that line the shore from the point into and around the cove are good places to find both seatrout and snook at most times of the year. Boat access is easy from either the South A1A Causeway or the Black Pearl Boat Ramp.

Although the western shore of the Indian River from Fort Pierce to Stuart is paralleled by Indian River Drive (CR 707) and the flats along here look appealing, access is very limited. There are few places to park, and much of the land is private, posted property. Surprisingly, the fishing is not particularly great either. Some of the grass flats regularly hold seatrout but are noted for little else. The eastern side of the river offers far more options through this part of the Treasure Coast.

To the south of Fort Pierce Inlet, Hutchinson Island has 8 miles of virtually undeveloped beach and river frontage. There are several good public access points from shore and a number of wading possibilities. As you travel south from Fort Pierce via FL A1A, the first of these you encounter is Bear Point Sanctuary. There is a parking area on the western side of the road on Bear Point Cove. The cove offers good wading on hard sand in an area that often attracts schools of red drum. At the northern end of the parking area a gated dike road offers 3 miles of foot access to the riverbank through the 13-acre preserve. Culverts under the dike connect the mosquito-control ditches to the east to the river. Each culvert is a potential holding area for snook, as is the entire mangrove-lined shore. It is possible to wade out into the river at many places along the dike, then cast back toward the pipes and mangroves. The bottom is almost entirely hard sand with sea grass. Seatrout, redfish, jack crevalle, and ladyfish also show up along the flats. The mosquito-control ditches on the other side of the dike are home to baby tarpon of up to about 10 pounds—but don't even think about wading into these ditches. They have soft mud bottoms, and if you stepped in you might simply disappear!

The Bear Point Sanctuary dike road ends at a no-trespass area, so you must simply walk back out along it. Be aware also that in the spring through fall, walking this dike (or any of those to the south that are discussed later) requires a heavy dose of insect repellent.

The Green Turtle Beach Access parking lot is located on the eastern side of FL A1A 0.7 mile south of Bear Point. Across the highway from it is the end of 3N Dike Road (the N denotes the northern end; all the dike roads are loops running off the highway, so an S designation indicates the southern end of the road), which, like all these roads, is gated. It offers more shoreline access to the river and the adjacent mosquito-control ditches. This road runs south around Middle Point before rejoining FL A1A.

At 0.6 mile south of Green Turtle Beach Access is the entrance to the Vitolo Family Park at Middle Cove Park Riverside. Obviously, when someone donates land for a park, it can result in a rather long and convoluted name! Still this 107-acre tract offers foot access to 4N Dike Road, as well as the 4S entrance 0.3 mile farther south. The entire loop road can be walked and features frequent access to flats, culverts, mosquito-control ditches, and mangrove shores.

At 0.2 mile south of the Vitolo Family Park 4S Dike Road, there is an access point directly to the Indian River flats from the roadside, with turnout parking. Then another 0.5 mile down the road is the Middle Cove Beach Access. Across the highway from this parking lot is 5N Dike Road, which runs for 1.2 miles south along the Indian River and offers access similar to that found on the other dikes. Its southern entrance at 5S is on the northern shore of Little Mud Creek. Across the stream on the southern side is the Blind Creek Beach Access and the entrance to 6N Dike Road. There is an unimproved sand launch site at the southwestern side of the FL A1A bridge over the creek. Limited wading is available along the mangrove shore of Little Mud Creek for trout and snook as well. Boating anglers often target the deep hole at the mouth of the creek to the west of the bridge for these species, too.

The Blind Creek Beach Access runs for 1 mile along the eastern side of the road to the point where Blind Creek comes under the road. The gate for 6S Dike Road is also on the western side of the highway at this spot. The dike road, which is gated at each end, provides a loop for access to the river along its entire length back to Little Mud Creek.

The St. Lucie II Nuclear Power Plant is 0.7 mile south of Blind Creek, with most of the area around it off limits. For boating anglers, the channel dredged to the plant from the main river and Big Mud Creek on the northern side of the plant provide fishing bonanzas. The channel is 4 to 7 feet deep, and the drops along its sides hold trout, redfish, and jack crevalle. Big Mud Creek holds tarpon in the summer, while the two deep holes at the warm-water discharge points from the plant hold tarpon, jack crevalle, lady-fish, trout, redfish, snook, and even permit on a year-round basis.

The nearest paved public boat ramps are at the South A1A Causeway at Fort Pierce (described earlier in this section) or to the south at Jensen Beach Causeway Park. The latter facility has a double-lane, paved ramp with parking on the southern side of CR 732. It also affords casting room from shore and seawalls along both sides of the causeway for trout and snook.

Immediately south of the St. Lucie II Power Plant property is roadside parking and access to Old Hermans Bay. The grass flats to the west gener-ally have clear water, are firm and shallow enough for wading, and yield seatrout and snook.

At 1.7 miles south of the power plant, FL A1A runs along the edge of Hermans Bay for a mile. There are frequent parking spots along the highway, as well as beach access parking lots on its eastern side. All of the bay is com-posed of shallow, wadable grass flats that mainly hold trout and snook.

The final point of shore access to the Indian River on Hutchinson Island before you reach St. Lucie Inlet is 4.6 miles south of Hermans Bay (and to the south of the Jensen Beach Causeway). The cove immediately north and east of Joes Point is right at the side of FL A1A, offering a place to wade onto the flats. This area is noted for holding trout, snook, jack crevalle, and mangrove snapper. Parking is in a pull-off on the western side of the road.

The vicinity of the St. Lucie Inlet at Stuart lies at the southern end of Hutchinson Island. It has a plethora of options for fly-casters to tangle with trout, redfish, snook, tarpon, jack crevalle, ladyfish, and permit. Having listed all these fish, it should be noted that tarpon and snook are the stars of the fishing world at St. Lucie.

On the northern fringe of this zone is the Stuart Causeway across the Indian River on FL A1A. You sometimes hear locals refer to this as the 20-Cent Bridge—a holdover from the days when tolls were collected on this bridge as well as on the FL A1A bridge to the west over the St. Lucie River. The Stuart Causeway Bridge did indeed cost 20 cents to cross, while the St. Lucie span is known as the 10-Cent Bridge.

There is parking and shore access on both sides of the Stuart Causeway, as well as a double-lane, paved boat ramp on the southern side of FL A1A. This landing is convenient for boating anglers to launch for fishing all the areas on the Indian and St. Lucie Rivers and the St. Lucie Inlet at Stuart. The northern side of the causeway's western end usually holds speckled trout and can be waded from the shore. The relief channel at the eastern end of the causeway often holds tarpon, while trout can be found in dredge holes along the northern side of the road. Docks in this area also harbor snook. The only problem with fishing here is that in warmer weather the causeway is crowded with swimmers, sunbathers, boaters, and folks riding personal watercraft.

To the south of the causeway, Bird Island sits on the eastern side of Sewalls Point (which separates the Indian and St. Lucie Rivers). This area has several attractive habitats for game fish and is well worth inspecting. Snook hang out under the docks on Sewalls Point, while the dredge holes between it and Bird Island hold trout and redfish. There are also grass flats all around Bird Island. A good approach for these is to anchor your boat and wade the shallows for reds, trout, and snook.

Rounding Sewalls Point to the west puts you in the St. Lucie River, which is famous for its spring and summer tarpon fishing, giving up fish that tip the scales at up to 100 pounds. You can find these fish rolling on the surface anywhere from the Roosevelt Bridge on FL A1A downriver to the channel just off the narrow spot known as Hells Gate. Through here you will also encounter ladyfish along the eastern side of the river, schools of jack crevalle roaming the entire area, and snook under the many docks. The tarpon and jack also move above the Roosevelt Bridge to the area around the mouth of Bessey Creek on the North Fork of the St. Lucie River. The fish venture even farther upriver, but this is at the border of St. Lucie and Martin Counties and also the demarcation line between salt and fresh water; if you go upstream after the tarpon and jack, you need to have a freshwater fishing license. You can find these fish in the South Fork of the river as well, but above the mouth of Mapps Creek you are again venturing into fresh water.

Shore access to St. Lucie Inlet from the north is a rather difficult proposition. Sailfish Point is an exclusive residential development on that side of the inlet, and only property owners are allowed in. This leaves you with a 1-mile walk down the beach to reach the inlet. Once you are there, the jetty is not accessible from shore, though you can wade out in the surf to fish around it. In fact, you are probably better off fishing the stretch of the beach known as the Bathtub to the north of the jetty if you are targeting summer snook. They often feed right in the surf along here.

For boating anglers, the options are better. From May through August, permit hang along the northern side of the inlet feeding on blue crabs being pulled out of the Indian River during falling tides. This action is best around the full moon of each of these months.

All summer the snook fishing in this inlet is what attracts most anglers. The fish stack up along the southern shore of the inlet, from the junction of the Indian and St. Lucie Rivers east to the southern jetty at the mouth of the inlet. Spots to pay particular attention to are just off Hole in the Wall and Toilet Bar. The first of these is a pass running back into the mangroves, while the other is a nearby rock bar on which a porcelain toilet sat for several years before washing away in a storm. Along the shore off these spots the bottom is littered with fallen trees and alive with juvenile snook.

Farther east on this side is a stretch of stone jetty detached from the shore. During falling tides it is a favored feeding station for big snook of up to 15 to 20 pounds.

Finally, on the northern side of the inlet target the water outflow from the Sailfish Point complex. Numbers of snook tend to stack up in the summertime when water is moving here.

As noted earlier, the best boating access for all of these sites is from the ramps on FL A1A at the Stuart Causeway.

Jupiter Island

Compared to its two sister islands on the Treasure Coast to the north, Jupiter Island is a fly-fishing wasteland. This is not to say that the waters around it do not hold fish, or that they cannot be caught on fly-rods. It is simply that these situations are in much shorter supply here than farther north.

At the northern end of the island lies the Hobe Sound National Wildlife Refuge, which runs all the way north to St. Lucie Inlet. Paying the $5 entrance free for the refuge entitles you to make a very long walk up the beach to the inlet. There are too many other easier, better, and cheaper options for fly-fishing in this region to get too excited about this one!

Farther south at Hobe Sound Beach there are some possibilities for surf casting for fly-anglers in boats. A shallow reef only 100 yards offshore often harbors permit of up to 35 pounds, though smaller ones are much more plentiful. Also, this is the northernmost point at which bonefish occasionally show up along the beaches. To the north of the pavilion at the public beach access, pompano are also regularly taken from the surf. As with any beachfront that holds pompano, look for places where the sand drops steeply into at least 6 feet of water for the best action.

At the southern end of Martin County near the Palm Beach County line lies the Blowing Rocks Preserve. Owned and managed by The Nature Conservancy, this preserve contains a stretch of beach dominated by bedrock protruding from the sand. The bottom offshore is also rocky and a haven for snook in the summertime, with literally hundreds of the fish stacked up here. It is possible to wade into the surf and cast to these fish in some places, but the main rock outcropping is pounded by waves, making this impractical. Boating anglers often target the fish by chumming with live bait fish; when the snook start feeding, streamers are tossed into the melee. Pompano are also taken regularly in this area.

The Nature Conservancy has a small parking lot on CR 707 and charges a fee for admittance to the beach. You can access the area for free by walking 0.5 mile up the beach and across the county line from the south after parking at Coral Cove Park. That park is a Palm Beach County facility with no parking fee. Be aware that the loose sand on the beach makes walking tiring.

The most practical access point for boating to Blowing Rocks is from Jupiter Inlet to the south in Palm Beach County. Burt Reynolds Park is located south of the US 1 bridge over the Loxahatchee River. The highway then crosses a small creek on which the park has a four-lane ramp on eastern side of the road and a two-lane ramp on the west. Both ramps have paved parking areas. From the ramp, run west into Lake Worth Creek (Intracoastal Waterway), then turn north into the Loxahatchee River. On that waterway head east out through Jupiter Inlet, then follow the shore north until you see the Blowing Rocks jutting up from the beach.

On the inland side of Jupiter Island only the waters of Hobe Sound are particularly noted for producing fish. While the western shore of the sound has a fair amount of development, the eastern shore is still lined with mangrove thickets. Ladyfish, pompano, jack crevalle, and snook are the main species encountered. Much of this fishing is done on flats barely a foot deep, but they tend to be inaccessible from shore, so you need a boat to reach them. The best area to target is just south of the CR 707 bridge over Hobe Sound; pay special attention to the eastern shore along the 1-mile stretch between ICW Channel Markers 36 and 40.

The nearest public boat ramp providing practical access to this area is, again, in Burt Reynolds Park at Jupiter Inlet, which was described earlier in this section. From the ramp follow the directions for Blowing Rocks, but before you exit Jupiter Inlet, turn north up the ICW through Jupiter Sound. Follow the ICW channel for about 6 miles to Channel Marker 40.

CHAPTER 18

The Gold Coast

MAPS
DeLorme: *Florida Atlas* pages 109, 115, 119, 123
NOAA: chart numbers 11462, 11466, 11474

South Florida's Gold Coast well deserves its name. It stretches from Jupiter Inlet to the north, across Palm Beach, Broward, and Dade Counties, to end on the southern edge of Biscayne Bay. Along the way it takes in some of the most glamorous and exclusive real estate in the South. Other forms of gold found along the shore come in the form of glitzy nightlife and sun-drenched beaches. As a result, it is a place where a lot of people want to live. From North Palm Beach at the northern end of Lake Worth to Miami's southernmost suburb, Cutler Ridge, the Atlantic coastline is one huge unbroken development spanning almost 100 miles. It is also home to more than 8 million people.

The major cities along the Gold Coast are West Palm Beach, Palm Beach, Lake Worth, Boca Raton, Pompano Beach, Fort Lauderdale, Hollywood, Miami, and Coral Gables. Ocean inlets occur at Jupiter, Palm Beach, Ocean Ridge (Boynton Beach), Boca Raton, Hillsboro (Pompano Beach), Port Everglades (Fort Lauderdale), and Haulover (North Miami). Inland saltwater fisheries are, however, in very short supply for such a long coast. The Loxahatchee River at Jupiter is joined to the south to Lake Worth via Lake Worth Creek (referred to locally as the Ditch). Then from Lake Worth south to Biscayne Bay the Intracoastal Waterway is a narrow, deep, and dredged channel. Its shores are mostly private property, offering no access for angling, and its waters are not noted for good fishing.

In the same vein, the beaches along this coast from Lake Worth to Miami Beach are beautiful, but most are also gently sloped and crowded with swimmers, sunbathers, sailors, and personal watercraft. None of this is conducive to good fly-fishing in the surf, and some beaches are even closed to fishing between 8 AM and 5 PM daily.

Having gotten the negative factors out of the way, it should be noted that the fisheries located on either end of the Gold Coast are very good ones, and there are some small oases of fly-fishing opportunities spread along the coast.

On the Gold Coast the populations of the various game fish species undergo a dramatic change. The spotted seatrout and redfish that are the staples of the fishery to the north become far less common or important. They still show up even into the Upper Florida Keys, but south of Lake Worth they are second-fiddle players, as are ladyfish and bluefish. Snook, tarpon, mangrove snapper, barracuda, and jack crevalle are more common in inshore waters here and, in the case of tarpon and snook, more sought after by fly-casters. Biscayne Bay sees another switch of emphasis. Snook and jack crevalle begin to fade a bit in numbers and prominence, to be replaced by bonefish and permit. In other words, the deep-south Florida fishery takes on a decidedly tropical face.

Jupiter Inlet

Jupiter Inlet, just south of the Palm Beach County line, anchors the northern end of Florida's Gold Coast. It serves as the outflow for the waters of the Loxahatchee River, as well as the Intracoastal Waterway from Jupiter Sound to the north and Lake Worth Creek from the south.

By far the main species of game fish targeted in Jupiter year-round is the snook, but bluefish and jack crevalle are plentiful in the Loxahatchee in the fall and winter, as are ladyfish. During the summer months tarpon also run into the river.

The inlet itself is the most popular place for intercepting snook. Most fly-casters use boats to drift through it when targeting these fish. A couple of factors aid fly-casting here. To begin with, the water is relatively shallow—only 8 to 10 feet deep—along the northern shore. It is also very clear, allowing you to spot the fish, which sometimes feed in the inlet by the hundreds!

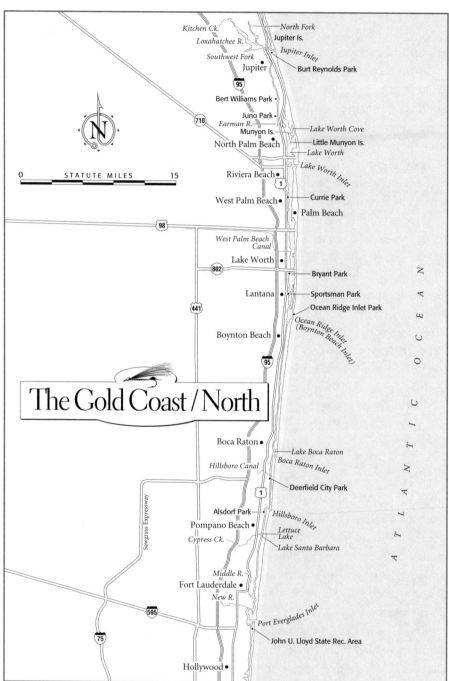

The Gold Coast / North

Kitchen Ck.
North Fork
Loxahatchee R.
Jupiter Is.
Jupiter Inlet
Southwest Fork
Burt Reynolds Park
Jupiter
95
Bert Williams Park
Juno Park
710
Earman R.
Lake Worth Cove
Munyon Is.
Little Munyon Is.
North Palm Beach
Lake Worth
Lake Worth Inlet
Riviera Beach
1
West Palm Beach
Currie Park
Palm Beach
98
West Palm Beach Canal
Lake Worth
802
Bryant Park
Lantana
Sportsman Park
Ocean Ridge Inlet Park
Ocean Ridge Inlet
(Boynton Beach Inlet)
Boynton Beach
95

N
0   STATUTE MILES   15

ATLANTIC OCEAN

Boca Raton
Lake Boca Raton
Boca Raton Inlet
Hillsboro Canal
1
Deerfield City Park
Alsdorf Park
Hillsboro Inlet
Pompano Beach
Lettuce Lake
Sawgrass Expressway
Cypress Ck.
Lake Santa Barbara
Middle R.
Fort Lauderdale
New R.
595
Port Everglades Inlet
75
John U. Lloyd State Rec. Area
Hollywood

Paul Woodward, © 2000 The Countryman Press

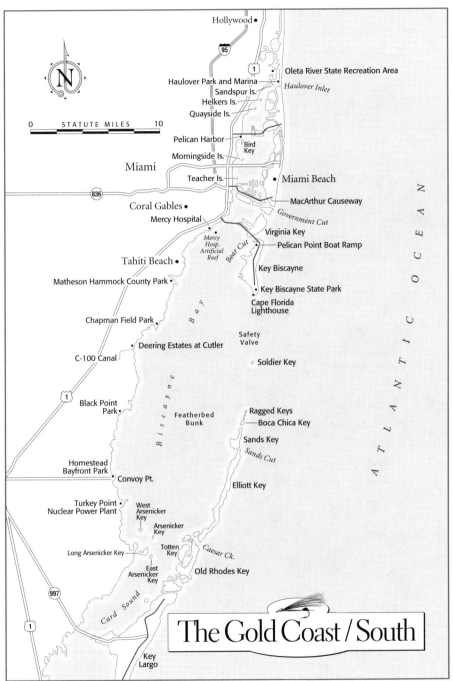

The Gold Coast / South

Paul Woodward, © 2000 The Countryman Press

Snook move in with the incoming tide looking for bait fish (croakers in particular), then drift back out with the tide. Pay special attention to the seawall along the northern side of the inlet and the old groin that sticks out from it at the western base of the northern jetty. This spot is known locally as the Bathtub.

On the southern side of the inlet you'll find good access from shore in Jupiter Beach and Dubois Parks. These sit adjacent to each other and provide access to the inlet, jetty, and beach. The water on this side of the inlet is deeper, currents are strong during moving tides, and there is usually a stiff breeze blowing, all of which make fly-casting difficult. Add to this a lot of palm trees right at the shore, areas cordoned off for swimming, and numbers of bait-fishermen—fly-casting here is not easy. Shore access, however, runs inland in the parks to the first boat basin on the southern shore. Bluefish are a possibility along here in the winter months. There is also a small tidal creek in the parks, with a bridge over it and concrete and manicured sand shores for swimming. It also has some mangroves along the bank, so if you can find it empty of swimmers, it probably harbors snook.

From Jupiter Beach Park access is available to the southern jetty, where fly-casting is possible but, again, difficult because of wind and other anglers. Snook, jack crevalle, bluefish, and ladyfish are all possible targets here, along with the occasional Spanish mackerel or tarpon.

These parks are at the end of Jupiter Beach Road to the east of FL A1A, south of the Loxahatchee River. Boating access to the inlet is easiest from Burt Reynolds Park. This Palm Beach County facility is on a small creek leading into Lake Worth Creek (Intracoastal Waterway) to the south of the Loxahatchee. There is a four-lane, paved boat ramp on the eastern side of US 1 where it crosses the creek, while a double-lane, paved ramp is on the western side of the highway. Both have large paved parking lots but are very crowded on weekends.

Once you are on the water, run west out of the creek into the ICW and turn north. At the junction with the Loxahatchee River, turn east to reach the inlet.

Just inland of the inlet and to the north of the Loxahatchee River, Coral Cove Park offers a stretch of access to the eastern side of the ICW as it flows through Jupiter Sound. For 0.5 mile the shore has a hard-packed sand bottom that allows you to wade out far enough to fly-cast toward the mangroves that grow sporadically along here. This is a popular fishing, sunbathing, and swimming area on weekends. Seatrout, snook, jack crevalle, and

JIMMY JACOBS

*Blue runners are one of the smaller inshore species of fish
along south Florida's Gold Coast.*

ladyfish are the most available species, but hooking a tarpon is possible in the summer.

The Loxahatchee River upstream of its junction with the ICW offers a couple of fisheries worth checking out. Tarpon range up into the river during the summer months, traveling into the Loxahatchee itself along with its North and Southwest Forks. Be aware that the forks of the upper river are brackish water; rainfall heavily affects the salinity. If you choose to fish up these, it is safest to have both a salt- and a freshwater fishing license.

In the winter months the Loxahatchee sometimes hosts a heavy run of bluefish, with some 20-pounders present. These fish show up all over the shallow flats from the Florida East Coast Railway bridge upstream to the confluences of the three forks of the Loxahatchee. When water salinity is high, blues have even been spotted as far up the main river as the mouth of Kitching Creek in Jonathan Dickinson State Park. The mouth of the North Fork of the Loxahatchee has a deep hole off its eastern side called Tarpon Bay. The water here drops to 12 to 18 feet and harbors big jack crevalle and bluefish in the winter, while holding tarpon in the hotter months.

Another oddity of the fishing here is that there is a resident, year-round population of bluefish in the river too. These 2- to 10-pounders are most often taken between May and September along the southern side of the river, 0.25 mile west of the railway bridge. Usually the best time to ambush the blues is during falling tides, particularly one that takes place near the break of day. During rising tides, look for schools of ladyfish on the same flats that hold the blues. In fact, the ladyfish is one of the species the big blues feed on.

The best boating access to all of these areas in the Loxahatchee is from Burt Reynolds Park's boat ramps, described earlier in this section. Run north on the ICW to the Loxahatchee and head west under the railway bridge.

To the south of Jupiter Inlet down to the northern end of Lake Worth, the fishing options are rather skimpy. Along the Atlantic shore the public access area of Juno Beach has a trough running along its shore that is fairly deep near the edge. This is ideal water for surffishing for pompano. Other than this, the inland channel of the ICW running through Lake Worth Creek is the only angling offered along this 6-mile portion of the coast.

Lake Worth Creek is lined with impassable mangroves on much of its shore, or private property where it is cleared, so public bank access is virtually nonexistent. There are no areas of the stream that provide wading access either. Boating anglers may find ladyfish, jack crevalle, snook, and trout on the deeper edges of the creek, but no specific areas are noted for holding fish on a regular basis.

Launch facilities for fly-casters who want to explore the creek are located in two Palm Beach County parks on the western side of Lake Worth Creek. The first of these is Bert Williams Park, off Ellison Wilson Road between Donald Ross Road on the north and PGA Boulevard to the south. It has a double-lane, paved boat ramp with plenty of space for parking.

To the south of Bert Williams Park, Juno Park is situated on Juno Road (this is actually the same thing as Ellison Wilson Road, but the street changes names as it approached North Palm Beach). This facility has a single-lane, paved boat ramp with a large parking lot.

Lake Worth

Lake Worth runs for just over 20 miles. Its western shore forms the waterfront for the cities of North Palm Beach, Riviera Beach, West Palm Beach, Lake Worth, and Lantana before ending at Boynton Beach in the south. To the east of the lake lies Palm Beach Shores to the north of Lake Worth Inlet (also called Palm Beach Inlet). South of the inlet are the ultra-exclusive beachside estates of Palm Beach. Although called Lake Worth, this body of water is actually a lagoon off the Atlantic Ocean with Lake Worth Inlet on the north and Ocean Inlet (sometimes referred to as Boynton Beach Inlet) in the south connecting it to the sea. It offers a number of places for anglers in boats to cast flies, a couple of shore-casting sites, and one excellent place for wade fishing.

At the northeastern corner of Lake Worth, the shore is in John D. MacArthur Beach State Park. This park contains 161 acres of land, providing shore access to both the beach and 174 acres of water on Lake Worth that are also in the park. A fee is charged for entering the park.

Reaching the beach requires a long trek from the parking areas across a boardwalk over Lake Worth Cove. The scenic beach lies at the foot of a sand bluff, is steeply inclined, has a reef very near shore, and usually sees fairly heavy surf action. Beach fishing can be good for pompano and whiting, with bluefish possible in winter.

On the inland side are two small arms of Lake Worth that run under bridges on FL A1A to the north into the park. The eastern arm is the larger and called Lake Worth Cove. To the west is Lake Worth Lagoon. Both of these are limited to nonmotorized boat traffic, creating ideal conditions for canoe or kayak fly-casting. This is especially true of Lake Worth Cove, whose mangrove-lined shores can give up snook, seatrout, and jack crevalle. The beach boardwalk bisects the cove, but fishing is not allowed from this structure. Its pilings, however, offer paddlers another target for their casting. The bottom of the cove has a very soft bottom not suitable for wading.

The most attractive area for anglers on foot in MacArthur State Park is Munyon Island, which offers wading flats and causeway fishing. Despite its name, this protrusion of land jutting out into Lake Worth from the east is actually a small peninsula. The flats around Munyon are by far the best place for wade fishing between St. Lucie Inlet and Biscayne Bay. The grass flat south of the island is extensive, running more than 0.5 mile south and bounded on the west by Little Munyon Island. The bottom through here is hard sand, offering good footing. At high tide the water is roughly waist-deep, providing good locations for casting to snook and barracuda along the mangrove-lined banks. As the tide falls the huge pods of bait fish in water little more than knee-deep are often attacked by large schools of jack crevalle that run from 6 to 10 pounds each. Ladyfish, seatrout, and tarpon are other species that show up on the flat.

Access to this flat is a bit of a hassle, since no parking is allowed along FL A1A in the southern part of the park or along the public bike path to the

POLLY DEAN

The flats north of Munyon Island at Burnt Bridge in North Palm Beach are good places to hook up with a hefty jack crevalle.

south. You can, however, use the parking turnout at the southern end of the Burnt Bridge (FL A1A) where it crosses Lake Worth Lagoon. This is part of MacArthur Beach State Park, but you do not have to pay the entrance fee to park here. From the parking area on the eastern side of the road, cross to the west and walk south along the bike path. At the end of the state park's fence a number of openings in the mangroves allow you access onto the flat.

To the north of Munyon Island is another flat, but one that has a different character. The bottom is softer, but still very wadable from the riprap west of the Burnt Bridge. There also are some deeper channels, so it is much wiser to wade here during lower tides, when these are clearly visible. Fishing to the mangrove shores during falling tides or the main channel edges at low tide can produce barracuda, snook, jack crevalle, seatrout, ladyfish, and tarpon. Snook and jack crevalle are the most dependable species. The bigger 'cuda are more prevalent on the flat in the fall, but smaller ones are here year-round.

When the tide is high, this northern flat is best fished from the riprap along the Burnt Bridge Causeway. It provides access on both sides of the highway, as well as both ends of the bridge, where seawalls line the channel into Lake Worth Cove. Also, be aware that there are small culverts though the causeway at either end of the bridge. These also attract bait fish and predators during moving tides.

As mentioned, parking is available at the southeastern corner of the Burnt Bridge Causeway. If you want to fish the area without getting your feet wet, the nearest public boat ramp is 3.5 miles south at Phil Foster Park in Palm Beach. This county-owned facility has a four-lane, paved boat ramp with a large paved parking area on the northern side of County Road (CR) 708 (Blue Heron Boulevard) at the eastern end of the bridge over Lake Worth.

One other place in the northern end of Lake Worth is known for holding concentrations of fish on a year-round basis. The mouth of the Earman River—which carries the Intracoastal Waterway from Lake Worth Creek into Lake Worth—is located on the western shore about 0.6 mile north of Munyon Island. The river itself attracts lots of snook in the warmer months, while the deep hole in Lake Worth immediately north of its mouth is a hot spot for trout, mangrove snapper, and bluefish in the winter months. The area around the Earman River is accessible only by boat. Like most of the other fishing sites in Lake Worth (except Munyon Island), its water is deep, ordinarily requiring weighted flies and slow presentations to get down to the fish.

South of the Blue Heron Boulevard Causeway are two more good fishing holes. One is Lake Worth Inlet between Palm Beach Shores on the north and Palm Beach to the south. This inlet attracts hundreds of snook in the spring and summer, while giving up jack crevalle and bluefish in the winter. The edges of the channel are the places on which to concentrate. Although there is beach access to the northern side of the inlet, there is no parking anywhere near the inlet in Palm Beach Shores. From Riviera Beach Municipal Park, you will have a long trek south down the beach to reach the inlet.

To the west of the inlet and south of Peanut Island lies the other hot spot—and in this case, that is a very accurate description of the site. Directly east of the red and white smokestacks of the Florida Power and Light Electric Plant is the Boil, the plant's warm-water discharge. It attracts tarpon and jack crevalle throughout the fall and winter. For tarpon, use shrimp or cockroach pattern flies tied on 1/0- or 2/0-sized hooks with fast-sinking line.

The Earman River, Lake Worth Inlet, and the Boil are all best accessed by boat from Phil Foster Park on the Blue Heron Boulevard Causeway, described earlier in this section.

About 2 miles south of the Boil, a seawall runs along the western side of Lake Worth on the West Palm Beach lakefront. The wall starts at Currie

Park on the north and continues along Flagler Avenue (with a couple of breaks for private property) for 6 miles to south of the city's downtown. The seawall along here is backed by a paved walkway, but parking is extremely limited along the entire distance, with the exception of Currie Park. It is possible to cast from the seawall, and the waters along it are famous for giving up jack crevalle in the 20- to 30-pound range in the early morning hours! In the summer snook may also show up around any of the boat docks, and tarpon sometimes can be seen rolling; in the winter some huge ladyfish are taken here. On rising tides it is even possible to sightcast to sheepshead along the wall. The downside to fly-fishing from the wall is you have to watch your backcasts to avoid hooking a passing jogger or bike rider.

For boating access to the seawall area, Currie Park has a six-lane, paved boat ramp with a large paved parking area. It is located at the intersection of Flagler Avenue and 23rd Street. The park is, however, a favored hangout for panhandlers and vagrants.

For boating anglers, the next stop moving south on Lake Worth is immediately north of the Southern Boulevard (US 98) bridges. Here a series of oyster bars just offshore can hold seatrout, ladyfish, jack crevalle, and snook. These shell beds offer your best shallow-water option for finding fish in the midsection of Lake Worth.

Next, 2.3 miles south of Southern Boulevard along the western shore of Lake Worth is the mouth of the West Palm Beach Canal. This is a good place to drop anchor and work the canal's mouth for jack crevalle, mangrove snapper, and snook, as well as bluefish in the winter.

In the city of Lake Worth, Bryant Park is a city facility sitting at the southwestern end of the Lake Avenue (CR 802) causeway and bridge across Lake Worth. The park has 0.5 mile of seawall with casting access to the water, as well as a small riprap-lined peninsula with fishing piers that juts into the lake. There is shoreline fishing access on the eastern end of the causeway as well. This area offers some prospects for jack crevalle and snook in the summer, but from the park north to the Lake Worth Municipal Golf Course, winter bluefish are the main attraction.

Also on site in Bryant Park is a double-lane, paved boat ramp with a large parking lot. This facility is a good jumping-off point for the Southern Boulevard oyster beds, the West Palm Beach Canal's mouth, and the municipal golf course shoreline, all of which lie to the north.

In the town of Lantana at the southern end of Lake Worth, Sportsman and Bicentennial Parks offer some shore and boating access. These Palm

Beach County parks are located on the downtown waterfront of Lantana. At the western end of the East Ocean Avenue bridge, Sportsman Park on the south side of the road and Bicentennial Park to the north have seawalls from which casting is possible. Again, summer snook and seatrout are possibilities, while jack crevalle, ladyfish, and bluefish show up in the cooler months.

The boat ramp at this site is a double-lane, paved facility with plenty of paved parking. It is also the closest public launch site for fishing Ocean Ridge Inlet, which lies about 2.5 miles south on the eastern shore of Lake Worth.

Ocean Ridge Inlet (also known as South Lake Worth Inlet) has a reputation for holding snook in the summer through fall, but it is a narrow pass with such swift, turbulent currents that fishing it from a boat is not very practical. Look instead for a hole about 25 yards to the northeast of the inside of the inlet. This can be fished from a boat, has 10 to 15 feet of water in it, and often holds numbers of snook.

Shore access is good at the inlet, through Ocean Ridge Inlet Park. There are parking areas on both sides of the pass on the western side of FL A1A. Seawalls along the pass and the jetties on either side of the inlet can be reached by foot, but, as mentioned, the current is extremely fast here, and fly-casting is not very practical.

Fort Lauderdale

In spite of the title of this section, the area actually covered is much larger than the city of Fort Lauderdale. Beginning at Boynton Beach and running south through Delray Beach, Boca Raton, Pompano Beach, Fort Lauderdale, and Hollywood, the coast is not a very good one for fly-fishing. The beaches along here have excellent access and do hold fish, with snook present in the spring through fall, bluefish in the surf in the winter, and jack crevalle cruising year-round. Still, the sands are crowded with sun worshipers and swimmers and not particularly attractive surf-fishing sites. Prevalent east winds make this shore particularly tough on fly-casters.

Inland, the ICW is a narrow, deep, dredged channel whose shores are almost exclusively lined by private property. Indeed, along this entire stretch only three inlets and one state recreation area offer very limited fishing options to fly-casters.

The first of these is at Boca Raton Inlet, situated between Boca Raton to the north and Deerfield Beach on the south. This small inlet provides limited access to the water from its southern side in South Inlet Park off FL

A1A. Parking (for a fee) is provided for fishing from the beach or southern jetty. As with most South Florida inlets, snook is the primary species to target in the spring through fall. Expect to find them in the inlet or the harbor inland of it that is referred to as Lake Boca Raton.

To the south of the inlet (about 1.75 miles), just south of the Palm Beach County–Broward County border, is the inflow of the Hillsboro Canal on the western shore of the ICW. The mouth of the canal and surrounding docks are places to check out for snook during the winter months. Boating access to this location is easiest from Deerfield City Park. Head east from US 1 on Hillsboro Boulevard (CR 810) to NE Fifth Avenue and the park, which provides a paved boat ramp and parking. Once you are on the ICW, the canal's mouth is immediately north of the Hillsboro Boulevard bridge over the waterway.

Roughly 5 miles south of Boca Raton Inlet lies Hillsboro Inlet. The fishing here has a bit more variety but is tough on fly-casters. Just outside the inlet along the beach to the south is a deep shoreline trough noted for attracting pompano in the early spring, with March the peak month. Then, in May through September, permit move into this region. These fish can run up to 30 pounds and hang near the mouth of the inlet. They like crab patterns, but you have to fish them very near the bottom.

Inside the inlet on its southern side is a little harbor area that can be a snook honey hole, with the best fishing taking place around the new and full moons, when the snook spawn in June through September. There is good shoreline access from a parking lot at the southwestern end of the FL A1A bridge over the inlet. Casting from the seawall to this area is possible, but difficult due to the number of palm trees along the shore and the skeletal frames of old docks cluttering the waterfront.

Approximately 2.6 miles south of Hillsboro Inlet on the ICW is the confluence of Cypress Creek on the western side of the channel. At this site the waterway bulges on either shore, with the western side referred to locally as Lettuce Lake and the eastern as Lake Santa Barbara. Lettuce Lake and lower Cypress Creek have depths of from 6 to 12 feet, and snook like to spend the winter around the shoreline docks. Fish of up to 10 pounds are possible, and there are probably going to be some jack crevalle in the area as well. Alsdorf Park, just off US 1 to the south of Hillsboro Inlet, offers the closest public boat ramp. After launching, run east to the ICW channel, then turn south to Cypress Creek.

The final Fort Lauderdale–area fishing location, and one actually in that city, is found around Port Everglades Inlet. This is the natural outflow site for the New and Middle Rivers, but the inlet has been dredged to become a major cruise-ship port. It is also known for producing big tarpon and snook, as well as for giving up the state-record mangrove snapper, a huge 17-pounder. March is the best time for tarpon, while the summer months provide plenty of snook, some of which run as large as 25 pounds. Also, in October when the mullet migration reaches Port Everglades, the entire harbor can be alive with feeding jack crevalle, bluefish, snook, and tarpon, many quite hefty. Targeting surface-feeding schools is your best option.

Needless to say, the water in the inlet is very deep, and it is usually turbulent from tidal currents and wakes from the heavy boating traffic it sees. Probably your best option for fly-casting from a boat comes in the summer, when you can target the areas just west of the inside end of the riprap on either shore. A shelf along the dredged channel is only 4 to 12 feet deep along here, and snook often congregate on it. But as mentioned, expect rough boating conditions.

There is a paved jetty on the southern side of the inlet that is in the John U. Lloyd State Recreation Area, but its height above the water, the strong prevailing winds, and the rough waters make fly-casting from it totally impractical. The park also provides beach access, but the sands are broad, flat, and much better for swimming than fishing. A small tidal creek cutting though the park to the south has mangrove-lined shores and could yield some tarpon or snook action for anglers in canoes. Access to the creek is from the recreation area boat ramp at the creek's mouth on the ICW. This is also the best public boating access for fishing the Port Everglades area.

To reach the John U. Lloyd State Recreation Area, take North Ocean Drive to the north off FL A1A at Dania. This street crosses the mouth of the tidal creek at the boat ramp, then continues to a parking area at the southern jetty on Port Everglades Inlet. A fee is charged for entering the park.

Once your boat is in the water, there is one other possibility for some snook action in the vicinity. Run north on the ICW past Port Everglades for 1 mile to the mouth of the New River and turn west. The shore of this deep stream is lined with upscale homes, all of which have docks that often harbor snook.

A bit farther on the ICW, north of the Las Olas Boulevard Bridge, the Middle River also enters the ICW from the west. This stream offers very similar conditions to those found on the New River, but the water here is not as deep. Again, target the shoreline docks for snook.

Biscayne Bay

Inshore fly-fishing in the Miami area is dominated by Biscayne Bay. This shallow, subtropical marine lagoon stretches 35 miles from North Miami south to Old Rhodes Key and the northern end of Key Largo. At its narrowest the bay is 1 mile wide, but it spreads to 8 miles across in the south, bordered on its seaward side by a coral reef that runs as far north as Cape Florida. Just inside the reef lies a string of islands that are, in fact, a northern extension of the Florida Keys. These consist, from north to south, of Soldier, Ragged, Boca Chita, Sands, Elliott, and Old Rhodes Keys. To the lee of these keys grass flats stretch for miles to the west, broken in the middle of the bay by a huge patch of hard bottom west of the Intracoastal Waterway. There is then another strip of grass flats along the western shore, fronting on miles of mangrove thickets.

When it comes to the game fish that are ordinarily taken on fly-fishing equipment, Biscayne Bay is loaded. It has spotted seatrout, bonefish, permit, and some redfish on grass flats; snook under docks; tarpon, jack crevalle, and ladyfish in channels and cuts; plus smaller barracuda and mangrove snapper virtually everywhere, though the really big 'cuda show up in the bay in the fall and winter. While most of these fish require a boat to locate and catch, there are a few surprisingly good areas for shore or wade fishing as well.

North Biscayne Bay

At the very northern end of Biscayne Bay lies the Oleta River State Recreation Area. The park is immediately south of the Sunny Isles Causeway (CR 826) on the western shore of the bay. It is positioned on a 993-acre peninsula between the bay and its namesake river.

The riprap shores on the eastern side of the park facing on Biscayne Bay offer some casting room from shore to sea grass beds where seatrout are likely to be found. A small cove intrudes into the park from the south, placing it to the west of the picnic and parking area in the state recreation area. This cove breaks up into several slender fingers of water that are lined with mangroves and form the facility's canoe trails. These narrow and usually shallow waterways connect with larger pondlike areas. It is possible to wade the edges of virtually all of them. Small barracuda, mangrove snapper, snook, tarpon, and seatrout show up at various times in the channels. Good access to these is

JIMMY JACOBS

To find many of the fly-casting opportunities along the Gold Coast you can't avoid the area's luxury condominiums.

from the children's playground area or from the mountain-bike trails that meander through the park.

A fee is charged for entering the Oleta River State Recreation Area. The area entrance drive is located on the southern side of CR 826, just west of the Sunny Isles Causeway.

A bit to the south and on the northern side of Miami Beach's Bal Harbour community sits Haulover Inlet. This is the only pass connecting the northern end of Biscayne Bay to the Atlantic. Although this narrow inlet has Dade County's Haulover Park and Marina on its northern shore, along with a rock jetty, there is no real fly-fishing access on that side. To the south a concrete seawall lines the inlet, but the fly-casting is no better than from the northern shore. A parking fee is charged in the park and at the lots under the FL A1A bridge on the inlet's southern side.

Boating anglers can target the inlet in the spring and summer for snook, with most of the action occurring during falling tides in the early morning. Another dependable option here from April through November is targeting the charter-boat docks just inside the inlet when the half- and full-day fishing vessels are docking. As they clean their catches, fish scraps are tossed into the water, which attract huge tarpon like a dinner bell. Fish of more than 100 pounds are common here.

Due east of Haulover Inlet and on the western side of the Intracoastal Waterway (ICW) channel lies Sandspur Island. It is the northernmost of a string of dredge-debris isles in the bay that are Dade County parks but accessible only by boat. On Sandspur's western side is a grass flat where seatrout are likely to be found, along with the ever-present barracuda.

The nearest public boat ramps for the fishing sites around Haulover Inlet are in Haulover Park and Marina. This facility has five paved ramps, totaling 10 lanes, with plenty of parking. This is just north of the inlet on the bay's eastern shore on Collins Avenue (FL A1A).

In the northern portion of Biscayne Bay, between the Broad Causeway (CR 922) on the north and the North Bay Causeway to the south, there are some extensive grass flats to the east of the ICW. The largest lies northwest of Normandy Isle and north of the green ICW Channel Marker 21. It has a couple of debris islands near its southern edge as well.

On the western side of the ICW channel and immediately south of the Broad Causeway is Helkers Island. This is another of Dade County's island parks. It has a grass flat to its west, and to sweeten the fishing along the western side of the flat, a rubble-pile artificial reef has been created in 7 feet of water. Farther down this side of the ICW channel is Quayside Island, which is also a park. It lies directly east of Miami Beach's Indian Creek Village community. Again, Quayside's western shore is bordered by grass flats.

All of these flats are good places to encounter spotted seatrout, mangrove snapper, barracuda, and roving pods of tarpon. Boating access for them is easiest from Pelican Harbor on the southern side of the North Bay Causeway off NW 79th Street. This facility has five paved ramps, with 10 lanes and plenty of parking.

South of the North Bay Causeway the fishing options on grass flats become even better. At 0.25 mile, almost directly south of the Pelican Harbor boat ramp lies Pelican Harbor Reef. This is another of Dade County's inshore, rubble-pile artificial reefs, again lying in only 7 feet of water.

Immediately south of the reef is Bird Key, a Dade County island park containing extensive wading bird rookeries. Boating around it is discouraged, but it does mark the northern edge of vast grass flats that run almost from shore to shore in the bay all the way south to Morningside Island, just north of the Julia Tuttle Causeway (NW 36th Street, I-195, FL 112). Morningside is another of the county-owned island parks.

These flats are excellent for seatrout, while also producing mangrove snapper, ladyfish, jack crevalle, and barracuda. Snook and tarpon also sometimes roam into these areas. A better option for these two species, however, is to target the western bridge on the Tuttle Causeway after dark. It is possible to sight-cast to snook and tarpon that cruise just along the edge of where the span's lights meet the shadow created by the bridge. This is boat-fishing-only territory, since no shore access exists.

The most convenient public boating access is from Pelican Harbor on the North Bay Causeway, which was described earlier in this section.

South of the Julia Tuttle Causeway and north of the Venetian Causeway are more grass flats. Some of these are along the eastern shore, just off of the Sunset Islands, while the largest concentration is along the eastern side of the ICW. In this latter location Teachers Island is the southernmost of the county-owned island parks and is completely surrounded by flats. The same species of fish are common here as on the flats north of the Tuttle Causeway.

South Biscayne Bay

The MacArthur Causeway (US 41, FL A1A) connects the mainland to the trendy South Beach area of Miami Beach and marks the transition from North to South Biscayne Bay. From the causeway all the way down to Key Largo at the Dade County–Monroe County border, the southern bay is filled with enormous and lush grass flats. Down the center runs a strip of hard bottom. These expanses hold spotted seatrout, bonefish, permit, mangrove snapper, barracuda, and ladyfish. In the channels crossing the flats, particularly in the northern portion of this region, tarpon are found along the edges of the shallows. Since 1990 a program of stocking redfish in the bay has introduced 1.6 million hatchery-reared fingerlings to the southern bay. The plantings appear to be bearing fruit in bringing these fish back to their native range, from which they disappeared in the 1940s.

On the southern side of the MacArthur Causeway, bordered on the opposite side by Dodge, Lummus, and Fisher Islands, runs a channel called Government Cut. It is the main thoroughfare for boat traffic entering and leaving Biscayne Bay from Miami. It is also a great place to find tarpon of up to 100 pounds. Due to the boat traffic, this is a fishery best challenged in early morning before the passing watercraft make the fish skittish. Similar conditions are found just to the south where Bear Cut forms the channel between Virginia Key on the northwest and Key Biscayne to the southeast.

The Rickenbacker Causeway (Crandon Boulevard) spans the western end of Bear Cut, as it connects Key Biscayne and Virginia Key to the mainland. The causeway to the west of Virginia Key is lined on both sides by parking and beach areas that have shallow, wadable flats, which are accessible from shore. These are, however, very popular swimming beaches, so early morning is the best time to fish here. Additionally, just north of the eastern end, Dade County's Brickell–North Rickenbacker Artificial Reef is just offshore of the causeway. This debris pile, along with the flats to either side of the roadway, holds seatrout, jack crevalle, ladyfish, mangrove snapper, and barracuda.

West Biscayne Bay

The western shore of the bay to the south of the Rickenbacker Causeway offers a number of fishing hot spots, some of which are best accessed by boat, while others are available for fishing from shore or by wading. The first of these sits just east of the stubby peninsula on which Mercy Hospital is situated. This site is just more than 0.5 mile south of the causeway. Along with patchy grass flats, the Mercy Hospital Artificial Reef is located here. The area is noted as a hotbed of spotted seatrout action, while the rubble pile of the reef is a good spot to target mangrove snapper. This is, however, a boat-fishing location with no shore access.

The closest public boat landing for fishing around Mercy Hospital is the Pelican Point Boat Ramp. This facility is located in Crandon Park on the northern end of Key Biscayne, west of Crandon Boulevard. The ramp is paved, as are the adjacent parking lots. From the ramp, run northeast across the bay to the mainland and Mercy Hospital.

The next fishing location to the south on this side of Biscayne Bay is Matheson Hammock County Park. The park's South Beach is marked with a WADING BEACH sign. It is, in fact, the most accessible wading flat for bonefish available to shorebound anglers north of the Florida Keys. Boats are not allowed to approach closer than 200 feet to the shore on this beach.

From the boat channel in the park, the flat stretches for about a mile to the south, with its hard-sand bottom covered with dark-colored sea grass. At low tide, particularly early and late in the day, bonefish can be found tailing here. Barracuda are present during all tide levels. Even at high tide the water on the flat is only 2 feet deep. The shoreline is edged with mangroves, while new shoots of the plant dot the flat. This flat can also be accessed from the South Picnic Area, next to the boat channel.

The northern side of the creek that carries the boat channel inland, which leads past the park marina, is lined with riprap and offers a casting platform for probing this deeper water. Barracuda, small jack crevalle, and mangrove snapper are most prevalent, but tarpon sometimes cruise the channel.

Upstream of the marina, which has a paved public boat ramp with parking lots, the the creek swings under the entrance drive and has a designated fishing area running along its western bank. There is a parking lot and casting room from shore for several hundred yards. Seatrout, ladyfish, jack crevalle, barracuda, mangrove snapper, and snook are all likely to be encountered here.

Matheson Hammock County Park is open daily from sunrise to sunset. An entrance fee is charged. The park entrance is off Old Cutler Road, which runs parallel to the bay's shore to the east of US 1, just south of Tahiti Beach.

Traveling 3 miles farther down this side of the bay brings you to another area of shallow grass flats. These run from Chapman Field Park on the north, past the Old Cutler Power Plant, to Chicken Key on the south. Chapman Field Park is a sports complex located at bayside but offering very limited access to the water. This site is easier to reach and fish using a boat. The flats here are hard sand with sea grass and noted for yielding seatrout and bonefish. The boat channel cutting through the flats to the power plant often holds numbers of mangrove snapper along its edges. Boating access to these flats is best from the ramp at Matheson Hammock County Park that was described above.

The next public access point for the western shore of Biscayne Bay is located in the Cutler community just south of Chicken Key. The Deering Estates at Cutler (South Addition) is a Dade County park not much bigger than its name! Tucked on the northern shore of the mouth of the C-100 Canal where it meets the bay, this site offers fishing from the canal's shore for about 100 yards up to a small lock. Also, there is access to the bay on a soft mud and grass flat that allows limited wading. This is a place to target mangrove snapper, seatrout, and jack crevalle. When rains cause the lock to dump water into the canal, snook, and tarpon can be caught as they take advantage of forage fish being swept along with the current.

The park is a fenced compound at bayside in a residential neighborhood. It has a large unpaved parking area just off Old Cutler Road, south of its intersection with SW 168th Street and to the east of US 1.

A little more than 5 miles farther down the coast on the western shore lies Black Point Park, which is another Dade County facility that has a marina with a paved boat ramp. There is a 0.25-mile boat channel running in from the bay to the marina with a walking trail along its northern side. This bank has room for casting to the deep water in the channel, where barracuda, mangrove snapper, redfish, and seatrout are all possible catches.

To reach Black Point Park, take Palm Drive east from US 1 at the Princeton community, south of Cutler Ridge. The park is at the end of Palm Drive.

The last shore access to the western side of Biscayne Bay is at a duo of federal and county facilities. Run by the National Park Service, Convoy Point is the main entrance to Biscayne National Park. It is separated by a boat channel from Dade County's Homestead Bayfront Park.

Convoy Point has a long, paved rock jetty running along the boat channel out into the bay. The jetty provides a good casting platform for fishing the deep water in this channel to the south. Barracuda, seatrout, mangrove snapper, jack crevalle, snook, and redfish all frequent this area. On the northern side of the jetty there is a shallow grass flat, but its bottom is too soft for wading. Occasionally it is possible to spot trout, reds, or even bonefish within casting distance on the flat.

Across the boat channel lies Homestead Bayfront Park. This side of the channel running into the park marina is lined with riprap; barracuda and mangrove snapper are usually present. It is possible to fish all the way up to a small lagoon beside the marina. Redfish, trout or snook may enter this area as well.

To the south of the boat channel is a saltwater lagoon cut off from the bay for swimming. West of this pool the bayshore is lined with riprap along a soft-bottomed grass flat. Barracuda, redfish, bonefish, and mangrove snapper are often found just off the rocks. Seatrout of up to 3 or 4 pounds have also been caught here in recent years. Unfortunately, this flat is too soft for easy wading.

At the far southern end of the park is a small cove that juts back into the mangrove-lined shore. It appears to be a creek mouth, but it runs only a few hundred feet inland. Access to the shore of the cut is available past the decorative stone wall sitting on the point at its mouth.

There is limited wading around the cove's mouth and up into it. At high tide the water is up in the mangroves. Casting to the far edge along these may produce snook, redfish, or trout. At low tide the cut often contains numbers of small barracuda anxious to attack anything that looks edible.

Homestead Bayfront Park has a paved, six-lane boat ramp with large parking lots. A fee is charged for entering the park and for launching a boat.

To reach Convoy Point and Homestead Bayfront Park, take SW 328th

JIMMY JACOBS

The Turkey Point Nuclear Power Plant looms in the distance while casting at Homestead Bayfront Park.

Street east from US 1 in Homestead. This road changes names, becoming North Canal Drive. The entrances to both parks are at the end of this road.

The final fishing destination on the western side of Biscayne Bay is one of the most remote angling sites on the coast of the southeastern states. The Arsenicker Keys lie 5 miles to the southeast of Homestead Bayfront Park and just north of the Dade County–Monroe County border. Arsenicker, Long Arsenicker, East Arsenicker, and West Arsenicker make up this group of islands. These uninhabited mangrove isles are surrounded by lush grass beds that have patches of marl mixed in where new mangrove shoots jut above the water.

The Arsenicker flats are known for giving up some of the biggest bonefish in the world. Fish of 10 to 12 pounds are taken here, with 6- to 7-pounders common.

It is also worth noting that these isles lie immediately east of the cooling canals of the Turkey Point Nuclear Power Plant on the mainland. These canals and the surrounding area are the last stronghold of the American crocodile. With the population of these large reptiles expanding, you face the possibility of running into one here. These crocodiles are a fully protected endangered species and best given a wide berth if spotted.

East Biscayne Bay

The eastern side of Biscayne Bay also provides some good options for fly-casters. At its eastern end the Rickenbacker Causeway delivers Crandon Boulevard onto Key Biscayne; Crandon Park covers this key's northwestern corner. The swimming beach here is actually a grass flat on the Atlantic Ocean often visited by tailing bonefish. Unfortunately, the beach is very popular and usually crowded, so your best option is to fish it very early in the morning. That also happens to be the most likely time of the day to find bonefish anyway.

On the other side of Crandon Boulevard from the beach lies the Pelican Point Boat Ramp, which is within the park on the bayside. This landing has a paved ramp and parking lot. It is the best jumping-off point for all of the fishing sites along the eastern side of Biscayne Bay.

The southern end of the island is contained in Key Biscayne State Park. On its eastern side this park has a popular swimming beach on the Atlantic Ocean. From the old Cape Florida Lighthouse west around the southern end of the island, you find more than a mile of seawall fronted by riprap and a deep channel, with several small fishing piers jutting out into the water. It is possible to cast from the seawall along most of its length, targeting the pilings of some of the piers.

Fishing in the channel can produce seatrout, mangrove snapper, barracuda, snook, and tarpon. The grass flats southwest of the park often contain bonefish of up to 7 pounds. These can be spotted at a low tide if it occurs early in the morning or late in the evening. You'll need a boat to reach these flats.

There is a fee for entering Key Biscayne State Park, but the park is very popular and stays crowded. It is located at the southern end of Crandon Boulevard.

To the south, permit become the glamour species—most prevalent and most often targeted by fly-casters. Between Key Biscayne and tiny Soldier Key is an area dubbed the Safety Valve. Through here there are a number of channels running east–west through the grass flats. Permit can be found cruising the edges of the flats, using the channels as travel routes during low tides. At the flood they move up onto the shallows to feed. On the southern side of Soldier Key there is also a deep flat where permit are often found. Along the ocean side of these same flats big tarpon can be found cruising during the months of May and June.

The next islands south of Soldier Key are the Ragged Keys. These small isles have a hard bottom to their west that attracts permit but also holds bonefish. Be aware, however, that these islands are privately owned, so do not go ashore. Their ownership is a vestige of the fact that as late as the 1970s Ragged, Sands, Elliott, Totten, and Old Rhodes Keys were all within the city limits of Islandia, Florida, with a population of 12! The rest of these keys are now part of the national park property.

Lying just south of little Boca Chita Key is Sands Key, which is almost entirely composed of mangroves. Another good flat lies inside Sands Cut, which separates Sands Key from Elliott Key to the south. This flat can be virtually dry at low tide, but bonefish move up on it when the water rises.

Elliott Key is a long, slender island that stretches 8 miles north to south. Along its ocean side are hard-sand flats that offer excellent wading, while often holding permit and bonefish. To easily fish here, however, a west wind must be blowing. On the bay side of the island, the grass flats produce permit and bonefish as well, with the added bonus of some redfish showing up.

At the southern end of Elliott Key, Caesar Creek separates it from Old Rhodes Key. This spot regularly produces some of the biggest mangrove snapper in Biscayne Bay. Fish of up to 5 pounds are caught here. Another option in the creek in the spring and summer months is to target the over-hanging mangroves at high tide. Tarpon often loll around under this natural cover and ambush careless forage fish—or well-presented flies.

Finally, one fishing destination worth mentioning lies out in the middle of Biscayne Bay. Featherbed Bank is located between Black Point Park on the mainland and Boca Chita Key to the west, and is bisected by the channel of the Intracoastal Waterway. The site is composed of three soft-bottomed grass flats, some of which go completely dry during extreme low tides but can be alive with fish during flood stages. This is not a wading area; you can sink up to your knees in the soft bottom.

Permit hang around on the hard bottom to the west of the flats, then move up onto the Featherbed near the red ICW channel marker that sits at the southern edge of the northern flat. The southern flat is south of the nearby green ICW channel marker, while the smallest of the flats is to its west. The northern flat is the most dependable of the three for fish. Often permit and bonefish tail in these shallows, but due to the soft bottom, you can also locate them by looking for the puffs of mud they stir up. It is not unusual for tarpon to cruise the edges of these flats, and the drop at the edge of the ICW channel is almost guaranteed to have mangrove snapper and barracuda along it.

Boating access to the Featherbed Bank is easiest from Black Point Park, which is just more than 5 miles east of the ICW channel.

CHAPTER 19

Florida Keys

MAPS
DeLorme: *Florida Atlas* pages 122, 123, 124, 125, 126, 127
NOAA: chart numbers 11442, 11452, 11462

Welcome to a different world! Whether you travel down US 1, take the back-door route to Key Largo on Card Sound Road, or fly into Marathon or Key West, once you enter the Florida Keys everything changes. Land or sea, fishing or people—all seem affected by island fever. After all, this is the Conch Republic.

Back in the 1980s during a downturn in the area's economy, the final straw for the local residents, or Conchs (pronounced to rhyme with *bonk*), was having the U.S. Drug Enforcement Agency set up roadblocks on US 1 at Florida City to search all vehicles headed into or out of the island chain. The law-abiding Keys folks were outraged. In response they seceded from the Union, formed the Conch Republic, declared war on the United States, surrendered, and asked for foreign aid to rebuild their economy—all in one day!

These islanders are just as serious about their fishing as they are about politics, and for good reason. Throughout this "strand of pearls" stretching southwest from the mainland near Homestead, some of the best saltwater angling in the world can be found.

Although the islands in Biscayne Bay from Soldier Key to Old Rhodes Key are technically part of the Florida Keys, normally the region is described as running from Key Largo to Key West, and beyond to the Marquesas Keys and Dry Tortugas. In all, the island chain stretches for 126 miles from Key Largo to Key West, including dozens of inhabited islands connected by 42 bridges carrying US 1 and the Overseas Highway. These bridges vary from a few hundred feet long to the Seven Mile Bridge, which spans the water from Knight Key south to Little Duck Key (identified on older maps as Pacet Key) near Marathon. Some of the bridges still use the rail trestles of the Florida East Coast Railway's Key West Extension. Henry Flagler's "Railroad That Went to Sea" was completed in 1912 and blown away in the most violent hurricane on record, which struck on September 2, 1935. The major towns and communities along the island chain are Key Largo, Islamorada, Marathon, and Key West.

The species of most interest to fly-casters in the Florida Keys are bonefish, permit, and tarpon. Additionally, in the Upper Keys there are some good areas for snook, redfish, and seatrout on the Florida Bay side of the islands. Other fish likely to grab your fly along the island chain are mangrove snapper and barracuda.

Snook, redfish, and trout are fairly rare around the islands touched by the Overseas Highway, and are almost never found west of the Big Pine Key area. The fish that are present and biting year-round in the Keys are bonefish, barracuda, mangrove snapper, and small tarpon. Snook also are active every month in the backcountry of the Upper Keys.

Among seasonal species, permit are at their best from March through August along the entire island chain, while redfish and trout angling is good these same months in Florida Bay near the Middle and Upper Keys. Finally, big tarpon are easiest to find in April through June.

The biggest problem with describing the fishing in the Florida Keys is that there are just too many good places to fish. Many of these, however, are in very remote regions. Unlike fishing around populated and accessible areas, if you have boat trouble on the backcountry waters of Florida Bay, you cannot simply flag down another angler for a tow back to the dock. You may end up waiting for the Coast Guard search-and-rescue helicopters to find you!

Exacerbating this problem are the shallow sand, mud, and marl flats that jut up everywhere. Boating in the Keys can be treacherous. The vast number of wrecks of all sizes lying on the bottom around these islands attests to this.

For these reasons, the scope of this chapter is the waters immediately surrounding the islands connected by road to the Overseas Highway, or in easy visual contact with the roadway. If you want to venture into Florida Bay, or

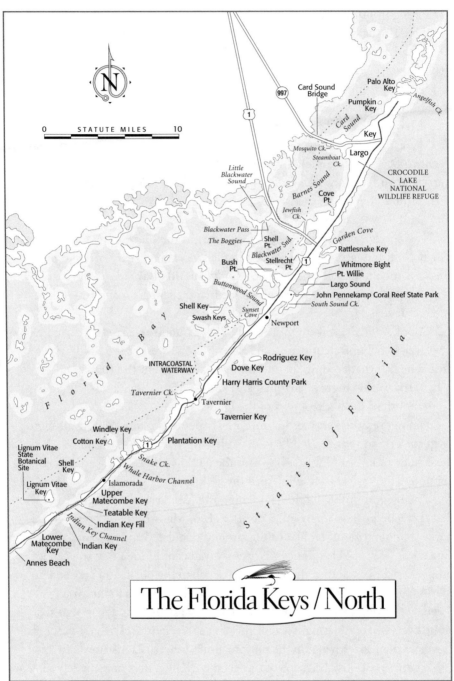

The Florida Keys / North

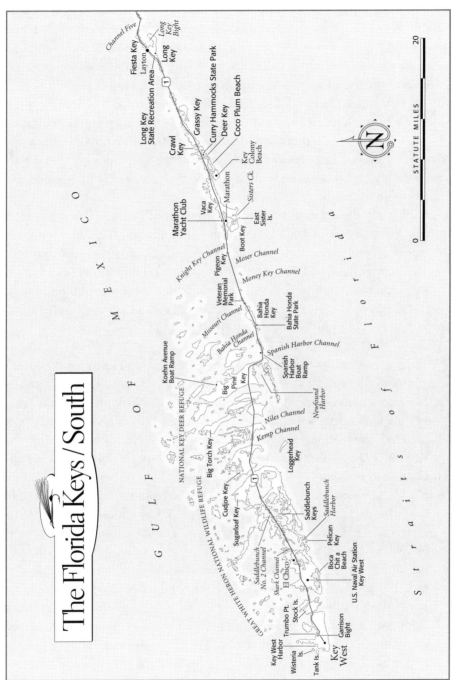

The Florida Keys/South

Channel Five

Long Key Bight

Fiesta Key

Layton

Long Key

Long Key State Recreation Area

Curry Hammocks State Park

Grassy Key

Deer Key

Coco Plum Beach

Crawl Key

Key Colony Beach

Marathon

Sisters Ck.

Vaca Key

Marathon Yacht Club

East Sister Is.

Boot Key

Knight Key Channel

Pigeon Key

Moser Channel

Veteran Memorial Park

Money Key Channel

Missouri Channel

Bahia Honda Key

Bahia Honda State Park

Bahia Honda Channel

Spanish Harbor Channel

Koehn Avenue Boat Ramp

Spanish Harbor Boat Ramp

Big Pine Key

Newfound Harbor

NATIONAL KEY DEER REFUGE

Niles Channel

Kemp Channel

Big Torch Key

Loggerhead Key

GREAT WHITE HERON NATIONAL WILDLIFE REFUGE

Cudjoe Key

Saddlebunch Keys

Sugarloaf Key

Saddlebunch Harbor

Pelican Key

Saddlebunch No. 2 Channel

Shark Channel

El Chico

Boca Chit a Beach

Trumbo Pt.

Stock Is.

U.S. Naval Air Station Key West

Key West Harbor

Garrison Bight

Wisteria Is.

Tank Is.

Key West

GULF OF MEXICO

Florida

Straits of

N

STATUTE MILES

0   20

Paul Woodward, © 2000 The Countryman Press

west to the Marquesas and Dry Tortugas, hire a veteran guide, at least for your first trip or two. For this book to toss out names of remote areas with general directions to them would be just as foolhardy as a visiting angler trying to find those regions by using such directions. We will stick close to shore—and still cover enough fishing spots to keep you busy for a very long time!

In this description of Keys fishing and how to reach it by boat, only the public boat ramps are mentioned. These are not overly plentiful on the islands, but there are a number of marinas that offer ramp privileges for a fee. Often these are more convenient to some of the fishing grounds, so a little research in the local phone book might save you some time running long distances on the water.

Finally, do not expect to find the same sandy beaches along the ocean that are on other South Florida shores. The Florida Keys are composed mostly of coral rock or marl (a crumbly mixture of sand, silt, clay, and calcium carbonates originally laid down on the seafloor). These are at best covered with a thin veneer of sand. A true beach is rare on the shores of these islands.

Upper Keys

There are two ways to enter the Florida Keys by road from the mainland. The back-door route is via Card Sound Road (County Road 977 to the Monroe County line, where it changes to CR 905A), which runs from Florida City across to the northern end of Key Largo. The other way in is the more conventional route down US 1 from Florida City to the town of Key Largo. Regardless of which path you take, there are some fly-fishing options along the way.

On Card Sound Road the angling begins as soon as you reach the toll booth for the Card Sound Bridge. At this point Card Sound is to the northeast, while Barnes Sound runs southwest. The area around the bridge is known for giving up snook, barracuda, mangrove snapper, tarpon, and permit. Big tarpon are here in the spring, while the smaller ones appear year-round. Expect to find snook and snapper around the bridge pilings or nearby power poles standing in the water. Permit are summer visitors here and they, along with barracuda, may be found in channels or on the mangrove-dotted flats near the western end of the bridge. These flats are cut off from the bridge causeway by boat channels along both shores.

The western end of the Card Sound Bridge has riprap that has been filled in with concrete to form a solid platform for casting to the ends of the boat channels. The access is much more extensive on the northern side of the bridge. Additionally, just up the channel on the southern side of the road is a single-lane, paved public boat ramp. This site provides the best boating access for Barnes and Card Sounds.

East of the Card Sound Bridge CR 905A crosses three smaller creeks that connect the two sounds. All three offer access for fishing around the bridges. The first is Mosquito Creek, which also offers some access to wadable Card Sound shoreline. At the second creek, whose name does not appear on any maps, about 0.25 mile of shoreline is available for casting from the southern side of the road east of the bridge. Finally, the road crosses Steamboat Creek before reaching Key Largo. This crossing also has limited shore-casting options. All the fish found at the Card Sound Bridge may be encountered in the creeks, but snook and mangrove snapper are most abundant.

These creeks also are good places to launch a canoe for paddling through their mangrove-lined channels, but they do have strong tidal currents. Be aware also that you are on the western edge of Crocodile Lake National Wildlife Refuge. If you enter it, approaching closer than 100 feet to any shoreline is prohibited between March 1 and October 1—the nesting season for endangered American crocodiles.

To the south in Barnes Sound the most prevalent fish are seatrout and mangrove snapper, which can be found on the extensive grass flats. Though the fish can turn up anywhere, the most consistent areas are found along the sound's eastern shore at the mouth of Steamboat Creek, and in the cove just south of Cove Point. The southern end of Main Key on the sound's western side also holds seatrout.

One final place worth a look at the northern end of Key Largo is Angelfish Creek. The entire tip of the island here belongs to the private Ocean Reef Club, which allows no public access. By boat, however, it is possible to enter the creek between Key Largo and Palo Alto Key to the north, where snook hide along the overhanging mangroves.

To reach Angelfish Creek, run north in Card Sound along the shore of Key Largo past Pumpkin Key. The mouth of Angelfish Creek is to the east 1,000 yards farther north.

Along US 1 headed to Key Largo, down the portion of highway referred to locally as the 18 Mile Stretch, there are several culverts under the roadway connecting Barnes Sound to Blackwater and Little Blackwater Sounds to the south. At some points roadside canals also offer casting room from shore. All of these sites hold mangrove snapper, snook, and small tarpon year-round.

JIMMY JACOBS

The mouth of Jewfish Creek, which separates Key Largo from the mainland, often harbors seatrout.

At mile marker (MM) 111 (these are measured from the end of US 1 in Key West and are the standard for locating everything along the Overseas Highway) is a paved public boat ramp with limited parking on the western side of the road on Little Blackwater Sound. To the west, Blackwater Pass connects south to Blackwater Sound, which has a number of good fishing sites. The area immediately south of the mouth of the pass on Blackwater Sound is good for seatrout, as are the waters off Shell Point and on both sides of The Boggies (the pass leading from Blackwater Sound into Florida Bay). This last location also gives up some snook to the south of the pass.

Down the eastern side of Blackwater Sound, look for seatrout in Sexton Cove south of Snake Point; mangrove snapper and trout to the south of Stellrecht Point; plus seatrout to the north of Bush Point on the southern side of the sound.

On the northern end of Blackwater Sound, Jewfish Creek connects to Barnes Sound. This 1.5-mile waterway is a good place to target redfish, mangrove snapper, and snook along its mangrove-shaded edges. Another advantage of fishing here is that it is usually sheltered from the wind.

After you cross Jewfish Creek, US 1 spans Lake Surprise before reaching Key Largo. The area of the lake that is north of the highway generally holds some seatrout and mangrove snapper. You can enter the lake from Blackwater Sound on the south.

All of these locations on Blackwater Sound, Jewfish Creek, and Lake Surprise require a boat for fishing. Boating access is best from the ramp on US 1 at MM 111.

Continuing down the western side of Key Largo, Buttonwood Sound offers more seatrout and mangrove snapper action. The best spots to try include Sunset Cove at the southern end of the sound for snapper. For trout, check out the grass flats east of the Swash Keys. Running around to the west of the Swash Keys puts you on a shoreline that extends down to Shell Key. Along both of these isles is good water for redfish.

Boating access to these sites on lower Key Largo is a bit difficult from public ramps. The closest one is on the Atlantic side of the island in Harry Harris County Park in Tavernier. This park has a double-lane boat ramp with paved parking lots east of US 1 at MM 93.5. There is also access here to wadable flats off the swimming beach that often hold bonefish.

A stiff $5 fee is charged for all nonresidents of Monroe County to enter the park, plus a boat-launch fee. To reach the bay side of the island from here, run south to Tavernier Creek, then turn west through its channel. On the bay side turn north to reach Buttonwood Sound.

The eastern side of Key Largo has a much different character. Here the main species of game fish are bonefish, permit, barracuda, and tarpon. In the spring big silver kings can be found just off the shore at Tavernier, El Radabob, and Rattlesnake Keys.

For bonefish, a good site is in Garden Cove. This is located directly east of the point where US 1 and CR 905 join beside Lake Surprise. There is no access from the shore, but by boat it is possible to target the northwestern shore of Rattlesnake Key, where the bones are most often concentrated.

Just to the southwest is Largo Sound, an almost landlocked body of water behind El Radabob Key. Bonefish work the flats on the northeastern corner of the sound, as well as in the extreme southern area at the mouth of South Sound Creek. These flats can be particularly good after winter cold snaps when the fishing at other sites in the Upper and Middle Keys is dead because of cloudy water. Although there is no shore access to these areas, the concessions and beach area of John Pennekamp Coral Reef State Park is at the southwestern corner of the sound. You can rent a canoe and easily paddle to these flats. The entrance to the park is off US 1 at MM 102.5.

Pennekamp State Park does not offer fly-casting access to any good waters within this portion of its boundaries, but it does have a double-lane, paved boat ramp with paved parking lots. A fee is charged for entering the park, as well as for launching a boat.

On the southeastern shore of El Radabob Key, to the ocean side of Largo Sound, there are good fishing spots for barracuda, bonefish, and permit. These flats have hard-sand bottoms that are ideal for wading but must be reached by boat. Try Whitmore Bight—an indentation on the island's coast just north of Point Willie—for bonefish and 'cuda, but right off Point Willie is the place to look for permit.

At the southern end of Largo Sound, South Sound Creek empties into a flat off the community of Newport. These shallows wrap all the way around the end of El Radabob Key, are wadable (though you will hit pockets of muck), and contain bonefish and barracuda. Again, however, there is no shoreside access to the flats, so they have to be approached by boat. Once you are on them, no gasoline motors may be used. The nearest public boat access to the flat is from the Pennekamp State Park ramps.

Roughly 4 miles southwest of the Newport flat lies Rodriguez Key. Off the island's northeastern end is a hot spot for cruising permit, while the sand flat that runs down the southeastern shore and around the southwestern end of the key usually attracts bonefish. Although bonefish show up around Dove Key, between Rodriguez Key and Key Largo, the immediate vicinity of this tiny isle is closed to access to protect shorebird nesting sites.

The final flats fishing location along Key Largo sits near the end of the island, around Tavernier Key, directly east of the mouth of Tavernier Creek. The flat runs along the southern side of Tavernier Key and continues west to the mouth of the creek. Bonefish commonly use this flat, as well as the shallows on both sides of the creek's mouth. These sites can best be accessed by boat from the ramp at Harry Harris County Park, described earlier in this section.

Plantation Key is the next island down the chain from Key Largo. This key has two spots that usually hold some bonefish on shallows. One is on the bay side where a narrow sand flat stretches west just off the end of Seminole Avenue, which runs west from US 1 between MM 89 and 90. Back on the ocean side, the flat on the northeastern side of the mouth of Snake Creek and the southern end of Plantation Key is also good for bonefish.

Across Snake Creek to the southwest there are more flats that hold bonefish on the ocean side of Windley Key. These run along this entire island to Whale Harbor Channel at its other end. In the spring big tarpon use

Whale Harbor Channel as a thoroughfare, while big mangrove snapper inhabit it all year. At the northwestern end of the channel on the bay side more shallow sand flats stretch all the way to Cotton Key. This is another good area for bonefish, as is the smaller flat that extends due west off Cotton Key.

Unfortunately, none of the flats off Plantation or Windley Keys is accessible by foot from shore. Access from a public boat ramp requires a long run north from the single-lane, coral rock ramp on Indian Key Fill at MM 79 on the southwestern end of Upper Matecombe Key. From the ramp it is a 7-mile run to Snake Creek, which separates Plantation and Windley Keys.

Middle Keys

The middle portion of the Florida Keys is famous for producing big bonefish, including monsters of up to 14½ pounds! March through June and August through November are the best times of year, while early and late in the day during mid-incoming through mid-outgoing tides are the best times of day. This portion of the Keys also has the best access from shore for wading anglers along the chain of islands. The Middle Keys run from Upper Matecombe Key to Bahia Honda Key. This is the area where the island chain begins swinging westward in earnest. By the time you reach Bahia Honda, the islands are running due west toward Key West.

For anglers fishing from a boat, the entire southeastern shore of Upper Matecombe Key, where Islamorada is located, is lined with shallow grass flats that often attract bonefish. This side of the island also has a number of hotels and motels on the oceanfront. By staying in one of these, you can also secure foot access to good fishing flats. An especially good flat is on this side of Upper Matecombe at its southern end, along the northeastern side of the small causeway that connects tiny Teatable Key to the Overseas Highway. This hard-sand flat is easily waded, but a boat channel cuts it off from the highway, while the drive on the causeway is private. A canoe or sea kayak can put you on this flat in seconds, however, and bonefish are usually present.

To the west of Upper Matecombe, Teatable Key Channel, and Indian Key Channel (these channels are crossed by US 1 just south of the island) lie extensive shallow sand and sea grass flats on the eastern side of Shell Key and running southwest to the eastern side of Lignum Vitae Key. The latter of these two small keys is in the Lignum Vitae State Botanical Site. The flats here are known for regularly yielding big bonefish of up to 10 pounds. Where Race, Indian Key, and Teatable Key Channels split these shallows, you can

Indian Key lies just southeast of the Overseas Highway between Upper and Lower Matecombe Keys. The shallows around the island are good bonefish habitat.

find tarpon cruising in the spring months. On all the flats around Upper Matecombe barracuda are encountered year-round during all tides.

At the southern end of the Indian Key Fill, which carries the Overseas Highway from Upper to Lower Matecombe Keys, tiny Indian Key sits to the ocean side and is not connected to the highway. This 10-acre island is a state historic site that holds the ghost town of what was once the second largest town in the Keys and the site of the only battle of the Seminole Wars to take place on the island chain. Burned by Indians in 1840, the village of Indian Key was never rebuilt.

For anglers today, the island marks the midpoint of more ocean-side bonefish flats. These are cut off from the highway by a boat channel along Indian Key Fill, but marinas at either end of the fill rent sea kayaks that can put you on the flats quite easily for wading.

Boating access to all these flats is best from the single-lane, rough coral rock public landing on the bay side of Indian Key Fill at MM 79. These is plenty of room for parking at the ramp. Additionally, parking is available all along the fill, where there is casting room on the boat channels running down either shore. Barracuda, mangrove snapper, and an occasional snook or tarpon are found in these.

Annes Beach at the south end of Lower Matecombe Key is one of the few true beaches in the Keys and is also a good flat to wade for bonefish.

The next island, Lower Matecombe Key, has all its good fishing sites on the ocean side. Like its sister island to the north, Lower Matecombe's entire southeastern side holds bonefish flats that are quite wadable. As a bonus, however, a couple of these flats can be reached from shore by anglers on foot. The first of these is located at MM 74.6 on the eastern side of the road. Parking is possible on the US 1 right-of-way, and the water is right at the roadside. The best wading is from this point south. There are some isolated mangrove shoots sticking up on the flat. When no bonefish are present, try running a popping or skipping bug quickly past these. Barracuda often lie near the plants and cannot resist the noisy flies.

At the southern end of Lower Matecombe on the ocean side is Annes Beach—one of only three or four spots in the Florida Keys that most people would recognize as a real beach. This is a public access area and does attract a lot of swimmers, particularly on weekends. It is also an excellent bonefish flat that is easily waded from shore. Fishing early and late in the day is recommended.

In all, the beach runs for 0.5 mile north from the end of the island. There are two entrances to the beach off US 1. At high tide the mangroves between the parking areas are inundated, but the lots are connected by a pedestrian boardwalk.

JIMMY JACOBS

*Long Key offers easy access to wading anglers searching
for bonefish in the Middle Keys.*

Between Lower Matecombe and Fiesta Keys lie Channel 2 and Channel 5. These two passes drop to depths of 8 to 13 feet and are beyond a doubt the best places in the Middle Keys to intercept huge tarpon during the spring months.

To the south of little Fiesta Key (which is covered with a KOA campground and shown on older maps as Greyhound Key) lies the next major island, Long Key. This isle has a long and venerated history as a saltwater fishing destination. In the early days of the 20th-century western novelist and angling fanatic Zane Grey discovered the shallow-water angling at Long Key when a yellow fever epidemic in Tampico, Mexico, caused him to abort a fishing trip there and land instead at Henry Flagler's railroad work camp on this island. The bonefish flats, tarpon and permit in the channels, and hordes of barracuda here led to his convincing Flagler to build the Long Key Fishing Club. This resort attracted other notable anglers, among them Ernest Hemingway, until it was destroyed, along with the railroad, in the Labor Day hurricane of 1935.

Today the southern side of the island is in the Long Key State Recreation Area, while the town of Layton occupies the northern portion. The angling here has not changed much since Grey first visited. Barracuda are everywhere around the island, on flats and in channels; bonefish can be found

The Long Key Fishing Club was founded by western novelist Zane Grey and often visited by Ernest Hemingway.

in Long Key Bight at the eastern end of the island and all along the ocean side in front of the state recreation area; tarpon and permit visit the channels on both ends of the island.

Though targeting bonefish in Long Key Bight requires a boat, the oceanfront flats in the state recreation area are accessible from shore. These are hard sand covered with sea grass. If you wade north toward Long Key Point where the shore is mangrove lined, the bottom gets softer, particularly close to the edge. Also, that portion of the flats near the area's nature trail seems to attract an inordinate number of sharks, some of which are 6 to 7 feet long. Still, smaller blacktips and bonnetheads are more common.

The Long Key State Recreation Area is located to the southeast of US 1 at MM 70. A fee is charged to enter the area. Parking is allowed at the shore just outside the northern edge of the designated campground. Or you can park at the boardwalk for the nature trail at the northern end of the park. If you choose this option, however, you have to walk along the boardwalk to the shore, then muck through 30 to 40 yards of soft bottom to get out to the hard-sand flat.

Boating access to all of Long Key is most convenient from the ramp on Indian Key Fill to the north, described earlier in this section.

At the southwestern end of 2.5-mile Long Key Viaduct, Grassy Key is the first of the islands that make up the greater Marathon area. This town is presently the second largest, behind Key West, on the islands. The area is another portion of the island chain that boasts many excellent fly-casting situations, most of which are accessible only by boat, though some can be reached easily by wading from shore.

As was the case in the Islamorada area, virtually all of the better close-to-shore fishing spots around Marathon are on the ocean side of the islands. The eastern end of Grassy Key (the islands are now running virtually east–west) is noted for attracting permit along its southern oceanfront, with some weighing up to 30 pounds. Bonefish, barracuda, and even tarpon show up along the shore as well. This area has a number of motels and guest cottages with access to the near-shore flats, so picking the right accommodations for a trip here offers the bonus of convenient fishing.

There is one spot where the flats are accessible from the US 1 right-of-way. At MM 58 you find room to park on the southern side of the road, where a path through the trees puts you on the water. At the edge the bottom is mushy (you may sink in up to your ankles or more), but 20 to 30 yards out it changes to hard sand, with patches of sea grass. Just east of the entry point the small stone remnants of some type of foundation sit about 50 yards offshore. Though this rock pile is almost out of the water at low tide, during floods it often holds a veritable school of barracuda ranging from 12 to 30 inches long around it.

To the west the flat continues for several hundred yards, but is then broken by a small boat channel coming into a private dock. This channel and the dock can give up some mangrove snapper and barracuda.

To the east, beyond the rock foundation, the flat continues along the shore for a mile to another, more substantial boat channel. Along this channel's eastern side is a small peninsula of dredge material. This channel is good for targeting barracuda and snapper. If you have a canoe or kayak, a short 30- to 40-foot paddle puts you across the channel to where the flat continues for at least another 0.5 mile.

At the extreme western end of Grassy Key, where it borders Crawl Key, sandbars jut out from the shore. Some of these are dry during ebb tides, and most are wadable at that water level. At high tide they are covered by 4 to 5 feet of water. This is a great place to anchor a boat and watch for singles or pods of permit to cruise past. Dropping a crab-patterned fly in front of them can provoke a furious fight!

To the west of Grassy Key lies Curry Hammocks State Park. This little-known 260-acre preserve is the largest undeveloped tract of land between Key Largo and Big Pine Key. The portion of it that gets the heaviest public use is on the ocean side, via a drive off US 1 between MM 56 and 57. A sign marks the park entrance on US 1. At the end of the road, which is actually on Little Crawl Key, it forms a loop, lined by picnic tables and parking spaces on the water. At present there is no fee for using this park.

The flat to the west of the rest room and concessions building runs out toward a channel separating Little Crawl from Deer Key. This flat—which is mostly firm sand, but does have some mushy spots—is a good place to find tailing bonefish for two hours on either side of an ebb tide.

At the eastern end of the park a small boat channel cuts between Little Crawl and Crawl Keys. The shelf along the shore of the channel is wadable, while the deep water of the channel itself holds barracuda, blue runner, and mangrove snapper. In the spring and fall medium-weight tarpon of up to 50 to 60 pounds show up in the channel or along the mangrove shore just inside it.

The other portion of Curry Hammocks that provides some fishing options is on Fat Deer Key and even less known than the beach side. Along Fat Deer Key US 1 is paralleled on its northern side by a dirt road that runs just behind a line of bushes. There are gaps where this road can be seen from the highway, as well as drives connecting to it. At MM 55.5 there is room to park on this dirt road and a sign for Curry Hammocks at the trailhead of a path leading north through the mangroves.

The trail strikes the water at a huge dredge hole, probably a remnant of the railroad days when the marl was needed to build up the railbeds. This hole has vertical walls dropping to depths of 12 to 15 feet, while it is surrounded by hard marl flats that are very wadable. The dredge hole holds mangrove snapper, blue runner, yellowtail snapper, and even an occasional small grouper around its edge. There are some of the ever-present barracuda, too. During the spring big tarpon enter the hole as well. Because of the hard bottom, the flats around the hole are likely to attract permit, along with bonefish.

*The trail to the dredge pit off Fat Deer Key's northern shore
begins in Curry Hammocks State Park.*

By wading beside the western side of the hole to the end of the mangrove shore, you can gain access to the flat paralleling the deep water to the north. Another option is to wade east along the southern edge of the hole, tight against the mangroves. Going this way puts you on a large marl flat on the opposite side of the hole from where the path strikes it.

To the ocean side of Fat Deer Key lies Key Colony Beach. This whole town sits on land created by dredging back in the 1950s and 1960s. Its most appealing aspect to fly-casters is Coco Plum Beach, which lines the midsection of the waterfront. This narrow strip of public beach is fronted by sand and sea grass flats where bonefish often cruise or tail. To reach Coco Plum Beach, drive south from US 1 at MM 54 on Coco Plum Drive. The road curves around to the east, with the entrance to the beach at 1.4 miles on your right.

Vaca Key, on which the town of Marathon is located, has Boot Key to its south, across narrow Boot Key Harbor. The entire ocean side of Boot Key from the harbor entrance east to the mouth of Sisters Creek is composed of shallow sand flats. Many portions of these shallows are firm and quite wadable, while others near the mangrove shores are too mushy and require a boat to fish. Bonefish commonly feed here, along with some permit.

At the eastern end of these flats, along Sisters Creek, hard sand runs out

Marathon's Sombrero Public Beach lies just across Sisters Creek from a good bonefish and permit flat. This flat is easily reached by canoe or sea kayak.

from the mangrove shore toward East Sister Island. Close to the mangroves or to the west of the tiny mangrove island here, the flat is too soft to wade. Some big bonefish cruise along the edge of the Sisters Creek Channel.

Across the creek channel lies Sombrero Beach, which is a public facility. The eastern end of the swimming beach is an excellent place to launch a canoe for a 100-yard paddle across Sister Creek to these flats. To reach Sombrero Beach, take Sombrero Beach Road (CR 931) south off US 1 at MM 50 in downtown Marathon. The beach is at the end of the road. You have to carry canoes and kayaks for about 100 yards from the parking area though a gated fence to reach the water.

To the west of Marathon are the twin spans of the old and new Seven Mile Bridge that carries the Overseas Highway to several small islands, then Bahia Honda Key. Beneath the eastern end of these long bridges lie Knight Key and Moser Channels, both of which are renowned as tarpon hot spots in the spring months. Separating the two channels is tiny Pigeon Key. This isle held the maintenance camp for the Overseas Railway in the early part of the 20th century, and its buildings are being restored as a historic site. To the south of the island along the new bridge, debris piles hold schools of mangrove and yellowtail snapper that can often be fooled with shrimp-imitating bonefish flies. Beyond the bridge the shallows of the Pigeon Key Banks are broken by channels. Bonefish and permit feed up on the flats, while barracuda and tarpon cruise the edges of the channels.

Boating access to all of the areas from Grassy Key west to Moser Channel is best from the public boat ramp located on the bay side of US 1 at MM 54, or from the Marathon Yacht Club ramp on the bay side at MM 49.

Near the western end and to the south of the Seven Mile Bridge are tiny Money and Molasses Keys. Both of these isles are surrounded by shallow sand flats where barracuda, bonefish, and permit show up. Between these keys tarpon can be found in Money Key Channel from April through June.

At the western end of the Seven Mile Bridge are Little Duck, Missouri, Ohio, Bahia Honda, and West Summerland Keys. These islands mark the western end of the Middle Keys and provide some very good wading options that are accessible from shore. The first of these isles is Little Duck Key (formerly called Pacet Key), which is a public park. On its eastern end on the bay side is a public boat ramp that provides access for boaters to the eastern end of these islands. The west end of Little Duck's ocean side is occupied by Veterans Memorial Park, which has a swimming beach that doubles as a wading flat. Bonefish, permit, and barracuda are often present here. On the bay side at this end of the isle is another hard-sand flat, but it is cut off from the road by a mangrove ticket. It is possible to wade along the channel from the bridge at the western end of the island to reach this flat, but the channel is mushy and you have a tough trek to get to the firm sand. Bonefish, permit, and barracuda can be found on this flat.

On Missouri Key, the western end on the ocean side has a hard marl flat jutting out along the Missouri Channel, which separates the island from Ohio Key. This hard bottom is a place to target both bonefish and permit. As you wade back to the east from here, the bottom changes to sand and sea grass but remains firm enough for continued wading. There is roadside parking and shore access to these flats.

Across Missouri Channel the eastern end of Ohio Key has a firm-sand flat sticking out on the ocean side. It offers very easy access from the highway and holds good prospects for bonefish during rising tides.

The final islands of the Middle Keys are Bahia Honda and West Summerland Keys, which are entirely contained in 524-acre Bahia Honda State Park. The southern shore of Bahia Honda facing the Atlantic Ocean is a continuous sand and sea grass flat, where bonefish show up regularly. On the western end is Loggerhead Beach, while Sandspur Beach lies to the east. Both of these have parking lots, but they are swimming areas that stay crowded. Between them no parking is allowed on the roadside, so you have to walk to get away from the bathers to fish. Also between the beaches is the outflow of a small tidal lagoon that drains across the flats and presents an interesting casting option during falling tides.

A fee is charged for entering Bahia Honda State Park. There is a paved, double-lane boat ramp in the marina boat basin at the park. From the ramp, it is a short run west to Bahia Honda Channel, where tarpon stack up in unbelievable numbers from April through June. The entrance to the state park is at the eastern end of the island on the southern side of US 1, east of MM 38.

On the western side of Bahia Honda Channel is West Summerland Key (also known as Spanish Harbor Key). As mentioned it is also within Bahia Honda State Park, but no entrance fee is charged for parking on it. On the ocean side of the island is a hard-marl flat that can hold permit, bonefish, and barracuda. At its eastern end, toward the old Bahia Honda trestle, this marl shore drops steeply into deeper water near shore. Mangrove snapper are common along this drop, as are barracuda. At the western end of the island on the bay side is the Spanish Harbor Boat Ramp. This single-lane, paved public facility is on US 1 and has plenty of parking.

Lower Keys

For the purposes of this book, the Lower Florida Keys run from Big Pine Key in the east to Key West. Through here the Overseas Highway touches a dozen major islands, crosses another dozen or so smaller ones, and skirts literally hundreds of tiny keys.

Although the Lower Keys offer some of the best saltwater fly-fishing in the world, a great deal of it is not very close to the Overseas Highway and the inhabited islands. The Content Keys to the north of Big Pine, along with the myriad small islands running west through the Great White Heron National Wildlife Refuge to north of Key West, are alive with a wide variety of fish in locations where they can be caught on flies. But as I discussed earlier, these are not places for grabbing a chart, launching your boat, and taking off on your own. The same applies to the Marquesas Keys and Dry Tortugas west of Key West.

While there are many good places to fish nearer civilization in the Lower Keys, they are admittedly fewer in number and lower in quality than those of the Upper and Middle Keys.

The first island you encounter upon entering the Lower Keys is Big Pine

JIMMY JACOBS

Little Palm Island is one of many isles in the Lower Keys that offer great fishing flats in a tropical setting.

Key, which is distinctive for a couple of reasons. First of all, it is the second largest of the Florida Keys, behind Key Largo. Second, its northern section makes up the bulk of the National Key Deer Refuge, where these endangered pygmy white-tailed deer have their last stronghold. When you drive on this key, go slowly. If you speed, you may hit one of the deer, and, if not, you will probably get a traffic citation. The speed limits are more closely monitored and enforced here than anywhere else on the southeastern coast of the United States.

Flats surround much of Big Pine Key's northern and southern ends, while deep channels brush its eastern and western shores. Bonefish and permit use the flats as feeding grounds; smaller tarpon cruise the passes.

There is only one wadable flat that can be reached by foot from shore—and this is no easy task. One other spot provides canoe access, while the others require a motorboat to properly fish. The shore access is on the southern end of the island. Immediately upon reaching the eastern end of Big Pine on US 1, turn south onto Long Beach Road. After this road turns sharply to the west, follow it to its end. From here you have to follow a path toward the water, but still wade through a band of mangroves to get to the flat. If you hit this site early or late in the day, the bonefish may make your effort worthwhile.

The Spanish Harbor Channel, which runs along the eastern side of Big Pine Key, is noted for holding a lot of medium to small tarpon, with larger ones showing up in the spring. This channel is easily accessible from the Spanish Harbor Boat Ramp on West Summerland Key, which was described earlier in the Middle Keys section. When boating this area, be aware of the many submerged pilings along the shores that are left over from railroad construction days. Another option for tarpon in this vicinity is to check out the waters of Newfound Harbor (also known as Coupon Bight) north of Long Beach Drive. The harbor juts into southern Big Pine Key from the west.

Near the northern end of Big Pine Key there is a public boat ramp at the end of Koehn Avenue. East of this ramp is a shallow sand and marl flat along the shoreline. It normally holds large numbers of barracuda, but also attracts some bonefish. It is best reached by using a canoe or kayak, since the bottom is rather mushy immediately beside the boat ramp. There are mangroves along the shore to the west of the ramp, where mangrove snapper and barracuda are also present.

This ramp is a good launch site for running west around the northern end of Big Pine to the channel separating it from an uninhabited mangrove island called Howe Key. The southeastern and southwestern sides of Howe hold bonefish on shallow flats.

The Koehn Avenue Boat Ramp is single lane and paved but has only limited parking space. To reach it, take Key Deer Boulevard north off US 1, between MM 30 and 31. At Big Pine Street turn east. Koehn Avenue runs north off this street.

West of Big Pine Key are Little Torch, Ramrod, Summerland, Cudjoe, and Sugarloaf Keys. Through here both fishing access and known hot spots are sparse. The southern tips of Little Torch and Ramrod, and the entire southern coast of Sugarloaf, all have shallow flats that are frequented by bonefish. A boat is needed to reach all of them.

The Niles Channel between Ramrod and Summerland Keys, Kemp Channel between Summerland and Cudjoe, and Bow Channel between Cudjoe and Sugarloaf are all good places to hunt tarpon with a fly-rod in deeper water during the springtime. The channels running through the flats off the eastern end of Loggerhead Key are good for tarpon, and you can expect to find a few bonefish using the shallows between the channels. Loggerhead Key lies 3 miles due south on the ocean side of Cudjoe Key.

Having covered the better-known places for fishing these keys, let's look at a couple of unusual situations that provide some fishing prospects in the area. By taking Middle Torch Key Road north from US 1 just west of MM 28, and then turning west onto Big Torch Key Road, you come to the causeway connecting Middle Torch to Big Torch Key. This causeway has three culverts running underneath, and deep holes have been washed out under each end. These holes are gathering places for mangrove snapper, blue runner, and other small fish that hit flies. To either side of the causeway are flats surrounded by mangroves where barracuda and bonefish cruise. There is wading access along the shore from parking spaces beside the road. Near the eastern end of the causeway a gravel stub of road runs out into the mangroves to the south. At its end it is possible to wade across a few yards of soft muck at the mangrove edge to reach a hard-sand flat.

The other unusual situation for fishing in this part of the island chain is found on Park Key in the enclosed waters of upper Sugarloaf Sound, immediately south of US 1. At MM 18.4 there is room to park on the southern side of the road; you then follow a trail for about 30 feet through the mangroves to the water's edge. At this site there is an old dredge pit right on the shore. To either side it is surrounded by hard-marl flats, which are lined with small mangroves on the east. It is possible to wade along these mangrove shoots for more than 0.5 mile to the south. Additionally, you can wade around the southern end of the dredge pit to reach the open-water flats to its east.

The deep water of the pit gives up mangrove snapper, jack crevalle, blue runner, tarpon, barracuda, and even a grouper or two. Meanwhile, the flats around the pit are alive with barracuda as well as bonefish. With such a hard bottom, do not be surprised to find tailing permit either.

To the west of Sugarloaf Key, the Overseas Highway skips across a series of tiny islands and channels known as the Saddlebunch Keys. Through here the flats on both sides of the road look inviting for wading and fly-casting. While you rarely see anyone accepting the invitation, this is a good wading area. Barracuda and bonefish are the species you are most likely to find here. The trick to the wading is to find the spots along the roadway where you can easily get through the narrow band of low mangroves growing at the water's edge. Most of the flats are either firm sand or hard marl, but there are some mushy spots. Parking is plentiful all along the highway right-of-way. The best area to explore runs for 2.8 miles along the northern side of US 1, from Saddlebunch Channel 2 west to Shark Channel.

The next major key you encounter as you move west is Boca Chita, and for its size, you would expect it to provide more fishing options than it does. However, most of the island is covered by the Naval Air Station Key West.

Just southeast of Boca Chita lies Pelican Key. To the east of this little isle is a channel running south from Saddlebunch Harbor. Tarpon are known to cruise this channel during the spring months. To reach this site, the best jumping-off point is the public boat ramp on Shark Key Fill on US 1 at MM 11. This is a single-lane, paved boat landing with very limited parking space. It is a 1.5-mile run due south to the channel beside Pelican Key.

The other option worth mentioning on Boca Chita is a good spot for wading for permit or bonefish of up to 12 pounds; it is accessible from shore. Although called Boca Chita Beach, this shoreline on the ocean south of the island is a much better fishing flat than swimming beach. For 1 mile Old FL 4A runs right along the shore, with parking at roadside. Be aware that you are wading at the end of the runway for the naval air station, where F-14 Tomcats come in for landings. This is where pilots train for aircraft carrier landings, which are often described as "controlled crashes." They come in low, loud, and fast over you. The fish may not mind the noise, but it can be rather unnerving the first time you experience it.

To reach Boca Chita Beach, take Old FL 4A (CR 941) south off US 1 between MM 10 and 11 on Big Coppitt Key. The road turns west to cross Geiger Key before reaching the southern shore of Boca Chita Key.

Finally, when you cross over Stock Island from Boca Chita, you reach the end of the line—Key West. Despite the reputation this town enjoys as a fishing destination, it has little to offer on its own. There is fantastic fishing to the west in the Marquesas Keys and Dry Tortugas, or to the north in the Great White Heron National Wildlife Refuge, but Key West is simply the launch site for this fishing. In fact, the only fly-fishing opportunity around this island is found in its harbor.

The harbor on the western end of the key, off the Old Town section, is one of the most consistent producers of big tarpon in Florida on a year-round basis. For fly-casters, the best time to ambush one of these 60- to 120-pound brutes is after dark, by casting to lighted docks. Flies with brown or rust colors work well, since they match the "palmetto bugs" (a Florida euphemism for a giant, ugly cockroach) that live on the docks and are snapped up like candy by tarpon when they fall in the water.

To reach Key West Harbor by boat, launch at the public ramp on Garrison Bight, on the northern side of US 1 between MM 1 and 2. Pass under the bridge to the north into the main body of the bight, then out the inlet at Trumbo Point. Turn west at Channel Marker 21 and run under the Fleming Key Bridge. The harbor area is to the south, inland of Wisteria and Tank Islands.

Index

Books from The Countryman Press and Backcountry Guides

Arizona Trout Streams and Their Hatches, Charles Meck and John Rohmer

Bass Flies, Dick Stewart

Building Classic Salmon Flies, Ron Alcott

Fishing Small Streams with a Fly-Rod, Charles Meck

Fishing Vermont's Streams and Lakes, Peter Cammann

Flies in the Water, Fish in the Air, Jim Arnosky

Fly-Fishing with Children: A Guide for Parents, Philip Brunquell

Fly-Tying Tips, Dick Stewart

Fundamentals of Building a Bamboo Fly-Rod, George Maurer and Bernard Elser

The Golden Age of Fly-Fishing: The Best of The Sportsman, 1927–1937, ed. Ralf Coykendall

Good Fishing in the Adirondacks, ed. Dennis Aprill

Good Fishing in Lake Ontario and its Tributaries, Rich Giessuebel

Great Lakes Steelhead, Bob Linsenman and Steve Nevala

Ice Fishing: A Complete Guide . . . Basic to Advanced, Jim Capossela

Michigan Trout Streams, Bob Linsenman and Steve Nevala

Mid-Atlantic Trout Streams and Their Hatches, Charles Meck

Modern Streamers for Trophy Trout, Bob Linsenman and Kelly Galloup

Tailwater Trout in the South, Jimmy Jacobs

Trout Streams of Pennsylvania and Their Hatches, Charles Meck

Trout Streams of Southern Appalachia, Jimmy Jacobs

Trout Streams of Southern New England, Tom Fuller

Trout Streams of Virginia, Harry Slone

Ultralight Spin-Fishing, Peter Cammann

Universal Fly-Tying Guide, Dick Stewart

Wisconsin and Minnesota Trout Streams, Jim Humphrey and Bill Shogren

---

We offer many more books on hiking, bicycling, canoeing and kayaking, travel, nature, and country living. Our books are available at bookstores and outdoor stores everywhere. For more information or a free catalog, please call 1-800-245-4151, or write to us at The Countryman Press, P.O. Box 748, Woodstock, Vermont 05091. You can find us on the Internet at www.countrymanpress.com